UNJUST BY DESIGN

Law and Society Series

W. Wesley Pue, General Editor

The Law and Society Series explores law as a socially embedded phenomenon. It is premised on the understanding that the conventional division of law from society creates false dichotomies in thinking, scholarship, educational practice, and social life. Books in the series treat law and society as mutually constitutive and seek to bridge scholarship emerging from interdisciplinary engagement of law with disciplines such as politics, social theory, history, political economy, and gender studies.

A list of titles in the series appears at the end of the book.

UNJUST BY DESIGN
Canada's Administrative Justice System

Ron Ellis

UBCPress · Vancouver · Toronto

21 20 19 18 17 16 15 14 13 13   5 4 3 2 1

Printed in Canada on FSC-certified ancient-forest-free paper
(100% post-consumer recycled) that is processed chlorine- and acid-free.

Library and Archives Canada Cataloguing in Publication

Ellis, S. Ronald
    Unjust by design: Canada's administrative justice system / Ron Ellis.

(Law and society, ISSN 1496-4953)
Issued also in electronic formats.
ISBN 978-0-7748-2477-4 (bound) – ISBN 978-0-7748- 2478-1 (pbk.)

    1. Administrative courts – Canada. 2. Administrative law – Canada. I. Title.
II. Series: Law and society series (Vancouver, B.C.)

KE5029.E45 2013   342.71'0664   C2012-907533-7
KF5417.E45 2013

Canadä

UBC Press gratefully acknowledges the financial support for our publishing program of the Government of Canada (through the Canada Book Fund), the Canada Council for the Arts, and the British Columbia Arts Council.

UBC Press
The University of British Columbia
2029 West Mall
Vancouver, BC V6T 1Z2
www.ubcpress.ca

This book is dedicated to

Nick McCombie

A remarkable tribunal member and colleague

Invitation to a Discussion

The author is hopeful that this book will provoke a serious debate within the legal profession, the administrative justice system, the executive and legislative branches of government, and perhaps within the public at large about the structures and quality of our administrative justice system – and also about the reforms proposed in this book. For the convenience of those who might wish to contribute to that debate, the author has organized an interactive website – administrativejusticereform.ca – and invites all interested parties to go there and talk to him and each other about these important issues. To facilitate free and frank discussions, the website will be structured to allow participants to elect to have their names held in confidence if they wish to do so.

Please note that the website is the author's undertaking and is separate from UBC Press's website.

Contents

Acknowledgments

There are a number of people whose contributions to this book I must acknowledge. Foremost is my wife, Ruth, who is my tireless support in all things, as well as my constant guide on readability issues.

The book emerged from my graduate program at Osgoode Hall Law School, York University, and I am indebted to the co-supervisors of my program, Osgoode Professor Mary Jane Mossman and H. Thomas Wilson, York University Professor of Public Policy and Public Law. After Professor Wilson's retirement from the university's full-time faculty, Professor Mossman took me over, as it were, and it was her encouragement, advice and direction, and editing and organizing skills that brought the PhD project to a successful conclusion. I am also indebted to Professor Liora Salter, the Director of Osgoode's Graduate Program at the time, for her support and encouragement, and to Professor Leslie Green for the stimulating directed-reading Theory of Law course I was privileged to take with him. I was also privileged to have an expert – not to say, intimidating – dissertation defence committee whose members encouraged me to think that there was a book in the dissertation. The members, in addition to Professors Mossman and Wilson, were Professor Salter, Osgoode Professor Eric Tucker, York University Professor Ian Greene, and the external accessor, University of Toronto Faculty of Law Professor Lorne Sossin, now Dean of Osgoode.

In a special category is Mary E. McKenzie of Nanaimo, British Columbia, a lawyer and judicial tribunal adjudicator. In the Introduction, the reader will find a full account of the McKenzie case in which I became involved as co-counsel, and of the influence that Mary and her case had on this book.

Two outstanding academics in the administrative law field read the book manuscript: David Mullan of Queen's University and Geneviève Cartier of the University of Sherbrooke. I thank them both for their important and constructive criticisms, comments, and questions. They would not want to be taken to have subscribed to all I have written, but the book is significantly better for their input.

I must also thank my family and friends who, aware of my interminable "book project," were always kind with their diplomatic inquiries and encouraging comment.

Finally, I need to acknowledge the kinship between the title of this book, *Unjust by Design*, and *Denial by Design*, the title of the 2001 report by Legal Aid Ontario's Income Security Advocacy Centre. That report is about the unfair bureaucratic obstacles facing applicants under the Ontario Disability Support Program, obstacles that were part of that program at that time. As the report indicates, it was researched and written, and presumably its title chosen, by John Fraser, Cynthia Wilkey, and JoAnne Frenschkowksi. The affinity between the two titles is based on more than just syntax. In the circumstances described in that report, the "denial" it references was "unjust." Thus, this book and that report are generically talking about the same thing: executive branch indifference to the principles of justice.

UNJUST BY DESIGN

Introduction

I begin with a story.

When I had been the chair of Ontario's Workers' Compensation Appeals Tribunal for a few years, a letter arrived on my desk from a mother living in a small Ontario town. The mother's young adult son had been seeking workers' compensation benefits for a major, disabling injury – benefits that would provide the income he could no longer earn for himself. Notwithstanding the seriousness of her son's injury, the Ontario Workers' Compensation Board had decided that the circumstances under which it had occurred did not bring the injury within the coverage of the *Workers' Compensation Act*; it had rejected his application. The Board's decision had been appealed to my Appeals Tribunal. A panel that I had assigned to hear the appeal had agreed with the Board. Her son's appeal had been rejected.

"Dear Mr. Ellis," the mother wrote, "I thought that as Chair of this so-called Tribunal you might want to see the enclosed." The "enclosed" was the last page of my Tribunal's decision in her son's appeal. The last line on that page read: "Appeal denied." Her son, the mother explained in her letter, had read the decision, gone out to the back shed, taken down the family shotgun, and killed himself. On the last page of the decision, below the words "Appeal denied," he had scrawled the words "Life denied." His mother had sent it to me in the blood-spattered condition in which she had found it.[1]

The Administrative Justice System in Context

The "so-called Tribunal" the grieving mother held responsible for her son's death is just one of hundreds of executive branch "administrative tribunals" to which Canadian legislatures have assigned the judicial branch function of making judicial decisions, decisions that are frequently of a life-altering nature. Currently, these tribunals are mainly referred to as "adjudicative tribunals" or "quasi-judicial tribunals," but for reasons to be explained later I choose to call them "judicial tribunals." Taken together, they add up to a surrogate system of justice – the Canadian administrative justice system – the system of justice that is the subject of this book.

This administrative justice system is the system to which Canadians are required to turn for the enforcement or vindication of their rights in a broad range of everyday matters. These matters currently include retirement pensions, disability pensions, veteran's pensions, compensation for personal injuries arising from automobile accidents, compensation for workplace injuries, enforcement of human rights laws, involuntary incarceration of individuals in psychiatric institutions, enforced medical treatment and withdrawal of medical treatment, mental competence issues, parole eligibility, social welfare benefits, residential landlord and tenant issues, labour relations issues, employment standards, the conduct or competence of medical practitioners, the validity of doctors' billings, access to assisted living accommodations, access to programs of special education, child and family services, compensation for victims of crime, immigration, asylum for refugees, employment insurance, cruelty to animals, compliance with building codes, and so on and so forth.

In any Canadian province, on any particular day, one will typically find over thirty executive branch judicial tribunals conducting hearings and exercising their specialized judicial functions. The total number of judicial decisions made by these tribunals across the country in the course of a year is unknown but is clearly very large indeed. In Ontario alone, for instance, one estimate puts the number of rights-related decisions by administrative tribunals at over a million each year.[2] In 2010, the Ontario Workplace Safety and Insurance Board dealt with a quarter of a million applications for the adjudication of new compensation claims, and the Landlord and Tenant Board dealt with 78,000 applications for the judicial determination of rights disputes between residential landlords and their tenants, a large proportion of which involved landlords applying for eviction orders.

Although the administrative justice system is the part of our justice system[3] to which Canadians must now look for the recognition or vindication of a majority of their everyday legal rights – the only justice system that most people are ever likely to encounter – it is, as a system, largely unknown. Lawyers, law professors, and judges know it, but even to them it presents an uncertain topography. It is an *ad hoc* system that has emerged over the past several decades as an unplanned consequence of the inexorable parade of new statutes creating important everyday rights and obligations in which the judicial function of adjudicating those rights and obligations has been routinely assigned not to the courts but to executive branch tribunals.

This uncertainty – even in the minds of academics, lawyers, and judges – about what the system consists of stems from the fact that Canada's administrative law landscape is awash with bodies that are authorized by statute to exercise rights-determining functions, only some of which are judicial functions. Thus, the judicial tribunals that constitute the administrative justice system are to be found mixed in with an array of rights-determining bodies that may structurally resemble judicial tribunals, may exercise functions that are rather like those of judicial tribunals, and, most confusingly, are often called by the same names – tribunals, boards, commissions, committees, and so on. It is always a puzzle to distinguish one from the other and it has not helped that in the administrative law conversation in Canada – in our literature and jurisprudence – it has rarely been thought necessary to do so.

For purposes of this book, I divide the myriad of statutory, rights-determining bodies found in the modern Canadian polity into four groups: (1) executive branch administrative *justice* bodies, (2) executive branch *regulatory* bodies, (3) non-government *regulatory* bodies, and (4) non-government *adjudicative* bodies.

Administrative justice bodies are the executive branch, non-court judicial tribunals whose principal statutory assignment is the exercise of judicial functions. They are the core constituents of the administrative justice system and are the principal focus of this book. They are typically the judicial arms of the executive branch's statutory rights enterprises. They have been known in the past as government "agencies," but are now more commonly referred to as "tribunals." As indicated above, in this book they will be called "judicial tribunals." This group, of course, includes the adjudicator members of judicial tribunals. The prototypical examples of judicial tribunals are the workers' compensation appeals tribunals.

Within this first group I also include the individuals appointed to government offices that exercise rights-determining functions that are in fact properly judicial functions. Here I am thinking principally of public servants employed in a government department or ministry[4] (including, perhaps in some instances, ministers themselves) to whose office a statutory provision may have assigned a rights-determining function that meets the definition of a judicial function. (As we will see, this definition includes, in part, the requirement that the rights-determining decision be a final decision – "final" in the sense that its conclusions concerning both facts and law cannot be appealed, as of right, to another judicial tribunal.)

In my view, the exercise of judicial functions of such final nature by public servants or cabinet ministers is neither compatible with the rule of law nor constitutionally permissible; where this has occurred, reforming the system will require these functions to be restructured. Fortunately, most of these in-house ministerial rights-determining functions are not judicial but only interim decision-making functions or administrative functions. The latter may often be of a "quasi-judicial" nature and so governed by the principles of procedural fairness (see below), but, as I will demonstrate in due course, a rights-determining function that is properly characterized as "quasi-judicial" is not a judicial function. (The differentiation of "quasi-judicial" administrative functions from "judicial" functions has in recent years been muted in the Supreme Court of Canada's jurisprudence, but it is a difference that in my view is constitutionally essential. In later pages I will be addressing at length the definition of quasi-judicial administrative rights-determining functions, and the importance of maintaining the distinction between them and *judicial* rights-determining functions.[5])

It is in the interest of completeness that I have noted the fact that in-house, ministerial rights-determining judicial functions are necessarily part of the administrative justice system, but in fact the exercise of such functions by public servants or ministers is rare.

The second of my four groups includes all government organizations that have been assigned regulatory functions. These functions are principally rights-determining functions of an administrative nature. Even when they are seen to be of a quasi-judicial nature, they remain fundamentally administrative in nature and are not part of the administrative justice system – not as that system is rationally conceived. These organizations are commonly referred to as "regulatory agencies" – a practice that I will follow – and prototypical examples are energy boards, securities commissions, the Canadian Radio-television and Telecommunications Commission (CRTC), and the like.

In this group of regulatory bodies, I also include the individuals appointed to government offices who have been assigned rights-determining functions that are in fact properly regulatory functions. Here, as before, I have in mind public servants employed in a government ministry (including, in some instances, ministers themselves), to whose office a statutory provision may have assigned a rights-determining function of a regulatory nature. These functions may also often be of a quasi-judicial nature but they are not judicial functions and the individuals exercising them are not part of the administrative justice system.

Associated with this group of regulatory bodies is the important sub-category of functions often assigned to regulatory agencies that are in fact judicial functions, properly so called. In my view, these functions are, by definition, part of the administrative justice system and they present especially difficult issues that I will deal with later. I will refer to these functions as "adjunct" judicial functions.

My third group, the *non-government* rights-determining bodies, are bodies that are not executive branch organizations and whose statutory rights-determining functions are principally regulatory in nature. Examples are law society disciplinary tribunals, or bodies dealing with disciplinary issues or academic rights within the college and university communities. I will refer to the bodies in this group as non-government regulatory agencies. As with the executive branch regulatory agencies, one will find many of these agencies exercising adjunct judicial functions but I do not include these functions as part of the administrative justice system for the purposes of this book. To them, different arguments apply.

The fourth and final group, the *non-government* adjudicators, I also leave out of the frame as far as this book is concerned. Examples of these decision makers are grievance arbitrators appointed under collective bargaining agreements, and commercial arbitrators appointed pursuant to an arbitration act by the parties to a business dispute. In these cases, because the decision maker is chosen by agreement of the parties, the usual constitutional concerns about independence and impartiality of bodies exercising judicial functions are by and large answered.

This categorizing of bodies exercising statutory, rights-determining functions into four separate groups is, of course, anything but a scientific exercise. At the margins, it will often not be clear into which group a particular function or tribunal properly falls. Eventually, the lines of demarcation will have to be drawn through a case-by-case consideration of the fit of the applicable principles in the marginal cases; meanwhile, my analysis of those principles and their application will be focused on that core of tribunals that are beyond question judicial tribunals – executive branch tribunals whose principal rights-determining function is obviously a judicial function.

To sum up, this book is about the executive branch's judicial tribunals and the administrative justice system of which they are the core components. This justice system looms over everyone's everyday life, waiting to be summoned to invasive action by the arrival of some exigent but everyday circumstance. Nevertheless, if one asks anyone who is not a lawyer about "judicial tribunals" and the "administrative justice system" one may expect only a blank stare. This is not surprising, since each judicial tribunal has a different appearance and a unique name, and none of them is actually called a "judicial tribunal." They are also easily confused with regulatory agencies; moreover, they are located in the executive branch of government, where no one should expect to find a judicial tribunal, much less a justice system.

The variability in the appearance and structure of judicial tribunals reflects the fact that there is no central design-coordination or any standard design principles or criteria, and the choice of names is purely arbitrary. Each tribunal is typically a one-off structure designed by the staff of the responsible portfolio ministry to reflect the particular political circumstances out of which the felt need for a judicial tribunal emerged in the first place. In these designs, the structural rule-of-law implications of the tribunal's role as an instrument of justice – as the surrogate for a court – have almost always been ignored.

That the design of each Canadian judicial tribunal is idiosyncratic and that their structures are, as we will see, typically unprincipled from a rule-of-law perspective is surprising enough, but even more remarkable is the fact that although their justice-system role is obvious as a matter of fact, as a matter of law their place in Canada's constitutional arrangements has yet to be determined.

Finally, since this book is most fundamentally about the rule of law in Canada, it is important to remind ourselves at the outset what the rule of law means. In its *Imperial Tobacco* decision[6] in 2005, the Supreme Court defined the role of the rule of law in Canada's Constitution:

The rule of law is "a fundamental postulate of our constitutional structure" that lies "at the root of our system of government." It is expressly acknowledged by the preamble to the *Constitution Act, 1982*, and implicitly recognized in the preamble to the *Constitution Act, 1867* ...[7]

This Court has described the rule of law as embracing three principles. The first recognizes that "*the law is supreme over officials of the government* as well as private individuals, and thereby *preclusive of the influence of arbitrary power*" ... The second "requires the creation and maintenance of an actual order of positive laws which preserves and embodies the more general principle of normative order" ... The third requires that "*the relationship between the state and the individual ... be regulated by law.*"[8]

My Own Experience of the Administrative Justice System

This book is in large measure a personal report from the trenches of the administrative justice system. It is, accordingly, important that I tell you something of my experience in those trenches – the experience that has provoked the writing of this book and that informs much of its content.

In the summer of 1997, my term as the chair of the Workers' Compensation Appeals Tribunal to whom the grieving mother wrote her poignant letter came to an end. I resumed the labour arbitration practice that I had previously pursued on a part-time basis, and commenced, as well, something of a career as a critic of Canadian administrative justice.[9] Six years later, I found myself enrolled in Osgoode Hall Law School's graduate program studying for a doctorate. My subject: administrative justice.[10]

I entered the graduate program motivated by my long experience with the administrative justice system, of which the grieving mother's blood-spattered missive was only the most wrenching part. I hoped that, in the academic environment of a PhD program, I might find my way to a coherent theory of administrative justice that would challenge the conventional wisdom that, in my view, supports an administrative justice system that, from a rule-of-law perspective, is truly beyond the pale.

Called to the Ontario bar in 1964, I had spent the first eleven years of my legal career with the Toronto law firm Osler Hoskin and Harcourt. I practised principally as a management labour lawyer, a practice that took me, as counsel, before the Ontario Labour Relations Board, very occasionally before the Ontario Workers' Compensation Appeal Board (as it then was), and before various grievance arbitration boards. I was also an employer nominee on many of the latter boards. Then in 1975 I was appointed an associate professor of law at Osgoode Hall Law School. Of my seven years there, five were spent as the director and then co-director of Osgoode's Parkdale Community Legal Services (Parkdale), a storefront poverty law clinic and clinical education program.

As the Parkdale clinic's director, I was responsible for the appearances of the clinic's law students on behalf of indigent clients before the numerous judicial tribunals that play such a critical role in the lives of the disadvantaged. In Ontario at the time, these included the Social Assistance Review Board, the Refugee Advisory Board, the Immigration Appeal Board, the Pensions Appeal Board, Employment Standards Officers, Boards of Referees under the *Unemployment Insurance Act*, the Workers' Compensation Board and its Appeal Board, the Criminal Injuries Compensation Board, the various iterations of the residential tenant and landlord tribunal, the Ontario and National Parole Boards, the Ontario Legal Aid Plan, the Ontario Labour Relations Board and the Canada Labour Relations Board, various public housing officials, Children's Aid Societies, and so on. While teaching at the Law School, I also had the experience of *being* a tribunal, as a labour arbitrator from time to time and as the occasional chair of university adjudicative committees.

In 1981, I left the law school and joined the Law Society of Upper Canada as head of the Bar Admission Course and Director of Education, and in the spring of 1985, I was appointed the inaugural chair of Ontario's new Workers' Compensation Appeals Tribunal (which I will hereafter refer to as WCAT, although in 1997 it was renamed the "Workplace Safety and Insurance Appeals Tribunal") and embarked on my twelve-year career as an administrative justice insider.

WCAT was created as an independent, tripartite tribunal to hear appeals from the decisions of Ontario's Workers' Compensation Board (WCB – since 1997, the "Workplace Safety and Insurance Board").[11] WCAT opened its doors on 1 October 1985, and for eleven years and nine months – through a series of four three-year appointments – I was its chair and chief executive officer. At the request of the Mike Harris government, I left the position in June 1997, three months short of the expiration of my latest term.[12]

Before joining WCAT, my impression of the quality of Ontario's administrative justice system had been mixed. Both employers and unions and their counsel respected the Ontario Labour Relations Board for its independence, impartiality, fairness, and competence. But, on the other hand, the lawyers and students working in the Parkdale clinic encountered many marginally competent and biased tribunals, and they knew only too well what life-altering damage these were capable of inflicting. Indeed, from the Parkdale vantage point, it seemed that most judicial tribunals were like that. Capable and trusted tribunals like the Labour Relations Board and a handful of other "elite" tribunals appeared to be anomalous.

At WCAT, however, I saw from the inside what a properly structured judicial tribunal could do and be, and my experience there greatly deepened my understanding of the administrative justice system generally. WCAT enjoyed a unique set of structural advantages – indeed, the proverbial "perfect storm" of structural advantages. And these advantages enabled it to become an exemplar of rule-of-law-compliant tribunal/government relationships, tribunal structural design, and administrative and operational practices.

I am confident that this claim is not contentious, and two particular "bookend" comments, one from 1990 and the other from 2008, are indicative. In 1989, the consulting firm of Coopers and Lybrand was commissioned by the Minister of Labour to review WCAT's performance as part of the Minister's "Green Paper" study of various aspects of the workers' compensation system. Coopers' 1990 report included this: "The Tribunal renders high-quality adjudicative decisions which are fair, balanced, consistent and fully-reasoned."[13] On 2 June 2008, the *Liversidge e-Letter* stated: "[T]he creation of the Appeals Tribunal in 1985, which for the ensuing 23 years delivered *the* archetypical standard of administrative justice in Ontario if not in Canada, was a leading edge and novel concept not that many years ago, that shook the Ontario workers' compensation regime to its roots."[14]

But, but – I can hear the question – what about the letter from the grieving mother to the "so-called Tribunal"? Good question. I did not, however, tell that story to point to a tribunal gone wrong. The son's appeal had been given a fair hearing by a tribunal that was, as we shall see, as independent and impartial – as rule-of-law-compliant – as one could hope for, and, although no one can ever be satisfied that any adjudicative decision is right in any absolute sense, I was, and am, confident that this decision was, at least in law, correct. Certainly, it was a decision that would have withstood court scrutiny on judicial review. I told the story to make the point that what judicial tribunals do truly matters – as much as what courts do – and I wanted to make that point as clearly as possible at the outset.

I have cited WCAT's exemplary status, and provided evidence in support of that status, to demonstrate that my experience of the administrative justice system during my twelve WCAT years was authentic and relevant. During those years, both as the management person responsible[15] and as one of the tribunal's adjudicators,[16] I was immersed in the problems, challenges, and opportunities of a sizeable,[17] capable, structurally principled, and eventually trusted administrative judicial tribunal.

My characterization of WCAT's structural advantages as a perfect storm of advantages suggests something unique, but the advantages WCAT enjoyed were unique, and unusual, only when compared with the structural, rule-of-law deficiencies with which most other administrative judicial tribunals were and are forced to cope.

One of WCAT's important advantages was having the Ontario Ministry of Labour as its "host ministry."[18] Of all Ontario's host ministries, the Ministry of Labour's relationship with its tribunals appears to have been uniquely enlightened. Over its long history of dealing principally with the always prestigious but also politically sensitive Labour Relations Board, there had developed a culture of respectful attention. In such a culture, no person would be appointed as tribunal chair without the Deputy Minister being satisfied that the candidate was acceptable to both employers and unions; and no tribunal vice-chair[19] would be appointed or, most importantly, reappointed without the tribunal chair's prior approval.

The ability to control appointments and reappointments is essential to a tribunal chair's management role and to a tribunal's institutional independence. Chairs known to have no say in their members' appointments, and expected to have little or no say in their reappointments, cannot win their members' allegiance or respect. Members who know they owe their appointment solely to their political connections bring to their work a sense of entitlement, and a sense of allegiance to those connections, that bodes ill for the culture of collegiality and allegiance to the tribunal and its goals and mission that an effective tribunal requires. Moreover, in a tribunal headed by such a chair, members faced with politically sensitive decisions will take no comfort from the chair's support and will know that if their decision makes the government or its friends unhappy, they will eventually have to face the government alone, typically when the expiration of their current appointment draws near. In view of these implications, one might have expected to find tribunal chairs typically empowered to control appointments and reappointments. But, no – the customary processes for appointment and reappointment of judicial tribunal adjudicators have historically excluded the chairs.[20] The chairs of tribunals hosted by the Ontario Labour Ministry were an exception. In that ministry, tribunal adjudicators always knew they owed their appointments to the tribunal chair and that if they performed to the chair's satisfaction – but only then – their reappointments were safe.

A second advantage of Ministry of Labour tribunals was that there was no limit on the number of reappointments. It was not unheard of for vice-chairs or members to retire twenty five years after their first appointment, having been appointed eight times to a series of three-year terms. This absence of a cap on the number of years of service was exceptional. Traditionally, governments have capped the number of total years of tribunal service at six or ten. (Ontario has recently reaffirmed its commitment to a cap – now applicable to all tribunals, apparently including Ministry of Labour tribunals – of ten years, the same as the federal cap.)

WCAT was the beneficiary of all aspects of this special relationship between the Ministry of Labour and its tribunals.

WCAT was also uniquely placed to assert its independence. Created for the sole purpose of providing the independence notoriously missing from the workers' compensation system's traditional adjudicative structures, independence was acknowledged to be WCAT's *raison d'être*.

WCAT was created at the end of a turbulent political era in the workers' compensation system that culminated in Professor Paul Weiler's iconic review of a troubled system and his recognition of the pressing need for a final-level appeals tribunal independent of the WCB.[21] WCAT became that tribunal – the independent, final adjudicator for which the injured worker organizations and unions had long fought and that Weiler had recommended. As a result, WCAT did not have to make the case for its independence nor, unlike most tribunals, did it have to deal with a government whose commitment to the tribunal's independence was merely rhetorical. For WCAT, independence was key; the government subscribed to it and the unions, injured workers' organizations, and legal clinics were all vigilant in ensuring that nothing was allowed to undermine it or give the appearance of doing so. WCAT became a truly independent judicial arm of the workers' compensation statutory rights enterprise, an enterprise that at the time employed some 3,000 people and processed approximately 450,000 new claims a year from workers employed by 155,000 Ontario employers.

One of the central needs of a statutory rights enterprise the size of the Ontario workers' compensation system, in which at the time nearly two thousand new claim files were opened every working day, is an efficient adjudicative strategy. Ascending levels of adjudication are required, with the first level focusing on screening out the obvious and routine. At this level, the goals have to be speed and low unit-expense – goals achievable only at the cost of quality and consistency. Large numbers of staff adjudicators managing large caseloads must be subject to rules and supervision that leave little room for discretion or independent judgment. Hearings as such are out of the question. At this level, efficiency is the priority, and to that priority the rule of law and the principles of natural justice must bend. In rule-of-law terms, however, this arrangement is acceptable provided the expedient decision making is backed by subsequent levels of review opportunities that add up to a fair hearing.[22]

The WCB's adjudication strategy involved four levels of decision making. All rejections of claims by claims adjudicators at the first level were automatically referred to a Claims Review Branch to be checked by senior claims adjudicators for errors before the decision was issued. After the decision was issued, either party – the worker or the employer – could appeal to an Appeal Adjudicator. The Appeal Adjudicators, who were also Board staff members, held *de novo* hearings[23] but were principally concerned with factual and medical issues. At this level, the "law" was not effectively an issue; everyone just "knew" the law. Typically, it was the worker who appealed, employers rarely participated, and lawyers tended not to be involved. The hearing process was rudimentary, and even complicated cases were typically dealt with in an hour or two.

Finally, the Appeal Adjudicator's decision could be appealed by either party to an internal Appeal Board composed of members of the WCB governing board designated as "Appeals Commissioners." The Appeals Commissioners sat in panels of three. Here again the hearing was a *de novo* hearing, and at this level it was common for the parties to be represented by counsel, often lawyers. Participation by employers resisting the claim was also more common, and it was before this Appeal Board that I had appeared on rare occasions on behalf of employer clients when I was in private practice and before which my Parkdale clinic students appeared on occasion on behalf of injured worker clients. Even here, however, legal arguments got short shrift, with the WCB's corporate conventional wisdom as to what the *Workers' Compensation Act* said being largely treated as gospel. It was the Appeal Board that WCAT replaced in 1985.

The WCB's multi-level adjudicative process was not merely a public relations strategy. There is no doubt that the work of the adjudicators at each level was sincere and necessary.[24] Unfortunately, however, the Board's policy was to give only *pro forma* reasons for its decisions, so the merits of those decisions could never be objectively assessed. By the time Weiler began his review in 1979, the WCB was, in his words, "an embattled institution," reeling from a continuous barrage of negative publicity and unrelenting attacks from injured workers' organizations.

Because the WCB's Appeal Board members, the Appeals Commissioners, were also members of the WCB's governing body – the WCB of Directors – they were inevitably perceived to be biased – one WCB person reviewing the work of another. Moreover, they operated under a conflict of interest.

The Board of Directors was responsible for both awarding benefits and setting employer assessment rates. The benefits decisions impacted on the assessment rates and, given the significance of the rate levels for the Ontario economy and for the competitiveness of Ontario employers, rate-raising decisions were fraught with political risk for the WCB, its chair, and its Board members, including the Appeals Commissioners.

It was WCAT's independence – both the reality and the perception – that at the final appeal stage eliminated both the perception of bias and the conflict of interest, and so independence was WCAT's main thing. But unstinting government commitment to its independence was only one of the sources of WCAT's culture of independence. There was also the unique circumstance that the debilitating conflicts of interest between tribunals and host ministries that typically characterize a judicial tribunal's operational environment were in WCAT's case all largely attenuated.

In the first place, the Labour Ministry's responsibility for workers' compensation policy was at one remove from that of the WCB itself. It was not the Ministry but the Board that planned the operational policy, drafted the rules and regulations, and made the original benefit decisions. WCAT decisions therefore did not address policy or operational decisions made by the Labour Ministry or its staff, so, unlike most tribunals, WCAT did not have to challenge its host ministry directly. When a WCAT decision appeared to question the judgment, or sometimes perhaps even the competence, of the initial decision makers, or impacted negatively on policy, it was the WCB and its staff that were affronted, not the Ministry.

Furthermore, although WCAT's annual budget was subject to the Minister of Labour's approval, the statute directed that the money come from the WCB's Accident Fund, which was derived from employer assessments and administered by the Board. The added costs arising from the Appeal Tribunal's decisions in individual cases were, of course, also paid from the Accident Fund. Thus, neither WCAT's administration nor its adjudicative decisions impacted on its host ministry's own budget. As things now stand in Canada, very few judicial tribunals are in that enviable position.

And, finally, with the Minister and Ministry, and government, known to respect the chair's recommendations on reappointment decisions, no threat to the tribunal's independence arose from that direction either.

In such circumstances, the tribunal's embrace of a robust independence came naturally and found support on all sides.

Finally, WCAT enjoyed the great advantage of having all of its administrative resources in-house. These included the registrar function, legal services, the financial and accounting function, the payroll and benefits departments, the personnel function, the library and publications departments, and the information technology (IT) and statistics departments. All were covered by WCAT's own budget and all were ultimately administered and supervised by the chair. Except for the chair, no WCAT person had any reporting relationship with the Ministry or with any of its officials. Moreover, WCAT staff members were not members of the public service and owed no allegiance, and had no rights or special opportunities of entry, to the public service.[25] Hiring, firing, and promotion decisions for staff were for the chair alone (although in due course, the firing power was fettered by a WCAT collective bargaining agreement).[26] Most importantly, the tribunal developed and defended its own annual budgets.

None of this was usual. There are only a handful of judicial tribunals that are stand-alone in all these respects.[27] In my experience, however, a judicial institution cannot be independent without being in all respects its own person – a fully realized adult person. In my view, WCAT's vibrant *esprit de corps* and culture of insouciant independence could not possibly have emerged had it not been such a person.

With all these advantages, and aided in the early days of the tribunal by the unstinting support of Dr. Robert Elgie, the Minister of Labour at the time, and by his Deputy Minister, Tim Armstrong, I was, as chair, able to recruit and keep a full complement of highly qualified and exceptionally talented tribunal members and staff, all selected by me in collaboration with my colleagues. When my own appointment was terminated in 1997, most of those members and staff were still there and still performing at a level of excellence; some are still with the tribunal as I write. It is axiomatic that to have a good tribunal you must recruit and retain good people, and we were allowed to do that.

This set of unique advantages continued for ten years. Then, in June 1995, the Progressive Conservative Party formed the government, and at once WCAT took its turn as an embattled institution. The new government's "Common Sense" election platform had included a commitment to reduce workers' compensation assessments and bring the system's unfunded liability under control. WCAT's elimination was widely anticipated.

As noted, I left the tribunal in June 1997, so for almost two years I headed a judicial tribunal operating within the gunsights of a hostile government. That experience proved, however, to be nearly as instructive about the mores of an administrative justice system as the preceding ten years of leading a uniquely advantaged tribunal.

The new government initiated a full review of the compensation system, with one of the foremost questions being whether WCAT's existence could still be justified. After an initial fact-gathering process, the responsible Minister published a discussion paper that again left the question of WCAT's continued existence explicitly open. In the end, the concept of an external, independent appeals tribunal survived. Its name was changed to the Workplace Safety and Insurance Appeals Tribunal (WSIAT), its jurisdiction was reduced to ensure that it would be, by law, bound by WCB policies that were themselves lawful, and its tripartite nature was diluted, but it survived in essential respects and continues to operate to this day. At various stages during the Minister's year-long review process, however, I found it necessary to make both private and public submissions correcting what I saw to be errors in the Minister's statements about the tribunal and its performance.[28] I did this with as much courtesy and circumspection as I could muster. Nonetheless, I experienced during this period what most judicial tribunal chairs and members experience routinely: the necessity of frequently disagreeing publicly with the Minister or Ministry on whom their tribunal depends for its life and the chair and members for their reappointments, obviously not a prescription for independent decision making.

During the month preceding my departure from WCAT, a number of my recommendations for the reappointment of WCAT members whose terms were expiring were rejected and three new members were appointed without consultation with either me or my replacement as chair,[29] the first such appointments in the tribunal's history.

The arbitrary denial of reappointment of meritorious members of judicial tribunals and the exclusion of chairs from the appointment and reappointment process, both of which were characteristic of the administrative justice system under the Harris regime, are inherently incompatible with the concept of an independent and impartial administrative justice system. About three months after leaving the tribunal, in a farewell address to the Workers' Compensation Section of the Ontario Branch of the Canadian Bar Association, I made my concerns in that respect public, and in the process rather launched my "career" as a critic of Canada's administrative justice system.[30]

Another aspect of my professional experience that has helped shape the lens through which I view that system is my involvement in the collegial organizations of tribunal chairs and members. These organizations began to evolve in the latter half of the 1980s and were devoted to the presentation of continuing legal education programs for administrative tribunal members and chairs and to the exploration of generic administrative justice issues.

The first such organization was, I believe, La Conférence des Juges Administratifs du Québec (CJAQ), first organized in 1985. The first and only national organization is the Council of Canadian Administrative Tribunals (CCAT), formally organized in 1986. I was a member of CCAT's first board of directors and served in that capacity until 1994. In 1986, I also became involved with an informal "circle" of Ontario tribunal chairs that met regularly to discuss common problems and issues, and in 1988 organized the first annual Conference of Ontario Boards and Agencies.[31] This informal organization morphed into the Society of Ontario Adjudicators and Regulators (SOAR), and I served as its inaugural president from 1992 to 1996. The CCAT and SOAR initiatives were followed in British Columbia by the organization of the BC Council of Administrative Tribunals (BCCAT), and in Manitoba there is now the Manitoba Council of Administrative Tribunals (MCAT).

I was frequently a member of training and conference planning committees for both CCAT and SOAR, co-chair of CCAT's annual national conference in 1990, and a regular presenter of papers at training programs and conferences, many of which were subsequently published. My involvement with these conferences continues to this day. One advantage of this type of involvement has been the opportunity to share confidences with colleagues in tribunals in other provinces and territories and in the federal jurisdiction, about the problems and issues we were all encountering in the administration and operation of our tribunals.

In 2005, I was asked to serve as a member of the Advisory Panel of the Immigration and Refugee Board of Canada (IRB). This was the Advisory Panel that was the central component of the IRB's merit-based appointment process that had been introduced circa 2004 by the IRB chair at the time, Jean-Guy Fleury.[32] This appointments process will be described at some length in Chapter 1.

Finally, there is my personal experience as counsel in the *McKenzie* case, which arose serendipitously in the midst of my graduate program at Osgoode Hall. The decision of the BC Supreme Court in *McKenzie* will figure prominently in the legal analysis to follow, but my experience with the case so enriched my understanding of the administrative justice system and its issues, and so quickened my concern about these issues, that it also belongs in this account of my formative administrative justice experiences.

In the winter of 2004-05, a senior and respected Residential Tenancy Arbitrator, Mary McKenzie, was adjudicating residential landlord and tenant disputes in British Columbia. She was a lawyer, a graduate of Osgoode Hall Law School in Toronto, with a master's degree in Public Administration from Queen's University. She had been appointed as a part-time Residential Tenancy Arbitrator in 1994, one of thirty selected out of three hundred applicants in what was at the time a unique, merit-based selection process. On 1 January 2004, she had been appointed to a new five-year term.

By 2002, McKenzie's residential tenancy arbitration work, while still notionally part-time, had become her sole source of income. She was by then the mother and sole support of two children, and circumstances had so conspired that she found herself living in Nanaimo on Vancouver Island and commuting to Burnaby in the Lower Mainland for arbitration hearings three days a week. Then, in March 2003, she was able to trade one day of her Lower Mainland hearings with another arbitrator for one day of his Nanaimo hearings, and so began to hold landlord and tenant hearings one day each week in her home city, Nanaimo.

This schedule continued for about twenty-one months, until December 2004, when, without warning, McKenzie was removed from all Nanaimo hearings and her Nanaimo hearings were assigned to other arbitrators. This decision, which effectively reduced her income by one-third, was particularly disturbing because the problem was obviously not a lack of cases in Nanaimo. She also knew that the quality of her work was not an issue because management had regularly complimented her work and encouraged her to seek additional hearing dates. Moreover, while suddenly barred from hearings in Nanaimo, she continued to be assigned to her two days of hearings in Burnaby.

Over the next five weeks, McKenzie's attempts to reach the Director of the program (who was based in Victoria) were unsuccessful, and her letter demanding an explanation went unanswered. Finally, she was summoned to a meeting with the Director at the Nanaimo office on 18 February. At that meeting, the Director handed McKenzie a letter advising her that her five-year, fixed-term appointment as a Residential Tenancy Arbitrator, due to expire on 31 December 2008, would be terminated effective 31 March 2005, the date on which her current fee arrangements would expire. The Director explicitly refused any reason or justification for this extraordinary decision, stating only that the government was acting under a new statutory provision that authorized it to terminate any tribunal member's fixed-term appointment at any time, without cause or reasons, upon payment of one year's compensation. The provision in question was s. 14.9(3) of the *Public Sector Employers Act*.[33] This section had been enacted in May 2003 and McKenzie was the first tribunal member whose appointment was terminated pursuant to its provisions.

Mary McKenzie had an unblemished service record of over ten years. She had no indication of management displeasure with her or her performance. In fact, at the 18 February meeting, the Director agreed to assign her additional hearings in Burnaby during the six weeks leading up to the termination date. After her termination, the previous Director, who had supervised her work for ten years, provided her with a glowing written reference; paradoxically, the new Director also provided a positive reference letter.[34]

The singling out of a tribunal adjudicator for termination in this fashion was unprecedented in British Columbia. For Mary McKenzie, it meant the destruction of her career as an adjudicator in her home province and a catastrophic disruption of her finances and personal life. She believed strongly that "they couldn't do this" and that in her own interests, and in the interests of the integrity of the administrative justice system in British Columbia, she "could not allow them to do this." She retained counsel and, in due course, after a period of futile discussion between her counsel and government counsel, she instructed her counsel to file a petition in the BC Supreme Court for judicial review of the government's decision.

An especially significant fact about these proceedings is that at no time – not during the pre-litigation discussion nor at any time during the course of the ensuing litigation – did the government attempt any explanation whatsoever for its original decision to bar McKenzie from presiding over residential landlord and tenant hearings in Nanaimo. The government did not suggest that the number of Nanaimo hearings had declined, nor did it express any concerns with the quality of her work. The Director who had written the termination letter was never called upon to explain why she had made such a recommendation, nor was she asked to confirm that the recommendation had in fact originated with her. The government filed no evidence of any kind. What, then, was the government's problem with McKenzie's holding hearings in Nanaimo? The government would not say; it has never said.

Of course, McKenzie and her legal team speculated at length about the government's motives for barring her from holding Nanaimo hearings. The obvious inference was that someone in Nanaimo with influential ties to the government had not liked her decisions. The team thought long and hard about how that probable motive might be made to figure in the litigation, but they ultimately decided against the attempt. There was no reasonable likelihood of proving what had really happened and, in any event, the importance of the case actually lay in its challenge to the constitutionality of the government's alleged power to terminate members of independent judicial tribunals without cause in the middle of their terms. From that perspective, the government's motives in this particular case were only of incidental interest.

McKenzie's Petition for Judicial Review was filed in the Supreme Court of British Columbia on 31 May 2005. Shortly thereafter, the BC Council of Administrative Tribunals (BCCAT) applied for intervenor status. The following paragraph from the affidavit of the BCCAT president filed in support of that application captures the public-interest nature of the issues raised by McKenzie's application for judicial review.

> BCCAT is of the view that the answers to each of the public law questions raised by the Petitioner, who has raised them as the first person respecting whom action has been taken under s. 14.9(3) ... will have implications for many administrative law adjudicative schemes. BCCAT thus does not view this Petition as being properly characterized as a dispute between private parties. Rather, BCCAT sees this as being a test case the outcome of which will transcend the particular dispute between the Petitioner and Respondents. BCCAT is of the view that the Petition raises public law issues whose outcome will have very significant implications for BC's administrative justice system.

Mary McKenzie's judicial review petition was successful. Mr. Justice McEwan of the BC Supreme Court held that the government's interpretation of s. 14.9(3) was incorrect. Most importantly for the thesis of this book, however, he also held that, if the interpretation had been correct, the section as it applied to Residential Tenancy Arbitrators would then have been incompatible with the constitutional principle of judicial independence, and therefore constitutionally invalid.[35] The order terminating McKenzie's appointment was quashed and her appointment thereby reinstated.

The government appealed. After a two-day hearing, the BC Court of Appeal reserved its decision and then surprised both parties by refusing to deal with either the interpretation or constitutional issues on their merits. The Court dismissed the government's appeal solely on the grounds that at the time of the hearing of the appeal the issues had become moot.[36] In addition, the Court, also on its own motion, went out of its way to cast doubt on the precedential value of Justice McEwan's decision. It took the position, without benefit of argument from either party, that the issues had also been moot (for different reasons) at the time of the lower court hearing.[37] It did not, however, comment on the substantive merits of Justice McEwan's decision.

McKenzie, whose role in the litigation had become by the time of the appeal only that of a public-interest litigant,[38] believed that the public interest required that at least the constitutional issue be resolved at the highest appeal level, and she therefore applied to the Supreme Court of Canada for leave to appeal the BC Court of Appeal's refusal to decide the substantive issues and its disparagement of the precedential value of Justice McEwan's judgment. Her application was dismissed in April 2008, and the *McKenzie* case came to an end. Justice McEwan's judgment remained intact on its merits, but its precedential value had been left in doubt.

So, where did I come into this? Within the tribunal community, the mid-term termination of Mary McKenzie's appointment without cause quickly became a national *cause célèbre*. I first heard of it in May 2005 in discussions with CCAT colleagues. It was perverse to be excited by the news, but it sounded to me exactly like the case the administrative justice system needed.

The case the system needed was a case that would present squarely the issue of constitutional protection for the independence of administrative judicial tribunals. I had come to despair of any realistic possibility of asserting justice-system principles in an executive branch–controlled justice system unless it could be established that the constitutional requirement of judicial independence applied to tribunals exercising judicial functions. On that issue, the Supreme Court of Canada had been giving confusing signals, at one time appearing to say it did not (*Ocean Port,*[39] 2001), and at another time suggesting that it might (*Bell Canada,*[40] 2003) or that it probably did (*Ell,*[41] also 2003).

In *Ocean Port,* the Court had seemed to say – indeed, had been understood by many to have said – that the implicit constitutional requirement of judicial independence first identified by the Supreme Court in 1997 in its *PEI Reference* decision[42] as applicable to "all courts" would not apply to administrative tribunals of any kind, not even to judicial tribunals. I had doubted, however, that, in the end, this view of the matter would hold. Speaking at a community legal services clinic training day in Toronto in April 2003, I had struck this hopeful note:

[T]en or fifteen years from now *Ocean Port's* place in the administrative justice system will be seen to have been principally important for the impetus it gave to a fundamental rethinking of our theory of administrative justice and to a more careful consideration of the nature of our [judicial] tribunals. In some future case, the Court will be faced with [a judicial tribunal] ... whose decision-makers, by reason of statutory provisions ... clearly do not qualify as impartial or independent. In that future case, the Court will ... be inevitably moved to reassert the role of the courts as the ultimate guardians of the rule of law in our administrative justice systems.[43]

From what I had learned from my CCAT colleagues, the *McKenzie* case appeared likely to be that future case.

McKenzie's counsel was Paul Pearlman, QC, of Victoria, British Columbia.[44] I e-mailed Mr. Pearlman, commenting on the constitutional importance of the case if the facts I had heard were true, and offering a memorandum of law that I had written on another occasion about the potential for asserting the constitutional principle of judicial independence in support of administrative justice system tribunals and their members. Mr. Pearlman forwarded my message to Mary McKenzie and I heard back from her the same day. I then learned that she was the same Mary McKenzie who had been a student of mine many years earlier, in the Parkdale clinic program; and when my interest in establishing the constitutional invalidity of the statutory provision under which her appointment had been terminated turned out to match her passionate belief that the termination of her appointment had placed the independence of the entire BC administrative justice system in question, my role as co-counsel in the *McKenzie* case began.

For the next three years, through researching and drafting the petition and appeal materials and preparing the Application for Leave to the Supreme Court of Canada, and while spearheading the funding campaign that would enable the proceedings to continue, Mary McKenzie and I spent countless hours working together.

From a doctrinal and theory of law perspective, my research and analysis on the issues presented by *McKenzie* were central to my graduate studies agenda. Just as important, however, was the extent to which my extended working relationship with Mary McKenzie enabled me to truly grasp the personal impact that a government's abuse of its powers has on the individual abused and to better appreciate the vulnerability felt by tribunal members faced with governments that brandish powers of arbitrary dismissal.

A mid-term dismissal of a tribunal adjudicator without cause is not a private event.[45] While the government is not alleging cause, the unusual nature of its action will inevitably suggest to the uninformed observer that the government must in fact have some serious reasons, and when the government declines to talk about those reasons, the observer is very apt to conclude that the government's reasons must be serious indeed. Few would suspect that the government is not talking about it because its own motives cannot stand the light of day.

Because the government has implicitly libelled them and refused any explanation, terminated members suffer severe damage to their professional reputations. Since the government also controls all future adjudicative appointments, the adjudicative career of terminated tribunal members in their home jurisdiction is effectively ended, and in applications for adjudicative appointments outside their home jurisdiction or for employment in other legal fields, they face the problem of having no explanation for their peremptory, and public, mid-term dismissal from a long-standing adjudicative position.

Mary McKenzie, through no fault of her own, was suddenly deprived of her income, her reputation, and, effectively, her career. The courage that it took, first to reject settlement offers fashioned as though her case was just another wrongful dismissal of a government employee, and then to persist in her fight for the independence principle all the way to the end of an unsuccessful application for leave to appeal to the Supreme Court of Canada, was remarkable.

In his opening statement in the hearing of McKenzie's petition (before Justice McEwan), Victoria lawyer Frank Falzon appearing for the Intervenor BCCAT, grabbed the attention of the Court – and, I might add, of his fellow counsel – by audaciously comparing Mary McKenzie's defence of the independence of administrative justice tribunals to Lord Coke's famous seventeenth-century defence of the independence of the common law courts against the depredations of King James I. The comparison appeared to provoke a tolerant smile from the presiding judge but, when looked at fairly in its modern context, was not far off the mark. Moreover, the comparison was tactically sound. With that bold metaphor, Mr. Falzon at one stroke laid bare for the Court the undoubtedly historic nature of the case and the daring and vulnerability of the protagonist.

In May 2007, speaking to the CCAT International Conference on Administrative Justice in Vancouver while we awaited the Court of Appeal's decision, I paid tribute to Mary McKenzie: "It is the system's rare good fortune that the burden of championing the constitutional independence of adjudicative tribunals happened to fall on a person with the courage and principled commitment of a Mary McKenzie."

At the annual CCAT conference in Halifax in June 2009, after the disappointing Court of Appeal decision and the dismissal of McKenzie's application for leave to appeal to the Supreme Court of Canada, the proposition that there was indeed no constitutional protection for the independence of adjudicative tribunals and that, yes, this was a good thing became the subject of a formal plenary-session debate. I was a member of the debate panel, arguing, of course, for the no side.[46] At the end of the debate, questions from the floor were invited. Heather MacNaughton, who was then the chair of the BC Human Rights Tribunal, asked the panel members supporting the "no constitutional protection" proposition: "Are you not aware of the chilling effect on the decision-making of tribunal members in B.C. and across the country of adjudicators having watched the treatment accorded to Mary McKenzie and what she was put through in her attempt to protect the independence of tribunal members? If there is no constitutional protection, what do you propose be done about that?" The pro side of the debate panel had nothing to suggest.[47]

What Experience Teaches

My experience with the administrative justice system recounted in this Introduction has led me to firm convictions on three fundamental points.

1. What judicial tribunals do really matters – often desperately. It was to drive this point home that I told the story about the blood-spattered missive from the grieving mother. What judicial tribunal members do is too important for them to be pursuing their own political or ideological goals, or dabbling in public service, or wending their way to a comfortable retirement; just like judges, they are engaged in serious business where the consequence of getting things wrong may be the infliction on the parties who appear before them, and on their families, of injustices and hardships of the gravest kind.

2. Canadian administrative judicial tribunals and their members are not independent, do not meet the rule-of-law criteria for impartiality, and cannot be counted on for competence.[48] The evidence for this will be found throughout this book.

3. Hardly anyone cares – on the evidence, certainly not the politicians or the bureaucrats. In the spring of 2003, Auditor General of Canada Sheila Fraser blew the whistle on the federal Liberals' sponsorship scandal. At or about the same time, Peter Showler blew the whistle on patronage abuse at the Immigration and Refugee Board. Showler knew whereof he spoke. He was the outgoing chair of the IRB and had been a member of that Board for nine years. Here are some of the remarkable things he said to a reporter:

> Political patronage is a devastating blight on the Immigration and Refugee Board ... [It] undermines the Board's work, the morale of its staff and the implementation of Canada's immigration and refugee policy ... Political influence ... is pervasive and pernicious ... [The Board's] real problem is ... mediocrity and incompetence among some of its members [caused by political patronage] ... The Board is hobbled by patronage ... [P]olitical infighting within the [federal] Liberal Party and caucus over who should get the patronage plums has often resulted in lengthy delays in filling vacancies, despite unprecedented pressure on the Board to perform ... Members who get mediocre or even bad [performance] ratings can find themselves appointed to a second term because of political connections, while members who have excelled are sometimes denied a second term ... The Board's internal process for evaluating the work of its members can also become tainted by political influence, with managers coming under political pressure to give positive evaluations to members who have more powerful political friends than they do.[49]

Federal government officials and politicians know that the competent implementation of Canada's troubled immigration and refugee policy depends on the quality of the people appointed to the IRB. They also know that these appointees are entrusted with adjudication of the immigrant or refugee status of individuals – frightened individuals, often in desperate straits, whose future and the future of their families, and sometimes their very lives, depend on a fair, competent, and timely adjudication of their rights.

In light of these facts, it seems to me that it should be plain for all to see that the patronage abuse of IRB appointments described by Showler is on moral and ethical grounds far more shameful than the mere misappropriation of public funds. Yet, unlike Sheila Fraser's revelations, Peter Showler's equally public and authoritative exposé appears to have startled no one; it certainly sparked no outrage, led to no inquiry, threatened no one's job, and brought down no government.

Nor, of course, was Showler the first to highlight the problem of patronage in appointments to administrative judicial tribunals; indeed, there had been a long history of known patronage abuse at the IRB itself. I cite this one instance as a particularly compelling demonstration of a general problem: except for its victims, no one seems to be concerned about our shameful administrative justice system.

That no one is concerned may be found writ large in the historical fact that, seemingly without political embarrassment and with no public criticism, Ontario governments were able to refuse any compensation increases to Ontario's administrative judicial tribunal members for over twenty years – a drought that did not come to an end until the spring of 2007. The salary of my successor as chair of WCAT was exactly the same in 2007 as mine had been when I left in 1997, and the same as I was earning in 1989.[50] There is no reason to think that, outside of Quebec (and the federal jurisdiction, where salaries for tribunal members were kept in line with the public service), the experience of members of judicial tribunals in other provinces or territories was very different.

In the category of evidence that no one cares, I must also respectfully place the decisions of the BC Court of Appeal and the Supreme Court of Canada in *McKenzie*. It is always problematic for lawyers to criticize court decisions in cases in which they have participated as counsel. Their motives will be suspect and their analysis viewed with the skepticism that extreme partisanship attracts and often deserves. It is not an activity in which any lawyer normally engages, but I believe the risk is necessary in this special case.

The Court of Appeal panel that heard the government's appeal in *McKenzie* had to know that the power claimed by the BC government – the power to terminate judicial tribunal members at any time without cause – was antithetical to either the appearance or the reality of their independence. The Supreme Court of Canada had said so, repeatedly.[51] But it was the Court of Appeal – not either of the parties – that raised the mootness issue. Both the government and McKenzie had urged the Court to decide the constitutional issue notwithstanding any concerns about mootness. It was also the Court that, again of its own volition, went out of its way to disparage the authority of the lower court's decision.

The law is perfectly clear that a court has jurisdiction to decide a moot issue, given exigent circumstances. The principles governing the exercise of that jurisdiction are known as the *Borowski* principles.[52] *Both* parties had argued that the constitutional and interpretation issues decided by the lower court were *not* moot in the appeal. But even if the issues *were* moot, the circumstances in which they were presented for decision to the Court of

Appeal were precisely the circumstances that the *Borowski* principles identify as authorizing a court to exercise its discretion in favour of deciding an
issue, despite its mootness.[53] If the circumstances of this case did not justify
the exercise of that discretion, it is difficult to imagine what circumstances
would. And, as mentioned, *both* parties had argued that, moot or not, it was
of critical importance that the issues be dealt with.

And yet the Court of Appeal, fully cognizant of the *Borowski* principles,
thought it right to effectively condone the continuation of the government's
power to dismiss judicial tribunal members at any time without cause until
some other victim of such arbitrary power should find the financial wherewithal and emotional fortitude to challenge the government again, in some
future litigation. On this point, the Court said:

> Further, it cannot be said that the issues are evasive of review. Section
> 14.9(3) ... applies to approximately 37 administrative tribunals. It defies
> common sense to suggest that another tribunal member, similarly ag-
> grieved, will not challenge the legislation.
>
> In my opinion, it would be wise to await that challenge and decide the
> merits of an appeal from that challenge on the specific facts and circum-
> stances of such a case and in their specific legislative context ... To do other-
> wise would, in my view, have the potential to create mischief.[54]

By this decision, the independence of virtually all BC tribunals was effectively destroyed for an indeterminate period of time, a period that has not
expired even as I write. The BC Court of Appeal was content to initiate such
a result, and the Supreme Court of Canada apparently saw nothing in that
contentment that was of sufficient public importance to warrant its granting
leave to appeal.

All of this, then, is what has moved me to write this book and also, of
course, is what has shaped the lens through which I view the need for transformative reform.

What This Book Is Not About

As indicated above, this book is *not* about the exercise of regulatory functions by regulatory agencies such as the energy boards. For reasons that I
will explain shortly, it is also not about Quebec. Neither is it about the fail-
ures or neglect of any particular government or political party. I am talking
here about a justice-system, rule-of-law train wreck whose provenance is

decades old – a train wreck for which all political parties; all Canadian governments, past and present, and their administrators; and, to some extent, the courts must take responsibility.

Why is my criticism of the administrative justice system not, for the most part, pertinent to Quebec's share of that system? Quebec's radical and progressive reform of its system of administrative law in 1996 dramatically changed the architecture of that system.[55] In terms of administrative law, Quebec is now a different case from the rest of the country. It is also the only province with a written constitutional requirement that administrative tribunals in general be independent and impartial.[56] I shall refer to Quebec in comparative terms from time to time, but by and large my analysis of the problems with the administrative justice system in the English-speaking jurisdictions of Canada does not apply to Quebec's current system. My concerns relate to the rest of Canada, where the Quebec reforms have had no discernible impact.[57] Note, however, that my exclusion of Quebec from this critique should not be taken to mean that I have concluded that there are no administrative justice problems left in that province. My point is that it is a different case. Whether it is in all respects a better case I leave for others to determine.

What This Book Is About

Given that administrative judicial tribunals are the only embodiment of our justice system that most Canadians will ever personally face, and that the decisions of those tribunals are often life-altering for the parties involved, casual admirers of Canadian justice would presumably expect to find in these tribunals what they expect to find in Canadian courts: a strong tradition of independence, impartiality, and competence. Instead, however, we have an executive branch system of judicial tribunals where the reality is typically an intransigent culture of government dominance and control, a system that ignores the rule of law and the Constitution, and a system that is, at a minimum, careless of competence. The executive branch proclaims its administrative judicial tribunals to be independent in their decision making, but requires that they operate in the ordinary course under the influence of pervasive conflicts of interest that are irredeemably toxic to any reasonable perception of independence or impartiality, conflicts that would not be tolerated in any other setting.

This book is about a national scandal, about Canada's long tolerance of a system of justice – the system of administrative justice – in which the rule of law's justice system requirements of structural independence and impartiality are simply absent.

The judicial functions that comprise this system are all deployed, controlled, and administered by the executive branch of government. From the beginning, the executive branch has understood that permitting these judicial functions to be protected by the structures required of a rule-of-law-compliant justice system – structures designed to ensure the independence and impartiality of the bodies exercising the judicial functions – would be inimical to its interests, and has simply chosen not to permit it. Thus, everywhere in Canada (with the exception of Quebec) we have a state-sponsored justice system to which the majority of our rights disputes have been assigned for final adjudication but where the rule of law has been willfully disrespected and actively resisted – by the government. As I say, a scandal.

For reasons I will address shortly, the structural flaws in Canada's administrative justice system generally lie below the surface, rarely causing public controversy of a general nature. Nevertheless, from time to time the evidence of the defective structures comes to the fore.

Of course, official assertions of the independence of tribunals are ubiquitous, but never more than empty rhetoric. In Chapter 1, I will present evidence of ruinously inadequate budgets; of patronage and partisan political preoccupations undermining appointments and reappointments; of competitive, merit-based selection processes for judicial tribunal members being the rare exception rather than the rule; of appointments that are invariably for short, fixed periods, typically of three or five years, with the reappointment power routinely exercised arbitrarily, and with expected reappointments of experienced, meritorious members and chairs often refused following decisions that were unpalatable to the government or its allies or merely to make way for the appointment of a government's importunate friends; of incoming governments refusing to reappoint judicial tribunal members on ideological grounds, not caring that the refusals are jeopardizing the tribunal's ability to meet its statutory responsibilities; of the tolerance of mid-term dismissals of members without cause or reasons; of judicial tribunal chairs and members being discharged allegedly for cause without an opportunity to be heard; of the administrative justice system routinely expelling its most qualified members at the end of an arbitrarily imposed maximum of six or ten or twelve years of service; and of egregious, structurally embedded conflicts of interest between judicial tribunals and their host ministries continuing to be the common reality.

Plumbing the depths of this embarrassment, I address the system's systemic, constitutional, legal, and structural impediments to justice. Building on my own experience of the system, and positing the elements of a theory of administrative justice on which transformative reform may be based, I propose a concrete blueprint for change. It is a blueprint for an administrative justice system that would be fully congruent with a principled, integrated, and rational rule-of-law-compliant justice policy, but one that would also be harmonized with its administrative roots and its policy role – a system that would live up to Canadian principles and traditions of justice and be worthy of the nation's respect, compatible with its international reputation, and congruent, finally, with its constitutional norms.

Why This Happened and Why We Don't Talk about It

Why has this train wreck of a justice system been allowed to happen? Principally, it is because politicians, governments, and the bureaucracies that serve governments all share deeply rooted interests in having it that way, and the rest of us have not noticed. We have not noticed because few of us are able to see the system in its entirety. Of course, most have yet to encounter the system at all, and even those who have will typically have dealt with only one or two of the system's large number of tribunals. Even administrative law professionals tend to do business with only a handful of particular tribunals.

There is typically no public discussion of any of this and the obvious question is, why not? If the system is this problematic, why do we not hear about it?

As discussed above, the existence of an administrative justice system has yet to enter the public consciousness. When things go wrong publicly at a particular tribunal, it is only the constituency actually served by that tribunal that is disturbed by that failure. Thus, when Ontario's Criminal Injuries Compensation Board is excoriated by the Ontario Ombudsman as a failed organization,[58] the only portion of the electorate the government has to appease consists of the victims of crime and their families. Members of the general public, unaware that the structural deformities that doomed the Criminal Injuries Compensation Board are systemic deformities that are also undermining the judicial tribunals to which many of them will eventually have to turn for the determination of their own rights, are only mildly interested, if at all.

Moreover, objective evidence of the system's structural deformities does not often present itself, and when bad things do come to light, it is typically portrayed by the government – and characterized by the media – as another idiosyncratic problem: the XYZ Tribunal needs fixing. Inevitably, however, the untold story is that of systemic structural deformities responsible for the failure – deformities that undermine the legality, independence, impartiality, and optimal competence of all judicial tribunals; deformities that only occasionally emerge into public view.

There is no mystery as to why the systemic implications of these events remain largely hidden. Knowledge of them is typically vouchsafed to only a few: the advocates appearing on a regular basis before particular tribunals, and the system's insiders, namely, the government and the tribunals' chairs and members. Moreover, as I have said, no one person's knowledge extends beyond one or two tribunals. Hardly anyone, professionals included, has a system-wide perspective on the administrative justice system writ large.

Moreover, for individuals who are in the know, speaking out about the rule-of-law problems they do see is rarely a desired, practical, or safe option. The politicians and bureaucrats that design and administer judicial tribunals see the tribunals' justice-system deficiencies, if they see them at all, as working in *their* respective interests, and are famously successful in their obdurate resistance to any justice-related reforms. Tribunal chairs and members are ineffectual as advocates for reform because their status and reputation are generically tarred in the public eye by the widespread perception that they are all the undeserving beneficiaries of a patronage system of appointments. Moreover, chairs and members are dependent on the government – on both the politicians and the bureaucrats. They know that if they are seen to put either group in a bad light, they will be vulnerable to reprisals at the time of their always pending reappointments.

Of course, advocates who appear before tribunals on behalf of clients experience the problems first-hand, but going public with criticism will put them at odds with the tribunal before which they practise, thus perhaps jeopardizing their clients' interests in future appearances. As prominent Toronto administrative law lawyer Andrew Roman once said: "Advocates have to be nice to tribunals, and tribunal chairs and members have to be nice to politicians."[59] Moreover, when advocates and/or their clients do make their concerns public, those concerns are routinely discounted as partisan advocacy.

The Exceptions to the General Rule

In this Introduction, I must, of course, not fail to acknowledge that there are administrative judicial tribunals that through a set of providential circumstances have managed to overcome the systemic, rule-of-law, and structural obstacles, and perform to standards that a principled administrative justice system would expect of them. But these are accomplishments achieved despite those obstacles and they remain, therefore, accomplishments that are not only fragile and implicitly transitory but, at bottom, still invalid in principle and very often at law.

I must also acknowledge those many individuals serving as judicial tribunal members and chairs who have providentially turned out to be competent (providentially, given the often problematic appointments processes and the many career-discouraging features of the system) and whose integrity impels them to ignore the career risks involved in making independent decisions in this system of executive branch justice. I regret the necessity of condemning a system in which they are so gallantly engaged.

It is also true that in the past decade or so, some provinces have reformed their appointments processes for judicial tribunals. But these are in important respects only partial or problematic reforms and I will be addressing them in Chapter 1.

The Enlightenment Sponsored by the Collegial Organizations

I should also mention a piece of positive news concerning the work of the professional collegial organizations referred to earlier.

These organizations have made a difference. Prior to CCAT's arrival on the scene, the judicial tribunal world, particularly the world outside Quebec, was in dire need of enlightenment. At that time, it had yet to be acknowledged that this was a *system* of tribunals with common functions, problems, needs, and vulnerabilities, and governed by common principles; much less that this system was an integral part of the justice system. Moreover, the concept of an *adjudicative* or judicial tribunal was largely unrecognized, with all tribunals, including judicial tribunals, being labelled and treated as regulatory agencies. Inter-tribunal collegiality was unheard of; each tribunal lived and did its business in an impenetrable silo. There was no tradition of inter-tribunal education or training in generic adjudicative skills; no recognition of the need for programs of continuing legal education for tribunal members; and, of course, no programs. There was also no forum where issues of administrative law and practice of generic interest to tribunals and tribunal members could be aired or analyzed – no annual conferences, no round tables, no academic journal devoted to those issues, and, within academe, little interest in the tribunals' rule-of-law structural deficiencies.

In all these respects, we have come a long way in the past twenty-five years, and the creation of CJAQ in Quebec in 1985 and CCAT in 1986 was the beginning of the gradual "enlightenment" of the administrative justice professional landscape. In the end, however, this enlightenment has not actually helped. In the real world, landscaping comes after the renovation of buildings. In the tribunal world, those who were active in the collegial organizations had the fond hope that enlightening the landscape – building a community of tribunals and their members, creating generic education programs, encouraging the professionalism of members, producing a literature of analysis and academic criticism – would so expose the dilapidation and barren architecture of the buildings that major renovations must needs follow.

But the renovations have not followed. The landscape is more pleasing but the buildings themselves are still a blight on the justice system with their medieval architecture still mocking the rule of law.

The Historical Context

The practice of assigning to non-courts the judicial adjudication of disputes about statutory rights has a lengthy history. In the common law system, it began in the United Kingdom before Canada came on the scene, and naturally it is there that one finds the antecedents of Canada's administrative justice system. In his book *Without the Law*[60] and in his earlier, famous article "Jonah and the Whale,"[61] Professor Harry Arthurs has provided a delightful, scholarly account of those antecedents as they unfolded in Great Britain in the nineteenth century.

By the end of that century, the practice of assigning judicial functions to statutory tribunals had caught the public's attention and was cause for growing concern among lawyers and judges who saw it as a practice pernicious to the rule of law. *The New Despotism*, a book published in 1929 by the Chief Justice of England, Lord Hewart, is notorious for its vituperative attack on the practice. The Chief Justice charged that there existed "a persistent and well-contrived system, intended to produce, and in practice producing, a despotic power which at one and the same time places Government Departments above the sovereignty of Parliament and beyond the jurisdiction of the Courts."[62]

Canadian lawyers and academics have traditionally disparaged Lord Hewart's book as self-interested, over-the-top rhetoric from an establishment court figure defending the status quo against competition from these newfangled rivals. Essentially the same criticism as Hewart's is found, however, in Professor A.V. Dicey's *Lectures Introductory to the Study of Law of the Constitution,* first published in 1885.[63] Dicey regarded tribunals – non-courts exercising judicial functions that he disparagingly equated with France's government-biased "official courts" – as incompatible with the rule of law.

Although Dicey is a persistent, iconic presence in Canada's administrative law conversation, he has not usually been seen as a positive influence. He figures most prominently as the Great Satan – the whipping boy for administrative law academics prone to see the replacement of courts by tribunals as modern and progressive and to dismiss judges resistant to the new structures as recalcitrant adherents of a reactionary and antediluvian – "Diceyan" – view of tribunals and courts.[64] Considered objectively in light of the state of Canadian judicial tribunals in the twenty-first century, however, Dicey's antipathy to judicial tribunals, an antipathy against which the Canadian administrative law academe has long railed, must now be considered rather more prescient than reactionary. Were Lord Hewart and Professor Dicey here today, I would respectfully suggest that both would have to be allowed a quiet "told you so."

This is not to suggest that judicial tribunals were not then or are not now an intrinsically good and necessary thing. In "Jonah and the Whale," Professor Arthurs asks how, in the teeth of such formidable opposition (as exemplified by Dicey and Lord Hewart), and with relatively little support, at least in legal circles, administrative law has not only survived but has become "the typical, the quintessential, the characteristic modern juridical mode." He answers: "[T]he tasks ... that all governments have set themselves, for the past 150 years, could not have been performed in any other way ... the civil and criminal law [being] totally inadequate for the administration and enforcement of ongoing social and economic policies."[65]

In that question and answer, Arthurs effectively defines the challenge for any viable, justice-focused criticism of our administrative justice system. Such criticism, including the criticism in this book, must accept the necessity of non-court tribunals in a "juridical mode" performing the tasks of "administration and enforcement of ongoing social and economic policies." We cannot do without them; that much is clear. The great question is how to answer Lord Hewart and Professor Dicey – how to have these tribunals *and* the rule of law.

The surge in the number of tribunals in Canada occurred between the end of the Second World War in 1945 and the 1980s, but the practice of assigning adjudication of rights disputes to tribunals had in fact first come to the fore during the First World War. Few wartime tribunals survived the end of that war, but the practice of giving tribunals judicial powers persisted and was sufficiently advanced by the mid-1930s for a leading Canadian administrative law scholar of the time, J.A. Corry, to write a significant article about the attitude of the legal profession and the courts towards these new tribunals, an article that would not have been out of place forty years later.[66] The Corry article provides an interesting insight into the state of play of administrative law when these new tribunals were first being confronted by the courts. Corry, one of the early Canadian critics of Dicey, viewed the courts as obstacles to the effective deployment of the new and necessary tribunals. It is a perspective that has dominated Canadian academic analysis for decades. The following passage from Professor Corry's article is of particular interest:

> [I]n many cases, Parliament has practically surrendered its legislative power to bodies better qualified to lay down rules of administration. In the same way, the jurisdiction of the common law courts over the relations between individuals and administrative authority is repeatedly ousted [by the legislatures' enactment of "privative clauses"]. Wherever this happens, it is because efficient administration is being embarrassed by judicial interpretation of the statute in question. Some serious students of the problem are advising that all judicial control be shorn away and that the courts be replaced by administrative courts after the continental model ... Force is being added to such suggestions by the accumulating evidence that such administrative courts are not solely guided, as Dicey thought, by their views of political expediency and the demands of efficient administration, but are also providing adequate protection to the rights of individuals. With such proposals in the air, it should be time to examine the part which the common-law courts play in this field of Public Law.[67]

I find two things in Professor Corry's article particularly notable. The first is the comfort that he takes from his impression that these "administrative courts" are "not solely [note the "solely"] guided, as Dicey thought, by their views of political expediency and the demands of efficient administration." The second is the absence in his commentary of any reference to rule-of-law or constitutional-law concerns about the transfer of judicial powers to the executive branch. The article implicitly assumes, without evidence and in the face of compelling indications to the contrary, that we can safely accept that executive branch "courts" are not the rule-of-law pariahs that Dicey saw them to be; that, when we entrust the executive branch with the administration and control of judicial functions devoted to deciding rights disputes in which the executive branch is an interested party, we are not endangering the constitution or risking our national sense of what justice expects. These implicit assumptions have been the underpinning of Canada's administrative law discourse throughout the history of the Canadian administrative law state to date,[68] and it is their unthinking acceptance by those who might have known better that principally explains why, in this second decade of the twenty-first century, the Canadian administrative justice system remains an in-house, executive branch justice system that is indeed "without the law."[69]

They Do It in the US, Don't They? No, They Do Not.

Canada's long acceptance of the executive branch, rule-of-law-deficient administrative justice system has been considerably influenced by the United States and its great agencies of the New Deal. To this day, many Canadians find reason for complacency about political appointments to Canadian administrative judicial tribunals in the thought that in the United States political appointments of agency chairs and members is an everyday practice, as one of the rites of passage of every newly elected President. This perception is incorrect, and because of its contribution to public and political apathy about our own administrative justice system, it is important to set the record straight.

In the United States, particularly in the federal administrative law system, the bulk of agency judicial functions are in fact exercised by "Administrative Law Judges" who are not patronage or political appointees and whose tenure is not subject to the whim of the President. These "judges" are appointed to life-tenured terms in a highly competitive and independent selection process administered by the US Office of Personnel Management based on a rigorous examination of relevant judicial qualifications. US Administrative Law Judges can be dismissed from their positions only after a hearing before the Merit Systems Protection Board, an independent agency.

1

Defeating the Rule of Law in the Administrative Justice System
Executive Branch Strategies and Tactics

When the executive branch implements a policy by having the legislature enact statutory rights and assign the adjudication of disputes concerning those rights to an executive branch tribunal, it has chosen as its instrument of policy an instrument of justice, and has thereby created two systemic conflicts. One is a conflict of interest: a conflict between the executive branch's interest in seeing its policy goals implemented efficiently without inconvenience or embarrassment in accordance with its own vision of that policy, and society's interest in ensuring that instruments of justice are structured and operated in conformity with the rule of law. The second systemic conflict is existential: the conflict between any government's deeply felt need for predictability and control and any justice institution's equally deep need for independence and autonomy.

The two conflicts present obvious obstacles to the structuring of a rational, rule-of-law-congruent administrative justice system, but the executive branch has never recognized or addressed those conflicts. It has opted instead for a Potemkin village system of apparently independent but in fact dependent judicial tribunals, a system that satisfies the executive branch's administrative and control needs while ignoring the rule of law.

Chapter-and-verse, tribunal-by-tribunal support for this book's condemnation of the executive branch's administrative justice system is beyond any individual researcher's reach. However, in the executive branch's design and administration of its judicial rights-determining bodies, one finds, behind the façade of independence and the rhetoric of independent decision making, a set of pervasive structural strategies and administrative tactics designed to optimize and protect the executive branch's interests and to serve its needs for predictability and control – strategies and tactics that subvert the administrative justice system's rule-of-law needs and its public promise of justice.

In this chapter, I examine those strategies and tactics, cite examples of their application, and expose their conflict with rule-of-law principles, beginning with the strategy of partisan patronage appointments.

Partisan Patronage Appointments

> *Political patronage occupies a grey area between amorality and immorality. In a sense, it is the "pornography of politics." Although it may ... "despise the official morality as hypocritical, fraudulent, or effeminate, it nevertheless knows that it is not itself the official morality." Patronage usually has no official status; it is not a right granted in constitutions, not a recognized method of management in the public sector, nor the official goal of political parties. Yet, patronage is a major method of political organization in democratic polities, including the United States, Canada, Italy, Ireland, Iceland, and many more.*
>
> *– Gunnar Helgi Kristinsson*[1]

As mentioned earlier, Canadian judicial tribunal adjudicators and chairs are typically appointed to short terms. The terms vary widely from one to ten years but typically range from three to five years. The terms are short but appointees are routinely led to expect that when their current term expires, the government will reappoint them for a further term, and then a further term, and so on. Governments do routinely reappoint members and chairs, but they may arbitrarily refuse reappointments and frequently do so. The egregious rule-of-law implications of this arbitrary reappointment regime will be dealt with at length shortly, but for now we need to focus on the partisan patronage factors at play in the appointment and reappointment decisions themselves.

The decisive influence of patronage and partisan political considerations in the selection of particular persons for appointment or reappointment to judicial tribunals is acknowledged to have been a long-standing scourge of

Canada's administrative justice system.[2] It is true that in the last decade or so there have been some improvements in the method of selecting appointees in the first instance. Such improvements have been initiated in four provinces. To understand the limited significance of these improvements, however, and the implications of no improvements in the other six provinces, three territories, and the federal jurisdiction, we need a clear picture of the endemic patronage abuse that has been the leitmotif of administrative justice appointment policies in Canada since time began.

There are two types of patronage appointments. There are the "jobs-for-the-boys" appointments to positions of public responsibility "bestowed on political friends of the governing party for past political services rendered, without appropriate regard for the qualifications and competence of the appointees."[3] And there is what author Chris Skelcher calls "motive patronage" – the process "by which those with political influence ensure that ideological or party supporters are allocated to key positions in the governmental machine."[4] In recent years, there has been a trend towards renunciation by some governments of jobs-for-the-boys appointments to tribunals, along with public commitments to new "merit-based" appointment policies. As we shall see, however, although these new policies may address the worst features of the old-style patronage appointments, they in fact continue to accommodate the core goals of government patronage regimes.

Skelcher sees motive patronage falling into two possible categories: the "patron-client" strategy of *exchange* or the "patronism" strategy of *gifting*.[5] The latter appears to be what is at work in the case of tribunal appointments and reappointments. In Canada's administrative justice system, governments consider appointments and reappointments of the chairs and members of judicial and other tribunals to be "in their gift,"[6] and the appointees understand that their governments see it that way. Skelcher describes the implications and significance of the gift mode of appointment as follows:

> The gift constitutes a social mode of exchange ... It is a special form of exchange because:
>
>> [S]eemingly, it is non-utilitarian and disinterested. At the same time, it is highly structured and based on relatively elaborated and specific rules of reciprocity.[7]
>
> Gifts help reinforce conditions of trust and solidarity and facilitate broad obligations for interaction within a social group. Through the gift of an appointment, therefore, the patron invites the individual into a social group

which apparently is not hierarchically ordered but, rather, collegial. The patron does not dominate the clientele but is *primus inter pares* – "first amongst equals" ... patronism encourages a sense of integration, unity and singularity of purpose ...

The offer of the gift of appointment invites a positive response by the recipient and is reciprocated through altruism and a willingness to defer to the judgment of the patron ... The informality and personalization of the approach encourages a bond between individuals and facilitates the creation of a sense of shared enterprise ... [T]he starting point of the relationship is one in which the patron has first-mover advantage and is able to co-opt the appointee towards his or her agenda.[8]

The appointments-as-gifts culture is endemic in Canada's administrative justice system. It is a culture rooted not only in the unique attractiveness of these jobs to both patrons and their clientele but also in the complete discretion exercised by ministers or cabinets in the granting of not only appointments but, even more importantly, reappointments. It is a culture freighted with government expectations of a tie between the government and the recipient of the gift, a tie characterized by loyalty and the acceptance of a shared agenda. When that tie is between a member of a judicial tribunal and a government minister or cabinet, it is patently incompatible with the rule of law. In Canada, it is also likely to be a particularly strong tie because members will understand that when their term is up, typically every three or five years, the government gets to decide – arbitrarily, privately, with no financial or political repercussions, and without giving reasons – whether reappointing a particular individual will continue to serve its interests.

The Goal of "Responsive" Competence

One of the goals of a motive patronage strategy to which Skelcher particularly refers is the development of a "responsive competence."[9] "The placing of allies through motive patronage acts as a mechanism," he says, "by which ... the development and implementation of particular lines of policy can more effectively be sustained." Such appointments facilitate a network of "political influence and commitment within government, *and between government and other bodies,* which reduces the uncertainty of relying on a merit or electoral system for the filling of posts."[10]

Skelcher's analysis was concerned with the public service, but it is readily seen that a search for responsive competence is implicitly an important factor in the executive branch's patronage-driven appointments and re-appointments of administrative tribunal chairs and members. Of course, for regulatory agencies, appointment policies designed to foster responsive competence are not unexpected. In the case of judicial tribunals, however, the particular kind of responsive competence that governments will be seen to be expecting is competence in the adjudication of issues in a manner that is *responsive* to the government's ideological perspectives, policy agendas, and political needs. It is an expectation that is plainly incompatible with the rule of law.

Naturally, the executive branch's penchant for "responsive" tribunals is rarely articulated in public, especially with regard to judicial tribunals. Premier Mike Harris's Progressive Conservative government in Ontario (June 1995 to April 2002) was never reticent about its position on any given issue, however, and in 1995 its expectation that judicial tribunal members would be biased in favour of government policy was made clear when both the Premier and one of his ministers had occasion to explain the government's interest in having a judicial tribunal's rights-determining function assigned to the government's ideological compatriots. The Minister of Community and Social Services in the newly elected Progressive Conservative government responded to criticism of egregiously partisan appointments to adjudicative positions on Ontario's Social Assistance Review Board (now the Social Benefits Tribunal) by explaining that "[t]hese appointments were done on the basis of principles, not politics." "We," he said, "wanted individuals who would take a tough stand on welfare and welfare fraud."[11] Speaking later on the same issue, the Premier assured reporters that one of the appointees in question had been selected for her new post not because she was a Conservative but because she "agrees with the Government's position on welfare." "It helps," the Premier told reporters, "that she has views similar to the government's views ... [w]hether she's a Tory or not is not as important as her belief that welfare should be a hand up."[12]

The National Parole Board Scandal

Thirteen years before Peter Showler's denunciation of the patronage culture at the IRB in 2003, another outgoing chair of a federal tribunal also spoke frankly about the patronage culture that had undermined the competence of his tribunal. William Outerbridge was chair of the National Parole Board from 1978 to 1990.[13] After his retirement, he was invited to speak at an administrative tribunal conference and chose as his topic "the diminished role of agency chairs in the appointment and re-appointment of adjudicators."

One newspaper reported:

> Dangerously inexperienced appointees have been foisted upon the National
> Parole Board by federal governments that saw the Board as an excellent
> pork barrel, former Parole Board chairman William Outerbridge said yes-
> terday ... The government showed less and less interest in seeking his aid to
> secure qualified "street-wise" board members who could solidly appraise
> criminal offenders ... The growing supply of positions and the generous
> salaries made the jobs too attractive as rewards to pass up, Mr. Outerbridge
> said ... "Not infrequently ... it was necessary to transfer seasoned members
> between regions ... *to attempt to retain a minimum level of perceived com-
> petence*," he said. "The larger the Board grew, the less was I consulted on
> appointment needs and the more predictable the products of the process
> became ..." Mr. Outerbridge said he found the lack of qualifications among
> appointees particularly distressing considering that "a great many of the
> 30,000 decisions the Board makes every year have serious consequences for
> the public and for the inmate."[14]

(It is telling that Outerbridge's description of the impact of patronage abuse
on the competence of the National Parole Board is virtually identical to that
of Showler's with regard to the IRB's performance: "[T]he real problem is ...
mediocrity and incompetence among some of its members [caused by political patronage]."[15])

Patronage consequences usually remain below the surface. In the case of
the National Parole Board, however, the consequences of the patronage
abuse to which William Outerbridge referred ended tragically for an innocent victim in Regina and became very public indeed. In January 1994, the
Toronto Star reported: "Solicitor General Herbert Gray is promising sweep-
ing reforms to the National Parole Board following a scathing report on the
freeing of a sex offender who later murdered a Regina woman ..."[16] And nine
months later:

> Members of the National Parole Board will soon be facing annual reviews
> of their performances after facing criticism for releasing inmates who later
> committed violent crimes. The reviews are part of an effort by the board's
> new chairman, Willie Gibbs, to re-establish confidence in it ... He was
> picked to take over the quasi-judicial body in August to re-place Michel
> Dagenais, a Conservative appointee who resigned in the spring amidst
> controversy over the actions of paroled convicts.[17]

Ratushny on Patronage Appointments

Concern among lawyers about the impact of appointment policies reflected in experiences such as the foregoing prompted the Canadian Bar Association (CBA) to commission University of Ottawa administrative law professor Ed Ratushny to inquire into the problem. Ratushny's *Report on the Independence of Federal Administrative Tribunals and Agencies* was delivered to the CBA annual conference in 1990.[18] In this report, one finds a particular reference to a notorious incident in 1986 when a public disclosure of the resumés of a number of new appointees to the Canadian Human Rights Tribunal confirmed that many of them had no qualifications for the position and knew very little about what it entailed. This disclosure prompted the CBA president to speak forcefully against the appointment of incompetent people to "quasi-judicial" tribunals. Ratushny's *Report* notes in that regard that "in private, there is no difficulty in confirming that a very real and persistent problem exists," and comments that "[a]lthough many well-qualified people are appointed there is no reason why our system of justice, and the people whom it serves, should tolerate the problems created by unqualified, inexperienced and often intemperate appointees."[19]

The IRB, 1989-95

As mentioned earlier, Peter Showler's indictment of patronage appointments at the IRB was not the first time such abuse at that tribunal had been noted. Indeed, refugee and immigration tribunals have always been notorious patronage magnets, and the modern IRB was itself born of a convulsion in partisan politics. On 1 January 1989, the Conservative government of Brian Mulroney abolished the Refugee Advisory Board and Immigration Appeal Board and replaced them with the IRB, simply, it appeared, as a means of getting rid of an immigration and refugee adjudicative regime that was dominated by the previous Liberal government's appointees, who were thought by the Conservatives and their supporters to be too soft, particularly with respect to refugee claims.[20] It took about three years for the Conservative patronage appointees to the new board to get into trouble in the public eye, and when the next Liberal government came to power in 1993 and began making motive patronage appointments to the IRB of refugee advocates, a regular free-for-all ensued.

Media reporting on the IRB during the 1992-95 period was rich in controversy and criticism.[21] Stories in 1992 were about patronage appointees who lacked expertise and who demonstrated bias against refugee claimants; about appointees who were alleged by refugee advocacy groups to be "crassly indifferent to human misery."[22] In 1994-95, on the other hand, stories were about the "capture" of the IRB by a pro-refugee lobby. In 1992, the complaint was that the proportion of claims being accepted was too low; in 1994, it was the reverse. The polarized performance was nicely summed up by an editorial in the *Globe and Mail* in January 1994:

> The problem with the Conservative-appointed Immigration and Refugee Board was that vacancies on the tribunal too often went to people with ties to the Tory party: aides, bagmen, relatives – in a word, hacks. The trouble with the twenty-eight new Liberal appointments is that many of them had been crusaders on behalf of refugee claimants, which means that although they were well versed on the issues, their take on the issues risked being decidedly one-sided – in a word, *engagé.*[23]

The very public conflict between the *Globe and Mail*'s holdover "hacks" and new "*engagés*" led finally to the noisy resignation of the new Liberal-appointed vice-chair, who came under fire for allegedly interfering with the independence of other members (i.e., presumably the Conservative holdovers).

An Unexpected Window into Problems with Ontario's Judicial Tribunal Appointments

Of course, the problem of patronage appointments is not confined to federal tribunals. In 1998, the report of an Ontario government commission inquiring into how changes might be made in the way that Ontario's regulatory and adjudicative agencies conduct their business provided an unexpected window into the reputation of Ontario's administrative justice tribunal appointments. The commission that produced that report was an Ontario government caucus commission consisting of five Progressive Conservative Members of Provincial Parliament (MPPs) and chaired by former Provincial Court judge and MPP Gary Guzzo. The commission's *Everyday Justice* report has come to be known as the *Guzzo Report.*[24]

The *Guzzo Report* made a number of unexpected recommendations for reforming the appointment process – unexpected because the appointment process had not been part of the commission's original mandate, the principal focus of which was on finding new cost-cutting measures. These recommendations themselves provide significant evidence of the deep flaws in the appointment policies of Ontario's administrative justice system, but the commission's account of its broad consultation process is of also of particular interest in that respect. It is an account that lays bare the serious concerns of a broad range of administrative justice consumers and stakeholders about the quality of tribunal appointments in Ontario.

After extensive consultations with "consumer and stakeholder groups, agencies and government ministries" (submissions were received from 247 separate organizations),[25] the commission took the unusual step of seeking the government's permission to expand its mandate to include the selection and appointment process. In its final report, it gave the following reasons for that initiative:

> *Throughout* the consultations, the commission heard that the [administrative justice] system is only as good as the people in it. At *virtually all meetings, and in the majority of written submissions*, the quality and training of adjudicators was raised as an issue. Most felt that, to ensure a high standard of administrative justice and credibility with clients and the public, changes are needed to the public appointments process. As a result of the consultations, the commission's mandate was expanded to include recommendations on improving the appointments process.[26]
>
> ... *[T]hroughout* the commission's consultations, the operation of the appointments process and the qualifications and training of appointees *were issues raised so often and so strongly* that the commission added recommendations on these issues.[27]

Having sought and won the expansion of its terms of reference to include the appointment process, the commission subsequently reported that it made its recommendations regarding appointments "with the belief that it is important to ensure" that appointees are "qualified and competent" and that the process "for appointments *and reappointments*" is "open and transparent."[28] The reforms it recommended included: (1) a clear application process; (2) publication of functions and job requirements; (3) selection criteria based on "core competencies (skills judged to be necessary to effectively do the job)"; (4) training to support and expand core competencies and expert knowledge; (5) minister consultation with chairs about "both appointments and reappointments"; and (6) a "screening committee of recognized, reputable people to evaluate applicants against the selection criteria and create pools of qualified candidates." These recommendations tell us quite a lot about the state of Ontario's administrative justice appointment process at the time.

The Progressive Conservative government's failure to implement the Guzzo recommendations is another distressing story, and I will come back to that when I deal with the general subject of the executive branch's indifference to performance standards for judicial tribunals.

Nova Scotia

The situation concerning patronage appointments of tribunal members in Nova Scotia in 1998 is summarized in a statement concerning Nova Scotia's executive branch justice system made to an annual CCAT conference by Moira McConnell, professor of law and former executive director of the Law Reform Commission of Nova Scotia (1992-97):

> Some provinces have a plethora of full-time appointees, however, many provinces, such as Nova Scotia operate virtually on a "volunteer" part-time basis and have very few resources to devote to this sector. The increasing number of Board-CEO difficulties encountered in Nova Scotia and the governance/accountability record of some agencies is perhaps now proving costly enough to ensure that appointments are *to a larger degree based on merit* rather than *entitlement* and that agencies have *some* resources available for training of [agency, board, and commission] personnel.[29]

McConnell's indication that entitlement rather than merit was the typical basis for tribunal appointments in Nova Scotia was subsequently confirmed by a report from the staff of the Nova Scotia Human Rights Tribunal filed in 2003 in the famous Archie Kaiser human rights complaint proceedings (of which more later). The report stated: "Evidence does support that [in Nova Scotia] there was a context of systematic political patronage in ABC [agency, boards, and commissions] appointments."[30]

New Brunswick

Express judicial acknowledgment of the impact of patronage appointments on tribunal competence is rare. In the same year as the Kaiser report, however, New Brunswick's Justice of Appeal Joseph T. Robertson, responding in a judgment to the question of what reasons the New Brunswick legislature might have had for providing employers and workers with what seemed a redundant statutory right to appeal decisions of the Workplace, Health, Safety and Compensation Commission to the courts (redundant given their statutory right to appeal those same decisions to the Commission's

Appeals Tribunal) noted dryly that "the right of appeal may signify the legislature's understanding that historically, the appointment of tribunal members has been influenced by factors not tied to legislative objectives."[31] That Robertson's observation was in fact fairly reflective of the public understanding in New Brunswick was confirmed in 2004 when the *Report and Recommendations of the New Brunswick Commission on Legislative Democracy* included the Commission's observation that there is a "widespread perception that patronage is the deciding factor in appointments [to New Brunswick's agencies, boards, and commissions]."[32]

Saskatchewan

Government commitment to non-partisan appointments seems especially thin in Saskatchewan. When I turn shortly to the executive branch strategy of idiosyncratic removals, I will describe the refusal in 2006 by Saskatchewan's New Democratic government to make an expected reappointment of a full-time vice-chair of the Saskatchewan Labour Relations Board because, it virtually admitted, the Saskatchewan unions did not like some of his decisions.[33] More recently, in 2008, the new Saskatchewan Party government made national news with its arbitrary mid-term dismissal without cause of the chair and two vice-chairs of the Saskatchewan Labour Relations Board – the three "neutral" members of the Board who had been appointed by the NDP government. Their replacements were perceived to be Saskatchewan Party loyalists.[34] In the litigation that followed those dismissals, the Saskatchewan Court of Appeal may be seen to have effectively acknowledged that the provincial government had intentionally compromised the independence of the Labour Relations Board by breaking the tenure of the chair and vice-chairs of the sitting Board and replacing them with persons chosen specifically "to give effect to the legislative policy choices" reflected in radically new labour legislation that the government was proposing.[35] These were persons whom Premier Brad Wall said he "expected" would "consider what the government has said publicly" and would maintain a "balance between the interests of unions and the interests of business."[36] And it is not only the Labour Relations Board that has been affected. The press reports that after taking office in November 2007, the Saskatchewan Party "axed" seventy chairs and members of boards and agencies across the province and replaced them with people of its own choosing.[37]

In removing the Labour Relations Board chair and vice-chairs as well as the chairs and members of the other tribunals, the Saskatchewan government relied on the Saskatchewan *Interpretation Act* provision that when a new government is elected, fixed-term appointments made prior to the election are automatically converted to at-pleasure appointments.[38] In the litigation referred to above, the Saskatchewan Court of Appeal was called upon to interpret that provision.[39] The Court characterized the provision as "extraordinary" but concluded that the legislature's intent was clear. It drew support for this conclusion from the following remarks of the Saskatchewan Attorney General, Gary Lane, in the legislature in 1982 in support of the bill at its Second Reading:[40]

> Mr. Speaker, the purpose of the amendment is quite clear. When any new government is elected, it cannot have its hands tied by the previous government's actions. This amendment will assist any new government ... to move to implement its policies through its various boards, commissions, and agencies, by changing memberships on those bodies as is necessary.[41]

Perhaps one cannot quarrel with Attorney General Lane's perspective if one is talking about regulatory agencies, but this provision did not distinguish between regulatory agencies and judicial tribunals and the fact that this failure was deliberate was demonstrated when a motion to amend the bill to exempt the Saskatchewan Labour Relations Board was soundly defeated.[42] (This persistent failure – refusal – to distinguish between regulatory agencies and administrative judicial tribunals is a hallmark of the executive branch's disregard of the principles of justice in its justice system, and we will see more of this as we go along.)

Side Note on the Constitutional Issue Presented by the Saskatchewan LRB Litigation

It should be noted that although the Saskatchewan Court of Appeal's decision was tantamount to an acknowledgement that, by virtue of s. 20(1) of the *Interpretation Act*, Saskatchewan adjudicative tribunals were in law biased,[43] the Court was careful to say that it had not considered the constitutional validity of the *Interpretation Act* provision. The issue of whether a constitutional requirement of judicial independence applies to the Labour Relations Board, and thus to s. 20(1) as it applies to Board appointments, had not been raised in the lower court. The unions had raised the issue in the Court of Appeal, but had raised it too late, in the Court's view. Subsequently, this constitutional issue was the explicit basis for a renewed judicial review application by the unions to the Saskatchewan Court of Queen's Bench. That court acknowledged the possible existence of a constitutional protection for judicial independence for some tribunals, but held that it would not apply to the Labour Relations Board, which it found to be an agency whose "primary purpose" was not to exercise judicial functions but "to formulate and implement policy intended to achieve the *Trade Union Act's* primary goals and objectives."[44] This decision is currently on appeal to the Saskatchewan Court of Appeal.[45] This vital issue of constitutional protection for the independence and impartiality of judicial tribunals is dealt with at length in Chapter 4.

An Authorative Summing Up

In November 2009, the Manitoba Law Reform Commission delivered its one-hundred-page report on the appointment process in Manitoba, titled *Improving Administrative Justice in Manitoba: Starting with the Appointments Process.*[46] To provide context for its assessment of the Manitoba appointment process, the Commission canvassed the state of the union, as it were, respecting government practices, policies, and legislation governing appointments to administrative tribunals in each Canadian jurisdiction. The administrative justice community is indebted to the Commission for a comprehensive, thoroughly researched report that is likely to be the baseline reference on this subject for many years to come.

On the subject of the history of patronage appointments in Canada, the Commission concluded:

> In spite of the need for public confidence in the independence and impartiality of administrative decision makers and the desirability of having certain decisions made by expert decision makers rather than generalist judges or politicians, governments across Canada have a long history of using board appointments as a means of rewarding political loyalties and ensuring that kindred individuals are in positions of authority.

In support of this conclusion, the Commission cites fourteen significant articles or studies published between 1985 and 2008, including, of course, the Ratushny report mentioned above.[47]

Illusory Modern Reforms

In the past two decades, some governments have claimed to have reformed their appointment processes, including, typically, adopting a "merit-based" selection process. Any such claims are to be measured against the following six principal features of a traditional patronage appointment regime.

First, the final decision concerning an appointment is always in the hands of senior political partisans. The constitutive statutes of judicial tribunals routinely specify that appointments are order-in-council appointments – appointments technically made by order of the Governor General or a Lieutenant-Governor. As a practical matter, however, the selection authority lies in the hands of either the Premier or Prime Minister, or the cabinet or the particular cabinet minister responsible for the statutory enterprise of which the judicial tribunal is a part. In most governments, there is also a central patronage office (never so called) staffed by senior political staff and reporting directly to the Prime Minister or Premier that vets the partisan credentials of all candidates being considered for appointment to these tribunals.

Second, governments committed to patronage appointments have traditionally allowed only limited access to information about the existence of vacancies. The fact that there are vacancies to be filled has rarely been advertised. Only the political staff and the associated bureaucracy know about them. The last thing an ideal patronage regime wants is for the public to know in advance that there is a vacancy to be filled. All sorts of people might end up inquiring about the chances of their being appointed, and so the political gains from the appointment of one deserving partisan would be diluted by the political cost of refusing other partisans who may be equally "deserving" and, perhaps, even more importunate. Furthermore, when appointments are made, the announcements are usually confined to the Official Gazettes, and the qualifications of the appointees are rarely made public.

Third, the qualifications required for appointment are typically not specified at all, or else are specified in such general terms that almost anyone can be said to be qualified. If one is running a patronage-driven appointment regime, one does not want access to positions to be unduly narrowed by sharp-edged qualification requirements.

Fourth, where qualifications have been specified – typically where modern governments have finally committed to a "merit-based" selection policy – there has rarely been a commitment to appointing the *best* candidate. Governments have felt themselves justified in appointing anyone whose qualifications can be seen to meet the requirements. Governments that have committed to merit-based appointments have typically asked themselves only this: Of those identified as "qualified," who has the most deserving or pressing partisan claim?

Fifth, patronage-driven appointment regimes run counter to the public interest principally because they have little or no chance of appointing the best persons. Not only do these regimes rule out any actual candidate, how-ever well-qualified, whose partisan credentials are non-existent or even not optimal but they also fail entirely to attract the interest of the majority of qualified potential candidates who, being apolitical or having no currently relevant partisan credentials, and understanding the nature of the game, will rarely waste their time applying.

Finally, where qualifications have been specified, the process for deter-mining which candidates are "qualified" will typically be structured to allow for partisan manipulation.

The Manitoba Law Reform Commission report identifies only British Columbia, Alberta, Ontario, and Nova Scotia as jurisdictions that have intro-duced meaningful reforms to the appointment process. It is therefore rea-sonable to infer that the other six provinces and three territories, as well as the federal government, have remained committed to patronage appoint-ments of either the jobs-for-the boys or the motive category. And, although the Manitoba report makes recommendations for the reform of Manitoba's appointment process, at the time of writing there seems to to be no indica-tion that the recommendations are being implemented.

New Brunswick's Failed Reform Attempt

The recent fate of a New Brunswick reform initiative demonstrates the typ-ical executive branch resistance to meaningful reform of the appointment process. In 2003, the provincial government appointed a "Commission on Legislative Democracy." Its terms of reference were broad, but its instruc-tions to make recommendations for strengthening and modernizing New Brunswick's democratic institutions and practices in the area of legislative reform included "opening up the appointments process for agencies, boards, and commissions." The Commission's *Final Report* is dated 31 December 2004. In its views as to why it was important to "look at" how appointments are made to agencies, boards, and commissions, the Commission may be seen to generally share many of this author's opinions, even if it expressed them in perhaps a more respectful tone. It cited three main reasons:

> First, there is an overall need to improve public trust and confidence in the integrity of the political process and ABCs [agencies, boards, and commis-sions] themselves, in the face of a widespread perception that patronage is the deciding factor in appointments. Second, there is a need to ensure the competence of arm's length governance boards that have significant regu-latory, adjudicative and service responsibilities. Third, there is a need to

ensure quality governance for these ABCs to avoid putting the public purse at risk.[48]

The New Brunswick Commission's recommendations concerning the appointment process were extensive, particularly for the "significant" agencies (in the definition of which the presence of an adjudicative function figured prominently). They included the establishment of a central appointments unit within the government's Office of Human Resources; a specified application and selection process; the development of qualifications descriptions to be published, with vacancies to be advertised; transparent selection processes; mandatory orientation training, and so on. The Commission implicitly recognized the shortcomings of the traditional merit-based appointment regimes, and identified the issue of whether the policy should be to select "*the most* qualified" candidate[49] rather than merely *a* qualified candidate. It recommended that the candidate selection process present to the appointing authority (effectively, the government) a short list in a "possible rank order," but was content to leave to the government the final ranking of the short list and selection from that list. Nevertheless, when the New Brunswick government released its response to the Commission's *Final Report* in June 2007 (three years later), it may be seen to have paid only lip service to the Commission's major recommendations concerning the appointment process.[50]

Periods of Renaissance in the Appointment Processes that Come and Go
It sometimes happens, in some jurisdictions, that tribunal appointment policies experience something of a general renaissance. Some new governments or new ministers arrive on the scene determined to do better, and for a while they may succeed. Certainly, this has been true in Ontario, which experienced such a renaissance period of about five years under David Peterson's Liberal government, and experienced a similar one now under the government of Premier Dalton McGuinty. The McGuinty government pursued a progressive appointment policy for "adjudicative" tribunals that included relevant qualification requirements, advertisement of vacancies, and full consultation with chairs. This policy culminated in 2009 with the enactment of new tribunal governance legislation: the *Adjudicative Tribunals Accountability, Governance and Appointments Act, 2009*,[51] which I will deal with at length later.

These periodic reforms, however, inevitably focus on merely improving the quality and representative nature of appointments, on being seen to be tamping down the role of patronage and giving tribunal chairs the right to influence appointments (although not always reappointments). They hardly ever address the underlying structural problems. In Ontario, for instance, although the *Adjudicative Tribunals Accountability, Governance and Appointments Act* has enhanced the appointments process, it has also dramatically tightened the portfolio ministries' control over their judicial tribunals.[52] Moreover, these periodic reforms are always ephemeral – slowly dissipating or quickly disappearing as new ministers or new governments with different policies and perspectives take over.

As noted earlier, public commitments by governments to so-called merit-based tribunal appointments have not been uncommon in recent years, but it tells us something about the "anyone will do" tradition that when the BC government enacted its new *Administrative Tribunals Appointment and Administration Act*[53] in 2003, the fact that it included a provision requiring a merit-based appointment process was considered big news. The Ontario government's 2009 legislation, referred to above, mandating both merit-based *and competitive* appointments of members of adjudicative tribunals was also regarded as a breakthrough.

The Chimera of "Merit-Based" Reforms

The IRB Appointment Process, 1995-2007
When a government announces that it has finally committed to a merit-based appointment process, experience suggests that one's natural skepticism is likely to prove justified. A classic case in point is the merit-based selection process for appointments to the IRB introduced by the Liberal government of Jean Chrétien in 1995 in response to the media criticism in the first half of the 1990s referred to earlier.

In that year, the government committed to a merit-based appointment process for the IRB and established a "Ministerial Advisory Committee on the Selection of Members of the Immigration and Refugee Board" (the Advisory Committee) and provided it with a set of qualifications by which it was to be guided when evaluating candidates. The Advisory Committee was not a statutory body but an *ad hoc* committee established by the Minister of Immigration; its authority depended on the Minister's commitment that no one would be appointed to the IRB who had not been recommended by the committee. By 2002, the year that Peter Showler retired from his three-year term as chair of the IRB, the Advisory Committee had been at work for seven years, with the government's commitment to this merit-based selection system in full sway all that time. And yet, as disclosed by Showler in his 2003 interview with the Toronto *Saturday Star*, political patronage remained "a devastating blight on the Immigration and Refugee Board."[54] Moreover, Showler tells me that at the time he retired, although 10 to 15 percent of the 170 appointed members in the Refugee Division of the Board were in his estimation excellent, 10 to 15 percent, or 17 to 25 members, were in his opinion incompetent, while the rest were "adequate."

In assessing the current "merit-based" reforms in Alberta, British Columbia, Nova Scotia, and Ontario, it is therefore important to understand how from 1995 to 2002 the federal government's patronage apparatus succeeded in effectively finessing an IRB appointment process that was supposed to be a merit-based system.

For the following analysis, I rely on information from the Hansard transcript of the appearance of the inaugural chair of the Advisory Committee, Gordon Fairweather, before the House of Commons Standing Committee on Citizenship and Immigration in 1996, when the Standing Committee was interested in learning about the Advisory Committee and how it was operating.[55] I have also relied on my own interview with Showler in 2011.[56]

Why is it, then, that over the course of its seven-year history this merit-based appointment system seems to have produced so relatively little merit?

In the first place, both the penultimate and the ultimate selection decisions were left in the hands of partisans. The members of the Advisory Committee (five originally plus the chair of the IRB and two IRB officials as *ex officio* members) were all chosen by the Minister, and although Fairweather himself was a well-known Progressive Conservative, even he recognized that his selection as inaugural chair was unprecedented in the tradition of party politics.[57] Certainly, during Showler's term as IRB chair it was known that the members of the Advisory Committee (by then twelve) were all Liberal Party partisans, with the Committee chair at the time being both a former judge and former Liberal Party candidate.[58]

Next, the system provided the Minister with a broad latitude in selecting the successful candidate. The goal of the Advisory Committee was to provide the Minister with as large a pool as possible of candidates certified by the Committee to be qualified. Thus, for appointments to be made in 1996, the Committee provided the Minister with 150 or 160 names for what was expected to be about 50 vacancies.[59] On what basis did the Minister select from this large pool of certified candidates? It could not have been through an objective assessment of their relative qualifications, because the Advisory Committee did not rank its recommendations and the only thing the Minister and the Minister's staff had to go on was a one-paragraph recommendation from the Committee. The Minister's office was not provided with the recommended candidates' resumés. Obviously, the only basis for selection was the relative merits of their partisan patronage credentials, the one thing the Minister's office would have known about.

Evidence of the determinant role that patronage continued to play in the final decisions can also be found in the fact that the Advisory Committee's work failed to speed up the pace of appointments. And what was causing the delays? As Peter Showler told the *Star* reporter in 2003, they were caused by political infighting within the Liberal Party as to which of the certified candidates "should get the patronage plums"[60] – which of them would actually be tapped for an appointment. Obviously, in such an environment the deciding factor was how one candidate's partisan credentials stacked up against the partisan credentials of the others – how one candidate's party patron measured up in terms of political influence compared with the patrons of the other candidates. In the Minister's office, partisan credentials were the only currency – the only *known* qualifications. Those whose names made it into the Minister's office but who had little or no partisan credentials had obviously been wasting their time.

On occasion, Showler told me, he would be aware that the Committee had sent to the Minister's office the name of a person with particularly strong qualifications but limited or no partisan credentials. In such cases, Showler might inform the Minister's office of the importance with which he viewed that person's appointment, and sometimes his intervention would succeed.

The formation of the new Advisory Committee had been announced in the *Canada Gazette* early in 1995, but there was a delay in getting it up and running.[61] It had its first working meeting in October. Except for the *Gazette* announcement, there was no public advertisement of the vacancies. Meanwhile, people who had approached their MP, the Minister or other cabinet member, or the IRB chair expressing an interest in an appointment to the IRB had been advised to apply to the Advisory Committee. By the time the Committee began its work, over 1,100 applications were awaiting its attention.[62]

The qualifications against which the applications were to be judged were classic in terms of their lack of specificity – or, if you will, their susceptibility to a well-meaning, positive interpretation by a friendly reviewer. As described by Fairweather to the Standing Committee, the selection criteria consisted of the "ability to write, ability to conduct hearings, linguistic proficiency in either of the official languages, and, of course, some knowledge of immigration and refugee matters."[63]

In the Committee's first year of operation, the 1,100 applications were first culled to 300 through a simple review of the applicants' resumés. Telephone calls to the candidates' references eliminated a few more. Then each member of the Committee personally interviewed a proportion of the applicants and administered a thirty-minute writing test. Finally, each member presented to the rest of the Committee (usually during a telephone conference) the names of those they had interviewed and felt were qualified, after which further names were eliminated by consensus. Through this process, 150 or 160 of the initial 1,100 applicants were eventually certified as qualified and their names presented to the Minister.[64]

By the time Showler became the IRB chair, the thirty-minute writing test had evolved into a three-hour "fairly rigorous" exam designed and administered by an outside contractor but graded on a pass/fail basis (thus enabling persons who had barely passed to present themselves to the committee on the same footing as those who had aced the exam), and the interviews were being conducted by a panel consisting of one Committee member and a human resources expert from the public service. The Advisory Committee members, all Liberal Party partisans, continued to be appointed by the Minister, and their goal was still to give the Minister as many names as possible, and always substantially more than the number of anticipated openings. The Minister continued to receive only a one-paragraph recommendation unaccompanied by any resumés. Showler characterizes the system as he experienced it as a "hybrid process – merit-based but patronage driven."

On 29 November 2002, Showler's term as IRB chair came to an end and he was replaced by Jean-Guy Fleury, a senior member of the federal public service. In 2004, under Fleury's direction, the IRB implemented fundamental structural reforms in the appointment process. At the time, Judy Sgro was the Minister of Citizenship and Immigration in the new Liberal government of Paul Martin. With Sgro's consent, the following changes were implemented:

- The Advisory Committee was renamed the Advisory Panel and reduced to six members, all of whom were to be selected and appointed by the IRB chair, not by the Minister.
- The new Panel's recommendations were to be made to the IRB chair, not to the Minister's office.

- A new selection committee within the IRB, chaired by the IRB chair, received those recommendations and, after an extensive personal interview of each of the recommended candidates, decided which ones the chair would recommend to the Minister.
- It was agreed that the chair would provide the Minister with only three names (unranked) for each vacancy.
- The qualifications were revamped and made much more specific.
- Invitations to apply for appointments were widely advertised in both the mainstream and ethnic print media and online, with the qualifications specified.
- The applications were initially screened by staff, not the Advisory Panel, for general compliance with the qualifications.
- Those who survived this screening were asked to take a serious, four-hour exam involving the writing of an adjudicative decision based on hypothetical facts.
- The exam was marked by IRB staff, and the applications of those who had passed the exam were forwarded to each member of the Advisory Panel, along with the exam answer itself, the mark, and the full resumé.
- At its periodic meetings (about three times a year), the Panel discussed the candidates and determined those whom it would recommend to the IRB chair. Each member of the Panel would come to the meeting having reviewed all the information for each candidate. (This was the panel on which I had the privilege of serving for one year.)

The Advisory Panel members resigned en masse in February 2007 when the new Conservative government's intentions to fundamentally restructure the selection process became clear.[65] The number of panel members was to be changed from six to seven, and the panel's name changed to the Selection Advisory Board. Three of the seven positions were to be reserved for persons to be selected jointly by the Minister and the IRB chair (it was this politicization of the process that seems to have precipitated the mass resignations), with the remaining four being the IRB chair, another person appointed by the IRB chair, and two members of the IRB management staff selected by the IRB chair. Fleury's internal selection committee was abandoned, and the recommendations now went directly from the Selection Advisory Board to the Minister. At the same time, the qualifications became less specific and the written exam was changed back to a pass/fail exam.[66]

So, with that trip through the byzantine world of a merit-based appointment process as a guide, what is one to make of the modern reforms in Alberta, British Columbia, Nova Scotia, and Ontario?

Alberta Reforms

The Manitoba Law Reform Commission report on appointments gives a positive impression of the reformed Alberta appointment process. Introduced in 2008 through a "Public Agencies Governance Framework," the process is said to be committed to transparent, non-partisan, and merit-based appointments for all, and the selection process includes the participation of the agencies and agency chairs. Vacancies and the required qualifications tailored to the specific needs of the agency are advertised. The selection process is also said to be tasked with identifying the "top" candidates. Since the publication of the Manitoba report, the Alberta government has enacted the *Alberta Public Agencies Governance Act,*[67] and its appointment regime can now be assessed in light of that *Act* as well as the Governance Framework.

In fact, however, there are reasons to doubt whether the Alberta selection process is producing appointments to judicial tribunals that are non-partisan and free from patronage, although the average competence level must surely have been enhanced. It seems likely that, like the IRB selection committee system, it too remains a hybrid system – merit-based but patronage-driven.

To begin with, the Manitoba report notes that "recent appointments do not appear to be readily accessible (and may not be available) on the website" and that "the names of current board members do not appear on many board websites," thus casting doubt on the "accountability" of the system. Moreover, the *Governance Act* appears to have taken a step back from the commitment to transparency; s. 13(2) of the *Act* reads: "The steps that are taken or intended to be taken in a recruitment process and any identified skills, knowledge, experience or attributes required of a member to be appointed must be made public *either before or after the member is appointed.*" The ultimate appointment decisions are still made by a senior partisan – the Minister to whom the relevant tribunal reports. The online information does not specify who appoints the selection committee; the only requirement is that the committee include the agency chair or a member of the agency. There is therefore no assurance that the committee will be free of partisan influence.

It is true that compared with the federal Immigration Minister's freedom in 1996 to choose 50 names from a pool of 150 candidates, the Alberta Ministers' ultimate discretion appears to have been dramatically curtailed. The Alberta system requires the selection committee to provide the Minister with an unranked but short list of 2 to 5 of the "top" candidates for each vacancy. As far as one can see, however, there is no reason for confidence that the Minister's ultimate choice will be based on the relative merit of the shortlisted candidates rather than on the relative strength of their partisan or ideological credentials. The system does nothing to encourage potential "top" candidates who have no partisan credentials, or the wrong partisan credentials, to throw their hats into the ring. And of course the names chosen do not need to have the approval of the agency's chair, which raises a question: If the goal is truly to appoint the best candidate for the position, why is it the Minister and not the chair who gets to make the final decision?

There also appears to be nothing in the structure of the selection process to prevent ministers from delaying appointments when the persons recommended on a particular day do not come with sufficient partisan or ideological credentials – that is, nothing to prevent an experience such as that of IRB Chair Jean-Guy Fleury when the list of candidates he had recommended on the basis of three recommendations for each vacancy became, through a new Minister's delays, a pool of over fifty recommended but still unappointed candidates, all available for any particular vacancy.

Pessimism over the reliability of the Alberta system's professed commitment to non-partisan appointments is especially warranted because of the province's failure to distinguish judicial tribunals from regulatory agencies. The appointment processes specified by the Governance Framework and the *Governance Act* are the same for both. It is doubtful that a government would voluntarily surrender its ability to fill its regulatory agencies with its ideological compatriots, and one must expect that the means that will be found within the new appointments process to ensure that such compatriots find their way onto Alberta's regulatory agencies will also be exploited with respect to its judicial tribunals.

Finally, it may be noted that all this structure is focused only on original appointments. Subsequent appointments – reappointments – are left entirely in the hands of the Minister. The only provision with respect to reappointments appears in s. 15 of the *Governance Act,* which provides that a Minister *may* reappoint a member if, in his or her opinion, "the member meets the requirements of the position."[68]

BC Reforms

The Manitoba Law Reform Commission report gives the BC appointment process better grades than any of the other provinces, although, it should be noted, this report predated the enactment of Ontario's *Adjudicative Tribunals Accountability, Governance and Appointments Act.* The BC transparency is good – tribunal websites advertise openings, specify the appointment process, announce appointments, and provide a professional biography for all appointees. The qualifications are publicly available and very specific. There is a stated "underlying" commitment to selecting the "best and most qualified" candidates, and a statutory requirement that appointments be merit-based and that tribunal chairs be consulted. There is overall supervision of the appointment processes by the Board Resourcing and Development Office located in the Ministry of Labour, Citizens' Services and Open Government.

In British Columbia, however, as in Alberta, the appointment policies do not distinguish between judicial tribunals and regulatory agencies, so the suspicion remains that the tactics that will as a practical matter have to be developed to ensure that regulatory agencies are populated by the government's ideological allies may well also infect the process for selecting judicial tribunal members.

The policy does allow for customized selection processes depending on the nature of the tribunal, and permits either the Minister or the chair to take the lead in the appointment process, with the choice of which being expressed in a memorandum of understanding between the chair and the host minister. A casual check of BC tribunal websites suggests, however, that information on who takes the lead in appointments to those tribunals is not always readily available.

In any event, it is clear that what is ultimately provided to the Minister is a list of recommended candidates – a list of unspecified length – and the names on that list are determined not by the tribunal chair but by a selection panel whose members are appointed either by the Minister in consultation with the chair or by the chair in consultation with the Minister. Either way, there is obviously room for partisan influence in the selection panels. There does not appear to be a requirement for candidates to write an exam. As in Alberta, it is not clear on what basis the Minister or the cabinet chooses from among the candidates on the approved list. Thus in British Columbia, as in Alberta, potential apolitical or wrong-party candidates are left with the impression that partisan or ideological credentials remain the final determinants.

Finally, like Alberta, British Columbia has no statutory requirement for merit-based reappointment decisions, and the statutory power to dismiss tribunal members in the middle of their terms without notice or cause – the power that the *McKenzie* case challenged – remains in place.

Nova Scotia's Reform

Nova Scotia's history of appointment reform is particularly interesting, highlighted as it is by the influence of Professor Archibald Kaiser's 1995 complaint to the Nova Scotia Human Rights Tribunal that the rejection of his several applications for appointment to tribunals within his area of expertise constituted discrimination against him based on his "political beliefs or affiliation." Such a complaint was possible in Nova Scotia, where the *Human Rights Act* prohibits discrimination on the basis of political beliefs or affiliation. Professor Kaiser was known for his support of the NDP.

Kaiser's complaint was settled in 2002 when the government, Kaiser, and the Human Rights Commission agreed to terms of settlement that were intended to be the basis for fundamental reform of the province's tribunal appointment process. The agreement was reached on the eve of Kaiser's Human Rights Tribunal hearing, and it is widely believed that the government was moved to settle by the prospect of leading politicians being cross-examined during the hearing about the nature of the appointment process at the time.[69] Nova Scotia's reformed appointment system largely reflects the Kaiser terms of settlement.

One of the most encouraging aspects of the Nova Scotia system is that the system does distinguish between adjudicative tribunals and regulatory and other agencies, providing a unique appointment process for adjudicative tribunals that is isolated from methods that can be counted on to accommodate a government's felt need for ideological allies in its regulatory agencies.

The Nova Scotia adjudicative tribunal appointment process touches many positive bases: the system is transparent – vacancies are posted and qualifications are publicly specified; appointments are announced and summaries of members' professional biographies are available on tribunal websites; the structure of the selection panels ("advisory committees") is elaborately specified in a way apparently geared towards eliminating partisan influence; and the government has made a public commitment to appoint the *best* candidate. And yet, public confidence has not been restored[70] and there are several obvious problems.

First, the qualifications are specified in such general terms that in a pinch virtually anyone can be said to be qualified. For example, the only qualifications specified for appointments to the Department of Community Services Assistance Appeal Board, acknowledged to be an adjudicative board, are: experience in human or social services, an ability to conduct meetings, communication and writing skills, an ability to apply and interpret enactments, and an ability to think analytically. The simplicity of the qualification requirements hark back to the IRB qualifications prior to 2002.

In addition to the published qualifications specific to the position in question, the advisory committees are also given generic instructions to use the following criteria when evaluating applicants:

[the demonstration] in their work, volunteer, or other life experiences of: respect for the essential dignity of all persons, regardless of their circumstances, and commitment to diversity and employment equity; ability to apply a broad perspective on issues, and work with a team to listen to others, constructively solve problems, make objective and fair decisions, and reach consensus in a timely manner; ability to deal professionally with confidential and sensitive information; ability to communicate effectively and write clear and concise board reports; ability to commit required time and effort, and if necessary, travel; peer/community recognition of high ethical standards and integrity in professional and personal interactions.

The advisory committees are also instructed to give preference to applicants with previous involvement/experience in matters related to the board's function, such as activities where one would acquire "an understanding of related issues, interests, practice, policy, legislation, and collective agreements," and to those who are a "former client of program or service, provided that [the latter preference] is not in violation of code of conduct and conflict of interest practices."

All of this is admirable but so all-embracing and generic that no one person could satisfy all the requirements, and a willing selection panel would have no difficulty in finding a significant match for any half-way reasonable candidate. There is no mention of an exam, and interviews are not mandatory.

Second, the advisory committees as structured are in fact subject to partisan influences. It is true that one member – the chair of the committee – is a human resource professional appointed by the Commissioner of the Public

Service, but two members are public servants employed in the department responsible to the Minister and selected by the Minister, and the other two are lay members appointed by the Minister from an unranked list of six volunteer candidates for those positions selected by the panel's human resources professional from names provided to him or her by the Executive Council Office.[71] Most importantly, tribunal chairs are not members of the selection committees, not even *ex officio*, and there appears to be no requirement or expectation that they will even be consulted.

Finally, in Nova Scotia, as in Alberta and British Columbia, the ultimate decision is left to the responsible partisan minister who in Nova Scotia is free to choose the successful candidate from a list of three to six candidates identified by the selection panel as qualified – a list that must be in alphabetical order only, and must be accompanied by only a précis of information about each.

In short, Nova Scotia's elaborate arrangements fail to give qualified apolitical or wrong-party candidates reason to think it would be worth their while to apply, or the rest of us reason to think that Nova Scotia's tribunals are now free of pro-government bias.

Ontario's Reforms

The necessary starting point in addressing Ontario's reforms is now s. 14 of Ontario's *Adjudicative Tribunals Accountability, Governance and Appointments Act, 2009*, which came into effect on 30 June 2011.[72] The first thing to note is that in Ontario, as in Nova Scotia, there is the recognition that the recruitment process for judicial tribunals must be different from that for regulatory agencies. Ontario chose not to attempt a statutory definition of "adjudicative tribunal" but to list the tribunals it considers to be adjudicative tribunals in a regulation enacted under the *Act*. The current regulation identifies thirty-seven such tribunals.

Section 14 also effectively commits Ontario to a best-candidate selection process, as it requires the process to be "*competitive* and merit-based." It also specifies a set of significant minimum qualifications. All appointees must have "experience, knowledge or training in the subject matter and legal issues dealt with by the tribunal," as well as an "*aptitude* for impartial adjudication [and for] applying alternative adjudicative practices and procedures."

This statutory requirement that appointees have an "aptitude" for impartial judging is, I believe, unique. Despite the obvious difficulties in demonstrating the existence of such a personal characteristic, the official

recognition that not everyone has what it takes to be a judge and that se-
lectors must at least be on the lookout for candidates who do not have that
capacity is an important – indeed, groundbreaking – contribution to what
is rationally needed in a process that selects members of judicial tribunals.

Besides these important minimum qualifications, s. 14 requires that
public notices of the intent to make an appointment include a description
of the additional qualifications pertinent to the particular appointment –
"the skills, knowledge, experience, other attributes and specific qualifications required of a person to be appointed." It also requires that such notices
include a description of the selection process.

But the particularly groundbreaking provision is the one that prevents
anyone from being appointed or reappointed unless the tribunal chair approves. Section 14(4) states:

> (4) No person shall be appointed or reappointed to an adjudicative tribu-
> nal unless the chair of the tribunal, after being consulted as to his or her
> assessment of the person's qualifications under subsections (1) and (2)
> and, in the case of a reappointment, of the member's performance of his or
> her duties on the tribunal, recommends that the person be appointed or
> reappointed.

In context, s. 14 represents a remarkably progressive advance in the appointment process. If administered in good faith – and the anecdotal
evidence that I have heard suggests that this is indeed happening – it will
address many of the traditional concerns. Nevertheless, as a shield against
patronage abuse, it has a number of inherent structural weaknesses.

In the first place, both the tribunal-specific qualifications and the structure of the selection process are subject to the host minister's approval.
Second, although s. 14 does give the final say on appointments and reappointments to the tribunal chair rather than the Minister, the power is a veto
power, not a selection power. Thus, the government is not *required* to appoint or reappoint candidates approved by a chair; it just cannot appoint or
reappoint anyone of whom the chair has not approved. Accordingly, chairs
who find themselves dealing with patronage-obsessed ministers may find
their Minister prepared to simply wait them out – to wait until the chair gives
them a candidate whose partisan or ideological credentials are acceptable.

Moreover, tribunal chairs, standing alone, are particularly thin reeds
to depend on as bulwarks against patronage abuse. It is true they have an

abiding interest in ensuring the competence of appointments to their own tribunals, and are the persons best placed to judge the merits of any proposed appointment or reappointment. It is also true, however, that they themselves have been appointed by the government and it is not inconceivable that a government would be influenced in its selection of chairs by its sense of a candidate's likely amiability on the patronage issue. Chairs are also dependent on their host ministers for their own and their members' reappointments, as well as for their tribunal's budget and administrative support. One cannot help wondering, therefore, how likely it is that, faced with a host minister's desire to appoint a government favourite, chairs would in fact find it politically feasible to exercise their veto power. The Ontario legislation, like all similar legislation in other provinces, is also notable for the absence of any provision to ensure the appointment of the best, apolitical candidates for the judicial tribunal *chair* positions.

The "Now It's Our Turn" Syndrome

Patronage appointment regimes really come into their own when a government is defeated at the polls and a new government arrives on the scene. The "now it's our turn" syndrome will now burn its way through the ranks of sitting tribunal chairs and members, leaving not only personal but also institutional havoc in its wake. We have recently seen this occur in Saskatchewan; it occurred in Ontario in 1995 when the Harris government came to power; and – no surprise – the IRB provides us with another convenient case in point.

After the Harper government came to power in 2006, Jean-Guy Fleury found that his recommendations concerning the reappointment of IRB members – even those whose excellent performance had been confirmed by the IRB's respected system of performance evaluation – were no longer being accepted; neither were his recommendations for the appointment of new members. A year later, the annual IRB report to Parliament[73] highlighted the impact of the new government's appointment policy on the Board's backlog. The Canadian Press reported:

> Canada's backlog of refugee claims is soaring to record numbers due to the government's failure to appoint sufficient adjudicators, says the chairman of the Immigration and Refugee Board. The backlog has ballooned along with the number of board vacancies since Prime Minister Stephen Harper took office in February 2006. The number of vacant positions has more than quintupled – to 58 from 10, according to the board. At the same time, the

number of claims waiting to be heard has more than doubled to 42,300 from just over 20,000. In its recent report to Parliament, the board projects that the number of pending claims will soar to 62,300 this year. That's more than triple the line-up when Harper took office and well beyond the previous record of 52,325 pending claims in 2002. Moreover, the numbers are expected to escalate to 73,300 next year and a whopping 84,300 the following year.[74]

The implications of the Harper government's refusal to reappoint meritorious members of the IRB went well beyond the impact on the backlog, however. And it is important to understand these implications, because in Canada they are experienced by many tribunals, judicial or otherwise, whenever there is a change of government.

The Conservatives' policy of not reappointing members who had been appointed by the previous Liberal government even though the chair was recommending their reappointment meant that the Board lost a generation of hard-won skills and experience that in the ordinary course would have provided the basis for training, supervising, and mentoring new appointees. The IRB's adjudicative function is complicated and difficult, and it is well known that it takes about a year or two of full-time experience under the guidance of experienced members and managers for even the best new adjudicators to get fully up to speed. Under the Harper government's reappointment policy, it is hard to know where that experienced training and mentorship will come from.

This policy will have dramatically reduced the Board's average adjudicative experience and overall competence, imposed large new administrative, personnel, and budgetary burdens for training, education, and supervisory activities (assuming that trainers and mentors with the necessary level of experience can be found). Moreover, the government must have known, but chose to ignore, the fact that the inevitable delays in filling the numerous vacant positions with up-to-speed replacements would lead the Board back to the unmanageable and unacceptable backlogs of previous years – an outcome that was confirmed, as we have seen, in the new chair's report to Parliament a year later.

Finally, there is the obvious human dimension. The impact on the personal lives and careers of Board members whose reappointments were unexpectedly denied without, it is important to note, any notice or financial compensation is obvious, but that is a tiny matter compared with the impact on the refugees and immigrants who depend on the Board for life-altering decision making that is impartial, credible, competent, and expeditious. In my opinion, the Harper government's determination to replace the Liberal appointees on the IRB with their own appointees will have jeopardized the Board's capacity to respond effectively and appropriately to that need, to some extent for many years to come.

At-Pleasure Appointments

Of all executive branch strategies for ensuring "responsive" judicial tribunals, "at-pleasure" appointments are the obvious gold standard. People appointed at pleasure hold their offices only as long as they remain in the government's good graces. They may be dismissed at any time without cause or explanation and without notice or compensation. Their status, as the Federal Court of Appeal has confirmed, is "inherently precarious."[75] Implicitly, at-pleasure appointments tell appointees that the government expects them to perform in a manner compatible with its needs; such appointments both presume and condition responsiveness to those needs. As might be expected, therefore, at-pleasure appointments of members of judicial tribunals do not conform to rule-of-law principles of judicial independence.

It is in this context that the executive branch's determination to control its judicial tribunals regardless of rule-of-law considerations is perhaps most clearly demonstrated. As I write, a number of provincial governments and the federal government are still ignoring rule-of-law principles, and by legislative action continuing to impose at-pleasure appointments on judicial tribunal adjudicators and/or chairs. Moreover, they are persisting in this policy willfully. The executive branch knows full well that at-pleasure appointments to offices exercising judicial functions are incompatible with the rule of law – with the common law principles of judicial independence – and that under the *Canadian Charter of Rights and Freedoms* at least some are likely to be constitutionally invalid.

The Sea Change in the Law of Judicial Independence: *Valente*, 1985

At-pleasure appointments of judges or tribunal adjudicators were not always incompatible with the common law of judicial independence. For the first 150 years or so of Canadian law, at-pleasure appointments of persons exercising judicial functions, including not only tribunal members but also provincial court judges, were not thought to be incompatible with judicial independence. This view prevailed, in fact, until the seminal decision of the Supreme Court of Canada in the *Valente* case in 1985.[76] Prior to *Valente*, the law managed, as implausibly as it seems, to reconcile at-pleasure appointments of judges and adjudicators with judicial independence.

In the pre-*Valente* era, while the *British North America Act, 1867*[77] specifically ensured the independence of superior court judges, it left the independence of provincial court judges, justices of the peace, and tribunal adjudicators squarely in the hands of the common law. And the common law simply presumed that anyone appointed to exercise judicial functions in Canada could be relied upon to act as though they were independent, even though, objectively speaking, they were not. The courts based that presumption on two informal factors that in their view effectively ensured independent decision making. One factor was simply *tradition* – what the courts referred to as the Anglo/Canadian tradition of governments respecting the independence of judges notwithstanding their inherently precarious status as at-pleasure appointees. The other factor was *duty* – the professional and ethical duty of individual adjudicators to make decisions as if they were independent, even though they were not.

Speaking a bit irreverently, one might call the pre-*Valente* doctrine of judicial independence a hope-and-a-prayer doctrine; more respectfully, it was effectively a doctrine of trust. The courts simply trusted that, on the one hand, the tradition of governments not exercising their powers to rescind at-pleasure adjudicative appointments for inappropriate reasons could be relied upon to hold,[78] and, on the other, that judges and adjudicators could be relied upon not to allow their decision making to be influenced by contemplation of the possibility that it might not.

The clearest statement of the pre-*Valente* doctrine of trust is found in the 1984 Ontario Court of Appeal decision in *Currie*.[79] Mr. Currie had been charged with an offence for breach of the *Niagara Escarpment Planning and Development Act* and was to be tried by a justice of the peace under the *Provincial Offences Act*. Section 11(d) of the newly minted *Canadian Charter of Rights and Freedoms* explicitly required that he be tried by a "tribunal" that was "independent and impartial." Mr. Currie applied to have the justice of the peace prohibited from hearing his case on the grounds that he was not independent. Currie's principal argument was that because the justice was appointed at pleasure he could not be seen to be independent. The application was granted. The government appealed, and in a unanimous judgment, a five-member panel of the Ontario Court of Appeal allowed the appeal, effectively certifying the independence of Ontario's justices of the peace notwithstanding their at-pleasure appointments.

In the following passages from its judgment, the Court of Appeal's comfort with a justice system that relied on tradition and duty as sufficient guarantors of judicial independence shines through:

> It is important that not only the legislation that governs be looked at but that the practice and traditions surrounding the office be considered in determining how reasonable persons, reasonably informed, would view justices of the peace in this connection, understanding always their position as laymen in the hierarchy of courts.
>
> Regard should also be had to the oath which each justice of the peace takes before entering upon his duties. The oath set out in s. 4(1) of the Justices of the Peace Act reads:
>
>> I ... do swear that I will well and truly serve Her Majesty Queen Elizabeth ... in the office of justice of the peace, and I will do right to all manner of people according to law, without fear or favour, affection or ill will. So help me God.
>
> The motions court judge was of the view that by virtue of the appointment at pleasure, regardless of the oaths taken by justices of the peace, they were dependent on the "whim" of the government which could revoke commissions at any time. This, in his view, bespoke judicial "dependence" not "independence."
>
> The effect of the oath should not be minimized in the individual case and must be a factor that any reasonable and informed person would take into consideration in determining the question whether all justices of the peace lack judicial independence. *If any justice of the peace felt from a subjective point of view and despite his oath, that he was not truly independent, his obligation surely would be to resign.*
>
> Turning back to the question of security of tenure, as already noted, we have inherited the tradition and expectation of judicial independence as part of our common law heritage. In England as here, there are different forms of tenure but that fact has not lead [*sic*] to an attack on the independence of those who appear less secure from government interference.[80]

Four years before the Court of Appeal spoke in *Currie,* the Supreme Court had had occasion to examine the law of judicial independence as it applied to a judicial tribunal – a court martial tribunal.[81] The case was *R. v. MacKay.*[82] *MacKay* was the first case in which the independence of an adjudicator – judge or tribunal adjudicator – had been challenged in a Canadian court.

The issue was whether the court martial tribunal was "independent and impartial" as required by the *Canadian Bill of Rights*.[83]

There is no doubt that, viewed objectively, the tribunal was not independent. As Chief Justice Laskin observed in his dissenting opinion, "both the officer constituting the Standing Court Martial and the prosecutor were part of the office of the Judge Advocate General ... [T]he accused was in the hands of his military superiors in respect of the charges, the prosecution and the tribunal by which he was tried."[84] A majority of the Court, however, embraced what I have chosen to call the trust doctrine of judicial independence. There was, it said, no *"proof"* that the tribunal had *"acted* in anything but an independent and impartial manner," or that the assigned officer "was otherwise unfitted for the task"; nothing to prove that his appointment was *"calculated* to ... deprive [the accused] of a trial before an independent and impartial tribunal";[85] neither was it reasonable to think that military officers are "less able *to adjust their attitudes* to meet *the duty of impartiality* required of them in this task than are others."[86]

Three years after *MacKay* and a year before *Currie*, another five-member panel of the Ontario Court of Appeal was called upon, in a case called *Valente (No. 2)*,[87] to consider the question of judicial independence in light of at-pleasure appointments, this time of provincial court judges. Mr. Valente was being tried for an offence under the *Highway Traffic Act*, an offence that s. 11(d) of the *Charter* required be tried by an independent and impartial tribunal. He had challenged the independence of the provincial court judge. In a unanimous judgment written by Chief Justice Howland, the Court of Appeal embraced the trust doctrine (as it would again, a few months later, in *Currie*).

Fortunately, the Ontario Court of Appeal's judgment in *Currie* proved to be the trust doctrine's last hurrah. *Valente (No. 2)* was appealed to the Supreme Court of Canada (which heard and decided the case after the Court of Appeal's judgment in *Currie*). The Supreme Court rejected the trust doctrine and made objective, structural guarantees of independence – guarantees established by law – the essential conditions of judicial independence. The judgment of Justice Le Dain, speaking for a unanimous Court, became the iconic Canadian judgment on judicial independence, now known simply as *Valente*.[88]

The important point is that, prior to *Valente*, the judicial independence of provincial court judges or members of administrative judicial tribunals appointed at pleasure was not, as a practical matter, an issue in law. As can be seen in *MacKay*, in *Currie*, and in *Valente (No.2)*, without evidence of actual interference or inappropriate conduct, any person assigned a statutory judicial function was simply *presumed* to be independent. The common law now holds, however, that independence must be ensured by objective, structural guarantees of at least the three "conditions" of independence identified in *Valente:* security of tenure, financial security, and administrative control (with administrative control being defined as "institutional independence of the tribunal with respect to matters of administration bearing directly on the exercise of its judicial function").[89] These guarantees are designed to ensure both actual independence and what the courts believe to be the equally important – the *appearance* of independence.[90]

Of course, *Valente* dealt only with the concept of "tribunal" independence constitutionally required by s. 11(d) of the *Charter,*[91] and only as this requirement applied to provincial court judges. However, the Supreme Court's subsequent adoption of the *Valente* principles in other cases – such as *Consolidated-Bathurst,*[92] *Matsqui,*[93] and *Généreux*[94] – have entrenched these rule-of-law principles of judicial independence as an essential component of the common law doctrine of procedural fairness and/or natural justice for both provincial court judges and administrative judicial tribunals and their members.

Généreux, in particular, underscores the fact that, post *Valente,* we have a new regime of judicial independence. In that case, in 1992, seven years after *Valente* and twelve years after *MacKay,* the issue of the independence of a court martial tribunal was considered once again by the Supreme Court, and this time the Court overturned *MacKay.* After citing the relevant passages from the majority judgment in *MacKay,* Chief Justice Lamer, writing for the majority, said:

> MacKay ... assists us by revealing various concerns with the independence and impartiality of the court martial system. The question raised in this appeal, however, is not resolved by this earlier case. First, the majority of this Court in MacKay seems to have applied a subjective test. It asked whether the Standing Court Martial actually acted in an independent and impartial manner. This is not, in light of Valente, the appropriate test ... We must now therefore undertake an analysis that was not undertaken in MacKay.[95]

The Court concluded that the court martial tribunal did not satisfy the *Valente* principles: there were no objective guarantees of security of tenure, no objective guarantees of financial security, and no objective guarantees of what the Court called this time the condition of "institutional independence."

Valente and the jurisprudence that it spawned has made it perfectly clear that the security-of-tenure condition of independence could not be satisfied by an at-pleasure appointment. Justice Le Dain summarized the requirements of security of tenure in *Valente* as follows: "The essence of security of tenure for purposes of s. 11(d) is a tenure, whether until an age of retirement, for a fixed term, or for a specific adjudicative task, that is secure against interference by the Executive or other appointing authority in a discretionary or arbitrary manner."[96] Thus, the modern law now fits with common sense: at-pleasure appointments are not compatible with the independence the rule of law requires for the exercise of judicial functions.

Governments Show True Colours in Response to *Valente*

Once the courts had made it clear that at-pleasure appointments of judicial tribunal adjudicators no longer conformed to the common law of judicial independence, one might have expected the legislative and executive branches of our governments to move to identify those tribunals to which they had assigned judicial functions, and, for those tribunals, to have abandoned the concept of at-pleasure appointments, thereby conforming the tribunals to the new law. Instead, however, the legislative and executive branches took to the barricades.

The legislative channels through which the pre-*Valente* tradition of at-pleasure appointments was principally made operational were the *Interpretation Acts* found in all provinces and territories and in the federal jurisdiction. These acts traditionally purported to render all appointments, including tribunal appointments, at-pleasure appointments. Although the practice of appointing tribunal members to fixed terms grew after *Valente*, such appointments were largely cosmetic in nature, since the standard provisions in most *Interpretation Acts* could be pointed to as authorizing the removal of an appointee mid-term without cause even if the appointment was said to be for a fixed term.

This view was challenged in 1992[97] when William Preston, chair of the BC Motor Carrier Commission applied to the courts to challenge the BC government's right to terminate without cause his three-year appointment, three months before the expiry of his term. The government argued that, notwithstanding Preston's appointment to a fixed term, it had statutory authority under the province's *Interpretation Act* to terminate his appointment at any time. It relied on the *Interpretation Act* provision that "words in an enactment authorizing the appointment of a public officer include power to (a) fix his term of office; (b) terminate his appointment.[98] (Asked by the trial judge during argument what meaning should be given to the fixed term if the Crown had nevertheless an absolute right to terminate the appointment at its pleasure, the government's counsel replied that the only effect of the fixed term was to provide an expiry date when the office would become vacant without termination.)

The trial judge held that, in appointing the Commission chair to a three-year term, the Lieutenant-Governor-in-Council (*i.e.*, the cabinet) had committed the government to a three-year contract of employment and, while the chair could be removed from the office at any time, the financial obligation to pay him for three years continued (subject possibly to mitigation, which, because the dismissal came so close to the end of the chair's term, was not a pertinent issue in this case). The government appealed and the BC Court of Appeal, although doubtful that the relationship between the chair and the government should be considered one of employment, upheld the trial judge's decision, holding that the provisions of the *Interpretation Act* authorized the Lieutenant-Governor-in-Council to commit the Crown to pay the plaintiff for the term of the appointment without impairing the Crown's right to declare the office vacant at any time.[99] (The impact of the latter conclusion on the Commission's independence was not raised as an issue in this case. Moreover, it may be that the BC Motor Carrier Commission is a regulatory agency, rather than a judicial tribunal.)

Two years later, the mid-term termination of four members of the Ontario Labour Relations Board (a board that, in my view, is clearly a judicial tribunal) brought the same issues before the Ontario courts in *Hewat.* The Ontario Divisional Court effectively followed *Preston,*[100] but the Court of Appeal held that, as a matter of interpretation, the statutory power to appoint at pleasure was superseded by the actual appointment for a fixed term, and that the power to remove was subordinated or exhausted by the inclusion of a fixed term in the original appointment.[101] (Significantly, the Court of Appeal did not agree that the government was entitled to terminate the appointments of Labour Relations Board vice-chairs contingent only on paying them for the balance of their terms. It held that the orders of the Lieutenant-Governor-in-Council terminating the appointments were null and void at their inception.[102])

In neither *Preston* nor *Hewat* did the courts consider the constitutional validity of the statutory powers to terminate. In both cases, the decisions were based on statutory interpretations, with fixed-term appointments being seen in *Hewat* to override the powers of dismissal, and in *Preston* to require compensation for the full term even if the appointment was terminated in mid-term. Thus, while these two decisions served to stick something of an oar into the executive branch strategy of appointing for a fixed term but continuing to rely on the standard *Interpretation Act* powers of at-pleasure dismissal, they did not prevent the resort to at-pleasure appointments *per se*. Explicit, statutory at-pleasure appointment powers were still enforceable, as would be new statutory provisions clearly authorizing such appointments. And, for judicial tribunal appointments, *Valente* and *Preston* and *Hewat* were seen by governments as challenges to be overcome, not as a reason to give up on the at-pleasure appointment strategy.

In making new appointments, some provincial governments now resorted to combining a fixed term with an explicit at-pleasure appointment, with members now appointed "at pleasure for a term of *x* years." This gave these governments the double advantage from a control point of view referred to by the government's counsel in *Preston:* they could terminate anyone at any time for no reason, or they could wait for the term to expire, not reappoint, and thus rid themselves of troublesome members, or create vacancies for their friends, without taking any active step against them. In some provinces, governments clarified the legislation to make the power of mid-term termination without cause clear; in others, they continued to apply *Interpretation Act* provisions that because of their particular wording had not been affected by the *Preston* and *Hewat* decisions.

After *Preston*, the Alberta legislature amended the *Interpretation Act* by adding s. 20(4):

> If the appointment of a person by or under the authority of an enactment is terminated, revoked or rescinded effective on a specified day, that termination, revocation or rescission, *whether or not that person holds office for a term of office that is to conclude, expire or otherwise come to an end on an expressed day*, is deemed to be effective immediately on the beginning of the specified day.[103]

In British Columbia, in the initial legislative step in that province's highly touted reform of its executive branch justice system – the *Administrative Tribunals Appointment and Administration Act*[104] – the government included s. 14.9(3) of the *Public Sector Employers Act*[105] as a consequential amendment. The government's intention to rely on the latter provision as rendering all BC judicial tribunal appointments as effectively at-pleasure appointments became perfectly clear in the *McKenzie* case (as recounted in the Introduction).[106]

In Saskatchewan, s. 20(1) of the *Interpretation Act* referred to above[107] was not affected by the *Preston/Hewat* interpretations and, as noted previously,[108] the Saskatchewan government and Court of Appeal continue to see it as operable – in the Court of Appeal's case, without considering the constitutional issue.

In Ontario, the Harris government responded to *Hewat* by making appointments to the Ontario Labour Relations Board (OLRB) explicitly at-pleasure appointments. It was a practice of short duration, however, as the uproar from both the union and employer communities at this break with tradition appeared to cause the government to rethink its position, at least as far as the OLRB was concerned.

An appointment policy commonly seen in the constitutive statutes of many federal administrative tribunals is to provide for the appointment of tribunal members to fixed terms on good behaviour – *i.e.*, not subject to dismissal during their terms except for cause – but then to select the tribunal chair from among the members and make his or her designation as chair an at-pleasure designation.[109] It is a practice that is subversive of the independence of federal tribunals generally.

Dunsmuir and the At-Pleasure Issue

One cannot leave this question of at-pleasure appointments without mentioning the possibly emerging argument that in its decision in *Dunsmuir*[110] the Supreme Court has converted all tribunal adjudicator positions to contract positions that can be terminated without cause or explanation on reasonable notice or with pay in lieu of notice. Appointments that can be terminated without cause at any time subject only to pay in lieu of notice are not quite as vulnerable as appointments that are purely at-pleasure, but they are effectively at-pleasure appointments and equally inconsistent with any viable concept of independence.

The argument one now hears in this respect is that, in *Dunsmuir*, in addition to breaking new ground on the standard of review principles, the Supreme Court also established – in passing, as it were – that the relationship between governments and the members of adjudicative tribunals is not arm's-length or independent at all but merely a standard, contractual relationship between employer and employee, a relationship that, as with any employment relationship, can be terminated without cause at any time during the term of appointment, subject only to the government's assuming an employer's liability for payment in lieu of reasonable notice.

That argument is, in fact, more apparent than real; the authorities referenced in *Dunsmuir* in this connection do not relate to adjudicative members of judicial tribunals, and it is surely inconceivable that the Court would
intend to overrule *Valente* and the vast jurisprudence on the judicial independence of judicial tribunals and their members that *Valente* spawned
without referencing those authorities and without hearing argument on that
critical issue. I mention the argument here only because it has a technical,
doctrinal plausibility about it and may turn out to be the next weapon that
one might find the executive branch deploying in defence of its power to
terminate judicial tribunal appointments at any time without cause.[111]

Secondments

The seconding of loyal executive branch public service staff to tribunal
positions is another tactic through which the executive branch ensures responsive tribunals. The problem with this tactic from an independence
perspective was once described in a Canadian Environmental Law Association (CELA) paper in 2001.[112] The association was concerned in part with
the independence implications for the Ontario Environmental Assessment
Board (now the Environmental Review Tribunal) of the Ontario government's seconding of a long-serving member of the public service to be the
"independent" board's new chair. (The Board needed a new chair because
the incumbent chair had been dismissed only a few days before the Board
was scheduled to review a highly politicized landfill site proposal.[113])

A long-standing, explicit legislative prohibition against government employees being appointed to this Board had been recently repealed, even
though, as the author of the CELA paper points out, the prohibition reflected the concern that public servants might have loyalties to their employer that are inconsistent with tribunal independence. For example, he
notes, future promotions and appointments of such persons would continue
to be within the control of the Ontario government as their employer. A
career government employee would probably also have loyalties to other
employees and colleagues, especially those from the same ministry.[114]
Robert Macaulay noted this problem as well. "[A] number [of tribunals]",
he said, "are chaired by or have members who are employed within the
Ontario Government Public Service [who are] not independent, with years
of service, and pension and tenure at stake."[115]

Another example of the secondment tactic at work may be found in the
Hansard record of a session of the Ontario legislature's Standing Committee

on Government Agencies in 1998.[116] The Standing Committee was reviewing a proposed appointment to the Social Assistance Review Board (now the Social Benefits Tribunal). The candidate was a "program supervisor" with the Ministry of Community and Social Services – the Board's host ministry and the ministry whose officials make the policy, rules, and decisions that the Board is charged with reviewing. He had been a career public servant with that Ministry for twenty-four years. The Standing Committee had been told that once the candidate's three-year appointment was confirmed, he would be granted a leave of absence from his position with the Ministry. The following question to the candidate from an opposition-party Committee member captures the issue squarely: "But you ... would be in a position where you are interpreting government policies, Ministry of Community and Social Service policies as enunciated by the minister, yet expecting to be able to go back to that minister's employment. What is your view of that in terms of conflict of interest?" The candidate responded that he would not be in a conflict because he would be on a leave of absence from the Ministry. The Standing Committee's government majority saw nothing to be concerned about in these circumstances, and the appointment was approved in the ordinary course.

The Standing Committee might want to rethink that decision now, however, and governments generally might want to rethink this practice. In 2001, the Federal Court of Appeal ruled that the appointment of an employee of the Ministry of Citizenship and Immigration who was on leave from that Ministry, to a panel deciding refugee claims created a reasonable apprehension that the member was likely to be biased and mindful of the effects of her decisions upon her career once she returned.[117]

Government's Untrammelled Discretion to Remove Adjudicators at the End of Their Terms without Notice, Cause, Compensation, or Reasons

From a rule-of-law perspective, by far the most objectionable of the executive branch's strategies for controlling judicial tribunals is its routine exercise of its power to remove adjudicators at the end of their terms without prior notice, cause, compensation, or reasons.

In a keynote address to the 1997 annual conference of Ontario Boards and Agencies, the Honourable Roy McMurtry, then Ontario's Chief Justice, endorsed the following principles concerning adjudicator independence:

1   Issues involving legal rights and obligations can at law only be validly
    determined by adjudicators who are independent and impartial and

whose circumstances do not provide any reasonable basis for an informed observer to think otherwise.

2 The confidence of the adjudicator, and of the parties, that the adjudicator is free to make a decision in their case without fear of personal consequences is a fundamental prerequisite for any independent and impartial adjudication.[118]

The Chief Justice then went on to say that freedom "from fear of *idiosyncratic removal*" is "integral" to the concept of adjudicator independence.[119]

Unfortunately, adjudicator fear of idiosyncratic removal is in fact one of the pervasive, defining features of Canada's administrative justice system. Whether or not their fixed-term appointments are protected from mid-term termination except for cause, all appointees know that their government sees itself as having an untrammelled power to arbitrarily refuse end-of-term reappointments – arbitrarily and without notice, explanation, or compensation. And it is well known that this is a power of removal that governments exercise.

The serious nature of the threat of idiosyncratic removals to the independence of a tribunal member's decision making was once uniquely captured by Supreme Court of Canada Justice Rosalie Abella when she was chair of the Ontario Labour Relations Board: "It takes," she said, "herculean feistiness for tribunal adjudicators to develop decisions of a potentially controversial kind ... when they know that at the end of the political telescope through which they are observed is a person with the power to renew or not renew a three- or five-year appointment."[120]

And, it is often meritorious members – respected members whose reappointments have been earned by good performance and recommended by their chair – who fall victim to these removals. Reappointments that tribunal colleagues expect them to receive in the ordinary course, and on which the members themselves have counted, are inexplicably refused. Typically such members learn the bad news only as their current term is about to expire, and despite often many years of dedicated service they are sent packing with no separation package. (For part-time members, an idiosyncratic removal of a virtual nature may also be accomplished by a chair's arbitrary decision to not assign them to any more cases. In such situations, the fact of their removal dawns on them only over a period of time.)

One hears the argument that the refusal of a reappointment cannot aptly be described as a removal or termination. However, refusals to reappoint in the administrative justice system occur in an organizational context in which tribunals could not operate if reappointments were not the rule. In most tribunals, it will take about two years for the performance of new appointees to fully mature. A tribunal's effectiveness and efficiency depends on retaining successful members for as long as possible. Routine reappointments are therefore an integral feature of the system. In this context, idiosyncratic refusals to reappoint meritorious members are in fact removals and are seen as such. They bring an individual's adjudicative career to an unexpected, arbitrary, and distressful end. Moreover, they are always institutionally jarring, with lasting effects on the morale and sense of security of the removed member's surprised colleagues.

While the reasons for idiosyncratic removals are known to include merely making room for patronage appointments of a government's friends or allies, they are also understood to include a government's unhappiness with a member's decisions, or with his or her politics. Every adjudicator in the system therefore comes to understand that good performance is never enough to ensure the continuation of an adjudicative career, and that a decision that treads too heavily on the toes of the government of the day or of any of its influential friends may well be the precipitating factor in bringing that career to a premature end. Mary McKenzie does not know which of her decisions led to the termination of her appointment, but she has no doubt that one of them did.[121]

The importance that governments attach to the discretionary power to arbitrarily refuse reappointments without giving reasons was especially evidenced in 2003 when the BC government, in the midst of a vaunted administrative justice reform project ostensibly devoted to improving tribunal independence, and priding itself on making consultation with tribunal chairs respecting appointments legally mandatory, could not bring itself to do the same for reappointments. Section 3(1) of the new reform legislation said that tribunal members were to be *appointed* only after a merit-based process and consultation with the chair, but with respect to *reappointments*, s. 3(2) said only that members "may be reappointed."[122] I was present at the BC Council of Administrative Tribunals (BCCAT) conference where Attorney General Geoff Plant was speaking and commenting on the new legislation. At question time, I asked about this discrepancy, and Plant had no pertinent explanation. Section 3(2) continues to read today the way it did then, and the arbitrary refusal of reappointments remains, as we will see, a well-known characteristic of the BC administrative justice system.

Matkowski v. Saskatchewan

Litigation of idiosyncratic removals rarely occurs. The prevailing legal opinion is that there is no point, that in refusing reappointments governments are exercising an unrestricted, sovereign power. As mentioned earlier, however, in Saskatchewan a full-time vice-chair of the Labour Relations Board sued the government in 2006 after he was refused a reappointment that he had been assured by the government would be available.[123] The government's refusal to reappoint appears to have been due to lobbying by Saskatchewan unions unhappy with some of his decisions. The following passage from the headnote of the decision that dismissed the vice-chair's claim makes abundantly clear the legally tenuous nature of an adjudicator's reappointment expectations:

> The Trade Union Act restricted the appointment of a vice-chairperson to five years,[124] and no contract term could be incorporated that guaranteed the extension of such employment beyond five years – The failure to re-appoint could not constitute a breach of contract – There was no place for the principles of procedural fairness and natural justice – The defendants adhered to the contract and were required to do no more ...[125]

A Plea from the Trenches

In March 1994, the shadow of the public wrath stirred up by the National Parole Board's decision in 1993 that had led, as we have seen, to the rape and murder of a Regina woman by a recent parolee[126] fell on an analogous decision-making process in Toronto. That month, an application to the Ontario Review Board by an involuntary patient to be released from the Penetanguishene Mental Health Centre was declined on the grounds that the likely result of a relapse by the patient would be serious bodily harm to other people. At the end of his written reasons for the decision, the respected Review Board panel chair, Michael Bay, was moved to add the following paragraph:

> It is clear that there has been enormous pressure on all of the institutions and professionals involved in this matter to conduct themselves in a manner that will not attract public criticism. Public interest in this issue is both understandable and justifiable. At the same time, we believe that it is perhaps time to take steps to ensure the integrity of our democratically

established institutions and processes by ensuring that decisions are made according to legal and professional criteria, not overt public pressure or a desire not to be subject to reprisals or criticism.[127]

Idiosyncratic Removal at the BC Human Rights Tribunal, 2010

It can rarely be proved that what led to a meritorious member's removal was an unpopular decision. Governments never give reasons, and, as I have said, it is understood that such a removal may sometimes be explained merely by a government's desire to create a vacancy for purely patronage purposes. Still, in the absence of reasons where none are obvious, tribunal members who are not reappointed and their tribunal colleagues are left to speculate, and inevitably the speculation turns to the question of which decisions so offended the government or its friends that it led to the refusal to reappoint.

In British Columbia in 2010, Judy Parrack, a respected member of the BC Human Rights Tribunal for a number of years was denied reappointment despite the recommendation of her tribunal chair and the fact that she had every reason to expect reappointment in the ordinary course. This idiosyncratic removal occurred while Parrack was in the midst of hearing an exceptionally complicated discrimination complaint. The case involved multiple complaints by thirteen Sikh veterinarians of discrimination against them by the BC Veterinary Medical Association (BCVMA) in which the complainants were attempting to prove a pattern of discrimination by the BCVMA in hundreds of individual decisions. At the time the reappointment was refused, the case had already consumed 200 hearing days and it was estimated that another 150 days would be required. Parrack's shocking removal from the case led the complainants to speculate publicly that the refusal of her reappointment was motivated by the BC government's wish to interfere in the complaint on behalf of the respondents. An eventually public exchange of correspondence ensued.

Parrack's appointment was eventually extended by the new, interim chair. (The original chair's appointment had expired at the same time as Parrack's, also as a result of the government's refusal of her request for reappointment.) The extension was to enable Parrack to complete the hearings in the BCVMA case. When that extension was announced, however, the respondents in the BCVMA case then asked her to recuse herself on the grounds that, because of the complainants' successful efforts to have her appointment extended, the respondents would now have a reasonable apprehension that she would be biased in favour of the complainants.

In an eighty-five page decision, Parrack rejected the respondents' request. The respondents then applied to the BC Supreme Court for a judicial review of her decision, and, in a detailed decision (*Brar v. College of Veterinarians of British Columbia*[128]), Justice Davies of the BC Supreme Court dismissed the application. Thus, in these two decisions – those of Parrack and Justice Davies – one finds the shamefulness of an arbitrary reappointment regime on full public display.

As in all such cases, the government's actual reasons for Parrack's idiosyncratic removal remain unknown. However, the administrative justice community's speculation as to the reasons for this spectacular removal would have been fuelled by contemplation of not one but two obvious possibilities. One of the possibilities would have been that the government did intend to affect the BCVMA case in the hope that it would benefit the respondents or perhaps cut short this prolonged hearing. The nature of this speculation is part of the record in the two published decisions, which I will return to shortly. The other obvious possibility, however, was a decision that Parrack had issued in a different case in 2007.

Parrack had had the misfortune of being assigned to adjudicate a human rights complaint against a McDonald's Restaurant in Vancouver. The complaint was that McDonald's had failed to accommodate an employee's disability – a painful hand condition that prevented the employee from continuing to comply with the restaurant's handwashing policies. In *Datt v. McDonald's Restaurants*,[129] Parrack found in favour of the employee and awarded significant damages. The decision caught the attention of Ezra Levant.

Levant is a crusader against what he sees as abuses by human rights tribunals. His book *Shakedown* contains extensive criticism of Canada's human rights tribunals, and characterizes Parrack's decision in *Datt* as a "crazy" decision. In various media outlets, he also described this "crazy" decision as granting an employee of McDonald's Restaurants the "human right" to refuse to wash her hands while working in McDonald's kitchens. He also publicly denigrated the decision's author as "a former divorce lawyer and left-wing lobbyist."[130]

Levant's description of the decision is unjustified. The complainant had been employed by McDonald's at the same restaurant in Vancouver for twenty-three years when she developed a painful skin condition on her hands that appeared likely to be attributable to the constant handwashing normally required of a McDonald's employee. From the evidence, a detailed description of which appears in the decision, Parrack found that there were, in fact, jobs in the restaurant that did not involve handling food and, if assigned to the complainant, would have substantially reduced the amount of handwashing required without breaching the handwashing policy. She identified a number of such jobs, and referred to established law requiring an employer to accommodate a disability even to the point of bundling parts of jobs to create a new job, if that could be done without "undue hardship" to the employer.

Parrack indicated in her decision that she could not be sure that such a bundling of work would solve the complainant's hand problem, or that it would not present undue hardship to McDonald's, but the evidence showed that there was a possibility that the problem could be solved without undue hardship on the part of the employer. At no time did she suggest that the restaurant could be criticized for refusing to employ the complainant in a food-handling position. Parrack's point was that the restaurant had steadfastly refused to even consider whether a bundling of a series of jobs that did not involve food handling and where less frequent handwashing was needed might be possible, and it was this refusal that, in her opinion, put McDonald's in breach of the BC *Human Rights Code*.

The decision demonstrates a competent, thorough, and careful consideration of the evidence and issues and of the applicable law. As an experienced adjudicator myself, I found it persuasive. Moreover, in 2011, its analysis of the law of accommodation was cited with approval by the BC Supreme Court.[131]

Levant's mockery of the decision and its author was in the media the year before Parrack's appointment came up for renewal. That appointment was due to expire on 31 July 2010, and the tribunal chair recommended renewal in the ordinary course. The recommendation went to the responsible Minister, the Attorney General, in November 2009. Seven months later, on 9 July 2010, three weeks before Parrack's appointment was to expire, she was advised that it would not be renewed. Her ten-year career as a human rights adjudicator would be ending.

In the absence of any official explanation for Parrack's removal, it would not be surprising if the community of administrative justice adjudicators in British Columbia were to conclude that the publicity concerning the *Datt* decision played a principal role. If that were the case, the decision not to reappoint will have ended Parrack's adjudicative career in the absence of cause, upon virtually no notice, without compensation, and with Parrack having no notice of the complaint or any opportunity to defend herself. For members of the adjudicator community who do attribute Parrack's removal to the public mocking of her decision in *Datt,* the rhetorical question asked in 2002 by human rights activist lawyer Robert Friedland on behalf of all BC human rights adjudicators is apposite: "Why dare to make a decision when every decision made brings a personal and professional attack, often with political override, and unhappy career consequences as well?"[132]

By the summer of 2010, Parrack was deeply engaged in the BCVMA case. At the beginning of July, there was a pause as the respondents prepared to mount their defence. The hearing was scheduled to resume on 12 July. On that day, Parrack announced a further one-day adjournment. The next day, she opened the hearing with a formal statement, later quoted in full by the BC Supreme Court in the *Brar* decision referred to above. The statement reads as follows:

> I have a statement that I would like to put on the record concerning a significant development that has an impact on this complaint.
>
> As you are aware, I am subject to a five-year appointment that expires on July 31, 2010. I sought a reappointment that was supported by the current chair of the Tribunal ... My request was communicated to the Attorney General in November 2009 ...
>
> I have been advised by the Chair that she made repeated requests to have the issue of my reappointment addressed. It was only on the afternoon of Friday, July 9, 2010 that the Chair was advised who then advised me that the Minister intended to let my appointment expire and that I would not be reappointed ... The Chair has also advised me that any further issues with respect to a continuation of my appointment, the only one being a possible six-month Chairs appointment pursuant to the Administrative Tribunals Act, would be addressed by the new Chair in August 2010 when that person will be appointed. [The incumbent chair's reappointment request had also been denied and her tenure also ended on 31 July 2010.]
>
> The effect of these decisions is that as of 31 July 2010, I will no longer be a member of the Human Rights Tribunal. I have had no written or direct oral communications from the Minister other than what has been communicated to me above and as such I am unable to provide you with any further information or answer any questions you may have. Clearly, having only been provided with three weeks' notice regarding the status of my appointment, I have not had a full opportunity to consider the professional impact that the Minister's decision has on me and the number of matters that continue before me including this hearing.

Given the circumstances, I am adjourning the balance of the hearing dates in July. I deeply regret that the decision communicated by the Minister results in me having to take this step. However, given this climate of uncertainty, I am of the view that it would be inappropriate and unfair to the parties to continue to expend their resources by continuing with this hearing at this time.

I appreciate the impact that this decision might have on the parties but the current circumstances are beyond my control.

The parties should maintain those dates that are scheduled in the fall until further notice from the Tribunal.

I would ask the parties to pack their materials and have them removed by close of business tomorrow. The witness copies of the exhibits must also be removed as I am unable to store them. The parties should decide who will take this responsibility.[133]

Of course, the story did not end with this statement. The adjournment and Parrack's explanatory statement led to public speculation by the complainants about the government's possible motives, and they lobbied the government and the new chair to extend Parrack's appointment so that she could complete the case, which had already consumed so many days of hearings. As mentioned above, the extension was eventually granted by the new, interim tribunal chair, electing to exercise the tribunal chair's own statutory power to extend an appointment to allow for the completion of any case in which a member was engaged at the time his or her appointment expired. Once the extension was granted, however, the respondents brought their application to have Parrack recuse herself.

The account in the BC Supreme Court judgment of the public speculation that followed the announcement of the non-renewal and of the ensuing correspondence should be deeply troubling to anyone concerned about our administrative justice system.[134] In para. 21, the Court quotes from a letter sent by the complainants's counsel to the Attorney General, dated 14 July 2010:

Further, the failure to re-appoint Member Parrack in the midst of one of the most significant human rights hearings in British Columbian history is a deep affront to the decision-making independence of this Tribunal member, to the integrity and independence of this Tribunal, and to the independence, integrity, authority and esteem of all administrative decision making bodies in this province. It undermines the fundamental role of the rule of law in our system of government. This failure to re-appoint has shocked and dismayed our clients and shaken their confidence in the legal structures of our province. It has also deeply troubled and dismayed us, both as counsel and as officers of the Tribunal. It is the gravest possible threat in this litigation to our clients' rights as litigants and as citizens.[135]

In addressing the argument of the petitioners (BCVMA and Osborne) that counsel for the complainants (the Sikh veterinarians) continued to "link" the actions of the government in not reappointing Parrack to the petitioners' agenda, the Court quoted from paras. 83 and 84 of the complainants' Response to the original Recusal Petition.[136] Counsel for the respondent complainants (the Sikh veterinarians) wrote:

83.
... there *were* certainly elements in the surrounding circumstances which might give rise, rightly or wrongly, to the concern that this case was a factor in the Government's decision not to reappoint. From our perspective, the confluence of these elements was unfortunate when coupled with this decision. As examples of these unfortunate circumstances we would point to: the discussions in the fall of 2009 between the BCVMA[137] and the Government about the Government funding of their defense in these proceedings; ... the representations by the BCVMA that their relationship with the government had rarely been better; the existence of a secret Governmental indemnity of the BCVMA, the details of which the BCVMA refused to disclose; the retention as new representation for the BCVMA in these proceedings [of] counsel ... who have frequently acted for the Government over a long period of time, including on very high profile matters; the central role of those Counsel in a Government initiative to investigate fundamental changes to the Tribunal, including perhaps its abolition; and the public role of those counsel in advocating for major changes to the Tribunal which the Government is investigating.

The Court also summarized the chain of reasoning on which the petitioners relied in their attempt to establish a reasonable apprehension of Parrack's being biased in favour of the complainants.[138] The chain was premised, the Court noted, on the following submissions by the petitioners:

1) In making the Statement [announcing that her reappointment application had been denied and adjourning the hearing (see above)]

the adjudicator, Member Parrack, deliberately failed to advert to the likelihood of an authorization by Chair McNaughton (sic) under s. 7 of the *Administrative Tribunals Act* that would allow her to continue and complete the hearing of the Complaint without re-appointment as a member of the Tribunal for a further five years.

2) Member Parrack "politicized" the hearing of the Complaint by making the Statement and "linking" it to her desire to be re-appointed.

3) Member Parrack thus "created a crisis where there was none" and in so doing "incited" a predictable response by the respondent complainants who then campaigned for her re-appointment, and made her appear beholden to them for their efforts on her behalf.

4) In their campaign on her behalf and in the conduct of the Recusal Application, the respondent complainants and their counsel "linked" the actions of the government to efforts by the petitioners to thwart the continued hearing of the Complaint by preventing Member Parrack from being re-appointed.

5) The actions of the respondent complainants in "championing" Member Parrack's re-appointment and supporting her continuation as the adjudicator of the Complaint in the Recusal Application align the respondent complainants with her interests and make her financially beholden to them for their continued support.

6) Similarly, in not supporting her re-appointment and pursuing the Recusal Application, the petitioners now appear adverse to Member Parrack's personal and financial interests.

7) In the totality of the circumstances, the Statement, together with the respondent claimants' reaction to it, has so compromised the appearance of Member Parrack's neutrality as the adjudicator of the Complaint that she must be disqualified.

The Court dismissed the petitioners' application for judicial review of Parrack's recusal decision, agreeing with her that her statement to the parties on 13 July was appropriate, understandable, and reasonable; that she was not responsible for the ensuing actions and communications by the parties; and that there were no grounds for a reasonable apprehension of bias on her part.[139]

Idiosyncratic Removals in Ontario

The impact of idiosyncratic removals on a tribunal's integrity, or at least on its perceived integrity, is particularly evidenced by what happened at the

Ontario Labour Relations Board during the tenure of the Harris government. The Board was the acknowledged flagship of independence and impartiality among Ontario's tribunals, and idiosyncratic removals were unknown. This changed when the Harris government came to power in June 1995. The following account is excerpted from a 2003 paper by Ron Lebi and Elizabeth Mitchell, both union labour counsel with the Toronto labour law firm of Koskie Minsky:[140]

> Not content merely to alter the statute, the previous provincial government made repeated changes to the complement of the OLRB which undermined its independence and its very ability to fulfill its statutory mandate. The Tory Cabinet's mid-term discharge of three vice-chairs in 1996 for so-called "budgetary reasons" attracted much attention at the time and, eventually, the opprobrium of the Court of Appeal for Ontario in *Hewitt* [*Hewat*] v. *Ontario*. Less attention, however, has been paid to other, equally destructive developments after 1996. These include the government's attempt to appoint and reappoint vice-chairs "at pleasure" rather than for secure, and definite terms, the appointment of new vice-chairs without the knowledge (or against the wishes) of the Board's Chair, and the failure to make vice-chair appointments and reappointments recommended by the Chair. After 1996, in addition to the three vice-chairs who were dismissed during their terms of office, the Conservative government failed to renew the appointment of at least seven others who wished to be reappointed and whose reappointments were supported by the Chair. Yet other vice-chairs, some senior, left the Board of their own accord in anticipation of the non-renewal of their terms.
>
> To be blunt, these changes have meant that fewer vice-chairs, with diminished security of tenure and less independence, must adjudicate cases that are often controversial and central to the government's concerns. These developments have seriously undermined the confidence that trade unions place in the Ontario Labour Relations Board as a tribunal that is willing and able to protect and advance the statutory rights of employees and unions.[141]
>
> If Labour rights are to be taken seriously ... [i]t is necessary that the Board's independence be restored so that adjudicators feel free, once again, to make decisions that may be unpopular with the government of the day.[142]

The idiosyncratic removals at the Ontario Workers' Compensation Appeals Tribunal in the spring of 1997 were mentioned in the Introduction, and I have personal knowledge that idiosyncratic removals occurred periodically elsewhere in Ontario's administrative justice system throughout the Progressive Conservative government's term in office and during the new Liberal government's term, as well.[143]

That the practice of idiosyncratic removals does not always escape public notice may also be seen from the July 2002 issue of the monthly newsletter of the Toronto administrative law firm Fink and Bornstein. That issue was devoted to an analysis of the decision record of an experienced and respected tribunal adjudicator whose appointment had been unexpectedly not renewed (this was not a Labour Relations Board appointment). The newsletter concluded that what must have alienated the "provincial political power brokers" and led to the adjudicator's "removal" was the fact that the adjudicator's decision making, while always competent and fair, was too often out of step with government interests.

It is also a fact that from 1995 to 2003, reserving the right to make idiosyncratic removals was the explicit policy of the Progressive Conservative government in Ontario. Clause 12 of a standard appointment agreement for adjudicators and regulators proposed by the government made the government's reservation of its power to engage in such removals explicit:

> The parties agree that consideration will be given to the renewal of the Appointee for one further term. Any such consideration will be based *in part* on the performance of the Appointee and the needs of the agency. *Nevertheless, the Parties acknowledge that any such renewals are at the discretion of the Governor in Council* [effectively, the Minister and/or the Premier's Office].[144]

The Invidious Comparison Even with Elected US State Judges

In many US states, a judge's position is an elective office, and Canadian lawyers have always been smugly dismissive of the US practice of electing and/or re-electing judges.[145] How, we ask, could one expect a fair trial from a judge whose career is dependent on his or her not losing the support of the electorate? Never do we stop and think that, in Canada, thousands of judicial tribunal adjudicators with as much power as elected US judges to decide rights disputes, inflict injustice, and cause harm are subject to a system of idiosyncratic renewal that is obviously far less principled than even an election-based system.

Imagine how Canadian observers of the US justice system would hold forth if state governors were constitutionally free to remove any judge without cause, reasons, or compensation, and to replace that judge with someone of their own choosing – and frequently did so. Imagine the derisive comments from north of the border! And yet those are exactly the powers that all Canadian executive branches wield in the part of our justice system where the majority of Canadian's rights disputes are now decided.

The Particular Implications for the Vulnerability of Tribunal Chairs to Idiosyncratic Removal

The vulnerability of tribunal members to idiosyncratic removal is bad enough but the same vulnerability of tribunal chairs has even more serious implications. A tribunal's institutional independence is embodied in its chair's independence. If a tribunal's chair has no commitment to independence, if he or she is seen, for example, to have a submissive or overly "collegial" relationship with the government, the tribunal's members will not feel themselves to be independent either. In any tribunal, the institutional culture of independence emanates from the chair.

And, of course, idiosyncratic removals happen to tribunal chairs as well as to members. When a tribunal's decisions inconvenience a government too often, and certainly when governments change, the tribunal chair is more vulnerable to removal than anyone, and chairs know this to be so.

We had the spectacle in 2009 of the former chair of the Royal Canadian Mounted Police Complaints Commission, Paul Kennedy, and former Military Police Complaints Commissioner Peter Tinsley joining with former Canadian Nuclear Safety Commission president Linda Keen in an appearance before a "Committee" of the famously prorogued Parliament in January 2010, where they asserted that the Conservative government was "at war" with its independent tribunals.[146] Kennedy and Tinsley had been the victims of idiosyncratic removals – Kennedy following what the government apparently saw to be an untimely release of a report sharply critical of the conduct of RCMP officers in the death by taser of Robert Dziekanski, and Tinsley in the midst of an ongoing inquiry into the politically sensitive issue of the treatment of Afghan detainees. Keen's removal was not technically an idiosyncratic removal as I have defined it, but a mid-term termination of an at-pleasure appointment; moreover, her commission was a regulatory agency, not a judicial tribunal. Nevertheless, it was a tribunal whose independence is of great public importance.

The Rule-of-Law Implications of the Arbitrary Removal Power

That the consciousness of his or her vulnerability to idiosyncratic removal

Unjust by Design

does have an impact on a tribunal adjudicator's decision making was demonstrated in a vivid way when, in the summer of 2009, federal Immigration Minister Jason Kenney made a series of public comments implying that refugee claims by members of the Roma community were in his opinion bogus. Before he made these comments, the success rate for Roma refugee appeals to the Immigration and Refugee Board (whose members' reappointments are known to depend on the whim of the Minister) was 97 percent. By April 2010, the success rate had dropped to 0.09 percent.[147]

For members who serve in full-time positions, or who serve on part-time but regular schedules and for whom such service provides their primary source of income, an unexpected denial of their reappointment not only disrupts their careers but also involves a significant financial penalty. Since governments believe that members have no right to notice of removals, they also believe that they have no right to payment in lieu of such notice, and the removals occur without compensation.

In the real-world context, where every two, three or five years tribunal members must petition a government for the gift of a reappointment in circumstances where reappointment decisions are known to be entirely discretionary, to be typically made *in camera* in an arbitrary manner and often refused for unknown reasons, and where the denial of such petitions means personal career disruption and financial hardship, the independence of such members is obviously in fact and in appearance entirely illusory. It is disingenuous to claim otherwise.

Moreover, the length of the term in question does not alter the argument. Time passes, and eventually a five-year term becomes a five-month, a five-week, and then a five-day term with the member still hearing cases and making decisions that have the potential to alienate the government on which he or she is relying for the gift of another appointment.

Chief Justice McMurtry's phrase "idiosyncratic removal" is in fact a precise description of commonplace events in Canada's administrative justice system that have had the cumulative effect of fixing in the minds of all judicial tribunal members a pervasive awareness of the real possibility of reprisals and personal career damage if they make decisions that inconvenience the government or its friends. It is an embarrassing thing to have to say, but that awareness makes a reasonable apprehension of bias a fixed, generic reality for all parties appearing before judicial tribunals in Canada's administrative justice system.

Harking back to the Supreme Court's three fundamental principles of the rule of law as described in its 2005 decision in *Imperial Tobacco*,[148] it is apparent that a system for reappointing judicial tribunal adjudicators and chairs merely by executive branch fiat cannot be reconciled with the principle of supremacy of law over "officials of the government." Neither is such a system *"preclusive* of the influence of arbitrary power"; rather, it is *inclusive* of that power. And when the state brandishes the threat of removal over the "judges" adjudicating disputes about the lawfulness of the government's determination of citizens' rights, the relationship between the state and the individual cannot be said to be "regulated by law." Thus, this administrative justice regime of arbitrary reappointments and idiosyncratic removals is plainly incompatible with the fundamental postulates of our constitutional structure.

And yet, my professional colleagues will ask, has not the Supreme Court itself found to the contrary? In *Valente* and later, particularly in *Régie*,[149] the Court has held that the security-of-tenure component of judicial independence is satisfied, as far as tribunal members are concerned, apparently by any fixed-term appointment.[150] All that is necessary, the Court has said, is that a member's appointment not be open to termination during the fixed term, except for cause. Fortunately, this opinion has not been given in cases where the impact on the independence of tribunal adjudicators of an arbitrary reappointment regime was directly at issue; moreover, this precise issue has been dealt with authoritatively elsewhere.

In its 2001 decision in *Barreau du Montréal*[151] – a decision with regard to which leave to appeal to the Supreme Court of Canada was refused – the Quebec Court of Appeal held that, for the *Tribunal administratif du Québec* (TAQ) to satisfy Quebec's *Charter of Human Rights and Freedoms'* requirement of tribunal independence and impartiality, it was not sufficient that its members have security of tenure during their fixed terms of appointment. They must also be the beneficiaries of a fair, objective, and independent reappointment process. Addressing the Quebec government's argument, based on *Régie*, that a fixed term, guaranteed to be free of intervention during the term except for cause, was all that was required, *Barreau* distinguished *Régie*[152] on the basis that in *Régie* the Supreme Court was dealing with a "multi-functional and essentially regulatory agency," not one that (like TAQ) "exercises a purely adjudicative function."[153] *Régie* could have been distinguished just as well, however, on the grounds that in that case the effect of an arbitrary reappointment regime on the independence of the tribunal was not at issue, and not argued.

Surprisingly, given the long Canadian tradition to the contrary, Quebec's 1996 administrative justice legislation that created TAQ had not left the reappointment of TAQ members solely to the discretion of the Quebec government. Instead, it had provided for a precedent-setting, transparent reappointment process. It had placed reappointment decisions in the hands of a special renewal committee, a committee that included, however, the president of TAQ and a member of the Minister of Justice's staff.[154]

Justice Dussault, writing in *Barreau* for a unanimous Court of Appeal, held that the presence of the TAQ president and the Minister of Justice's representative on the renewal committee meant that the legislated renewal process did not meet the *Valente* requirements of judicial independence. He also held that with members having no right to participate in the process – no right to notice of the grounds of complaint and no opportunity to respond – the process did not meet the procedural fairness requirement either.[155]

Significantly, however, having made this decision, the Court of Appeal did not then accept the argument by TAQ members[156] that for the tribunal to meet the constitutional requirement of independence their appointments needed to be life-tenured, like the appointments of provincial court judges. Acceptance of that argument would have taken Quebec's administrative judicial tribunals a long way down the road to judicialization. Instead, the Court held that fixed terms are valid provided that the reappointment process is merit-based, transparent, fair, and independent.[157] The Quebec National Assembly eventually responded to *Barreau* by amending its legislation to remove the TAQ president and the representatives of the Minister of Justice from the renewal committee and to give TAQ members the right to be heard by the committee.[158]

The latter is a precedent the Supreme Court might well embrace. If the security-of-tenure aspect of the reappointment issue is perceived by the courts as presenting them with the unhappy choice between, on the one hand, security of tenure during a fixed term followed by the traditional, arbitrary reappointment regime, or, on the other, life-tenured appointments,[159] one can readily surmise that the courts, wary of being accused of judicializing tribunals, might opt for the former. *Barreau* now presents a third option, and when the opportunity does arise for the Supreme Court to address the rule-of-law implications of having judicial tribunal adjudicators with fixed terms routinely subjected to arbitrary reappointment processes and, often, idiosyncratic removals, it will find an acceptable model of a merit-based, transparent, fair, and independent process ready at hand in the post-*Barreau* version of Quebec's *Administrative Justice Act*.[160] Moreover, for the Court to ensure the security of tenure of judicial tribunal adjudicators by requiring reappointment decisions to be made by independent reappointment committees would not be very different from what the Court has already done to protect the financial security of judges by requiring the intervention of independent compensation committees.[161]

It is true that *Barreau* was addressing a quasi-constitutional requirement of judicial independence. The Quebec *Charter of Human Rights and Freedoms* explicitly requires tribunals to be independent and impartial. However, by virtue of the now settled law that the *Valente* principles define both the constitutional and common law requirements of judicial independence,[162] *Barreau* ranks as both a constitutional and common law authority. Outside of Quebec, *Barreau* is, of course, no more than persuasive authority. Nevertheless, given that it is a unanimous decision of the Quebec Court of Appeal written by Justice Dussault, the same René Dussault who prior to his appointment to the Quebec bench was one of Canada's pre-eminent administrative law experts,[163] it is an authority that might well be thought especially persuasive.

Until the independence of administrative judicial tribunals is confirmed to be a constitutional requirement, the executive branch will no doubt continue to see the *Valente* principles as inconvenient obstacles to its control of judicial tribunals – obstacles that can be overridden when necessary by legislation. In the meantime, absent such legislation, the principles apply as if there were a constitutional requirement, and there is currently no Canadian legislation that unequivocally authorizes an arbitrary reappointment regime for members of administrative judicial tribunals. Moreover, where the applicability of the constitutional requirement of judicial independence is clear – and it is already clear with respect to tribunals that fall within ss. 7 or 11(d) of the *Canadian Charter of Rights and Freedoms*, s. 23 of the Quebec *Charter of Human Rights and Freedoms*, perhaps the due process requirements of s. 1 of the *Alberta Bill of Rights*,[164] and within ss. 2(e) and (f) of the *Canadian Bill of Rights* – arbitrary reappointment regimes are open to challenge by reliance on the *Barreau* analysis, whether or not they are seen to have been authorized by legislation.

Abolition of Wayward Tribunals

Idiosyncratic removals take on a whole new meaning when a particular judicial tribunal's performance so provokes the government of the day that by legislation it abolishes the entire tribunal and replaces it with a new entity staffed by new appointees. The prototypical example in Canadian history was the Mulroney government's abolition of the Refugee Advisory Board and Immigration Appeal Board, referred to above.[165] More recently, in Saskatchewan, the government abolished the Saskatchewan Human Rights Tribunal in 2011 and transferred its jurisdiction to the Saskatchewan Court of Queen's Bench. In the latter case, the government explained – irony of ironies – that the problem was the Human Rights Tribunal's lack of "judicial independence"; that its members "do not have security of tenure or financial security"; and that the Tribunal "does not benefit from administrative independence."[166] This explanation was in line with a recommendation from Judge David M. Arnot, Chief Commissioner of the Saskatchewan Human Rights Commission, who was appointed to his position on secondment from the Saskatchewan Provincial Court in 2009. Arnot is a highly regarded public servant, and his explanation of why he recommended that the government abolish its Human Rights Tribunal is a telling indication of the public and professional reputation of judicial tribunals both in Saskatchewan and generally. In an article published in the 16 December 2010 issue of Saskatoon's *Star Phoenix*, Arnot wrote that human rights complaints "are too important to be relegated to administrative adjudicator bodies overseen by lawyers who act as part-time quasi-judges ... These cases should be heard by full-time judges whose neutrality and fairness is guaranteed by their judicial independence." One is left to wonder whether Judge Arnot might not also think that the adjudication by Saskatchewan's Labour Relations Board of, say, charges of unfair labour practices would be another set of matters too important to be relegated to adjudicators whose neutrality and fairness is now not only without guarantee but, in fact, confirmed to be absent.[167]

Discharge without Recourse

> *[The] essentials of security of tenure [are] that the [tribunal member] be removable only for cause, and that cause be subject to independent review and determination by a process at which the [member] affected is afforded a full opportunity to be heard.*
>
> – R. v. Valente

Another gaping rule-of-law deficiency in the current administrative justice system is the absence of any procedural protection for judicial tribunal chairs or members against mid-term discharge for alleged cause. I have found no *Valente*-specified protections against termination for cause in any Canadian administrative justice jurisdiction outside Quebec.

The vulnerability of tribunal members and chairs to arbitrary dismissal based on claims of misconduct was made especially clear in the 1999 decision of the Federal Court in *Weatherill v. Canada (Attorney General)*.[168] The case involved the discharge for alleged cause of Ted Weatherill, chair of the Canada Labour Relations Board (CLRB). Weatherill, a highly respected labour arbitrator, had been appointed in 1989 to a ten-year term as the full-time chair of the CLRB, an appointment to be held on good behaviour. Thus, his appointment could not be terminated except for cause.

Weatherill famously engaged in an epic, years-long battle with the Board's five vice-chairs over the control of the Board's executive powers. It is a battle that is, in and of itself, an object lesson about the vagaries of the federal government's appointment policies and the exclusion of chairs from the appointment process. His battle was lost when, in April 1997, the *Ottawa Citizen* published negative allegations relating to what were said to be excessive travel and hospitality expense claims made by him, as well as certain allegations of bias in the exercise of his adjudicative functions. These claims prompted the Minister of Labour to ask the Auditor General of Canada to review Weatherill's expense accounts and the Federal Ethics Counsellor to review the bias allegation. The Ethics Counsellor found no merit in the bias complaint, but the audit found that Weatherill's expense claims were not compatible with the expense rules applicable to the federal public service.

The published audit report precipitated the spectacle of Lawrence MacAulay, the Minister of Labour at the time, announcing *on the floor of the House of Commons* on the day that the report was issued that he was firing Weatherill and that the legal steps required for the Governor-in-Council to terminate his appointment had been initiated. Hansard captured the moment:

> *Mr. John Williams (St. Albert, Ref.):* Mr. Speaker, the auditor general trashed Ted Weatherill and the Canada Labour Relations Board this morning in his report.
>
> On 1,300 occasions Ted Weatherill went away beyond the Treasury Board guidelines on his expense account. This guy is completely out of control.

My question to the Minister of Labour is will he stand up right now and tell us that that guy is gone?

Hon. Lawrence MacAulay (Minister of Labour, Lib.): Mr. Speaker, I have received and reviewed the report and agree with the report.

Members of the Canada Labour Relations Board are appointed by governor in council and hold office during good behaviour. There are legal steps required in order for the governor in council to remove an appointee and I initiated these steps this morning.

Some hon. members: Hear, hear.[169]

The judge who heard Weatherill's subsequent application for an interim injunction[170] was reported by the press to have said from the bench that the firing procedure was like throwing Weatherill "to the lions": "I'm concerned as a citizen that with immunity, a minister of the Crown can get up in the House – on the basis of I don't know what – and say, 'I'm going to fire this guy' and everybody is up and cheering. I don't know whether I have a right to intervene but it left a bad taste in my mouth."[171]

Weatherill believed that, in light of the status and duties of the office of the Canada Labour Relations Board chair, the public service rules pertaining to expense claims did not apply to him, and claimed that it had been agreed at the time of his appointment that they would not apply. He also argued that relative to the status of his office and the nature of his public duties, his expense claims had not been excessive. Given the Minister of Labour's public pronouncement in Parliament that he would be fired, he would have had no reason to expect an unbiased hearing from the Governor-in-Council (the cabinet), the body that would issue the order removing him from office, and he turned to the courts. His initial move was to seek an interim injunction, but his application was denied on the rather surprising ground that he had not satisfied the judge on the issue of irreparable harm.[172] By the time his appeal of that decision came before the Federal Court of Appeal, the Governor-in-Council had issued the order terminating his appointment and the application for injunctive relief was seen to be moot. He then applied to the Federal Court for judicial review of the Governor-in-Council's decision to remove him from office.[173]

The application relied particularly on the argument that Weatherill was entitled to have the issue as to whether there was "cause" for his dismissal heard and decided by the Canadian Judicial Council. Section 69(1) of the federal *Judges Act*[174] reads:

> The Council [Canadian Judicial Council] shall, at the request of the Minister [of Justice], commence an inquiry to establish whether a person appointed pursuant to an enactment of Parliament to hold office during good behaviour other than
>   (a) a judge of a superior court or of the Tax Court of Canada, or
>   (b) a person to whom section 48 of the Parliament of Canada Act applies,
> should be removed from office for [misconduct, among other things].

Justice Sharlow, the Federal Court judge who heard and decided Weatherill's application, agreed that s. 69(1) applied to Weatherill – he was a person other than a judge appointed pursuant to an enactment of Parliament to hold office during good behavior.[175] Sharlow also held, however, that under the statute, the referral to the Canadian Judicial Council was in the discretion of the Minister of Justice. The Minister of Justice was not required to proceed by that route, and had not done so in this case.

There is, I believe, no comparable provision in any of the provinces and territories, and, as I have said, as far as I know, no other legislated provision specifying any particular process for the dismissal for cause of a chair or member of a judicial tribunal.

Justice Sharlow held that Weatherill was entitled only to the procedural protections afforded any public officer whom the government proposes to dismiss for cause. But Weatherill was not just any public officer. He was the chair of an administrative judicial tribunal exercising judicial functions. And the problem the case presents for the administrative justice system is that Justice Sharlow failed to acknowledge the special procedural protections that the *Valente* principles have established for tribunal members in that position.

It would appear from Justice Sharlow's judgment, and from the judgment of her Federal Court colleague, Justice MacKay, in *Wedge*,[176] on which Justice Sharlow relied, that the Federal Court has read out of the security-of-tenure principles any special procedural protection for members or chairs of administrative judicial tribunals. Neither the requirement for a review of the allegations by an independent body nor the requirement for a "full opportunity for a hearing" is to prevail. Justice Sharlow said this:

Similarly, the removal of a person from an office held during good behaviour cannot be done without affording that person procedural protection. I do not accept, however, that a full hearing, with examination and cross-examination of witnesses, and full disclosure of documents, is essential to the fair exercise of the power of removal.[177]

In this regard, I agree with the following statements of MacKay J. in the *Wedge* case (*supra*) at page 282:[178]

> ... the requirements of procedural fairness were satisfied in this case in that the applicant was apprised of the substance of the allegations against him, and of the investigation report and the final Report about those allegations, and he was accorded a fair opportunity to respond orally once ... and twice thereafter in writing.

From the description of the process in *Weatherill*, it is apparent that the allegations against Weatherill were never reviewed on their merits by an independent body – much less a judicial body – and that he was never afforded a "full opportunity to be heard." In Justice Sharlow's decision, Weatherill suffered a personal defeat of major proportions, while the executive branch chalked up another victory over the justice-system pretensions of the members of its judicial tribunals.

If the Federal Court's view of the rules governing the mid-term dismissal of tribunal adjudicators appointed to fixed terms as set out in *Weatherill* and *Wedge* were to prevail over the *Valente* jurisprudence, the independence of judicial tribunals and their chairs and members, such as it is, would be even further diminished.

The problem is, of course, not unique to the current federal scene. When public controversy engulfs a particular tribunal, there is in Canada a history of casualties among the leaders. As we have seen, the idiosyncratic removal of chairs through the denial of reappointment applications is common, but removal in the middle of a term is also not unusual, especially for chairs of judicial tribunals dealing with controversial matters. In 2008-09, the new Saskatchewan government notoriously dismissed the incumbent chairs of most of Saskatchewan's tribunals, as the Harris government had done in Ontario in 1995-96. It has been reported that in British Columbia, prior to 2000, the chairs of the Labour Relations Board rarely if ever completed their full five-year terms.[179]

Executive Branch/Tribunal Integration

You will remember the employee of the Ministry of Citizenship and Immigration, seconded from that Ministry to be a member of the Immigration and Refugee Board of Canada and whose appointment was held by the Federal Court of Appeal to have created a reasonable apprehension that, mindful of the effects of her decisions upon her career prospects when she returned to the Ministry, the member could reasonably be perceived to be biased.[180] Well, that basis for apprehending bias is as nothing compared with the abject dependency of virtually all judicial tribunals and their chairs and members on their host ministries. The possible worries of a seconded member about his or her career prospects back at the ministry when the justice gig is over pales in comparison.

The structural integration of tribunals with the executive branch is the deepest root of executive branch control of tribunals – the executive's heartland strategy. Traditionally the crown jewel of that strategy has been the assignment of the tribunal hosting function – the care and feeding of a tribunal – to the portfolio ministry whose decisions and policies the tribunal is charged with reviewing. With a few recent exceptions, administrative judicial tribunals are nestled in the bosom of their portfolio ministries – sometimes physically located in the same office space but in any event routinely viewed as an integral component of the ministry's establishment and imbued with its culture. Ministries regard tribunals as "their" tribunals, part of their ministerial fiefdom.[181] Judicial tribunals are no exception.

These ministries have operational responsibility for the policies underlying the legislation, regulations, and policy guidelines from which arise the rights disputes the tribunals are mandated to adjudicate. Some even participate as parties in the tribunals' hearings, yet the tribunals charged with these adjudicative duties are dependent on these same ministries for their budget, for the compensation levels of their chairs and members, for their administrative support, for their housing, for the training of their members, for, as a practical matter, the selection and appointment and, most ominously, as we have seen, the reappointment every two, three, or five years of their chairs and members. Their chairs report to the host ministry's minister, or perhaps the deputy minister, or assistant deputy minister, or to all of these; and, most disturbingly, the tribunal's chief administrative officer often reports not to the tribunal chair but to an assistant deputy minister.

It is into this overwhelmingly dependent operational environment that parties seeking vindication of their rights must come. Those parties are asking the tribunal for decisions that will run contrary to the interests of its host ministry, probably impact negatively on that ministry's budget, potentially anger one or more of its staff or senior managers, possibly distort its intended policy, and perhaps politically embarrass its minister.

The Rhetoric of Independence
Governments believe – certainly they always say – that the only thing required for executive branch justice is a government's rhetorical commitment to the independence of a tribunal's *decision making*. This perspective may be seen particularly in the Macaulay report on Ontario's regulatory agencies.[182] Robert Macaulay had been a prominent Ontario politician for many years, a senior member of cabinet, and, for a time, chair of the Ontario Energy Board. His 1989 review encompassed both regulatory agencies and judicial tribunals, but, like the Ontario government itself at the time, he lumped them all together under the category of "regulatory agencies." On the subject of the "Independence of Agencies," he stated: "Agencies are not independent. Agencies have *independence of decision-making*, but are accountable to ministries and Ministers who are themselves accountable to the legislature."[183]

Shortly after the release of the Macaulay report, I had occasion at the annual Conference of Ontario Boards and Agencies to offer a public comment on the disingenuousness of that statement. Coming back to that comment over twenty years later, I find it still cogent and, regrettably, still clearly relevant:

[A] major deficiency in the Macaulay Report is its failure to make explicit the undoubted reality that institutional arrangements devoted to control of agencies, and to the assurance of their accountability, must be balanced by institutional structures devoted to providing agencies and their members with the capacity – both real and apparent – for independent decision-making. *Saying* that agencies are, and must be, independent or arms-length in their decision-making does not make them so. And an administrative-law system design that provides no protective structures but relies for the system's capacity for truly independent decision-making solely on the expectation that, within the secret corridors of agency members' minds, integrity may be counted on to routinely triumph over obvious and compelling self-interest, is a system design that is ... so disingenuous as to not be creditable.

It is a design that may be expected to achieve whatever truly independent decision-making it proves to be capable of on the backs of sacrificed heroes.[184]

Integrated Control, the Leitmotif of the New Ontario Governance Legislation

That the latter criticism is still relevant is evidenced by Ontario's new *Adjudicative Tribunals Governance Act*,[185] in which the Ontario legislature has demonstrated that the Macaulay view that a rhetorical commitment to "independent decision-making" is all that is needed is still pertinent. The stated purpose of the *Act* is to "ensure that adjudicative tribunals are accountable, transparent and efficient in their operations while remaining *independent in their decision-making*."[186] And although, as we have seen, the *Act* presents radically progressive provisions concerning the qualifications-driven, merit-based, competitive, and chair-controlled appointment process, it is positively antediluvian in its confirmation and extension of host ministry control over tribunals. The list of strategic policy and operational management decisions for which, under the *Act*, adjudicative tribunals will require their host/portfolio minister's explicit, prior approval includes everything of importance to the tribunal's operation except for the adjudicative decisions themselves.

The explicit requirement of prior ministerial approval applies specifically to the following: the tribunal's arrangements concerning financial matters, staffing and administration, and member orientation and training; the "accountability relationships of the tribunal," including its duty to account to its responsible minister (there are no limits to these requirements); the tribunal's "planning and reporting"; its committee structure and business plan containing "prescribed" contents – now by regulation including "performance standards" (the latter presumably including the time to be allotted to tribunal members for hearings and decision writing) plus any matter specified in a Management Board directive; its mandate and mission statements, consultation policy and service standards, and complaints procedure; its "job descriptions" for incumbent tribunal members, vice-chairs, and chair, and the qualifications required for appointment to the tribunal; its members' "code of conduct"; and "any other matter" specified by cabinet in regulations or in a "directive of Management Board." Finally, the *Act* makes the extent to which the tribunals are in the hands of their host ministries doubly plain by arming the Minister with a sword of Damocles power to "at any time" choose "any person" and commission him or her to review the tribunal and its performance and to report, among other things, whether the tribunal should be discontinued or "changed."

All of this is spelled out specifically in the *Act,* and in August 2010 the Ontario Bar Association released a commentary on the *Act*[187] that expressed its concerns about the impact of these host ministry ties on the independence of the tribunals. The commentary includes this:

> It seems to us to not be overstating the matter to observe that by the provisions of this new Act the legislature has effectively converted adjudicative tribunals to ministerial departments. If this degree of control is deemed to be necessary, why, one is moved to ask, do we have "tribunals" at all. If the facades were torn down and the reality displayed, the issue of governments exercising judicial functions could then be addressed directly.[188]

It is a good question. Given this degree of integration, why do we have judicial tribunals at all? Why not just assign the adjudicative functions to portfolio ministry staff and be done with it?[189] Why make the effort to maintain what is, indeed, only a façade of independence?

There are only three answers that one can think of, and better and more independent decision making is not one of them. Most importantly, experience tells executive branch officials – cabinet ministers and senior bureaucrats – that the public rarely sees the government behind the independence façades, thin as they are, and so ministers and bureaucrats continue to be shielded from responsibility. Presumably, there will also be the executive branch's fear that, absent the façade, the public might indeed wake up to the issue of governments' exercising judicial functions. Finally, there is no doubt that the positions of chair and members of notionally independent judicial tribunals comprise a significant proportion of any government's inventory of patronage opportunities.[190] Without these façades, these positions would revert to public service positions beyond the reach of the patronage regimes.

Judicial Tribunals: Judges in Their Own Cause

The hand-in-glove integration of judicial tribunals with their ministries also leads to inappropriate operational collaboration in the drafting of the rules and regulations and statutory provisions governing the rights and obligations of the parties appearing before the tribunal. It is a common law axiom that no one can appropriately be a judge in his or her own cause, but judicial tribunals will be judges in their own cause if they themselves have written the laws that they are then called upon to interpret and apply. However, with judicial tribunals working in the bosom of their portfolio/host ministries, when it is time to revise the rules, regulations, and statutory provisions applicable to the statutory enterprise of which a tribunal is the judicial arm, it is tempting for governments to have the chairs or members of that tribunal assist in the drafting process. "Who else," they can reasonably ask, "has better skills or more relevant experience?"

This collaboration makes perfect sense when one is talking about a regulatory agency, but involving the leaders of judicial tribunals in the drafting of laws for which their tribunal will eventually be the adjudicator not only offends the rule against being the judge in one's own cause but is also a means of co-opting the tribunal and thus minimizing the likelihood of surprises for the government when the meaning of the legislation eventually comes up for adjudication – in other words, it is a means of imbuing a judicial tribunal with a pro-government bias.

In Alberta, in 2006, the Alberta Federation of Labour (AFL) learned that the chair and a vice-chair of the Alberta Labour Relations Board had apparently worked privately with Ministry of Labour officials and government lawyers in drafting new regulations in 2003. These were regulations designed to implement a new collective bargaining regime for Alberta health services employees, a regime that the labour movement regarded as restrictive and pro-employer. In the course of responding to AFL freedom of information requests, the Ministry released, perhaps inadvertently, copies of e-mail traffic that appeared to confirm, among other things, that both the Board chair and a vice-chair had been directly involved in drafting these regulations.

The AFL asked Professor Lorne Sossin, then of the University of Toronto Faculty of Law, for his opinion. Sossin published his report in 2006.[191] The report assumes as its starting point that the AFL's factual allegations are true, and addresses the question of what involvement of labour tribunals and their chairs and members with their host ministries in the development of legislation would be legal and/or appropriate. The report concludes in part that "unless expressly authorized by statute or contemplated by guidelines, no member of a labour board should have a direct role in drafting labour legislation which is undisclosed to unions and employers."[192] It is a conclusion that is clearly relevant to all administrative judicial tribunals, but one that, if accepted, would mark a definite change in practice for many.

With great respect for Sossin, however, his conclusion that advance disclosure of the collaborative role will make things right fails to take account of the principle of judicial independence applicable to judicial tribunals. While the disclosure of a collaborative drafting role by a judicial tribunal may, absent constitutional restraints, enhance the legality of the collaboration, it will nevertheless give the parties compelling reasons to doubt the tribunal's independence and impartiality and thus subvert the common law requirement of judicial independence in which the manifest impartiality of the tribunal is of critical importance.

Alberta governments seem to have a particularly proprietary view of their tribunals, adjudicative or not.[193] It was not unexpected, therefore, to find the Alberta government taking steps to fix the Sossin crack in their integrated tribunal structures through legislation that would give parties to adjudication by Alberta's judicial tribunals explicit notice of the tribunals' collaborative role in the drafting of the laws they will be interpreting and applying. The *Alberta Public Agencies Governance Act,* enacted in 2009,[194] now explicitly authorizes a minister to request the advice or comment of any public agency (which explicitly includes agencies exercising "adjudicative functions") on any matter respecting "the *development,* establishment, amendment, termination or repeal of any *enactment,* program, directive, guideline or policy that is related to the public agency's mandate." The *Act* also authorizes the agency to "volunteer" any such advice or comment.[195] And, in controlling its adjudicative tribunals, Alberta even surpasses Ontario. The *Alberta Public Agencies Governance Act* explicitly prohibits the chairs of "agencies that perform only adjudicative functions" from being the chief executive officer of their own tribunals.[196]

Employment Insurance Appeals Regime

As an example of tribunal integration with their government handlers, however, nothing beats the integration of the appeals system in the federal Employment Insurance (EI) adjudicative regime circa 2002 as described by Professor Gaile McGregor in her thoroughly researched, closely reasoned, and very detailed study of that system. It is a study that provides information and insights that are rarely available for particular tribunals, and it identifies issues concerning the independence and impartiality of judicial rights-determining tribunals that resonate broadly with administrative justice issues generally. Here is another poster child for the damage the executive branch is capable of when it turns its hand to designing and running a justice system. The discussion in the following paragraphs references Professor McGregor's article.[197]

Canada's EI system is administered by the Canada Employment Insurance Commission. In this system, the Commission is effectively the portfolio ministry. At the time of Professor McGregor's study, EI claims were decided in the first instance by Commission staff, whose decisions were appealable to Boards of Referees. The Boards of Referees were said to be "independent" tribunals and were composed of chairs selected by the Commission from a roster of chairs appointed by the Governor-in-Council, plus two members selected by the Commissioner for Employers and the Commissioner for Workers from rosters established in consultation with appropriate employers' associations and central labour bodies, respectively. This adjudicative regime was abolished by the Conservative Government in 2012 and replaced by appeals to the new federal Social Security Tribunal.

The Boards of Referees had no legislative or regulatory power; their duty was to apply the provisions of the *Employment Insurance Act* "as they stand."[198] Here, then, were true judicial tribunals.

The Boards were required to provide written decisions, and these decisions were appealable to the Office of the Umpire. Umpires were generally judges of the Federal Court of Canada but could also be judges or former judges of a provincial court. Umpires' decisions were appealable to the Federal Court of Appeal.

McGregor found a remarkable degree of administrative influence by the Commission over the Boards of Referees and their decision making in 2002. This influence was derived from three factors: Commission control over the process; Commission influence over the Board chair and members; and Commission influence over the adjudication.

McGregor reports that the Commission – the respondent in every appeal – had the marked advantage of effectively picking the judge who would hear any particular appeal, selecting from the roster of chairs the individual to be appointed as chair in any particular case. The Commission also made the regulations that governed the conduct of hearings. As well, since the Boards were allowed to consider only the issue defined by the record, the Commission was able to limit the issues by the way it framed its decision.[199]

As to how the Commission influenced the adjudicators, McGregor reported that the Commission relied on its control of the Boards' training and reference materials. The training program for newly appointed chairs and panelists (few of whom were lawyers) was designed and administered by the Commission, as were the permanent reference materials on which, as a practical matter, the Board members had to rely principally in the development of their decisions. In the training and reference materials prepared by the Commission, McGregor found "limited coverage" of the issues; deficiencies in the "quality of judgments" selected for inclusion in the reference material; "bias" in the selection of the past decisions to be included; and finally the arbitrary exclusion from the reference materials of most decisions at the Umpire level.[200] McGregor comments:

> The last set of features bridges the line between appropriate and the improper. Given the foregoing, this is perhaps predictable. The fact is, thanks to its situational and propaganda advantages the Commission is in a position to exercise a problematic and unhealthy degree of influence, not just over general attitudes, but over the process of adjudication. Even after the orientation period is over, because of the breadth of its administrative mandate, it continues to function for the Referees as everything from facilitator to intellectual resource. What is easy to lose sight of – and what the evidence suggests many Referees do lose sight of – is that the role of the Commission in actual appeals is that of an interested party, not a "disinterested advisor."[201]

McGregor notes that the inappropriateness of the Commission's efforts to influence the Boards of Referees was often commented upon by the judges appointed as Umpires. In a representative sample of Umpire decisions on the availability-for-work issue, for instance, totalling around eighty cases, McGregor found more than a dozen clear-cut examples.[202]

McGregor concludes that the Board members and their adjudication are administratively controlled by the Commission to the point of obvious breach of the principles of natural justice.[203] To the Supreme Court's "institutional bias" question in *Lippé*[204] – "will there be a reasonable apprehension of bias in the mind of a fully informed person in a substantial number of cases?" – the answer with respect to the Boards of Referees in 2002 was, in McGregor's opinion, a resounding "yes!"[205]

McGregor also studied the impact of this integrated adjudicative environment on the quality of the Boards of Referees' decisions, reviewing and evaluating over 1,200 of them. The decisions were characterized, she says, by "conspicuous formalism" and "perfunctory reasons," and were "short, superficial ... light on analysis" and "mechanistic to the point of bizarreness."[206] The overwhelming sense she got from her review of these cases was, she reports, of "an unremitting series of small injustices resulting from a mechanical application of blanket rules."[207]

The Eviction Machine

In 1997, by provision in the Ontario *Tenant Protection Act, 1997*,[208] the jurisdiction to order the eviction of residential tenants was transferred from its traditional home, the Ontario Superior Court, to a newly created executive branch tribunal, the Ontario Rental Housing Tribunal (ORHT); thus, another executive branch justice system was born. From 1998 to 2003, the new tribunal evicted over 150,000 residential tenants from their homes without a hearing. These tenants were disproportionately single mothers, elderly women, immigrants, refugees, non-citizens, and persons with disabilities; many were barely literate in the English language.

How this happened is documented in the remarkable fifty-page tenant advocates' *Submission to the Ontario Ombudsman Concerning the Failure of the Tenant Protection Act and the Rules and Procedures of the Ontario Rental Housing Tribunal to Meet Ombudsman Fairness Standards* of June 2002 (hereinafter called the *Fairness Complaint*).[209] The *Fairness Complaint* is couched in restrained, professionally respectful language, and is technically complex, but it portrays in dismaying detail what a justice system train wreck looks like. It is an eye-opening read and especially remarkable in view of the fact that it was written by advocates who were continuing to represent tenants in proceedings before the ORHT on a daily basis and whose organizations were ultimately dependent on the government's goodwill for their funding.

The ORHT's mandate was to adjudicate rights disputes between landlords and residential tenants, but its principal business was evictions. Seventy-four percent of the orders it issued were eviction orders – approximately 60,000 of them per year. Of these, 58 percent, about 35,000 per year, were default orders issued without a hearing.[210] Given the importance of the matter – the removal of people from their homes – this rate of default orders was remarkable. It was made possible by two executive branch strategies: a statute drafted principally to ensure an efficient and speedy eviction process, and a tribunal structurally integrated with the Ministry of Municipal Affairs and Housing.

The statutory supports for the expedited eviction strategy included:

- the requirement that the ORHT's notice of hearing respecting the landlord's application for an eviction order be served on the tenant by the landlord, not by the ORHT[211]
- the requirement that a default eviction order be issued unless a written notice of the tenant's intention to dispute the landlord's application was

received by the ORHT within an impossibly short five calendar days from the service by the landlord of the ORHT's notice of hearing on the tenant[212]

- the virtual elimination, in the case of a default eviction order, of the availability of the ORHT's statutory discretion to relieve from forfeiture – or to postpone the enforcement of the order, on terms.[213]

The short time allotted for filing a written dispute following the landlord's service of the notice of hearing was unprecedented and surely incompatible with the reasonable notice requirements of the principles of natural justice. Compare this five-day limit with the twenty days that defendants in Small Claims Court debt-collection proceedings get for filing their responses, or to the measured pace in mortgage foreclosure proceedings before possession orders are issued. And while the statute specified five days, it was five *calendar* days; and, as a practical matter, by careful attention to the manner of serving the hearing notice, landlords had good hope of reducing the time the tenant had for writing and delivering the dispute to at least half that. If the landlord served the tenant on a Friday afternoon, the tenant would have until the end of business on the following Wednesday to meet the deadline – three business days. But if the landlord served the notice by leaving it "at the place where mail is ordinarily delivered" to the tenant – which by provision in the *Act* was deemed sufficient "service" – and happened to leave it there on Friday evening, after the normal time for mail delivery, with the reasonable expectation that the tenant would have no occasion to look in that place until he or she came looking for mail the following Monday afternoon, the tenant would have only *two days* or fourteen business hours within which to seek advice, write the notice of dispute, and deliver it to the ORHT office. Since under the *Act* a successful eviction eliminated the rent restrictions on the vacated apartment,[214] landlords could not be counted on to be fastidious about their service of the notice of hearing. Indeed, legal clinics acting for low-income tenants reported commonly encountering clients who had received eviction orders in the mail without ever receiving a notice of a hearing.[215]

The statutory requirement that the landlord serve the ORHT's notice of hearing on the tenant was also an unprecedented aspect of the eviction procedure. The standard practice in Ontario's administrative justice system is for such notices to be delivered by the tribunals that issue them, as specified in Ontario's *Statutory Powers Procedure Act*.[216] As mentioned above, however, this practice was changed in the *Tenant Protection Act* and the ORHT was explicitly exempted from doing so.[217]

This, then, was the principal statutory foundation for the Ministry's policy of expediting eviction orders. Evidence of the ORHT's responsiveness to this policy includes the following. The endnotes reference the evidence presented in the *Fairness Complaint.*

- the ORHT's persistence, despite frequent complaints from tenant advocates, in using a standard notice of hearing that was clearly confusing about the tenant's need to file a timely written dispute as a condition for having a hearing[218]
- its policy of refusing to countenance a tenant's failure to understand the notice of hearing as justification for setting aside a default eviction order[219]
- the striking absence of ORHT information directed at assisting tenants, in contrast with a comprehensive set of instructions for landlords[220]
- the ORHT's unprecedented restrictive use of the statutory power to grant equitable relief from an eviction order[221]
- its refusal to publish its decisions or decision data that would allow the neutrality of its decision making to be gauged[222]
- its dramatically limited use of time-consuming mediation procedures despite their obvious potential for resolving the need for eviction orders in many cases[223]
- its limited commitment of resources (an average of eight to fifteen minutes of adjudicator time per case) to hearings of eviction applications on their merits[224]
- generally, the ORHT's espousal of speed and efficiency in issuing eviction orders as its principal goal.[225]

Throughout its history, the ORHT, known within the tenant advocacy community as the "Eviction Machine," was furiously criticized by tenant organizations and tenant advocates for its perceived consistently unfair treatment of tenants.[226]

Following the election of Premier Dalton McGuinty's Liberal government, the ORHT's procedures and the terms of the *Tenant Protection Act* that it administered were substantially amended. The tribunal's name was changed to the Landlord and Tenant Board, and its reputation was repaired – it was no longer the Eviction Machine. But the Eviction Machine was the face of justice for all of Ontario's residential tenants for nearly five years, and it stands as an exemplar of what we all risk when we allow the executive branch to design, administer, and control justice systems.

Adjunct Judicial Functions of Regulatory Agencies

One of the executive branch's pervasive strategies for structurally integrating executive branch judicial functions with administrative functions is to assign the judicial functions needed in the enforcement of regulatory rules directly to members of the regulatory agency that is responsible for the administrative enforcement of those rules. These are the "adjunct" judicial functions to which I referred in the Introduction.

In March 2004, an eminently qualified "Fairness Committee," chaired by the Honourable Coulter Osborne, with Professor David Mullan and senior Toronto litigator Bryan Finlay, QC, as its two members, reported on an inquiry undertaken at the request of the Ontario Securities Commission (OSC).[227] The Committee had been asked to review and provide advice on the Commission's current structure, "in particular, its adjudicative function in light of increased sanctioning powers [fines of up to $1 million and disgorgement orders] that had been proposed for the Commission."

The Fairness Committee's report identified a serious problem with the perception of bias concerning the exercise of the Commission's adjudicative function, and recommended very strongly that the adjudicative function be separated from the Commission. The report stated:

> We would strongly advise the Commission to take steps to separate its adjudicative function from the Commission. *The arguments supported by the evidence in favour of this separation are persuasive, indeed overwhelming.* The evidence to which we refer goes beyond the now familiar complaints of some members of the securities litigation bar. Apart entirely from what might be characterized as anecdotal evidence, we received considerable expert opinion evidence on the governance issues we were asked to consider. A substantial preponderance of that evidence supports our central recommendation – that the Commission should do what is required to be done to establish an adjudicative tribunal that is separate from the Commission. *We are satisfied that the nature of the apprehension of bias has become sufficiently acute as to not only undermine the Commission's adjudicative process, but also the integrity of the Commission as a whole among the many constituencies that we interviewed.* Matters of institutional loyalty, the involvement of the Chair in the major cases, the increased

penalties, the sense that "the cards are stacked against them," the home-court advantage, the lengthy criminal law-like trials, and the Commission's aggressive enforcement stance, which likely will only increase over time, *all combine to make a compelling case for a separate adjudicative body.*[228]

The case for a "separate adjudicative body" made in the Fairness Committee report is, it may be noted, one that can be made for the adjunct judicial functions of most regulatory agencies.[229] It accords with the case Paul Weiler made in 1979 (described in the Introduction), for a separate adjudicative tribunal in the workers' compensation system.[230]

The OSC's adjudicative function, so heavily criticized by the Fairness Committee, had been in place since the Commission's inception and, despite the report's devastating and authoritative criticism, it remains in place.[231] And, of course, having regulators double as adjudicators when the need arises remains a common practice in the administrative justice system, generally. I will come back to this practice again later in the book.

The Criminal Injuries Compensation Board of Ontario and the Ministry of the Attorney General

The negative impact on the performance of judicial tribunals resulting from their structural integration with their host/portfolio ministries was given another public face when in 2007 the Ontario Ombudsman published his devastating report on Ontario's Criminal Injuries Compensation Board and another executive branch justice system train wreck came to light.[232] The following passages from the report's executive summary are so evocative of the pervasive problems within our executive branch administrative justice system generally that I have quoted many of them in full.[233]

Ontario's criminal injuries compensation scheme is impressive – on paper. *The Compensation for Victims of Crime Act* provides for compensation to a broader range of victims, in larger amounts, and for a greater range of injuries than most other provincial plans. This Cadillac program establishes *the only purely adjudicative model in the country in which claims are determined on their legal merits by an independent, quasi-judicial tribunal*[234] – the Criminal Injuries Compensation Board.

By law, the Board is obliged to receive claims and determine appropriate awards, unfettered by extraneous influences. *Unfortunately, it has never been permitted to do so.* One government after another has hindered its statutory mission by giving the Criminal Injuries Compensation Board *an unrealistically low budget and then forcing it to pay out of that budget not only its own operating costs, but any compensation it awards.*

This has had predictable consequences. First, it has undermined the Board's independence, leaving it vulnerable to Ministry direction and governmental interference. *On a number of occasions, the Board has been told by the Ministry of the Attorney General* to place a moratorium on its awards, or delay payment, so it will not exceed its budget ... Third, and of most concern, underfunding has created within the Criminal Injuries Compensation Board a bureaucratic culture that is harming those who are in need of help. Here are the cold facts:

It takes, on average, three years for an application to be processed. Of those applications that are received – approximately 4,000 to 5,000 per year – the Criminal Injuries Compensation Board succeeds in adjudicating, on average, only 2,500 per year. The Attorney General has predicted that by October 2007, there will be 17,500 backlogged compensation claims worth $109 million ... [T]he Criminal Injuries Compensation Board budget cannot come close to paying the type of compensation promised by law.

It is crystal clear that the Board has had to embrace delay to survive ...

The Board depends, shamefully, on attrition as well ... This report chronicles an embarrassing series of hurdles placed in the path of vulnerable victims of violent crime.

Each year, the Board receives 35,000 calls from victims, and sends out 7,500 new applications for compensation. Close to half of those will ultimately give up ...

... This is a shocking state of affairs. The Criminal Injuries Compensation Board is not an institution to be celebrated. *It is an embarrassment.* To understand why, we need only look at the human side of this sad story: [Here the report details six cases as particular examples of the suffering that the Board's maladministration has inflicted.] ...

Neither this Government, nor any of its predecessors, can plead ignorance. The Government did not need my investigation to uncover the problems I have identified, or their human toll. My Office has fielded numerous complaints over the years which have been brought to the Ministry. As this report shows, many cabinet documents and official missives have recounted how applicants are being "revictimized" and left frustrated and dispirited by the Board. There is no denying that successive governments have stood by, posing as victims' rights advocates, watching the process harm the very people it was meant to help. They have stood by with eyes wide shut, know-ing that they were breaking the promises made in the laws of this province.

This report details a cascade of proposals and initiatives for reforming the Criminal Injuries Compensation Board – revealed in documents uncov-ered during this investigation – which have been batted about over the years in what amounts to a game of policy ping-pong ... Meanwhile, nothing has been done.[235]

What makes all of this most troubling is that successive governments, though fully aware that the Criminal Injuries Compensation Board has been in perpetual crisis, have responded either with Band-Aids or no aid. They have stood frozen with fear and indecision at the same fork in the road. The first of the two paths before them – to ensure the Criminal Injuries Compensation Board has the funds it needs to do its legislated task – has not been taken because it is uninviting for governments averse to increasing spending. But the alternative path – reducing costs by scaling down victim compensation – is politically frightening. No government wants to be seen as the one that reduced the rights of crime victims.

Indifferent Standards

In addition to the problems of bias and dependency arising from these vari-ous executive branch strategies and tactics, administrative justice cannot be counted on to be optimally competent. As I have been careful to acknow-ledge in the Introduction, there are, of course, many individual exceptions. Generally speaking, however, the flaws in the design and administration of the administrative justice system ensure generally a level of competence for judicial tribunals that is rarely, and only providentially, optimal, and often marginal.

The Ontario Ombudsman's Criminal Injuries Compensation Board re-port is a vivid and uniquely public portrayal of a willful, long-running de-basement of a judicial tribunal's performance standards by successive host ministers based on putting their government's political interests ahead of any concern for justice. It is no doubt a particularly serious instance, but it is not unique; indifferent or providential performance standards are an inte-gral aspect of the administrative justice system in general and no one should be surprised.

The executive branch sets up administrative judicial tribunals as a means of ensuring that a host ministry's policies are applied in a manner that is responsive to the ministry's wishes. Most ministries would prefer to be

making those decisions themselves, but it has been deemed politically inexpedient or unwise for them to do so; instead, a ministry tribunal has been
set up to make the decisions. What the host ministry therefore seeks in its
tribunals are organizations that, behind the façade of their independence,
are responsive to the ministry's policy goals and generally respectful of its
decisions. It is therefore not in the interest of a host ministry to have judicial
tribunals that think too much for themselves – or *of* themselves; not in its
interest to have tribunals that are overly competent, too prone to independent thinking, excessively observant, unnecessarily insightful, or too effective. In short, the last thing a ministry wants to find in its judicial tribunal is
a competitor – or, perhaps worse, a judge.

This primal feeling within the hearts of portfolio ministries everywhere
that it is unnatural – contrary to their basic interests – to have an actual
competitor or a judge within their own office family, as it were, has spawned
a pervasive culture of portfolio ministry indifference to judicial tribunal
standards – an indifference bolstered by the fact that the façade of tribunal
independence can usually be counted on to shield ministries from responsibilities even when that indifference in fact leads to things going publicly
wrong.[236] There is therefore no pressing reason for ministries to be overly
concerned about the performance standards of their tribunals.

The influence of this careless-of-competence culture can be seen in
many places. In an operational environment characterized by finite resources, the money that a host ministry budgets for its judicial tribunals cannot
be devoted to the things for which the minister and deputy minister themselves are directly responsible. Not long ago, the chair of a senior judicial
tribunal recounted to me his experience of being told by a senior official of
his tribunal's host ministry that while he, the official, acknowledged the
statutory responsibility of the chair's tribunal to hold a hearing on a particular matter, the chair should nevertheless understand that "we do not have a
statutory obligation to fund that hearing."

The history of non-competitive compensation for tribunal members and
the various other executive branch strategies and tactics that discourage
professionalism and keep administrative judicial tribunals in their place, as
it were, are all in one way or another opposed to what a commitment to a
standard of excellence would call for.

The Enervating Populist View of Tribunals

Another phenomenon that has long been a source of indifference to performance standards in the administrative justice system is, in my experience,

a pervasive view among politicians both old and young that administrative judicial tribunal positions should be seen as opportunities for public-spirited amateurs to devote themselves for a time to public service. The thought that judicial tribunals might need to be staffed with professional adjudicators is not one that politicians or host ministries find attractive.

Anne Freedman's book about the patronage tradition in the United States refers to President Andrew Jackson's historical impact on the way government service is viewed. "The real shift in attitudes towards parties and patronage," she writes, "came in 1828 when Jackson was elected President." Jackson was "highly in favor of a 'rotation' system." He believed that "men who stayed too long in office are likely to become indifferent to the public's interests." To those who were concerned that rotation in office would damage the government's capacities, Jackson's response was that "the duties of all public officers are, *or at least admit of being made,* so plain and simple that men of intelligence may readily qualify themselves for their performance."[237]

The advice on appointments by a Standing Committee of the Ontario Legislature[238] written in 1986 resounds with that populist perception of tribunals and their appointments.[239] After agreeing that "one of the principal objectives of the public appointment process in Ontario should be that such appointments reflect the demographic, socio-economic and multicultural diversity of Ontario," and, in support of that proposition, agreeing that "openness" should be the first principle of a new appointment process so that *"everyone in Ontario* who has an interest in serving on Ontario's agencies, boards and commissions should be able to apply for a particular position," the Committee offered this disturbing, patronizing treatment of the significance of "qualifications" in the selection process:

> In addition to recommending that the public appointments be made open, the committee will also make recommendations concerning the selection process. It wishes to emphasize that selection should be the result of a fair and equitable process that *places stress* on appropriate qualifications. The committee believes that the public interest is best served when qualified individuals are appointed to Ontario's agencies boards and commissions. Those who are appointed feel a better sense of accomplishment if they have the knowledge or expertise to deal with the matters before an agency. The public gains a better respect for public institutions when it *knows* or deals with individuals who are qualified to make decisions. This is not to suggest that the committee envisages only professional experts to be appointed.

On the contrary, the committee believes that ordinary Ontario citizens as a result of their work experience, interests and accumulated knowledge and experience will have the necessary qualifications for appointments to Ontario agencies. At the same time, the Committee does not expect that only non-partisan appointments will be made. Those involved directly with particular political parties often have excellent qualifications, and the Committee would not want to discourage their participation in the public life of Ontario.[240]

Here, then, it would appear, is a significant underlying source of much of the resistance to a principled approach to the selection and appointment of members of administrative judicial tribunals and to the commitment to excellence in performance standards – the Jacksonian populist opinion that tribunal appointments, including adjudicative appointments, are opportunities for short-term public service by amateur, well-meaning citizens who if they stay too long in office are likely to become indifferent to the public's interests.[241]

Indeed, how else can one understand the condescending nature of the interest in qualifications reflected in the foregoing passage from the Standing Committee's report, or the following official explanation by the Ontario government in 2000 (in the course of "implementing" the *Guzzo Report*) as to why "at least some level of basic orientation and training [three days of training] early in the term of new appointees" [including persons appointed as judicial tribunal adjudicators] is important: "Early orientation and training is important because appointees come into the agency sector from many walks of life, and are *commonly* unfamiliar with government, the role of administrative justice agencies, the agency decision-making process, and particularly with the expectations associated with the role of an appointee."[242]

The same view is also manifest in the following "principle of remuneration" that is of long standing in the Ontario Management Board Secretariat's Directive on "Government Appointees"[243] and that is currently part of the Public Appointment Secretariat website's information for potential applicants:[244]

An element of public service is expected in all appointments to agencies of the government of Ontario. Consequently, rates of remuneration are not competitive with the marketplace. There is no requirement that appointees be paid, nor that they be paid at any maximum rate which may be established by Management Board of Cabinet. In fact, appointees to many of

Ontario's agencies do not receive any payment for their services beyond, in some cases, the reimbursement of out-of-pocket expenses.

This policy of non-competitive remuneration applies to all executive branch "agencies," including those in both the "regulatory" and "adjudicative" categories.

Presumably, it is this populist perspective on tribunals and tribunal appointments that also explains the politicians' insistence on limiting service in tribunal positions to a maximum of six or ten or twelve years. In Ontario, a general rule limiting appointments to two three-year terms had long existed even though it had never been applied consistently. For instance, it had never been applied to either Labour Relations Board or WCAT/WSIAT appointments. As mentioned earlier, however, in 2006 the Ontario government adopted a ten-year cap on appointments to particular positions that is to be of general application subject only "to the recommendation of the ... Chair in exceptional circumstances."[245] In the federal jurisdiction, there has been a long-standing cap of ten years, and experience has shown that the traditionally rigid enforcement of that cap ensures the annual, mid-career exodus of the federal tribunals' most useful members. In Alberta, the cap for adjudicator members is now twelve years.

It is this populist perspective on who should be tribunal members that also begins to explain the otherwise truly inexplicable lack of any concern on the part of Ontario's politicians and governments about the previously mentioned absence of *any* compensation increases for tribunal positions in that province for *over two decades.*[246] It also explains why it is commonplace for tribunal adjudicators and chairs to be earning substantially less than senior members of the tribunal's professional staff.

The Tribunal from Hell

I mentioned earlier the Guzzo Commission's apparent surprise at uncovering in 1997-98 a deep widespread concern about the quality of appointments to Ontario's administrative tribunals. No one in the administrative law field in Ontario at the time was surprised, however. Rather, the surprise was that a review of the appointment process had not been part of the Commission's mandate in the first place. Certainly, no one familiar with Margot Priest's famous 1992 "tribunal from hell" paper (and the formal comments on that paper, most notably by Andrew Roman, a prominent and respected Toronto administrative lawyer, who famously said that the tribunal in question was "not from Hell but from Ontario"[247]) would have been under

any illusion about the efficacy – or lack thereof – of the appointment processes prevailing in Ontario when the Guzzo Commission began its study.[248]

The "tribunal from hell" is a hypothetical construct that Priest used to
dramatize the distressing structural and administrative arrangements by
which administrative tribunals and agencies are often oppressed. It speaks
eloquently of the debased tribunal standards that Ontario's executive branch
was content with at that time. Priest's paper was originally presented as a
keynote address at the Law Society of Upper Canada's 1992 Special Lecture
on Administrative Law. At that time, she was the chair of the Ontario
Telephone Service Commission (a regulatory agency, now defunct) and had
previously been the vice-chair of the Ontario Highway Transport Board.
She was also an active member of the circle of Ontario tribunal chairs[249] and
a member of the board of directors of the Council of Canadian Administrative
Tribunals (CCAT). Following the publication of the paper, Priest was elected president of the CCAT and served two terms. There is, accordingly, every
reason to believe that she knew whereof she spoke.

In speaking to the Law Society audience, Priest was obviously speaking
truth to power, with personal and professional career interests clearly at
risk. She was careful not to claim that her description of the "tribunal from
hell" applied in full to any particular tribunal. It was, she said, a compilation
of characteristics, each of which was drawn from a real situation and could
be found in at least one tribunal. The complete description applied, she
said, to "few."[250] It is significant, however, that Andrew Roman, who was on
the same program for the purpose of commenting on Priest's paper, thought
that she had pulled too many punches.

Priest described the "tribunal from hell" in the following terms. True, her
paper is twenty years old, but, as will appear from the endnote references,
most of the issues she addressed have their modern counterpart and her
description still resonates today.

- The decision-makers change on average every three years.[251]
- Continuity of decision-makers is not considered to be important.[252]
- Incoming decision-makers have no background or expertise in the
  work of the tribunal, and are not familiar with it before joining it.
- They are not chosen on merit.[253]
- Indeed, some are chosen because they cannot find viable employ-
  ment elsewhere.
- Often, their appointment is a payoff for past favours.

- Some decision-makers work for the tribunal only in their spare time, and their salary does not cover their expenses on the days they do work.[254]
- Full-time decision-makers are not compensated on the basis of their performance. In 1991, their pay raise equalled the raise of those public servants whose work had been found to be unsatisfactory, or they received none at all.
- Tribunal staff advisors to the decision-makers are likely to be earning significantly more than the decision-maker.[255]
- The pensions of the full-time decision-makers are often not portable[256] and the three-year contribution does not provide pension security.
- The decision-makers are only guaranteed three-years of work, but they often are barred from actively seeking a new job during that time and are often barred from taking a job for which their tribunal experience would be relevant for six months or a year after they leave the tribunal.[257] If they are not re-appointed, they receive no compensation on leaving the tribunal.[258]
- The tribunal has no money to train the decision-makers, especially the new ones who arrive every few months. There is no specific place they can be sent for training.
- The lack of training may not worry newcomers because no one told them the job would require training; indeed, some resent being asked to attend training sessions. And, often, the part-time decision-makers cannot afford to attend training sessions.
- The Tribunal Chair is held publicly responsible for the decision-makers' decisions, but has little or no say in who becomes a decision-maker. The Chair first learns of a new appointment in a newspaper report or when the new person shows up in the office.[259]
- Decision-makers accept appointments to the tribunal without ever having had the duties of the job explained to them. There are no job descriptions for either the Chair or the decision-makers.[260] In fact, some new members are shocked to discover the complexity of the job and/or the size of their workload. Some want to reject part of the job, such as traveling or writing decisions.
- The Chair although publicly accountable has little control over the actions or decisions of the decision-makers. The decision-makers are sometimes separated by hundreds or thousands of kilometers, may

not be thought able to talk to one another[261] but their decisions must
be consistent.

- There are no rules or procedure for the Chair to follow in disciplining
  the members; indeed, it is not clear the Chair has any disciplining
  powers, and neither is there any apparent recourse for members who
  believe they have been unfairly dealt with by the Chair.[262]
- If the tribunal or its work is criticized publicly, the Chair and the
  members are prevented from replying or correcting any misconcep-
  tions or errors.[263]
- The tribunal's statute requires it to do certain work and it has to respond to public demands for that work which it cannot control, but
  its resources are determined, in practice, by public servants who have
  no responsibility of their own for the tribunal's performance. Often
  these public servants do not understand the work or the needs of
  the tribunal, and often the tribunal's approved resources are taken
  away to provide funding for unrelated purposes for which the public
  servants are responsible.[264]
- It has been known for the public servants to refuse to disclose the
  tribunal's budget to the Chair.
- The tribunal relies on outside public servants for administrative support, such as paying bills, ordering supplies or hiring staff. But these
  public servants being unfamiliar with the tribunal and its needs, give
  this work a low priority, so services are cut because bills go unpaid,
  work is delayed because supplies are not ordered and staff vacancies
  remain unfilled.
- These public servants often work for the same organization that is
  typically one of the parties whose interests the tribunal decision-
  makers are routinely asked to decide against.[265]
- The Chair, however, is the person held publicly accountable for any
  delays or poor service resulting from underfunding, budget cuts or
  poor support.

When Priest's paper was presented, no dissenting voice was heard – neither
then nor later. Three experienced observers were provided with an advance
copy of the paper and their prepared comments were presented as part of
the Law Society program and subsequently published along with Priest's
paper. The commentators were: (1) Toronto administrative lawyer Andrew
Roman; (2) Sheridan Scott, then Vice President, Planning and Regulatory
Affairs, Canadian Broadcasting Corporation; and (3) George M. Thomson,

then Ontario's Deputy Attorney General.[266] None of the three took serious issue with the pertinence of Priest's characterization of the "tribunal from hell." As mentioned, Roman criticized Priest, perhaps somewhat tongue-in-cheek, for being too reticent. Scott, speaking from her knowledge of the Canadian Radio-television and Telecommunications Commission (CRTC), addressed particularly the issue of tribunal independence, but evinced no particular surprise at the "tribunal from hell" depiction generally. Neither did she take issue with the suggestion that many tribunals suffer from the problems portrayed in Priest's paper. The overall tone of her reaction is reflected in her comment that "[t]he CRTC cannot be characterized as a tribunal from hell, as described by Ms. Priest. However, it does suffer to some extent from the shortcomings she has described."[267]

Thomson's comment was particularly interesting. The opening paragraphs of his comment read as follows:[268]

> Let me begin by stating that I support much that is written in Margot Priest's paper. At a minimum it demonstrates that there should be no more studies dealing with the structure and accountability of administrative agencies and tribunals until there has been at least a modest increase in the implementation of past studies.[269]
>
> Her description of the tribunal from hell is an effective way of demonstrating how far we have to go in creating a sound and defensible system of administrative justice. However, I think it also masks the fact that, in Ontario, a number of tribunals have worked extremely hard, with inadequate support from government, to create bodies that come very close to meeting the standard she would set for them. The three tribunals I dealt with at the Ministry of Labor [prior to becoming the Deputy Attorney General, Thomson had been the Deputy Minister of Labour] – the Ontario Labour Relations Board, the Pay Equity Tribunal and the Workers' Compensation Appeals Tribunal – are, I think, three excellent examples. However, it is also true that many fall short and probably all do to some degree, and so there is much to learn from her vivid example.

Given Thomson's official position as Ontario's Deputy Attorney General and his obvious need for circumspection, these comments might be thought particularly instructive of the true state of Ontario's administrative justice system at the time.

Of course, there has always been a consensus that some elite tribunals are good performers. The OLRB is, as I have mentioned, one tribunal whose performance has usually been respected. And within the community of members and chairs present at the Special Lecture, it was known that, as Thomson had suggested, under the approach of the Liberal and then the New Democratic Party governments, some Ontario tribunals were experiencing a renaissance in which many of the problems were being addressed. The Ontario Labour Relations Board, WCAT (my own tribunal at the time), the Ontario Securities Commission, perhaps the Ontario Municipal Board, the Pay Equity Tribunal, and the reformed Social Assistance Review Board fell into this category. Nevertheless, the insiders in the audience knew that by and large Priest had called it as it was.

The Promise of the *Guzzo Report* Dashed

Unfortunately, the renaissance in Ontario to which Thomson referred did not last. It ended abruptly in 1995 when the New Democrats were defeated by the Progressive Conservatives and the bad old administrative justice days returned full blown. The *Guzzo Report,* commissioned by the new government and published in 1998, gave reformers some hope that Premier Harris might have a progressive reform agenda for tribunals. In November 1999, the government announced that it would implement the report's recommendations. Two years and seven months later, in November 2000, at the twelfth annual Conference of Ontario Boards and Agencies, the new Attorney General and the chair of the Management Board of Cabinet jointly presented an informal collection of tools, templates, and guides[270] with the endorsement that these, "together with the other tools developed to assist agencies in enhancing service quality," were part of the implementation of the *Guzzo Report* and would "establish a firm foundation for excellence in the delivery of administrative justice in Ontario."[271]

Among the issues addressed by the documents in the government's binder was the question of the selection criteria – the "core competencies" – that Guzzo had recommended be developed to identify the minimum qualifications for persons being appointed to tribunals. When the government turned its attention to the development of the selection criteria, an existing authoritative prescription for such criteria was available. It could be found in the 1995 report on performance management in the administrative justice system written by a committee of the circle of chairs of the Society of Ontario Adjudicators and Regulators (SOAR).[272]

Recognizing that the essential foundation for any effective system of performance management must be the appointment of qualified people in the first place, the SOAR report specified what it called the "Generic Selection Criteria for Tribunal Members":

- A good understanding of the mandate of the tribunal and other relevant legislation;
- Experience with public hearings;
- Experience in a field related to the subject matter of the tribunal's hearings or in law;
- A good understanding of procedure, including the Statutory Powers Procedure Act if applicable to the tribunal's hearings, and the common-law concepts of natural justice/fairness;
- An awareness of, and sensitivity to, the various interests and issues represented at the tribunal's hearings;
- An aptitude for adjudication, including fairness, good listening skills, open-mindedness, sound judgment, tact, and an ability to interpret legislation;
- An ability to organize and analyze evidence (written and oral);
- Good writing skills – the ability to write a clear, well-reasoned decision that takes into account the evidence, the submissions, the Law and policy ...

(It should be noted that the current Ontario government's "Governance Tools" for regulatory and adjudicative agencies now specify core competencies that are similar to this list.[273])

At the time the *Guzzo Report* was issued, there was reason to believe that SOAR's generic selection criteria would influence development of the recommended core competencies. The SOAR criteria were known to have been developed by an expert and respected committee, and approved after a broadly based consultation with the people who were likely to have the best understanding of what was required; moreover, the *Guzzo Report* itself had publicly commended SOAR for the general quality of its work.[274]

The Progressive Conservative government turned out to have a markedly different perception of what was required, however. This perception was borne out in an indirect but very revealing way by the official explanation, previously quoted, that the reason the government thought new appointees to tribunals required some initial training was that they commonly came to their new positions without relevant experience.[275]

The government's limited expectations concerning the qualifications required for tribunal adjudicators was only one of the many disappointments experienced by those who had seen promise in the *Guzzo Report* and in the government's declared intention to implement it. The recommended screening committee never materialized. The selection process remained in its traditional closed and opaque state, and the important reappointment process remained arbitrary and secret and continued to be characterized by idiosyncratic removals. Instead of adopting the recommendation that all chairs be consulted on appointments and reappointments, the government began ignoring the chairs who had traditionally been consulted. All chairs now frequently learned of new appointments for the first time when the government announced them, and their recommendations concerning re-appointments were also frequently ignored – even when they recommended against a reappointment on the grounds that a member had proven to be incapable of doing the job.[276]

Thus, with the election of the Progressive Conservative government in 1995, the improvements for some tribunals that Thomson referred to in his 1992 comment on the Priest paper evaporated, and the grounds for overall optimism about the future of administrative justice in Ontario that he had suggested might be warranted disappeared as well. The pervasive concerns among Ontario tribunal stakeholders and client constituencies about the quality of appointments that the Guzzo Commission had unwittingly tapped into were not addressed at all; indeed, the general situation went from bad to worse. As we have seen, however, when the Liberal government returned to power, the appointments policies were again reformed.

Ontario's Medical Review Committee

In 1996, the Ontario Ministry of Health assigned the responsibility for auditing physicians' billings under the Ontario Health Insurance Plan (OHIP) to its Medical Review Committee (MRC), bringing one more executive branch justice system to the fore. The MRC was a judicial tribunal established under the *Health Insurance Act*[277] and integrated with the Ministry of Health and Long-Term Care. It had the power to review or audit physician fee claims and to direct the General Manager of OHIP to require physicians to repay all or part of any payment received from OHIP. Each year it heard approximately one hundred complaints brought by OHIP against individual physicians, and issued repayment orders totalling millions of dollars.[278]

The MRC was for a long time the subject of bitter complaints from medical doctors about the unfairness and arbitrariness of its proceedings and the devastating effects of its decisions, but when in April 2003 a respected doctor committed suicide after being the target of one of the

Committee's repayment orders, the new Liberal government commissioned a public inquiry by Peter Cory, a former justice of the Supreme Court of Canada. Christie Blatchford's column in the 23 April 2005 edition of the *Globe and Mail* describes the run-up to the inquiry:

> Calls for an overhaul of the MRC, long the subject of quiet but desperate complaint by physicians, came to widespread public notice only after the April 2003, drowning suicide of a gentle Welland, Ont., pediatrician named Dr. Anthony Hsu.
>
> Audited by the MRC, forced to cash in his RRSPs to repay $108,000 for services that allegedly were incompletely detailed in his billings, the 57-year-old Dr. Hsu was despondent and "felt the audit had tainted his name," his widow, Irene, tearfully told Mr. Cory at hearings in Toronto last fall.
>
> Dr. Hsu's experiences were mirrored by other physicians who appeared before the judge and described a process that saw them attend their audits without knowing the nature of the allegations against them and leave without being given reasons for the decisions that sometimes saw them ordered to repay huge sums.

In April 2005, Cory delivered his report.[278] His comments on the MRC included the following:

> In many cases, the cumulative effect of the billing and audit requirements now under review was to subject physicians to recoveries of more than $100,000, with devastating effects on those physicians, their patients and their families. The negative consequences reach even deeper into the medical system on which all Ontarians rely. Many physicians, who view the results of the audit system as arbitrary and unfair, have determined to avoid the process at all costs. I have thus heard from some physicians that, despite the unmet need for medical services, and their desire to provide dedicated service to their patients, they have concluded that it is necessary, for the protection of their families, or at the very least preferable, to curtail their practices so as to stay within average billing patterns. In that manner, they hope to avoid being singled out for investigation and audit, with the resulting devastation that can ensue. Accordingly, an audit system that is perceived as inflexible, arbitrary and unfair has a negative impact on the availability of medical services in Ontario. Not only have I heard that some physicians are grudgingly limiting their practices, but I have also heard that

the audit system is a factor in the decisions of some physicians to leave the jurisdiction. It is essential, for our health care system, that we have a fee billing system that is based on clear criteria and a medical audit process that is itself fair and is fairly administered.[280]

The report's recommendation makes clear what Cory saw to be the problems and addresses many issues endemic to the administrative justice system generally:

> The responsibility for conducting audits should be conferred on a new body that I will call the "Physician Audit Board." This body must, to the extent possible, be completely separate from and independent of the Ministry, OHIP, the [Ontario Medical Association] and the [College of Physicians and Surgeons]. It must have its own premises and staff, and a budget sufficient to cover its reasonable expenses. The budget should not be within the sole control of the Ministry, but should be prepared by the Board and submitted for approval to the College and the [Ontario Medical Association]. The budget, together with the approvals or comments, should then be submitted to the Minister.
>
> When OHIP refers a physician to the Physician Audit Board, an independent Inspector should investigate, and the matter should then either be settled or heard by an Audit Hearing Panel. The Hearing Panel should hold a hearing that provides all the procedural protections afforded by the Statutory Powers Procedure Act. At the hearing, OHIP should be responsible for proving the case for the recovery of funds paid as fees to physicians.[281]

Eventually, the MRC was replaced by the "Physician Payment Review Board,"[282] and it is understood that most of Cory's recommendations have been implemented.

The Fleeting Nature of Administrative Justice Reforms

It is true that for Ontario some of the foregoing flaws have once again been addressed by the current Liberal government. A set of core competencies has been adopted that are everything an ardent reformer would want. It is apparent, however, that under the current statutory and constitutional arrangements, the next time a new regime takes over in Ontario everything could quickly revert to the *status quo ante*. Indeed, we have two recent object lessons in that respect. In British Columbia, notwithstanding a highly touted Administrative Justice Project that was said to be focused on improving the independence of the province's executive branch judicial tribunals, the government has, as we have seen, asserted a statutory right to dismiss any tribunal member at any time without cause, and continues to exercise its reappointment powers arbitrarily. In 2009, it closed its Administrative Justice Office, a once-vaunted component of its administrative justice reform. And in Saskatchewan, under the Saskatchewan Party government, we have recently seen the public affirmation that judicial tribunals are partisan institutions to be populated with friends and allies of the party in power.[283]

The Tribunals' Reputations and Judicial Review

The impact of indifferent standards of competence and performance on the tribunals' reputations, particularly their reputation in the courts' eyes, is another feature of our administrative justice system that is not much talked about but which cannot be ignored. In 1992, in his comment on Margot Priest's controversial "tribunal from hell" paper,[284] Ontario's Deputy Attorney General, George Thomson, took official note of the relationship between what courts must think of tribunals generally and how they treat tribunal decisions – a point that has long been the elephant in the room when standard of review issues are discussed. He said: "I think it is true that the absence of uniform standards of administrative justice is one of the major reasons why courts are unwilling or, at a minimum quite changeable over time in their willingness, to show real deference to the decisions and procedures of administrative tribunals."[285]

Not long ago, I attended an administrative law conference in which a plenary session panel composed of a number of very senior justices from across the country had been asked to discuss judicial review issues from the judiciary's perspective. In the course of a discussion concerning whether the quality of the actual expertise of particular tribunal adjudicators should be an issue when deciding upon the degree of deference to be accorded a tribunal, one of the august panel members commented: "Of course, we all know tribunals you wouldn't let decide what day of the week it was." From the silent and studied reaction of the rest of the panel – and of the audience – it was apparent that the elephant in the room had just been glimpsed.

Defeating or Finessing Reform Recommendations

Misgivings over how the growing number of rights-determining bodies to be found outside of the traditional structures of the legislature and the public service have led to a pervasive and seemingly permanent disquietude in

the halls of both academe and government about their legitimacy, their reporting relationships, their accountability, their performance, and how they
might be seen as usurping the roles or powers of the legislative and executive branches of government.

This disquietude has led to an astonishing number of official studies and
reports over the years, in which the entrails of the administrative justice
system and the executive branch's regulatory agencies have been pawed
over from every conceivable angle. The number of official studies and reports is so remarkable that their accumulated weight – to say nothing of
their actual content – provides especially cogent evidence that, in constitutional terms, administrative tribunals and their members continue to be a
puzzle. Obviously, we need to find a place within our constitutional arrangements that they can rightfully call home. (And, of course, for judicial
tribunals, I argue that that home is in the judicial branch.)

Consider the following list of officially sanctioned or commissioned reviews of the nature, role, and constitutional status of our conglomeration of
administrative tribunals. The list is largely limited to those studies and reports that focused on the genre of either provincial or federal tribunals
or agencies, and does not include studies or reports related to individual
tribunals. Thus, for example, the reviews in Ontario of the Securities Commission, the Medical Review Committee, and the Criminal Injuries
Compensation Board are not included in this list:

1   the 1888 report of the Galt Commission[286]
2   the 1940 report of the Royal Commission on Dominion-Provincial
    Relations (the Rowell-Sirois report), Book I, Canada: 1867-1939
3   the 1959 report of the Gordon Committee on the Organization of
    Government in Ontario
4   the 1963 report of the federal Glassco Royal Commission on Govern-
    ment Organization
5   the 1968 report of the McRuer Royal Commission Inquiry into Civil
    Rights in Ontario
6   the 1971 report of the Dussault *Groupe de travail sur les tribunaux ad-
    ministratifs* in Quebec
7   Report Number 9 of the Ontario Committee on Government Produc-
    tivity, dated March 1973
8   the 1974 Management Board of Cabinet report on Agencies, Boards and
    Commissions in the Government of Ontario in 1974

9   the 1978 Ontario Economic Council report on *Government Regulation: Issues and Alternatives*

10 twenty-three "annual" reports of the review of "agencies" by Ontario Standing Committees of the Legislative Assembly from 1978 to 1996

11 the 1979 federal Lambert Commission report

12 the Economic Council of Canada's Interim Report on the "Regulation Reference" in 1979, and its Final Report in 1981

13 the 1980 report of the Ontario Williams Commission on Freedom of Information and Individual Privacy

14 the 1981 Peterson report (of the Special Parliamentary Committee Task Force on Regulatory Reform)

15 the 1981 Final Report of the Privy Council Office Review Group on Regulatory Reform of Crown Agencies

16 two reports from the House of Commons Standing Joint Committee for the Scrutiny of Regulations – the second report in 1976 and the fourth Report in 1982

17 the 1984 Ontario Legislative Library Current Issues Paper (no. 22) titled *Agencies, Boards and Commissions in Ontario: Accountability and Control*

18 the 1985 federal McGrath Committee report in 1985

19 the Law Reform Commission of Canada's extensive series of commissioned studies of administrative agencies commencing in 1975 and culminating in its 1980 *Report on Independent Administrative Agencies* (Working Paper 25), and its final, 1985 *Report on Independent Administrative Agencies* (Report 26)

20 the 1985 Gracey report on the Agencies, Boards and Commissions Project, prepared for the Ontario Ministry of Treasury and Economics and the Management Board of Cabinet by C.G Management and Communications Inc.

21 the 1985 report of the Nielsen Task Force Agencies Study Team, and the 1986 report of the Nielsen Task Force on Regulatory Programs

22 *Regulations, Crown Corporations and Administrative Tribunals*, one of the volumes of research by the MacDonald Royal Commission on the Economic Union and Development Prospects for Canada, on Law and Constitutional Issues[287]

23 the 1987 Ouellette report in Quebec[288]

24 the 1988 Ontario Branch of the Canadian Bar Association report on Appointments to Administrative Tribunals

25 the 1989 Macaulay report *Directions: Report on a Review of Ontario's Regulatory Agencies* (Ontario Management Board of Cabinet)

26 the 1990 Ratushny *Report on the Independence of Federal Administrative Tribunals and Agencies in Canada* to the Canadian Bar Association

27 Chapter 9 of the 1993 *Touchstones for Change: Equality, Diversity and Accountability,* the report of the Task Force on Gender Equality (chaired by Madam Justice Bertha Wilson) to the Canadian Bar Association

28 the 1994 Garant report in Quebec[289]

29 the 1996 research studies for the Ontario Civil Justice Review, written by Margot Priest

30 the 1997 Wood *Report on Restructuring Regulatory and Adjudicative Agencies* (Ontario Government Task Force on Agencies, Boards and Commissions)

31 the 1997 Law Reform Commission of Nova Scotia *Final Report on Reform of the Administrative Justice System in Nova Scotia*

32 the 1998 Guzzo report *Everyday Justice* (Agency Reform Commission on Ontario's Regulatory and Adjudicative Agencies

33 the 2002 BC Administrative Justice Project, culminating in the white paper *On Balance – Guiding Principles for Administrative Justice Reform in British Columbia*

34 the 2004 *Final Report* of the New Brunswick Commission on Legislative Democracy (dealing extensively with the issues of appointments to agencies, boards, and commissions)

35 the 2009 Manitoba Law Reform Commission report *Improving Administrative Justice in Manitoba: Starting with the Appointments Process*

36 the 2010 *Report of the Special Advisor on [Ontario] Agencies* by Rita Burak.[290]

Andrew Roman, after reading the list as compiled by Margot Priest in 1992, expressed "astonishment" at the "shocking number of studies, reports, and committees there have been examining administrative agencies." He had "no idea," he said, "of [their] sheer volume and repetitiveness."[291] Roman's understanding of the reason that reform recommendations go unimplemented matches my own. In his concluding comment on the Priest paper, he offers this:

> Why do so many of our tribunals resemble the tribunal from hell? Why have so many proposals for reform resulted in so little reform? The only explanation is that those who control the situation – ministers and senior

officials – really want to preserve the status quo. They want to be able to say that it isn't the minister who has created a problem in transportation or communications or human rights or whatever, because that power has been delegated to an independent agency over which the minister has no effective control; the decision has been depoliticized. But the politicians also want to preserve the power to make political appointments, both for political reward and to try to ensure that future decisions made by their friends, and appointed by them to the tribunal, will be more to their liking. And the senior bureaucrats want to control policy development in the area of their ministry. Hence, most reform proposals, which are directed to enhancing the independence, training, and status of tribunals, are resisted by bureaucrats and ministers alike. Until a principled politician announces and implements the end of "it's our turn now," studies will proliferate and reform will languish.[292]

As evidenced by the thirty-six Canadian studies and reports listed above, the pattern has persisted in Canada. Since Priest assembled her list in 1992, there have been at least eight more major studies in Canada, four in Ontario (Macaulay, Wood, Guzzo, and Burak), one in Nova Scotia, one in British Columbia, one in New Brunswick, and one in Manitoba – and all of these have seen their recommendations for reform largely ignored.[293] The official investigators who produced these reports all made major recommendations derived from theoretical analysis of the obvious shortcomings in the system's structures and arrangements from a principled perspective. In her "tribunal from hell" paper, Priest summed up the history of reform recommendations as it stood at the time:

In one form or another, all the Canadian reports and studies allude to the problems that occur in the tribunal from hell: poor quality appointments, a mysterious or closed appointment process, lack of training for members, uncertainty of tenure or other problems with the terms and conditions of office, poorly defined reporting relationships, difficulty of defining the need for or meaning of independence, inappropriate relationships between the executive (political and bureaucratic) and the tribunal members, and various problems with procedures or delivery of services. Not all of these problems exist with all agencies or tribunals and not all the problems exist all the time. There is, however, general agreement on either the reality or potential of these problems. There is also a surprising degree of agreement on possible solutions or approaches to solutions.[294]

Priest describes those agreed-upon "solutions or approaches to solutions" under the following headings: (1) Appointments and Tenure, (2) Training, (3) A Tribunal Council, (4) Reviews by Cabinet and Policy Directions, and (5) An Administrative Procedures Act. After describing a number of relatively nominal responses to these proposals for reform, Priest concludes that "[t]hese efforts and reforms are neither trivial nor futile. They are, however, fairly minor in comparison to the general body of suggested reforms and the potential problems that can occur when the tribunal from hell makes decisions."[295]

Thus, we have a history of independent and expert commissions and task forces regularly agreeing on concerns related to the appropriateness of the structures and arrangements pertaining to these tribunals, and, just as regularly, these concerns being largely ignored.

Ignoring Canada's International Commitments

Finally, Canada's executive branch can maintain its in-house, controlled justice system that is willfully non-compliant with the rule of law only by turning a blind eye to Canada's international undertakings and tarnishing Canada's reputation and role in the global promotion of the rule of law. Canadian administrative law professors Gerald Heckman and Lorne Sossin provide a succinct summary of the administrative justice requirements in international law in their 2005 article "How Do Canadian Administrative Law Protections Measure Up to International Human Rights Standards? The Case of Independence." The article summarizes the international human rights law requirement that individual rights and obligations be determined by "independent and impartial tribunals":

> It is well established that international human rights law entitles each individual to a fair and public hearing by an independent and impartial tribunal in the determination of his or her rights and obligations. This right is expressly guaranteed in several international declarations and conventions, including the *Universal Declaration of Human Rights*, the *International Covenant on Civil and Political Rights*, the *European Convention for the Protection of Human Rights and Fundamental Freedoms*, and the *American Convention on Human Rights*. It has been observed, based on a wide-ranging review of state constitutions, legislation and supporting state practice regarding judicial independence, that "the general practice of providing independent and impartial justice is accepted by states as a matter of law" and is thus a customary norm of international law.[296]

With its political patronage and at-pleasure appointments; with its se-conding of dependent government employees to "independent" tribunals; with its policy of short, fixed-term appointments, arbitrary reappointments, and, especially, idiosyncratic removals; with the exposure of tribunal chairs and members to discharge for alleged cause without procedural protection; and with the conflicted structural integration of tribunals with executive branch structures, Canada cannot even begin to pretend that the rights and obligations of its citizens are determined by tribunals that meet the inter-national standard of independence and impartiality. Canada's justice am-bassadors, trumpeting its judicial justice system to the world as the embodiment of all that is good from a rule-of-law perspective, dare not mention this country's system of administrative justice.

2

Administrative *Justice*
Getting the Context and Terminology Clear, the Concepts Straight, and the Prescription Right

And so it is that we have an executive branch system of administrative justice in which the rule of law is a stranger; a justice system that is, as I reference in the book's title, unjust by design. Since it is a system that has effectively displaced our system of courts for most of our rights disputes, it is not a system that in its present form we can continue to tolerate. Transformative reform of this system is a transcendent necessity. And such reform must begin with the recognition and acceptance of a principled prescription for administrative justice that is rule-of-law compliant and constitutionally protected – enforceable by the courts and safe from legislative override. This chapter is devoted to the development of such a prescription.

As I continue to emphasize, the administrative justice with which I am concerned includes only the exercise of *judicial* rights-determining functions by executive branch tribunals and their members. It does not include the exercise of *administrative* rights-determining functions by regulatory agencies and regulators, not even if the latter functions are of a "quasi-judicial" nature.

Statutory Rights Enterprises
Judicial tribunals must be understood in context, and their most important context is the statutory rights enterprise of which they are a central component.

When governments implement policy through a rights statute, the statute creates the rights, privileges, and corresponding obligations needed to effectuate that policy, and it also structures the "delivery" system – the organizations and mechanisms required to deliver and administer the policy. The totality of those institutional arrangements and structures can be conveniently referred to as a "statutory rights enterprise."

Such enterprises are, of course, ubiquitous. As we have seen, they deliver benefits or services, grant and administer statutory licences, vindicate rights and enforce obligations, and regulate various economic activities, to mention only a few categories. The workers' compensation system is a classic instance.

The components and structures of a statutory rights enterprise are specified by its constitutive statute. There is the "line ministry" or, to use, as I have been using, the more pertinent British terminology, the "portfolio ministry." This is the ministry headed by the cabinet minister responsible to the legislature for the administration and success of the enterprise. It is the portfolio ministry that, in Canada, traditionally hosts[1] the enterprise's judicial tribunal, and it is in the portfolio ministry that one finds the headwaters of the enterprise's overall direction.

Of key importance is what one might call the enterprise's policy and legislative department – the department that distills from the statutory text the particulars of the legislature's policy intentions, and drafts and "enacts" the directives and the rules and regulations necessary to give effect to those particulars. In Canada, this department is often found within the portfolio ministry itself, but it is also often found within a regulatory agency. The latter is the case with workers' compensation enterprises and securities regulation enterprises, and in the United States it is the invariable practice.

The Rights Deciders in Statutory Rights Enterprises

Beyond the policy and legislative functions, and central to the statutory rights enterprise's operation, are the people or institutions exercising the enterprise's rights-determining functions and deciding the disputes or issues respecting the rights of particular individuals, businesses, or corporate bodies arising in the ordinary course of the enterprise's administration. It is among these deciders that one finds the administrative judicial tribunal, the judicial arm of the enterprise.

The administrative judicial tribunal concept emerged from the fact that the judicial, rights-determining tasks demanded by the social and economic statutory right enterprises of modern governments were simply not appropriate for the traditional courts. The courts were seen to be too un-wieldy, too costly, or otherwise inappropriate, ineffective, or inexpedient.

Since the assignment of judicial functions directly to government port-folio ministries would have been too obvious an affront to the rule of law, the idea emerged of assigning these functions to specialized, separate, exec-utive branch rights-determining organizations that promised to be more efficient, more practical, more specialized, more expert, less august, less costly, and, from a government's perspective, more amenable and malleable than courts, but still organizations that could be held out to be independent.

As we have seen, these juridical organizations now comprise the core of the administrative justice system, and it is symptomatic of the current *ad hoc* and constitutionally unfixed nature of that system that there continues to be debate over what these organizations ought to be called. In this book, I have been calling them "administrative judicial tribunals," or "judicial tri-bunals" for short. But while that now seems to me to be the natural thing, the informed reader will know that it is not the usual thing. "Quasi-judicial tribunal" or "adjudicative tribunal" are the generic labels currently in vogue, and I expect that administrative law experts may well be disconcerted by my adoption of the "judicial tribunal" label.

In fact, I have had great difficulty deciding what they should be called. "Quasi-judicial" is the most obvious candidate because of the Supreme Court of Canada's current usage, but that is not a label I can accept. In my view, applying the "quasi-judicial" label to tribunals whose principal role is the exercise of judicial functions is misconceived, misleading, and pregnant with trouble to come. Not long ago, Frank Falzon suggested that we call them "justice tribunals,"[2] and in early drafts of this book I adopted his sug-gestion. It is a label with no firm antecedents in the law, however, and in the end I concluded that it was not a sufficiently full-bodied or focused indica-tor of the tribunals' judicial role.

In the past, including in my PhD dissertation, in which this book has its origins, I had elected to distinguish these tribunals by calling them "rights tribunals." I now think that choice ill-advised, however, as the "rights tribu-nal" label also has no common law provenance and contains its own meas-ure of ambiguity.

"Adjudicative tribunal" is the label on which the Ontario government has most recently settled. In the past few years, Ontario moved away from the practice of labelling all tribunals "regulatory agencies." It began by dis-tinguishing between regulatory agencies and "adjudicative *agencies*,"[3] but with the enactment of the *Adjudicative Tribunals Accountability, Governance and Appointments Act, 2009*,[4] the "adjudicative tribunal" label has become official. It is a label that is also used in Newfoundland and Nova Scotia. On the other hand, the new Alberta legislation respecting the governance of public agencies refers to "adjudicative functions" of "Public Agencies," and British Columbia's *Administrative Tribunals Act* does not distinguish between regulatory agencies and administrative judicial tribunals, preferring to call them all "administrative tribunals."

With Ontario's recent lead in the matter, I was tempted to adopt "adjudicative tribunal" as the generic label. Nevertheless, although that label does reflect what judicial tribunals do, it does not sufficiently reflect the fact that the important thing about the adjudicative functions of such tribunals is their status as an integral part of our justice system.

"Judicial tribunal" is the label the *McRuer Report* applied to these tribunals in 1968.[5] It is a label that evokes the essential role of these tribunals in the justice system while conveying a robust sense of that role. Moreover, the courts themselves have from time to time applied it to tribunals exercising judicial functions, so that it has a respectable common law provenance as well.[6] It is for these reasons that I have decided to continue as I began, referring to these statutory, non-court organizations whose functions are purely or mainly judicial as "administrative judicial tribunals," or, for convenience, "judicial tribunals."

One drawback of this label is that it risks suggesting that one wants or expects these tribunals to be "judicialized" – that is, fashioned to look and act as much like a court as possible. Of course, this is exactly what is not wanted; what is wanted is only for these tribunals to be *justicized*. In my opinion, however, the advantages of the "judicial tribunal" label outweigh the risk of its contributing to some misunderstanding of the goal of the proposed reforms, so "judicial tribunals" it will continue to be.

The judicial tribunals on which this book focuses are the same executive branch organizations that, as noted above, were called "judicial tribunals" in the *McRuer Report*; the same organizations that, in 1990, Ed Ratushny's *Report on the Independence of Federal Administrative Tribunals and Agencies* described as "tribunals which are adjudicative" and for which it recommended the label "tribunal" be exclusively reserved;[7] and the same organizations that in 1991 the late Chief Justice of Canada Antonio Lamer, in a keynote speech to the conference of the Council of Canadian Administrative Tribunals, referred to as bodies that are "created to operate essentially as

adjudicators ... in a manner that is similar to the function of the judiciary ...
[and] expected to dispense justice in the same sense as the courts of law."[8]
They are also the same organizations that, in 1998, in a speech to a conference of the BC Council of Administrative Tribunals (BCCAT), Supreme
Court of Canada Justice Beverley McLachlin (as she then was) described as
"dispute resolving bodies" [that are not] "regulatory or licensing bodies"
[and that] "seem to be doing what the courts have traditionally done."[9] More
recently, the Supreme Court of Canada has, carelessly and wrongly, I believe,
labelled these same organizations "quasi-judicial tribunals"[10] but described
them accurately as bodies whose "primary purpose" is to "adjudicate disputes" and who are "not involved in crafting policy."[11]

For the *individuals* exercising *judicial* rights-determining functions as
members of judicial tribunals, I use the traditional label: "adjudicator."

Since my definition of the administrative justice system is particularly
marked by the exclusion of regulatory agencies and regulatory functions, a
few words about the inherent nature of these agencies and their functions
are necessary.

In a 1978 report on the role of regulatory agencies in the economy – the
Trebilcock Report[12] – one finds a particularly useful statement of the traditional view of the nature, powers, and functions of regulatory agencies,
together with an early acknowledgment of the separate existence of judicial
tribunals. The report's subject was "autonomous regulatory agencies," and
its authors observe that the functioning of many regulatory agencies does
not raise fundamentally different questions from any other form of "political
decision-making." In the first place, they say, "with many agencies the entire
policy-making or legislative function has been delegated by government to
the regulators, and in this respect regulators perform the same roles as politicians."[13] They cite as examples the powers delegated (at the time of the
report) to the National Transportation Board, the federal Foreign Investment
Review Agency, and the Ontario Milk Marketing Board. "In all of these
cases," they say, "the primary policy-making responsibility is left, at least
in the first instance, to the agency." Thus, "regulators are transmuted into
politicians, and analysis of the functioning of this form of public decision-
making should not differ sharply from political decision-making at large."[14]
They conclude:

> [Q]uestions of institutional design and political accountability [of regula-
> tory agencies] cannot usefully be examined separately from such issues

across the whole spectrum of political decision-making. Hence, concepts of political due process become much more important [for regulatory agencies] than formalistic concepts of judicial due process."[15]

The report provides, however, a qualifier in which it concedes the existence of – and unwittingly does a fair job of defining – the "agencies" that are in fact "administrative judicial tribunals":

> The foregoing analysis is not intended to suggest that all regulatory agencies can be viewed in this political dimension. Obviously, agencies such as Workmen's Compensation Boards and Land Compensation Boards, *where the necessary political brokering of public policy is already reflected in their detailed statutory mandates,* and the application of those mandates involves relatively technical adjudications on relatively confined inter-party disputes, are most usefully modeled along judicial analogues, given that generally *the only realistic substitute policy instrument for the administration of such statutes is the courts.* Concepts of judicial due process are obviously, therefore, highly appropriate institutional reference points.[16]

I will continue to refer to tribunals whose rights-determining functions are mainly of an administrative or quasi-judicial administrative nature as "regulatory agencies," and will call the individuals exercising a regulatory agency's *administrative* or *quasi-judicial administrative* rights-determining functions "regulators."

Based on the foregoing taxonomy, workers' compensation appeals tribunals are judicial tribunals and their members are adjudicators, whereas energy boards are regulatory agencies and their members are regulators. Where I do not intend any distinction among the various categories of rights determiners, I will talk about "rights deciders" or "deciders."

A statutory rights enterprise's initial decisions on rights issues are made by what I will call "first deciders." Where these deciders are regulators exercising administrative rights-determining functions rather than judicial rights-determining functions (and I will define the distinction between these functions shortly), they are often both the first deciders and the final deciders, and they can be found either in an "independent" regulatory agency or within the portfolio ministry itself. An example of the former category is energy board members deciding whether or not to grant gas-marketing licences.

First deciders who are exercising what is effectively a judicial function – the "claims adjudicators" at the Workers' Compensation Board described in the Introduction come to mind – will be making initial decisions that are typically appealable – indeed, should be appealable – up the line to second, third, and perhaps fourth deciders. (The Workers' Compensation Appeals Tribunal was the fourth decider in the Ontario workers' compensation system.) As I have mentioned before, where judicial decisions at lower levels are interim and appealable to another judicial tribunal as the final decider, the adjudicative processes at the levels below the final decider can be simplified in the interest of efficiency. Lower levels of a multi-level judicial decision-making process may adopt expedient procedures that do not fully conform to the principles of natural justice[17] provided that the process at the final level of decision making is a *de novo* hearing[18] that does fully conform to such principles.

The History of Administrative Justice in Canada

For Canadian lawyers and academics, not to mention Canadian governments and bureaucrats, recognition that there was such a thing as administrative *justice* was remarkably slow to dawn. Until the last decade of the twentieth century, Canadian law conversation and jurisprudence was replete with references to administrative *law*, administrative *agencies*, and administrative *tribunals*, but rarely would one encounter references to administrative *justice*.

Quebec was something of an exception, as administrative *justice* had become part of the currency of academic thought in Quebec at least by 1971.[19] In the rest of Canada, however, we find, even as we speak, the idea that tribunals are part of the justice system to be – what can one say? – a bit unexpected. And, if we are to now embrace the legitimacy of that idea, we need to understand why Canada waited until nearly the twenty-first century to make the connection.

The different experience in the United States, where Americans understood the point very early, provides one illuminating contrast. The policy of assigning judicial functions to political appointees in agencies was strongly resisted during the 1930s and early 1940s by the forces of civil libertarianism, as well as by the Republicans.[20] The outcome of that resistance can be seen in the subsequent US requirement referred to earlier, dating from 1946, that the adjudicators of justiciable issues in the application of a federal agency's rules must be "Administrative Law Judges," selected by an independent body through a rigorous and competitive selection process and appointed to life-tenured terms, conditional only on good behaviour.

In the United Kingdom, the still-remembered 1957 Franks Committee recommended that tribunals be regarded as part of the judicial branch rather than the executive branch:

> [T]ribunals should properly be regarded as machinery provided by Parliament for adjudication rather than as part of the machinery of administration. The essential point is that in all these cases Parliament has deliberately provided for a decision outside and independent of the Department concerned, either at first instance ... or on appeal from a decision of a Minister or of an official in a special statutory provision ... Although the relevant statutes do not in all cases expressly enact that tribunals are to consist entirely of persons outside the Government service, the use of the term "tribunal" in legislation undoubtedly bears this connotation, and the intention of Parliament to provide for the independence of tribunals is clear and unmistakable.[21]

In his maiden speech to the House of Lords, the famous Lord Denning had this to say about the Franks Committee report: "[I]t contains and reaffirms a constitutional principle of first importance – namely, that these tribunals are not part of the administrative machinery of government under the control of departments; they are part of the judicial system of the land under the rule of law."[22]

The response to the latter perception was obviously slow to develop, however, even in the United Kingdom. In 1973, the respected British administrative law professor W.A. Robson was moved to comment that while the number of administrative tribunals in the United Kingdom was "growing apace," there had still been no discussion of the "principles that should inform a system of administrative justice" and that "neither Parliament nor the government had felt able to rise to the height of a general proposition on this vital subject" and so had "failed to evolve a coherent system of administrative justice."[23]

The modern view in the United Kingdom may be seen in Professor William Wade's observation that "despite the 'diversity of species,' it has long been recognized that statutory tribunals are an integral part of the machinery of justice in the state, and not merely administrative devices for disposing of claims and arguments conveniently,"[24] and that:

the decisions of most tribunals are in truth judicial rather than administrative, in the sense that the tribunal has to find facts and then apply legal rules to them impartially, without regard to executive policy. Such tribunals therefore have the character of courts, even though these are enmeshed in the administrative machinery of the state. They are "administrative" only because they are part of an administrative scheme for which a minister is responsible to Parliament, and because the reasons for preferring them to the ordinary courts are administrative reasons.[25]

In 2001, the report of Sir Andrew Leggatt, commissioned by the British government to conduct a comprehensive review of tribunals, asserted flatly that "tribunals are an alternative to court, not administrative, processes."[26] The *Leggatt Report* led, in 2007, to a radical – indeed, revolutionary – legislated restructuring of administrative justice in the United Kingdom that effectively "de-enmeshed" the tribunals from the administrative machinery of the state and fully recognized their judicial branch status. I will talk more about this development in due course.

In Canada, outside of Quebec, administrative law literature began to take notice of the existence of such a thing as administrative *justice* only in the early 1990s, and it remains true to this day that no Canadian government other than Quebec has ever felt able, in Robson's words, "to rise to the height of any general proposition concerning the principles that should inform a system of administrative justice."[27] Certainly, until Falzon spoke up in 2006, no Canadian had ever suggested that the administrative justice system's judicial tribunals were properly a part of the judicial branch of government.[28]

In Ontario, not until the year 2000 was there any official recognition of a difference between regulatory agencies and "adjudicative" tribunals. In the Ontario Management Board Secretariat's *Agency Establishment and Accountability Directive* issued in February of that year, the categorization of Ontario tribunals differentiated for the first time between "regulatory agencies" and "adjudicative tribunals." Previously, adjudicative tribunals – or "quasi-judicial agencies," as they were then called – were included in the regulatory agency category.

The absence in the 1970s of any concept of administrative *justice* was especially evident in the official descriptions of government "agencies" in existence at the time. Consider the "broad administrative definition" of "agency" in the Ontario Management Board's 1974 study *Agencies, Boards and Commissions in the Government of Ontario* – a definition that encompassed both regulatory agencies and what were called regulatory agencies but were in fact judicial tribunals. It is obviously a definition that had been carefully thought through, to say the least. Its particular significance from a modern perspective is its confirmation that, at that time, the executive branch was not prepared to acknowledge – or did not appreciate – that some of its agencies were surrogates for courts. The definition reads as follows:

> An organizational unit of government which is a component part of a min-
> isterial portfolio receiving a particular form of delegated authority and
> representing *one alternative to the departmental structure* as a means of
> assisting in the formation of government policy, or delivering government
> programs, or executing the government's regulatory responsibilities.[29]

The Canadian "coming out party" for the administrative justice concept *per se* – a very quiet and diffident party, to be sure – really occurred in 1991, fifty-three years after it had been officially recognized in US legislation and thirty-four years after the Franks Committee's assertion that tribunals were to be properly regarded as machinery for adjudication, and not part of the machinery of administration. In that year, Chief Justice of Canada Antonio Lamer was invited to speak at the annual conference of the Council of Canadian Administrative Tribunals (this was the speech I referred to earlier in this chapter). He chose as his topic "Administrative Tribunals – Future Prospects and Possibilities," and after the reference to tribunals created to operate not as "regulatory agencies" but as "adjudicators" and "*expected to dispense justice in the same sense as the courts,*" he observed that, "as a result [of the proliferation of the latter type of administrative tribunal], the term 'administrative justice' has become relevant."[30]

It is not the case that previous to this it had not been observed that some administrative tribunals were exercising *judicial* functions; no, that had always been well understood. What Canadians had always seemed able to ignore was the inescapable role of those functions – and of those who exercised them – as integral components of the justice system, as well as the incongruity, from a justice theory and constitutional point of view, of treating them as though they were legitimate executive branch functions.

Chief Justice Lamer's suggestion that it was time to think of some administrative tribunals in justice terms had no immediate impact. Six years later, in 1997, when Chief Justice of Ontario Roy McMurtry told an annual Conference of Ontario Boards and Agencies in Toronto that it was time to recognize that administrative tribunals were part of our justice system – in fact, the administrative part of the justice system[31] – his audience perceived him to be breaking radically new ground, if not actually preaching heresy.[32]

The pace of recognition quickened, however. A year later, in 1998, there came the acknowledgment by Justice McLachlin at the BCCAT conference referred to earlier, that there was a distinction to be drawn between "regulatory or licensing bodies" and "dispute resolving bodies" that are "doing what the courts have traditionally done."[33] Four years after that, in 2002, the Supreme Court of Canada, in a unanimous judgment in the case of *Paul v. British Columbia (Forest Appeals Commission)* written by Justice Michel Bastarache, finally acknowledged that our "justice system" comprised both courts and tribunals.[34]

What accounts for this Canadian blind spot? In my view, the long delay in the arrival on the Canadian scene of the idea of administrative *justice* can be attributed to three seminal features of Canada's unique administrative law landscape. First, there was what one might call the Diceyan distraction; second, there was the battle for the constitutional legitimacy of provincial tribunals in light of s. 96 of the *British North America Act;* and, third, there was the now archaic but previously long-lived trust-based doctrine of judicial independence.

The Diceyan debate was particularly distracting because, during the formative period of Canadian administrative law,[35] under A.V. Dicey's influence Canadian courts were excessively conservative in defining the room within which the tribunals would be allowed to operate without judicial supervision. In this era, the courts were seen to be almost willfully obstructing the legislatures' attempts to implement their new social and economic policies. It was a judicial attitude that triggered a strong reaction among administrative law academics, with Professors John Willis of the University of Toronto Faculty of Law and Professor Harry Arthurs of the Osgoode Hall Law School leading the charge.[36] (Professor J.A. Corry's previously quoted criticism of the courts' approach to tribunals in the 1930s[37] was, as I have said, an early expression of what became the mainstream of academic thought.) As a result, the issue of overriding interest for Canadian administrative law scholars, tribunals, and courts became, and largely remains, the relationship *between* courts and tribunals – the degree of deference owed by the courts to these upstart tribunals, and the tribunals' degree of independence from the self-absorbed courts.

With that issue at the forefront, the emphasis was always on the *distinctions* between tribunals and courts. And with the tribunals and the courts and their respective supporters in warring camps, as it were, there was little room for an objective discussion about the awkward fact that, yes, a significant proportion of such tribunals had been assigned a purely judicial, justice-system function that a principled justice policy could not really countenance being left in the hands of the executive branch.[38]

By now you may be wondering how I myself propose to reconcile Dicey's theory about the inherent illegitimacy of tribunals with the recognition of a justice-system/judicial branch status for Canada's judicial tribunals. In my view, the answer comes easily. Such recognition can be reconciled with Dicey – and with Hewart – if it is accompanied by an appropriate redesign of the tribunals' structures. It is the assignment of judicial functions to entities that are not structurally compatible with rule-of-law norms of independence and impartiality that is at the bottom of Dicey's rule-of-law objection to tribunals.

The second circumstance that obscured the justice-system role of administrative judicial tribunals in Canada is, as mentioned, s. 96 of the *British North America Act*.[39] Section 96 gives the federal government the exclusive power to appoint the judges of "Superior, District, and County Courts" in each province. And, whenever provincial legislatures gave one of their own tribunals a rights-determining function resembling a judicial function, the constitutional validity of the legislation was often challenged on the basis that the province had unconstitutionally usurped the federal power by creating what the challengers would argue amounted to a "s. 96 court."

Whether a particular provincial tribunal will be seen to be tantamount to a s. 96 court ultimately involves a number of arcane issues. In dealing with any s. 96 challenge, however, a court must first decide whether the tribunal's rights-determining function in fact constitutes the exercise of a "judicial power." In that legal environment, particularly as it existed in the early stages of tribunal development, when tribunals were novel and in many quarters controversial, the idea that a tribunal was an instrument of justice and part of the justice system was the last thing that its proponents would want to suggest. If the provincial tribunals were to survive the constitutional challenge, it was the *difference* between tribunals and courts that, as a tactical matter, counsel – and the courts – had to emphasize, even embellish.

But, you might ask, if we are to now, as it were, "out" a large proportion of administrative tribunals as closet judicial tribunals, may we not find that for those tribunals we are reigniting the s. 96 issue? There is little doubt that the characterization of a provincial tribunal as a judicial tribunal would at

one time have presented a significant s. 96 problem. The modern s. 96 jurisprudence, however, has ample room for provincial judicial tribunals as long
as their powers do not intrude on the "core" jurisdiction of the superior
courts. It is now recognized, for example, that it is constitutionally valid to
grant judicial jurisdiction to a provincial tribunal where that jurisdiction is
"novel" – unknown at the time of Confederation – or where, at the time of
Confederation, that jurisdiction was exclusive to inferior courts or shared
between the superior and inferior courts.[40]

Quebec's *Tribunal administratif du Québec* (TAQ) is a case in point.
TAQ, as described by the Quebec Court of Appeal in *Barreau*,[41] is acknowledged to be exclusively an adjudicative tribunal, with no "social or economic mission," with broad judicial powers, and a range of jurisdiction that
includes many matters that would originally have been found to be within
the jurisdiction of s. 96 courts. Nevertheless, although various aspects of
TAQ's constituent legislation have been challenged, at no point has there
been any suggestion that the tribunal presented a s. 96 issue.[42]

Finally, also hindering recognition of the existence and importance of
administrative justice in Canada was the trust-based doctrine of judicial
independence (discussed at length in Chapter 1[43]), pursuant to which anyone assigned a judicial function was deemed to be independent and impartial regardless of his or her structural ties to the executive branch. Under
that happily now defunct doctrine, the control of judicial functions by the
executive branch was not seen to present any justice-system issues, and it
was therefore immaterial whether the rights-determining functions exercised by executive branch bodies were or were not judicial functions.

The System of Administrative Justice

Once the concept of administrative justice entered the conversation, it became natural to refer to the "administrative justice *system*." As things now
stand, however, it is a reference that is disingenuous at best. In Canada,
other than in Quebec, there is no extant, operational *system* of administrative justice. Administrative judicial tribunals typically stand alone, each in
the ministerial silo occupied by its own statutory rights enterprise and each
in the hands only of its own ministry. Structured coordination of tribunals
is largely unknown except for the happenstance of judicial review.[44] The absence of a properly structured system of administrative justice is both a
symptom and a source of the problem, and the reforms that this book proposes will create a proper *system*.

Administrative Justice and Justice

Administrative justice must naturally find its roots in the foundational concepts of the traditional system of judicial justice – that is, of "formal" justice, the justice that is seen to happen when disputes about rights under the law are determined by courts, pursuant to rule-of-law-compliant court structures and processes. In the judicial justice system, the quality of that justice is judged by the extent to which the determination process measures up to courts doing properly what rule-of-law-compliant courts do. In the administrative justice system, the administrative role of the system mandates fewer traditional structures and more procedural flexibility in the determination of rights than is typical of the judicial justice system. In essential respects, however, the quality of justice in the administrative justice system must measure up to the quality of justice in the judicial justice system. The core elements of the rule of law must prevail in both.

Impartial Deciders – The Foundation of Justice

The *Grundnorm* of a rule-of-law-compliant justice system is the principle that like cases be treated alike and different cases be treated differently. As legal philosopher Joel Feinberg put it, "many writers hold that the principle of like treatment for like cases is more than simply one among many ethical principles vying for our allegiance, but is rather an instance of a more general principle that is constitutive of rationality itself."[45]

Where the matter at issue is the application of a statutory law (which is virtually always the matter principally at issue before judicial tribunals), the relevant criteria for determining whether cases are alike or different are found in the statute itself. However, both the facts against which conformity with those criteria is to be measured, and the meaning of those criteria as they were intended to apply to those facts, fall to a "judge" to determine, and, as legal philosopher Professor H.L.A. Hart points out,[46] the key to the "legitimacy of the determination" of "alike or different" is "the perceived impartiality" of the judge. A law is justly applied only, Hart says, if it is "impartially applied to all those and only those who are alike in having done what the law forbids [or permits]," which is to say that "no prejudice or interest has deflected the administrator from treating them 'equally.'" It is for this reason, he says, that "the procedural standards such as '*audi alteram partem*' [and] let no one be a judge in his own cause, are thought of as requirements of justice." "This is so," in Hart's view, "because they are guarantees of impartiality or objectivity designed to secure that the law is applied to all those and only to those who are alike in the relevant respect marked out by the law itself."[47] "[T]o apply a law justly to different cases is simply," Hart says, "to take seriously the assertion that what is to be applied in different cases is the same general rule, *without prejudice, interest, or caprice.*"[48]

To be seen to be applying laws justly to different cases, therefore, we must, according to Hart, have at the core of our justice system a manifest commitment to "take seriously" the requirement that bodies exercising judicial, rights-determining functions are, and are perceived to be, impartial. If one accepts Hart's analysis in that respect – as I do – it follows that the core foundational requirement of constitutional legitimacy for a person or entity exercising judicial functions is an objectively guaranteed impartiality.

But one might want to ask Hart: Have you not forgotten independence? Isn't the independence of courts and judges at least as important as their impartiality?

Judicial independence has a large profile in constitutional law analysis, and it is a concept that in rule-of-law terms applies to administrative judicial tribunals and their adjudicator members as much as to courts and judges. Judicial independence is important, however, only because without it no one can be confident about the impartiality of those exercising judicial functions. As the Supreme Court has said, judicial independence is not to be regarded as an "end in itself."[49] It is a cornerstone of the rule of law only because of its indispensable role in the establishment of "a protected platform for impartial decision making."[50]

The nature of the structures required for the protection of that platform is now well settled. As we saw in Chapter 1,[51] since the Supreme Court decision in *Valente* in 1985, our courts have recognized that the essential structural conditions of independence – conditions that apply to administrative tribunals and their adjudicators as well as to courts and judges – include at least the objective, structural guarantees of the three conditions of independence identified in *Valente:* "security of tenure," "financial security," and "administrative control"[52] – guarantees that ensure both actual independence and public confidence in that independence.[53] It is important to note, however, that these conditions are not necessarily the only requirements of judicial independence. In 1989, in a majority judgment written by Justice McLachlin (as she then was), the Supreme Court observed:

> Having enunciated these conditions [in *Valente*], Le Dain J. makes it clear that he is not attempting an exhaustive codification of the elements

necessary for judicial independence: identification of the essential conditions, he confesses, is a matter of some difficulty; moreover, the conditions themselves may vary and evolve with time and circumstances.[54]

And, as we have seen, there is at least one other common law requirement for independence that has been recognized subsequent to *Valente* (by the Quebec Court of Appeal). This requirement applies where adjudicators are appointed to fixed terms with the expectation of subsequent renewals. The requirement is that those renewals be determined in a merit-based, objective, independent, and fair process.[55]

It is also important to note that the individual independence of the adjudicator members of an administrative judicial tribunal is not enough. The judicial independence jurisprudence, beginning with *Valente,* recognizes two equally important "aspects" or "dimensions" of judicial independence: "individual" independence and "institutional" independence.[56] If there is to be public confidence in the independence of the members' decision making, the tribunal itself must be independent. The *Valente* reference to institutional independence reads as follows:

> The objections in the present case to the status of provincial court judges ... raise issues of both individual and institutional independence. The relationship between these two aspects of judicial independence is that an individual judge may enjoy the essential conditions of judicial independence but if the court or tribunal over which he or she presides is not independent of the other branches of government, in what is essential to its function, he or she cannot be said to be an independent tribunal.[57]

And, as one might expect, there is also an institutional aspect to the requirement of impartiality. This was first confirmed by the Supreme Court in *R. v. Lippé:*

> Notwithstanding judicial independence, there may also exist a reasonable apprehension of bias on an institutional or structural level. Although the concept of institutional impartiality has never before been recognized by this Court, the constitutional guarantee of an "independent and impartial tribunal" has to be broad enough to encompass this. Just as the requirement of judicial independence has both an individual and institutional aspect (Valente, *supra,* at p. 687), so too must the requirement of judicial impartiality.[58]

The test for determining whether a tribunal has an institutional bias is to ask the following question: "Will there be a reasonable apprehension of bias in the mind of a fully informed person in a substantial number of cases?"[59]

Impartiality is as much the keystone of administrative justice as of judicial justice. And, in both cases, it is about both the reality and the perception.

Impartiality has two components, both of which have to be present. First, there must be reason to be confident that the judges and adjudicators – and their courts and tribunals – in fact enjoy judicial independence. This confidence requires at least the known presence of the above-mentioned objective, structural guarantees. Without objective reasons for confidence in their independence, and in the independence of the institutions of which they are members, neither judges nor judicial tribunal adjudicators can feel themselves to be independent, nor can they be perceived to be impartial.

Second, there must not be any basis for a reasonable apprehension that the individual judge or adjudicator, or the court or tribunal of which he or she is a member, is consciously or subconsciously actually biased – no reasonable apprehension, that is, that the judges or adjudicators or their institutions have a "personal" interest in the outcome of the dispute that may consciously or subconsciously influence the decision. If such an apprehension of bias is reasonably justified, neither the judge nor the adjudicator nor the institutions to which they belong can be seen to be impartial, even if their independence is not disputed.

Process

It is not only public confidence in the impartiality of courts or judicial tribunals that makes their decision making constitutive of justice. Justice also depends on the manner of its doing. Parties who turn to the courts or to administrative judicial tribunals for the determination of their rights are entitled under the rule of law to a determination process that conforms to the "rules of natural justice."

As with justice in the judicial justice system, so it is with justice in the administrative justice system: conformity with at least the core rules of natural justice is as fundamental to justice as the manifest impartiality of the decider.

Tribunal Functions: Legislative, Administrative, Judicial

The statutory rights-determining functions assigned to administrative tribunals fall into three main categories – legislative, administrative, and judicial – but these functions are not assigned in any uniform or predictable manner. Some tribunals have been entrusted with all three functions but most do not have a legislative function, some tribunals with administrative rights-determining functions also have judicial functions,[60] and a large proportion of tribunals have only a judicial function.

Since what defines the constitutional status of any individual or institution exercising statutory, rights-determining functions is the nature of those functions, it is of primary importance that we fully understand the distinction between rights-determining functions that are legislative and therefore part of the legislative branch of government; rights-determining functions that are administrative and therefore part of the executive branch of government; and rights-determining functions that are judicial and therefore not part of the executive branch but part of the judicial branch of government.

The Legislative Function

The exercise of a legislative function involves a tribunal's determination of rights by "enacting" written regulations, rules, directions, and so on. Such enactments define or clarify general rights or obligations for all individuals or businesses or corporate bodies falling within the category addressed by the enactment. By contrast, in exercising either an administrative or a judicial rights-determining function, tribunals determine specific rights or obligations of a particular individual, business, or corporate body. A convenient example of the exercise of a legislative function is an energy board's implementation of a statutory authority to make rules governing the conduct of any person selling or offering to sell gas to a consumer.[61]

Legislative rights-determining functions of tribunals are not a concern from a justice perspective. The rules and regulations enacted in the exercise of those functions may in particular instances present justice-system or legal issues – they may, for instance, be seen to be unfair or otherwise inconsistent with justice-system principles, or perhaps beyond the jurisdiction of the tribunal – but the legislative function itself is, as we know, not a justice-system function; it is not any part of the judicial branch's role. This is a function of the legislature that, for practical reasons, has been delegated by the legislature to some of the executive branch's administrative tribunals.

Administrative versus Judicial Rights-Determining Functions

In any analysis of the administrative justice system, one must focus on both administrative and judicial rights-determining functions. The former, being exclusively executive branch functions, are not part of the justice system, but they cannot be ignored in the analysis of administrative justice, for the failure to recognize or respect the distinction between administrative and judicial rights-determining functions is one of the fundamental sources of Canada's administrative justice problems. Any attempt to find a viable prescription for administrative justice must therefore begin with an understanding of the essential differences between administrative and judicial rights-determining functions.

A prototypical example of a tribunal's exercise of an *administrative* rights-determining function would be an energy board's granting a particular applicant a licence, perhaps a licence to market gas. A prototypical example of a tribunal's exercise of a *judicial* rights-determining function would be a workers' compensation appeals tribunal deciding that an injured worker is entitled to workers' compensation benefits. So here's the question: why do we classify acceptance of an application for a gas-marketing licence as the exercise of an "administrative" function but classify the acceptance of an injured worker's compensation claim as the exercise of a "judicial" function? In both cases, a tribunal is deciding the specific rights of a particular individual, business, or corporate body in particular circumstances – a particular licence applicant gets a right to market gas or not, and a particular injured worker gets a right to receive benefits or not – and both decisions are made after the decision maker has held a "hearing" in the course of which argument and evidence have been presented. In fact, in both examples, a hearing is typically a statutory requirement.

The Supreme Court of Canada has had considerable experience in distinguishing between administrative and judicial rights-determining functions. This experience stems principally from the Court's dealing with the s. 96 issue referred to earlier. The question of whether a particular provincial tribunal that has been assigned a rights-determining function is the equivalent of a s. 96 court ultimately presents a range of issues, but in dealing with any s. 96 challenge, a court must decide in the first place whether the tribunal's rights-determining function in fact constitutes the exercise of a judicial function. If not, that is the end of the matter.

A leading authority on this issue is the Supreme Court of Canada's 1981 judgment in the reference on Ontario's new *Residential Tenancies Act* (*Ontario RTA Reference*),[62] in which the issue was the constitutional validity of provincial legislation that created a new Residential Tenancy Commission. The legislation included authority for the Commission to issue eviction orders or orders enforcing landlords' obligations. In the judicial justice system, the latter would be characterized as mandatory injunctions. And, of course, traditionally, these powers had been within the exclusive jurisdiction of

Ontario's federally appointed superior courts. The judgment was written by Justice Brian Dickson (before he became the Chief Justice).

In the course of deciding that the Residential Tenancy Commission had been assigned judicial functions in breach of s. 96, Justice Dickson cites with approval the 1949 decision of Lord Simonds in *Labour Relations Board of Saskatchewan v. John East Iron Works, Limited*,[63] in which the constitutional validity under s. 96 of a rights-determining function of the new Saskatchewan Labour Relations Board was in issue. While not purporting to propose a "final" answer to the "definition of judicial power," Lord Simonds "suggested" that "the conception of the judicial function is inseparably bound up with the idea of a suit between parties, whether between Crown and subject or between subject and subject, and that it is the duty of the court to decide the issue between those parties, with whom alone it rests to initiate or defend or compromise the proceedings."[64] After quoting with approval the foregoing passage from Lord Simonds's judgment, Justice Dickson added:

> The primary issue is the nature of the question which the tribunal is called upon to decide. Where the tribunal is faced with a private dispute between parties and is called upon to adjudicate through the application of a recognized body of rules in a manner consistent with fairness and impartiality, then, normally, it is acting in a "judicial capacity." To borrow the terminology of Professor Ronald Dworkin, the judicial task involves questions of "principle," that is, consideration of the competing rights of individuals or groups. This can be contrasted with questions of "policy" involving competing views of the collective good of the community as a whole.[65]

Against these criteria, therefore, how does an energy board's decision to grant a gas-marketing licence measure up against a workers' compensation appeals tribunal's decision to grant benefits?

In my view, the principal indicator that the energy board is not exercising a judicial function is that, in deciding the licensing question, it and its regulator members are not called upon – and are not expected – to be impartial. The energy board and its management and members have been charged with the responsibility for making the energy sector work effectively, efficiently, and fairly in the community's interest. They are committed to meeting those goals and will, as individuals and as an organization, be judged on how well those goals are achieved. In the consideration of any licence application, therefore, the board and its members must be seen to have their own "personal" institutional interests at stake – to be implicitly in the position of defending or promoting those interests. While the board may have one of the components of impartiality because it may be thought to be independent, it lacks the second component because it is not, in law, unbiased. Like a general contractor in a large construction project deciding whether or not to accept a particular tender from, say, one of several contending paving contractors, the energy board has both the interests of the community – the "owner," if you will – and its own interests to consider. It is not an *adjudicator* of other people's rights; it is a *manager* of its own – and its principal's – interests.

Thus, the key point in identifying an energy board's licensing function as an administrative and not a judicial rights-determining function is, I argue, that the nature of the licensing function is such that the law does not expect or require the board to be impartial. The issues it must determine do not invoke the treat-like-cases-alike principle. Even if, on its merits, this week's licence application were identical to an application the board granted last week, the board would be free to make a different decision this week, to find this week that another view of the collective good is more persuasive: economic factors may have shifted; market reaction to last week's decision may have been negative; the board may have changed its mind as to the relative weight to be given to the various criteria. At the very least, the market context is no longer the same: the market has one more gas marketer than it had the week before.

A workers' compensation appeals tribunal, on the other hand, is adjudicating a dispute – between the injured worker and his or her employer and/or the workers' compensation board – about the existence of a statutory *right.*[66] The tribunal confronts no policy issue requiring a choice between competing views of the collective good. The political brokering of the policy questions of whether – and when and how – from the point of view of the collective good the livelihood of workers injured at work are to be safeguarded has been completed. The legislature has answered those policy questions and incorporated the details of that answer in a workers' compensation statute that has created rights. The only responsibility of a workers' compensation appeals tribunal is to hear the evidence, find the facts, and determine, by the application of the principles of statutory interpretation, what the law intends concerning this applicant's entitlement to those rights, given these facts. It has no "personal" institutional interest in the decision other than to do its best to get the law and the facts right and to be seen to be doing so.

The appeals tribunal's assignment clearly invokes the treat-like-cases-alike principle. Justice implicitly demands that two injured workers, alike in all relevant respects, receive a like decision[67]and, moreover, are left with no reasonable ground for doubting that they have done so. And the only way this can happen is if the decider is, in fact as well as manifestly, impartial – that is, if he or she is deciding, and is seen to be deciding, without, in Hart's words, "prejudice, *interest* or caprice."[68]

Neither the literature nor the jurisprudence of administrative justice talks much about the fact that the distinction between administrative and judicial rights-determining functions turns most importantly on whether or not principle requires the tribunal exercising the function to treat like cases alike and therefore to be impartial. Typically, the treat-like-cases-alike principle is lost in the arcane reaches of legal philosophy, and day-to-day talk is typically about the fact that impartiality is a requirement *because* a tribunal is exercising a judicial function. But this, with all due respect, is circular.

When Justice Dickson says in the *Ontario RTA Reference* that a tribunal is seen to be "acting in a judicial capacity" when it is "called upon to adjudicate through the application of a recognized body of rules in a manner consistent with fairness and impartiality," one is left with the question of what it is that "calls upon" a tribunal to adjudicate in a manner consistent with fairness and impartiality? The answer, in my opinion, is that the tribunal is called upon to exercise the rights-determining function in a judicial manner – to be a judicial body – when circumstances invoke the treat-like-cases-alike principle.

What are those circumstances?

It is tempting to define them in these terms: that a law has defined a right or an obligation, a dispute has arisen concerning the validity of the right or obligation, and the duty of the rights decider is to determine what the law must intend, given the found facts. If we go with this definition for a moment, then, by contrast, the circumstances that would identify a rights-determining function that is not judicial but administrative would be those in which the law is seen to expect that the decider will decide not on the basis of what he or she, or his or her institution, thinks the law intends, but on the basis of what he or she or the institution personally thinks would be most *advisable* given those facts, *in the institution's own interest.*

But, of course, this too begs the question, and also leaves an unanswered question. In short, what are the circumstances that will demonstrate that the law expects a decider to decide what *the law* intends instead of what the decider thinks is advisable in the institution's own interests? This is, in effect, the same question left unanswered by Justice Dickson.

The answer cannot be only what the legislature may be seen to have intended in this respect. The legislature's intention – to the extent that such intention is apparent from the rights-determining structures the legislature has devised for the purpose – is obviously helpful. It can be taken to reflect the majority's views on the subject, views that are entitled to respect. But judicial functions are entitled to constitutional protection of their independence and impartiality, and so the identification of a judicial function entitled to that protection cannot be left to the legislature alone. In the end, it can come down only to the courts' judgment of what is *fairly* expected in the circumstances. If, from the point of view of the affected parties, the fair question for the authorized decider in all the circumstances is what *the law* intended (not what he or she thinks is advisable), then the like-cases principle is invoked and the decider must be seen to be exercising a judicial rights-determining function.

In those circumstances, if our rights-determining system cannot give a claimant (as well as any person disputing the claim, or the general public) manifest reasons for confidence that his or her entitlement will be resolved in a "like" way to the way that the entitlement of every other person making a like claim based on like facts would be resolved, then we cannot claim to have a system of justice at all. And the seminal point is that no one can possibly have that confidence unless there are manifest reasons to be confident that the tribunal resolving that dispute, and its members, are impartial – that is, that it and they are both perceived to be independent and cannot reasonably be apprehended to have an interest of their own in the outcome.

On the other hand, if it is not unfair for the decider to decide on the basis of what the decider thinks is advisable in the decider's interest without being concerned with what the law intended, and the decider is seen to have been authorized to do so, then the like-cases principle is not invoked and the decision maker may be seen to be exercising an administrative rights-determining function. In that case, the deciders are clearly regulators – managers – not adjudicators, and the requirement of impartiality does not apply.

The latter fundamental points are sometimes obscured by the complexity of the connection between impartiality and independence. As we have seen, from a justice perspective, the two go hand-in-glove. A person exercising a rights-determining function cannot be, or be seen to be, impartial unless that person is, and is seen to be, independent – independent, that is, of irrelevant influences, most notably the influences of government or its friends. And it is in the nature of things that the executive branch always claims that its administrative tribunals are independent. Those claims, and the public's acceptance of them at face value, are one of the executive branch's main reasons for having tribunals. However, because one intuitively equates independence with impartiality, it seems paradoxical to accept that a tribunal, such as an energy board, may be independent while at the same time recognizing that it is not impartial – not impartial because, though perhaps independent, it is not unbiased, not disinterested.

Why do we specify independence for tribunals if not to ensure their impartiality? Of course, with respect to tribunals exercising judicial functions, we do specify independence for that purpose. However, with respect to tribunals exercising administrative rights-determining functions, independence is not asserted to ensure impartiality but for other reasons. We want an energy board to be independent in order to take valuable licences out of the reach of the destructive temptations of political patronage and ensure that they find their way into the hands of competent and competitive businesses. We also want to ensure that energy policy decisions of a technical nature are vouchsafed to persons qualified to make sound, evidence-based, objective professional decisions that are beyond the reach of irrelevant political influences. Thus, we want the Canadian Nuclear Safety Commission to be independent so that expert, professional judgments on what is required to guard against nuclear accidents are not dangerously overridden by politically expedient considerations.

These policy reasons for stipulating that a tribunal exercising an administrative rights-determining function shall be independent are obviously important for public-interest reasons, but such reasons are not justice-related reasons; they have nothing to do with treating like cases alike, and they do not entail a requirement of impartiality. If there is a constitutional requirement for their independence, it is not likely to be found in the Constitution's justice mandate.

Thus far, we have recognized that a statutory rights-determining function must be recognized as a judicial function if in fairness the issues it addresses must be seen to invoke the treat-like-cases-alike principle, with the resulting requirement that the deciders be, and be seen to be, impartial – both independent and disinterested. And this analysis holds, it may be noted, regardless of the nature of the body to which the function has been assigned. If it is a judicial rights-determining function, it remains a judicial function whether it is exercised in a court by a judge or in a tribunal by a tribunal adjudicator – or in a tribunal by a decider who is ostensibly a regulator. This is the underlying premise of Justice Dickson's reasons in the *Ontario RTA Reference,* and direct authority to the same effect may be found in the Supreme Court's approval in *Baker v. Canada (Minister of Citizenship and Immigration)*[69] of the following passage from the UK Court of Queen's Bench decision in *R. v. Higher Education Funding Council:*

> While the judicial character of a function may elevate the practical requirements of fairness above what they would otherwise be, for example by requiring contentious evidence to be given and tested orally, *what makes it* "judicial" in this sense is principally the nature of the issue it has to determine, not the formal status of the deciding body.[70]

I have said that the treat-like-cases-alike principle is invoked and impartiality is required whenever the tribunal's predominant issue is seen in fairness to be the *law's* intention concerning the availability of a right to a particular party in a particular fact situation, rather than what the decision makers may think advisable from a policy perspective. That, in my view, is the general principle, but there are also a number of practical, tell-tale markers indicative of a judicial function at work.

We have seen, for instance, that one of the principal objective indicators is the fact that the rights decider is engaged in resolving a *lis inter partes:* a dispute about legal rights between parties – individuals, business or corporate parties, or government parties. Other such markers include the following:

- The tribunal's involvement is not optional; it is by law bound at the instance of a party to resolve the dispute.
- Parties who need to assert their rights have no legal option but to apply to the tribunal.
- The tribunal has no authority to involve itself in a rights dispute of its own motion, but only on the initiative of a party, and, once engaged, it is unable to discontinue its involvement except by making a final decision or by agreement of the parties.
- The rights-defining law that the tribunal is required to apply is "recognized" law – that is, existing law.
- The tribunal's resolution of the dispute is enforceable by law.

Rights issues that cannot be appropriately determined except through the exercise of a judicial function are commonly referred to as "justiciable" issues. Thus, whether a worker is to receive workers' compensation benefits is a justiciable issue; whether an applicant is to be granted a licence to market gas is not.

A particular objection that one finds classically urged against a tribunal's rights-determining function's being seen to be a judicial function is that the tribunal's enabling statute has accorded the tribunal a degree of "discretion" that is not typically accorded to a court. This objection was raised in the *Ontario RTA Reference,* and in specifically rejecting it, Justice Dickson noted that such "discretion" is also not atypical of courts:

> It is true that the Commission is given a certain degree of discretion when performing its adjudicative function. Under s. 93(1) for example, the Commission is instructed to decide "upon the real merits and justice of the case"; s. 93(2) provides that the Commission "shall ascertain the real substance of all transactions and activities ..."; s. 110(3) states that the Commission "may include in any order terms and conditions it considers proper in all the circumstances." Yet such terminology is certainly not foreign to courts within the purview of s. 96. The County Court under The Landlord and Tenant Act has the power to "make such further or other order as the judge considers appropriate" (s. 96); to make an order "granting relief against forfeiture on such terms and conditions as the judge may decide" (s. 106(1)); and to "refuse to grant the application [for possession] unless he is satisfied, having regard to all the circumstances, that it would be unfair to do so (s. 107(2)) ...[71]

I believe a better way of describing issues that require an adjudicator to, as Justice Dickson said, exercise a degree of discretion is to describe them as issues that require an adjudicator to exercise a broad judgment. And a better answer to that same objection, I respectfully submit, would have been that, however broadly based the judgment the Commission was authorized to exercise was, there is no doubt that for the central questions assigned to that Commission (for instance, should this tenant be evicted or shall that landlord be ordered to perform its obligations under the lease?) fairness plainly required a decision about what the law intended, not what the Commission wanted, thus invoking the like-cases principle and the attendant impartiality imperative. And that, I argue, is the essential point.[72]

In distinguishing between judicial functions and administrative functions, it is important not to be confused by the *breadth* of some of our legal concepts – by, to use Justice Dickson's language, the "degree of discretion" they seem to accord an adjudicator. Thus, the question of what is in the "best interests of the child" in a family law context is a legal question even though it is tempting to see from the breadth of the question an invitation to family court judges to consider themselves as having been accorded a discretion. But the question child welfare statutes ask is not what the judge personally thinks is in the child's best interest; it is what the law requires if the court's decision is to accord with the child's best interest, with precedent playing its usual role. In the same way, the labour board issue of what constitutes an "appropriate" bargaining unit is a question of what the law intends, not what particular board members think would or would not be a good idea. And the workers' compensation appeals tribunal question of whether the contribution of a worker's employment to his or her injury is "significant" is a legal question, not an invitation to tribunal members to go off on frolics of their own. These are questions about what the law intends and the answers are to be found in the "fields of answers" to which all judges must look when there is no "plain meaning" – the relevant statutory text, legislative history, precedent, jurisprudence, doctrinal literature, scholarly literature, and so on.[73] When the law asks our judges, adjudicators, courts, and judicial tribunals to make these broad judgments, we must resist the tendency to confuse those mandates with grants of discretion.

In 2010, I had occasion in my private practice to address the same contention that Justice Dickson dealt with in the above quotation – that is, that an administrative tribunal could not be seen to be exercising judicial functions because of the "degree of discretion" accorded to it by its constitutive statue. And, by way of bolstering Justice Dickson's point that these "degrees of discretion" or breadth of judgments are also routinely accorded to courts, I visited the Saskatchewan Courts website and made a random selection of the decisions of the Saskatchewan Court of Appeal issued in the month of January 2010. In those decisions, the issues that the Court of Appeal decided in which it clearly had been required to exercise, in Justice Dickson's terms, a "degree of discretion," and what I believe would be better called a "broad judgment," included the following: What is a "reasonable inspection timetable"?[74] Is a person over the age of eighteen a "child" for purposes of the *Divorce Act?*[75] "Should" a DNA order be made?[76] Did certain publications "cross the boundary of freedom of expression" and contravene the

Saskatchewan Human Rights Code?[77] And one can be sure that, in any collection of the decisions of any courts, similar examples of the law requiring judges to exercise broad judgments where the policy impact of the decisions are significant will abound. Put another way, there is a difference between deciding what the law intends an existing policy defined by the law to mean – and how it intends it to impact – in the context of a particular case, which is what courts and judicial tribunals do, and crafting a policy in pursuit of one's own institutional interests and deciding how, in one's own interest, that policy should be interpreted and applied in a particular case, which is what regulatory agencies and regulators do.

Next question: What does a *non-justiciable* rights issue look like?

For a convenient example of the kinds of non-justiciable rights issues that regulatory agencies typically face, see the following partial summary of the Ontario Energy Board's powers as they were once officially described:

> The [Energy] Board is given the power to improve and fix rates and charges for the sale, transmission, distribution and storage of gas. Moreover, it can grant leave to construct transmission pipelines, production lines, distribution lines and stations, and can grant authority to expropriate land for pipelines and stations. The board can recommend which lands are to be designated as gas storage areas and can authorize the storage of gas in a designated gas storage area. It can require the joining of interests in gas and oil pools, and order the sharing of storage capacity and facilities and the approving of terms of storage agreements. It can also grant leave to discontinue supply of gas, and hear applications with respect to the selling, leasing or conveying or other disposition of gas transmission and storage facilities or the acquisition of more than 20% of the shares of a gas transmitter, gas distributor or storage company.[78]

These are rights-determining powers that are not judicial in nature. Instead, they require what legal philosopher Lon Fuller has called an "intuitive exercise of managerial discretion."[79]

The telltale indicators that a particular rights-determining function is an administrative rather than judicial function include the inherent policy-driven nature of the determination and the absence of a requirement or expectation of impartiality. Perhaps the clearest possible indicator, however, is when the issue is "polycentric."

The Supreme Court described a polycentric issue in its 1998 decision in *Pushpanathan v. Canada (Minister of Citizenship and Immigration):*

A "polycentric issue is one which involves a large number of interlocking and interacting interests and considerations" (P. Cane, An Introduction to Administrative Law (3rd ed. 1996), at p. 35). While judicial procedure is premised on a bipolar opposition of parties, interests, and factual discovery, some problems require the consideration of numerous interests simultaneously, and the promulgation of solutions which concurrently balance benefits and costs for many different parties.[80]

The Ontario Energy Board responsibilities described above raise innumerable issues of a polycentric nature. With respect to such issues, what is required is the exercise of a management function, not a judicial function. The treat-like-cases-alike principle and the impartiality imperative are self-evidently not invoked.

For an instructive example of an inappropriate assignment of a non-justiciable issue to a judicial body, we have the reference in Ontario's 1968 *McRuer Report* to provisions in the Ontario *Expropriation Procedures Act,* at the time whereby expropriation decisions by a conservation authority, hospital, or university could be appealed to the County Court and subsequently to the Court of Appeal. McRuer comments:

> The exercise of a power of expropriation is an administrative power to make policy decisions affecting the rights of an individual, and should be subject to approval by a political Authority. The decision requires the consideration of many factors affecting the public interest; e.g., the need to expand public services or facilities; the suitability of the land in question; the availability of other suitable land; competing public demands for the lands, such as for highways, schools, other public buildings, pipelines and electricity transmission lines. The county judge, an independent judicial officer, is clothed with political power to make policy decisions with respect to conservation, health and education, or functions of government. In this way the initial tribunal is wrongly constituted.[81]

But we do not have to go back as far as 1968 to find an example of a court inappropriately assigned the decision-making role for issues that are clearly non-justiciable. Remarkably, until 1998, Ontario's legislature had assigned decision making respecting the granting or refusing of licences, certificates, or registrations required under the *Energy Act,* and respecting the refusal to renew, or to suspend or revoke, such licences, certificates, or registrations, to a judge of the Ontario Court (General Division) and then, on appeal, to the Divisional Court. The "Director" appointed under the *Energy Act* was required by the *Act* to give persons affected notice of his or her intention to refuse to grant or renew, or to suspend or revoke, a licence, and those persons were then invited to appeal the Director's proposal to the courts. Both the judge and the Divisional Court were authorized to substitute their own opinions for the opinion of the Director, and to make any order that the Director was authorized to make.[82]

The principal focus of this book is on the structure and status of administrative judicial tribunals and their adjudicator members, and their relationships to the judicial branch and the justice system, respectively. As we have seen, however, it is impossible to consider those issues without also having regard for the regulatory agencies and their regulators.

What is especially confusing in justice terms in the current administrative justice system's landscape is that rights deciders assigned to decide disputes about non-justiciable rights issues – regulatory agencies and their regulators, in my taxonomy – have traditionally worn the mantle of "adjudicative" institutions. The processes through which they inform themselves about the issues on which they are called upon to make their management decisions have been typically given the structure and trappings of a justice-system adjudicative process. Thus, in considering whether or not to grant an application for a gas-marketing licence, an energy board is usually required by statute to hold a "hearing" – a hearing that will have most of the hallmarks of an adjudicative proceeding. Indeed, Fuller specifically noted that it was in the field of administrative law that the solution of polycentric problems by adjudication has most often been attempted: "The instinct for giving the affected citizen his 'day in court' pulls powerfully toward casting exercises of government power in the mold of adjudication, however inappropriate the mold may turn out to be."[83]

A particularly arresting example of the Supreme Court's penchant for confusing administrative functions with judicial functions is the Court's 1992 judgment in *Newfoundland Telephone Co. v. Newfoundland (Board of Commissioners of Public Utilities)*,[84] in which the Court characterizes as "adjudication" a hearing-based exercise of what is clearly a regulatory function by Newfoundland's Board of Commissioners of Public Utilities. To that function the Court applied principles of impartiality pertinent to the exercise of a judicial function.

The issues before the Board were whether recent increases in the salaries and pensions of the Newfoundland Telephone Company's senior executives should be allowed as costs that could be appropriately included in the cost structure on which the company was entitled to rely in justifying rate increases. These were not, by any stretch, justiciable issues. The question for the Board could not rationally or fairly be what "the law" intended. The Board was tasked with deciding what was advisable in its own interests and in the interests of Newfoundlanders, and it allowed the salary increases but disallowed the pension increases. Both decisions were self-evidently policy-driven decisions. The Supreme Court, however, set aside the decisions on the basis that an informed person would have a reasonable apprehension that one of the Board members who participated in the "hearing" was biased.[85]

A truly classic example of the failure of our courts to maintain a clear distinction between administrative and judicial rights-determining functions is the Supreme Court's well-known decision in *Committee for Justice and Liberty et al. v. National Energy Board et al.*[86] The issue was whether Marshall Crowe, chair of the National Energy Board, should be disqualified from sitting as chair of an Energy Board panel assigned to decide which of two applicants should be authorized to build a Mackenzie Valley pipeline.

Prior to his appointment as chair of the Energy Board, Crowe had been part of a previous study of the feasibility of a northern pipeline bringing natural gas to southern markets, and one of the parties to the Board's current hearing had questioned whether Crowe's participation would be seen to be appropriate, given the possibility of a perceived bias arising from his involvement in the previous study. The Board referred the question to the Federal Court of Appeal, which held that Crowe was not disqualified. The Supreme Court, however, in a majority judgment written by Chief Justice Bora Laskin, allowed an appeal on the basis that there were reasonable grounds for apprehending a bias.

In considering the two pipeline applications, the Energy Board had convened a hearing that had all the trappings of an adjudicative hearing, but of course the Board was not engaged in the exercise of a judicial function: which applicant's pipeline proposal should be approved could not be a question of what the law intended. The Board was a regulatory agency, not a judicial tribunal, and the issues before it were quintessentially polycentric, requiring, as Fuller says, an intuitive exercise of managerial discretion. Nevertheless, a majority of the Supreme Court characterized the Board as an "adjudicative agency" and applied a definition of bias that had been developed in jurisprudence dealing with the exercise of judicial functions. Chief Justice Laskin said this:

This Court in fixing on the test of reasonable apprehension of bias [in earlier cases] ... was merely restating what Rand J. said in Szilard v. Szasz at
pp. 6-7 in speaking of the "probability or reasoned suspicion of biased
appraisal and judgment, unintended though it be." This test is grounded
in a firm concern that there be no lack of public confidence in the impartiality of *adjudicative agencies,* and I think that emphasis is lent to this concern
in the present case by the fact that the National Energy Board is enjoined to
have regard for the public interest.[87]

With all due respect, it is obvious that Chief Justice Laskin misconceived the
Energy Board's role, and in his dissenting judgment, Justice Louis-Philippe
de Grandpré, with Justices Martland and Judson concurring, made that mis-
conception clear when he described the Board's hearing process in the following terms:

The Board is not a Court *nor is it a quasi-judicial body.* In hearing the objections of interested parties and in performing its statutory functions, the
Board has the duty to establish a balance between the administration of
policies they are duty bound to apply and the protection of the various
interests spelled out in s. 44 of the Act. The decision to be made by the
Board *transcends the interest of the parties and involves the public interest
at large.* In reaching its decision, the Board draws upon its experience, *upon
the experience of its own experts, upon the experience of all agencies of the
Government of Canada and, obviously, is not and cannot be limited to
deciding the matter on the sole basis of the representations made before it.* It
is not possible to apply to such a body the rules of bias governing the conduct of a court of law.[88]

There can be no better description than this of the role a regulatory agency
plays when it holds a hearing structured as an adjudicative hearing.

I do not say that the concept of bias has no purchase of any kind in the
hearings and deliberations of regulatory agencies, but I believe the concept
requires a different standard, perhaps the standard traditionally applied to
elected boards – that is, that members not be seen to sit in the hearing with
a closed mind.

Go back for a moment to my earlier hypothetical energy board example
and consider the nature of that board's rights-determining function when it
subsequently appears that the company to which it issued a gas-marketing
licence may have engaged in misconduct and the board must exercise its

statutory authority to decide whether it should revoke the licence. The first thing to note is that, in making such a decision, the board could not claim to be impartial. The board's responsibility for the energy sector requires it to defend its own institutional interests. Its position in this situation would be akin to that of a general contractor deciding whether a paving subcontractor should be removed from the job for failing to perform in accordance with its contract, or that of an employer deciding whether or not an employee should be fired for cause. Just as no one would suggest that the general contractor or the employer could be, or could appear to be, impartial, so no reasonable person would think that, in deciding whether or not to revoke a gas-marketing licence, an energy board could be, or could be seen to be, impartial.

If my general argument is otherwise sound, this means one of two things: either the treat-like-cases-alike principle is not invoked in the litigation of an alleged breach of a gas-marketing licence condition or it is bad justice policy to have an energy board dealing with that issue.

I do not claim any first-hand energy board expertise, but one can readily imagine a number of factors that an energy board would have to identify, consider, and balance in deciding an issue such as this. There is, on the one hand, the disruption that would surely follow the revocation of the licence. Affected consumers would have to make another contract with another licence holder and the board would have to make arrangements to ensure that there would be no disruption in the supply of gas. The revocation may reflect badly on the board since it selected the licence holder in the first place, and it may undermine the confidence of other licence holders in the security of their own licences and thus impact on the board's working relationship with those licensees and conceivably on the economics of the industry. The decision to revoke may prove publicly embarrassing to the board and by extension to the government, potentially shaking the government's confidence in the board and impacting negatively on the board's relationship with the government on which it depends for so much. The board would also have to anticipate that its decision might provoke litigation, with the management distractions, legal costs, and risks of liability that litigation inevitably entails.

On the other hand, a decision not to revoke may put the licence holder's customers at risk, may set an undesirable precedent for other licensees, may only postpone the matter to another and potentially worse day, and may undermine the board's reputation in the eyes of the other people with whom it deals.

Against these considerations, the board would have to weigh the seriousness of the offence itself, and that would involve an assessment of the available evidence. How reliable is the evidence? Does the evidence establish with certainty – with a certainty that is "sufficient" from the board's perspective – that the conduct constituting the breach of the condition in fact occurred?

Obviously, one is very much inclined to see this as an exercise of managerial discretion by the regulator, where the legislature may be seen to have intended the board to decide what *the board* thinks would be advisable in its own interest, not what the law would have intended based on these facts. Surely this is an administrative rather than judicial decision – a management decision made by a system manager who no one could say was, or should be, disinterested.

There is a problem lurking in this analysis, however. It overlooks the point that the board's decision will depend on findings of fact concerning what the licence holder has done or failed to do that might warrant revoking the licence. In determining those facts (assuming they are in dispute), the board *is* arguably exercising what is classically a judicial function. In making those findings of fact, the board will have to determine what evidence the law considers reliable and admissible, assess the evidence impartially and fairly, and apply the law's rules of natural justice, including the standard-of-proof and burden-of-proof doctrines.

I will be dealing with the general problem of the exercise of judicial functions by regulatory agencies at greater length shortly, but in the meantime you might begin to contemplate the possibility of separating the fact-finding elements in the decision making of regulatory agencies from the other elements and transferring the former to a judicial tribunal.

Regulators are birds of quite a different feather from adjudicators, but as the Supreme Court's decisions in *National Energy Board* and *Newfoundland Telephone* show, they have long flown largely unremarked in the "adjudicator" flock of rights deciders. As a result, they have been a confounding influence on our understanding of the structural norms applicable to our adjudicators. When tribunal designers, commentators, and the courts consider regulatory agencies to be as integral to our "administrative justice system" as judicial tribunals, they must also see the system's structural norms as necessarily including the justice-adverse structures appropriate for regulators. Any attempt to define a coherent Canadian theory of administrative justice will require paying careful attention to that confounding influence.

Another confounding circumstance is that the distinction between justiciable rights issues and non-justiciable rights issues is not always clear. Usually it will be perfectly clear, but at the margins it will be arguable, and this argument will always be complicated by the fact that in the course of over a hundred years of *ad hoc* operational design of Canada's innumerable non-court rights deciders, the designers have rarely acknowledged the existence of this distinction. As a result, a tribunal's structures and processes are not always appropriately matched to its function, and the core character of a particular tribunal cannot be reliably defined or discerned by the nature of those structures or processes.

So much for the distinction between rights-determining functions that are judicial and those that are administrative; we might hereafter disagree as to the appropriate categorization of a particular rights-determining function, but we should now at least be speaking the same language.

Corporate Judicial Functions

The exercise of judicial functions in the administrative justice system is complicated by the fact that the functions are usually corporate functions – that is, the judicial functions have been assigned to a corporate entity, a tribunal. For reasons that will become clearer in Chapter 3, where I deal in detail with the nature and role of administrative judicial tribunals, judicial tribunals are, in effect, corporate judges, with their members – the individuals who do the actual adjudicating – being the tribunal's agents responsible to the corporate entity for doing its work. This is not something that one would say about judges. When judges hear and decide cases, they are not thought of as the court's agents; when judges sit to hear a case they *are* the court – they are themselves the embodiment of the court. The administrative entity that is in other respects known as "the Court" – for instance, the Ontario Superior Court – has no corporate interest or role in how a judge of that court hears a particular case or in what he or she decides, beyond perhaps how long it takes. Only the Court of Appeal has such an interest. This cannot be said of a judicial tribunal.

This is a perspective on the nature of administrative judicial tribunals and of the role of their members that I expect will be somewhat controversial. Certainly it is not a conventional view. I will not pause to argue it here, however, leaving that for Chapter 3. I raise it here, on my way to formulating a comprehensive prescription for administrative justice, because of the problem for such a prescription when a tribunal's corporate activity includes the exercise of both administrative and judicial rights-determining functions.

As we have seen in the analysis of the hypothetical energy board engaged in determining whether or not to revoke a gas-marketing licence, mixed functions are not uncommon, and the perception that the rights-determining functions assigned to a particular tribunal may not always be entirely one thing or another has led to the courts' practice of categorizing tribunals on the basis only of their "primary" function or purpose. Thus, in *Ocean Port*, the Supreme Court identified the "primary function" of the BC Liquor Appeal Board as policy making,[89] whereas in *Bell Canada* it identified the "primary purpose" of tribunals like the Canadian Human Rights Tribunal as one of "[adjudicating] disputes through some form of hearing."[90] This is not a wholly satisfactory basis for categorizing tribunals, as it leaves in limbo any rights-determining function of the tribunal that is not part of its primary function or purpose.

I do think, however, that the problem is usually more apparent than real. Most tribunals that the courts would identify as having adjudication as their primary function will be found, in fact, to have adjudication as their only rights-determining function. Ontario's Workplace Safety and Insurance Appeals Tribunal, its Social Benefits Tribunal, and the Canadian Human Rights Tribunal are all clear examples of this form of judicial tribunal.[91]

There is a problem, however, where a tribunal has both a regulatory function and a judicial function. It is the problem identified in the 2004 Fairness Committee report concerning the adjudicative functions of the Ontario Securities Commission.[92] The Commission – the corporate entity – is perceived to be biased in its exercise of its judicial functions by reason of its regulatory responsibilities. And this is a problem even if it is the regulatory function that is the adjunct function. If a judicial tribunal's corporate responsibility includes the exercise of an adjunct regulatory function, the latter function may well be perceived to bias the tribunal in the performance of its principal judicial role.

As suggested earlier, the solution may be to transfer either the adjunct regulatory function or the adjunct judicial function to another institutional setting. As we have seen, this is the solution that was proposed by Professor Paul Weiler in his study of the Ontario workers' compensation system that led to the creation of the independent WCAT,[93] and it is the solution strongly recommended in the Fairness Committee report with respect to the adjudicative functions of the Ontario Securities Commission. It is a solution that will no doubt be thought by most to be too drastic an intervention, too dramatic an interruption of the long-established structures of Canada's regulatory regimes. But, given the political will – or the arrival of a newly recognized constitutional necessity – it could be implemented without undue disruption of the regulatory world. The reform proposal in Chapter 5 includes a solution for this particular problem.

Quasi-Judicialism – The Cuckoo Chick in the Administrative Justice Nest

I turn now to what, in my view, is a doctrinal error in the development of Canada's law of administrative justice – the emergence of what might now be called the "doctrine of quasi-judicialism."

In the avian world, many cuckoo species are known to lay one egg in other birds' nests; when the extra-large cuckoo chick hatches, it shoulders the host mother bird's own chicks out of the nest, taking their place. In Canada, the developing doctrine of quasi-judicialism is the administrative justice system's equivalent of a cuckoo chick. In its modern form, the doctrine appears to be shouldering aside the very idea that tribunal rights-determining functions can be judicial – not quasi-judicial – functions. It is a doctrine that is obscuring the constitutionally protected role of judicial tribunals as part of the judicial branch of government. The problem is arcane and the analysis, I regret to say, is inescapably technical.

The distinction between judicial and administrative rights-determining functions, while fundamental, turns out not to have been sufficient. A subcategory was needed. The courts ultimately found it necessary to distinguish between tribunals exercising administrative rights-determining functions that were purely administrative and those exercising functions that, although administrative and not judicial, were "akin" to judicial functions. The latter came to be characterized by the courts as "quasi-judicial" administrative functions.

The courts' use of the label "quasi-judicial" changed dramatically in 1979 with the Supreme Court's seminal decision in *Nicholson v. Haldimand Norfolk (Regional) Police Commissioners*,[94] and I will deal with this change and what followed from it shortly. The law regarding the nature of quasi-judicial decision making that held sway prior to *Nicholson* continues to be of critical relevance, however, and I will deal with that first.

Originally, the courts' judicial review jurisdiction was seen to exclude the review of rights decisions of an administrative nature. However, the role of government broadened and the courts began to be confronted with requests for review of administrative decisions that, despite being policy-driven and by no means judicial in nature, had nevertheless impacted very seriously on the property or other rights of individuals or businesses. A

classic example may be seen in the 1954 decision of the Ontario Supreme
Court in *Re Knapman and the Board of Health for the Township of Saltfleet*
– a judgment of Justice Gale that was affirmed by the Supreme Court of
Canada in 1956.[95]

In *Saltfleet*, the township Board of Health had issued an order closing a
number of rental cottages housing itinerant farm workers after deciding
that the cottages were unfit for human habitation. The Board acted in response to a report by the township's medical officer of health. The owner of
the cottages and several of the occupants had learned that the Board had
convened a meeting to consider closing the cottages, and went to the meeting. They were not permitted to participate, however, and had no opportunity to respond to the medical officer's report. The effect of the order was
a substantial interference in the owner's use of his property, and the owner
applied for judicial review, asking the court to quash the decision because,
in effect, it had not been made fairly.

Justice Gale's understanding was that the Saltfleet Board of Health was
not exercising a judicial function – it was not deciding a dispute *inter partes;*
the Board itself, not any party, had initiated the proceedings; and the Board's
decision making was in the Court's view policy-driven. The Board's function
was seen to be administrative. To quote Justice Dickson in *Ontario RTA
Reference,*[96] the Board was seen, in effect, to be addressing a question of
"policy involving competing views of the collective good of the community
as a whole." It is also important to note that the Board of Health in *Saltfleet*
could not be seen to be unbiased: it was duty bound to "defend" its own interest, namely, the health of the residents of the Township of Saltfleet. Justice
Gale framed the issue in this way:

> The first question to be determined is whether this local board is the type of
> tribunal or body whose actions are liable to supervision by means of cer-
> tiorari proceedings [*i.e.,* by the courts]. It has been well established [citing
> here a 1924 decision of the English Court of King's Bench] that before an
> application of this kind can succeed, the inferior "Court" against which the
> order is sought must have authority to decide issues affecting the rights of
> others and must also be under a duty *to act* judicially. It is plain, of course,
> that this local board possesses the capacity to render decisions which ser-
> iously affect the rights of members of the public. That much cannot be dis-
> puted; indeed, the closing of the cottages in this case amounted to a great
> interference with their use. What is more difficult to determine, however, is

whether the board was under a duty to *act judicially* in disturbing those rights. *Unless it was, then the court is powerless because its process cannot be invoked to invalidate administrative, executive or legislative functions ...*

... [N]otwithstanding that its function may be largely administrative, I am satisfied that this board had imposed upon it the obligation of *acting in a judicial manner* when deciding whether to order these buildings to be closed ...

Even without those requirements for such an issue, it is obvious that this local board had cast upon it the moral responsibility of *conducting itself in a judicial manner.* It had to decide whether it was "satisfied" after "due examination" that certain conditions existed and surely it was never intended by those who enacted the statutes that in coming to a mental conviction as to the propriety of an order the members of the board such as this were to have conferred upon them the right to act capriciously or upon considerations merely of expediency, and yet that would be the result if it were held that they were not endowed with *quasi-judicial functions* [and thus amenable to judicial review] ..."[97]

With the *Saltfleet* facts in mind, the description of the quasi-judicial function that one finds in the following passages from the *McRuer Report* makes clear the law's original understanding of the rights-determining function that had come to be labelled "quasi-judicial." (The *McRuer Report* has been criticized for what is seen by many to have been excessive respect for Professor Dicey's views on tribunals, but the reliability of its understanding of administrative law as it existed in 1968 has never been questioned.) The report identified three categories of tribunal functions existing in Ontario jurisprudence at the time: judicial, purely administrative, and quasi-judicial administrative:

We adopt the expression "tribunal" as embracing corporations, groups of persons or single persons *exercising either administrative or judicial powers ...*

It is, however, *necessary ... to distinguish between tribunals exercising "administrative" and "judicial" powers.* If the power conferred on a tribunal is *administrative* we will refer to it as an "administrative tribunal." If the power so conferred is *judicial* the tribunal will be referred to as a "judicial tribunal" ...

The terminology in this branch of the law of Ontario is further complicated by a subdivision of administrative powers. In legal parlance it is said in some cases *administrative powers* must be exercised by "acting judicially." That is, the decision, although *administrative because it is arrived at on grounds of policy, is to be made after compliance with certain minimum standards of fair procedures, somewhat resembling judicial procedure.* For example, the tribunal exercising the power may be required to hold a hearing not unlike a trial before it reaches its decision. *In these cases, the administrative power is termed "quasi-judicial."* In other cases no obligation to act judicially – no requirements to follow any minimum standards of fair procedures – is imposed ... In such cases the power is termed *"purely administrative."* Although the use of this terminology raises other problems in addition to the initial difficulty of distinguishing between administrative and judicial powers, the classification of "quasi-judicial" and "purely administrative powers" is recognized in current usage ...[98]

Thus, originally, a "quasi-judicial" function was a policy-driven, *administrative* rights-determining function whose exercise impacted on rights to such a degree that considerations of fairness required it to be exercised in a *somewhat* judicial manner.

(Before leaving the *Saltfleet* case, it should be noted that Justice Gale never considered whether the function being exercised by the regulatory board might better have been seen as a judicial function. A more careful analysis might have identified the decision to close buildings used as residences, and thus to evict the residents from their homes, on the grounds that the buildings were unfit for habitation, to be the exercise of a judicial function – the deciding of an issue that invoked the like-cases principle and required a determination of what *the law* intended, rather than what the Board of Health considered advisable. If such had been the conclusion, it would have been seen that this was a function that ought not to have been assigned to the Board, given its own institutional interests and responsibilities. In those circumstances, the Board's proper role as a regulator would have been to identify what it saw to be a health problem of sufficient importance to warrant bringing an application for an order closing the buildings to an independent tribunal or to a court, where an independent and disinterested judicial decision could be made as to whether the evidence proved that the home was, *in the law's eyes*, "unfit for habitation.")

The recognition that a particular decision-making *process* might have to be a "quasi-judicial" process led to the labelling of the administrative rights-determining functions to which this requirement applied as "quasi-judicial" functions, and to the labelling of decisions made in the exercise of those functions as "quasi-judicial" decisions. But – and this ultimately becomes one of the sources of confusion – the "somewhat judicial" process that was to be followed by a quasi-judicial decision maker came to be referred to as a "judicial *or* quasi-judicial" process. This usage reflected the understanding that the content of the fairness requirement for particular quasi-judicial decision making ranged from process that was equivalent to a court process (*i.e.,* one that required the protection of the full panoply of the rules of natural justice) to process that was only mildly judicial in nature.

The content of the fair process required of a tribunal exercising a quasi-judicial administrative rights-determining function depended on the nature of the tribunal, the nature and seriousness of the potential impact of the decision, the circumstances in which the decision was to be made, and so on. Typically, however, there would be at least a requirement that parties likely to be affected by the decision be given reasonable notice that a decision was contemplated as well as of the issues, and that there be some kind of a "hearing" in which the parties would have a reasonable opportunity to respond to the issues. This hearing was not typically the full-blown, court-style hearing; it might not have to be held in public, and in some circumstances a mere exchange of correspondence sufficed.

Let me illustrate the original quasi-judicial concept by looking at it in the context provided by a hypothetical example.

Assume that in the earlier example of the hypothetical energy board's exercise of statutory administrative rights-determining functions the board ends up revoking the licensee's gas-marketing licence. Obviously, this decision would eliminate the licensee's right to market gas in that market, possibly terminate its gas-marketing business, probably threaten it with bankruptcy, negatively impact its business reputation, imperil its shareholders' investment, and result in the layoff of its employees. This is the kind of statutory rights-determining function that is obviously an administrative function but one that in the pre-*Nicholson* days would have been seen to fall within the quasi-judicial category, requiring a fair, court-supervised process of a "judicial or quasi-judicial" nature.

It is important to emphasize that, prior to *Nicholson,* the law concerning what was required of a tribunal identified as exercising a quasi-judicial administrative function focused principally on the *process* of decision making. Like the energy board in the foregoing example, tribunals exercising quasi-judicial rights-determining functions were administrative bodies and, although they might be independent, by definition they could not be disinterested; at stake in their decisions were always their own policy interests or those of their principal – for example, the portfolio minister to whom they typically reported. So the process had to be fair but the concept of fairness varied in the manner described above, and it had to accommodate the fact that the decisions were policy-driven and, as in the case of my energy board example or the Saltfleet Board of Health, the deciders were, by definition, not disinterested.

A clear recognition and acceptance of the foregoing distinction between judicial and quasi-judicial functions of tribunals as it existed in the law three years before *Nicholson* can be seen conveniently expressed in Justice Louis-Philippe Pigeon's majority judgment in the Supreme Court's 1976 decision in *Howarth v. Canada (National Parole Board).*[99] This judgment dealt with the newly enacted s. 28 of the *Federal Courts Act,*[100] which had given the Federal Court of Appeal jurisdiction to review certain decisions of federal boards, commissions, or other tribunals. At issue was whether s. 28 authorized the Court of Appeal to review a National Parole Board decision revoking a parole. Justice Pigeon interpreted s. 28 as distinguishing between (1) "*judicial* decisions" [by federal tribunals] and (2) "*administrative orders* [by federal tribunals] that are required by law to be made on a judicial or quasi-judicial *basis.*"[101]

At the time, s. 28 of the *Federal Courts Act* read as follows:

28. (1) Notwithstanding section 18 or the provisions of any other Act, the Court of Appeal has jurisdiction to hear and determine an application to review and set aside a decision or order, *other than a decision or order of an administrative nature not required by law to be made on a judicial or quasi-judicial basis,* made by or in the course of proceedings before a federal board, commission or other tribunal ...[102]

Justice Pigeon wrote:

[T]he new remedy created by s. 28 is restricted in its application to *judicial decisions* or *to administrative orders required by law to be made on a judicial or quasi-judicial basis* ... thus the clear effect of ss. 18 and 28 is that a distinction is made between two classes of orders of federal boards. Those that for brevity I will call judicial or quasi-judicial are subject to s. 28 ... The other class of decisions comprises those of an administrative nature not required by law to be made on a judicial or quasi-judicial basis ...[103]

But s. 28 was to be the graveyard of clear thinking on the distinction between tribunal judicial functions, on the one hand, and tribunal administrative functions that had to be exercised in a judicial or quasi-judicial
manner, on the other. Already, in *Howarth*, in the dissenting opinion of
Chief Justice Laskin and Justices Spence and Dickson (written by Dickson),
one finds this:

> The word "judicial" may refer to those *duties* which are discharged in public
> *by a judge* following formal legal procedures in resolving a lis inter partes or
> it may refer to administrative *duties* which need not be discharged in public
> and to the discharge of which a large measure of policy and expediency may
> properly be applied but in respect of which certain elemental norms of jus-
> tice and fair play must be brought to bear, minimally the right to know and
> to respond before suffering serious loss."[104]

Note that in this instance Justice Dickson is calling *administrative* duties "judicial" because "norms of justice and fair play must be brought to bear" on the
decision-making process. Under the law relating to the distinction between
judicial functions and quasi-judicial functions as it stood before this dissent
in *Howarth*, the "duties" Justice Dickson describes as being both "administrative" and "judicial" would have been classified beyond doubt as both "administrative" and "quasi-judicial." Here – I believe for the first time in the Supreme
Court's jurisprudence – are three leading members of the Court, including
Chief Justice Laskin, effectively ruling out the idea of tribunal functions being *ever* anything but administrative functions. Here, in this dissent, is where
the unravelling of the Court's recognition that some tribunals exercise purely judicial functions may be said to have begun in earnest.

Three years later, in 1979, this unravelling engulfed the rest of the Court.
In *Minister of National Revenue v. Coopers and Lybrand,*[105] another s. 28
case, we find Justice Dickson, this time speaking for the whole Court, saying
flatly that "judicial decisions [are] those made by the courts, and administrative decisions [are] those made by other than courts," and that "government
ministries and agencies carry out a different form of work than that done by
the courts ... Their primary concern is with policy objectives, rather than
adjudication inter partes."[106] This is a description of "government agencies"
that ignores the existence of tribunals such as the workers' compensation
appeals tribunals, the landlord and tenant boards, the social benefit tribunals, the human rights tribunals, and so on, whose primary concern *is* with
adjudication *inter partes*.

The *Coopers and Lybrand* Court goes on to make it perfectly clear that it is refusing – or at least failing – to acknowledge that some tribunals exercise judicial, not administrative, functions:

> *Administrative* decision does not lend itself to rigid classification of func-
> tion. Instead, one finds realistically a continuum. As paradigms, at one end
> of the spectrum are *rent tribunals, labour boards and the like,* the decisions
> of which are eligible for judicial review. At the other end are such matters as
> the appointment of the head of a Crown corporation, or the decision to pur-
> chase a battleship, determinations inappropriate to judicial intervention.[107]

Here we have the Court conceiving of all tribunals being located on a spectrum of functions that are all administrative, and ignoring or not accepting the fact that some tribunals – particularly the "rent tribunals, labour boards and the like" cited by Justice Dickson as examples of tribunals exercising administrative functions – in fact exercise judicial functions, not adminis-trative functions. This was the unravelled state of the law's understanding of tribunal judicial functions when *Nicholson* fell to be decided.

Coopers and Lybrand was argued in June 1978 before *Nicholson,* but re-leased after *Nicholson. Coopers and Lybrand* makes no reference to *Nicholson* and *Nicholson* makes no reference to *Coopers and Lybrand,* but both em-brace the same novel view that tribunal functions cannot qualify as non-administrative, purely judicial functions – the view first suggested in Justice Dickson's dissent in *Howarth.* Since Justice Dickson wrote both the dissent in *Howarth* and the Court's judgment in *Coopers and Lybrand* and joined Chief Justice Laskin in the majority judgment in *Nicholson,* perhaps we should not be surprised.

Dickson, who succeeded Laskin as Chief Justice, is a revered figure in Canadian legal history. I venture to think, however, that these three deci-sions, in which the previously established understanding that some tribunal functions are in fact judicial functions was effectively aborted, do not mark his finest hour in the jurisprudence of administrative law.

The ban against judicial review of administrative decision making that had spawned the Canadian jurisprudence that permitted such review as long as the decision making qualified as quasi-judicial had for a number of years been unique to Canadian law. In *Nicholson,* in 1979, the Supreme Court, having had enough of dealing with the artificial distinctions between administrative decision making that was purely administrative and adminis-trative decision making that was quasi-judicial, put an end to the exercise. It overruled the ban on judicial review of administrative decision making and adopted the modern English view that the process leading to *any* administrative rights-determining decision had to conform to the principles of procedural fairness, with any such decision open to review by the courts if it was claimed that the decision-making process had failed to comply with those principles. Thus, at this point, the technical need for the "quasi-judicial" concept as the common law's stratagem for opening the door to judicial review of non-judicial administrative decisions disappeared.

Although the courts' strategic need to distinguish between pure and quasi-judicial administrative rights-determining functions evaporated with *Nicholson,* the law continued – and continues – to have important substantive reasons for distinguishing between tribunal administrative functions and tribunal judicial functions. These reasons are, I argue, principally the need to distinguish between rights-determining functions that, subject to statutory override, must be exercised in conformity at some variable level with the principles of procedural fairness but do not require – or typically have – disinterested deciders, and those that, if the integrity of our justice system is to be sustained, must be exercised in conformity with the core rules of natural justice by impartial deciders, with both the process and the impartial status of the deciders protected from statutory override by the constitutional requirement of judicial independence and impartiality.

Nevertheless, in the process of ridding the Canadian common law of the courts' dependence for their judicial review jurisdiction on the artificial distinction between purely administrative functions and quasi-judicial administrative functions, the *Nicholson* court and the jurisprudence that followed seem also to have intended to eliminate the distinction between tribunal *administrative* functions and tribunal *judicial* functions, the distinction whose validity had first been thrown into doubt three years earlier in *Howarth.* The following is one of the oft-quoted passages from Chief Justice Laskin's majority judgment in *Nicholson:*

> What rightly lies behind this emergence [of a general notion of fairness] is the realization that *the classification of statutory functions as judicial, quasi-judicial or administrative is often very difficult,* to say the least; and to endow some with procedural protection while denying others any at all would work injustice when the results of statutory decisions raise the same serious consequences for those adversely affected, regardless of the classification of the function in question: see, generally, Mullan, Fairness: The New Natural Justice (1975), 25 Univ. of Tor. L.J. 281.[108]

See also the conclusion by Justice Claire L'Heureux-Dubé, speaking for the majority of the Supreme Court in 1990, in *Knight v. Indian Head School Division No. 19*, that "[t]here is no longer a need, except perhaps where the statute mandates it, to distinguish between judicial, quasi-judicial and administrative decisions."[109]

If we lived in an ideal administrative law world, after *Nicholson* the concept of a "quasi-judicial" rights-determining administrative function – no longer needed to provide legitimizing cover for judicial review of administrative rights-determining functions – would have been decorously retired to the status of a historical footnote and we would have heard nothing more about it. But, no, in the aftermath of *Nicholson*, the "quasi-judicial" label, freed from its traditional common law moorings, was still to be found floating in unamended pre-*Nicholson* legislation, and the courts were called upon to continue to assign some meaning to it.[110] This dissonance led eventually to the label's metamorphosis into a label of convenience for any quasi-judicial *or* judicial function exercised by non-court tribunals and to its current status as a historically anomalous and constitutionally flawed label for any tribunal whose main function is *either* judicial or quasi-judicial (in the original sense of the term). Thus, both the Canadian Human Rights Tribunal and the Canadian Nuclear Safety Commission are now referred to as "quasi-judicial" tribunals. The connotation of "quasi-judicial" as a non-judicial *administrative* function requiring a *somewhat* judicial process disappeared, and in the administrative law context "quasi-judicial" became the new "judicial."

That the Supreme Court has in fact merged the judicial and quasi-judicial labels when it comes to the *nature* of tribunals as well as to the requirements concerning their process – now labelling judicial functions exercised by tribunals as "quasi-judicial," perhaps to signify that the function is exercised by a tribunal rather than a court – is confirmed most clearly by its 2003 decision in *Bell Canada*.[111] In *Bell Canada*, the Court was called upon to assess the degree of judicial independence that the law required for the Canadian Human Rights Tribunal. In analyzing this question, the Court was moved to locate administrative tribunals along a spectrum of *administrative* functions running from tribunals exercising functions that were closest to executive branch functions, which the Court suggested might be labelled "quasi-executive tribunals," to tribunals exercising functions closest to the functions of a court, which it labelled "quasi-judicial tribunals."[112]

If one applies the definition of a judicial function in the *Ontario RTA Reference*[113] to the Canadian Human Rights Tribunal's functions described by the Court in *Bell Canada*, it is perfectly clear that the Tribunal is exercising a judicial function. (This has recently been confirmed in practical terms by the Saskatchewan legislature's abolition of the Saskatchewan Human Rights Tribunal and the transfer of its functions to the Saskatchewan Court of Queen's Bench.[114]) And, since the *Bell Canada* Court applies the "quasi-judicial" label to the tribunals at the "highest" end of the executive-judicial spectrum (thus, for instance, including not only human rights tribunals but also implicitly other classic judicial tribunals that in anyone's understanding exercise judicial functions that are no different from the adjudicative functions of provincial courts – tribunals such as workers' compensation appeals tribunals and landlord and tenant tribunals), we must now conclude that as far as the Supreme Court is concerned "quasi-judicial" is, indeed, the new "judicial." The cuckoo chick does appear to have pushed the natural chick out of the nest.

This merging of judicial and quasi-judicial tribunal functions into the single quasi-judicial category is the doctrinal error referred to at the outset of this section – an error fraught with danger for a rational and constitutionally sound law of administrative justice.

As we have seen, the unravelling of the notion of tribunals exercising judicial functions appears to have begun with Dickson's dissent in *Howarth*. But it was *Nicholson* itself that laid the foundation for the transmogrification of the judicial to the quasi-judicial. In his majority judgment in that case, Chief Justice Laskin not only criticized the "artificial" distinction between administrative functions and judicial functions but also quoted with approval a passage from an English decision that had within it the source of the trouble to come: "I accept, therefore, for present purposes and as a common law principle what Megarry J. accepted in Bates v. Lord Hailsham [[1972] 1 W.L.R. 1373.], at p. 1378, 'that in the sphere of the so-called quasi-judicial the rules of natural justice run, and that in the administrative or executive field there is a general duty of fairness.'"[115] In this passage, there is clearly no place for the concept of a tribunal that, while not in the "administrative or executive field," is exercising a *judicial*, not a quasi-judicial, function. Chief Justice Laskin's acceptance of Justice Megarry's view that the "rules of natural justice" – heretofore in Canada applicable only to the exercise of *judicial* functions – apply where the tribunal function is "quasi-judicial" is alien seed that vexes us to this day.

The ground for the reception of that seed had already been prepared, however, through the Canadian courts' persistent failure to distinguish between regulatory agencies exercising administrative functions that may or may not be of a quasi-judicial nature and administrative judicial tribunals exercising judicial functions – a failure that persists even as I write. We had seen this in Chief Justice Laskin's judgment in *National Energy Board* referred to earlier, in Justice Peter Cory's judgment in *Newfoundland Telephone,* and in Justice Dickson's dissent in *Howarth* and his judgment in *Coopers and Lybrand.* More modern evidence of this failure may be found in the Supreme Court's observation in *Paul v. British Columbia (Forest Appeals Commission)* that *"administrative tribunals"* are part of the justice system,[116] and also in the Supreme Court's confirmation in its recent decision in *R. v. Conway*[117] that any tribunal with the authority to decide questions of law has the implicit jurisdiction to decide *Canadian Charter of Rights and Freedoms* issues and to award remedies for *Charter* breaches.

I doubt very much whether the Ontario Energy Board or the Canadian Radio-television and Telecommunications Commission (CRTC) can appropriately or usefully be said to be part of any "justice system," as *Paul* appears to suggest, although workers' compensation appeals tribunals obviously are. And in *Conway*'s comprehensive analysis of the jurisdiction of administrative tribunals to deal with *Charter* matters, it is surprising that no thought appears to have been given to whether the nature of the *Charter* jurisdiction might differ depending on whether the tribunal is a regulatory agency or a judicial tribunal – whether, for instance, the fact that the former will inherently always be engaged in defending its own institutional obligations and interests makes it an ideal arbiter of *Charter* rights for others.

When one considers the provenance of the "quasi-judicial" label as a name for administrative functions that merely resemble judicial functions and for the "somewhat judicial" process that the courts imposed on administrators exercising such functions, it is clear that its current application to tribunals exercising what are in fact judicial functions will eventually cause trouble. The tribunal function of authoritatively determining justiciable rights disputes is not *somewhat* similar to the function of a court, as the label "quasi" naturally suggests: it is *identical* to that function. The *powers* of such tribunals are not as extensive as those of a court, and, like provincial courts, these tribunals have no *inherent* jurisdiction, but within the jurisdiction they have been given their adjudicative function is a judicial function, no different in nature or principle from the adjudicative functions of any provincial civil law court.

The courts' post-*Nicholson* eradication of the administrative law's distinction between tribunal judicial functions and tribunal administrative rights-determining functions creates problems for the theory and law of administrative justice that the courts have not foreseen and have yet to face. Both the common law rules of natural justice and the constitutional requirements of judicial independence (as they will eventually have to be recognized) require that any non-court person or institution exercising a judicial function be impartial – that is, they must be, and must be perceived to be, both independent and disinterested. In the past, however, before *Nicholson*, in dealing with bodies exercising administrative rights-determining functions for which the label "quasi-judicial" was originally coined – such as boards of health, university boards of directors, municipal councils, and regulatory agencies – the courts never addressed the issues of the independence of those bodies and only rarely considered whether they could be perceived to be impartial. In their review of the exercise of quasi-judicial functions, the courts' concern was focused, as we have seen, on the *process* of decision making – on fair notice and opportunities to respond that were comparable to hearings, and so on – not on the qualities of the deciders.

This made perfect sense since, pre-*Nicholson*, tribunals seen to be exercising quasi-judicial rights-determining functions were always administrators of one kind or another who would rarely meet the structural criteria of judicial independence and who, because of their administrative agenda and assigned policy missions, could never be seen to be disinterested. They could be expected to treat people *fairly* – which is what the courts were looking for – but they inevitably had a mandated *bias* and their decisions were policy-driven. What is apparent here is that the Supreme Court is taking its elimination of the need to distinguish between judicial and administrative tribunal functions for the purpose of making the *process* for exercising administrative rights-determining functions reviewable, as also eliminating the need to make such a distinction for other purposes, such as identifying when impartiality is a requirement.

The long-term administrative justice implications of the courts' conflation of quasi-judicial and judicial tribunal functions have so far been flying below the radar. This has been possible because, as far as the *common law* of judicial independence is concerned, the standard of independence has been held since *Valente*[118] to be contextually variable and is tailored by the courts to fit the practical independence requirements of any rights deciders, regardless of whether they are exercising judicial or quasi-judicial functions. For functions that are truly quasi-judicial in the original sense, the common law standard of independence is set lower; for those that are now called quasi-judicial but are in fact judicial, the standard is set higher.

This stratagem works as far as the common law of independence is concerned, but it is constitutionally unsound; other than courts, it is only tribunals exercising judicial functions in the traditional sense of the term that are constitutionally required to be independent.[119] Thus, when the time comes – as it inevitably must come for most tribunals – for the Supreme Court to decide whether a particular tribunal's statutory rights-determining function is protected by the constitutional requirements of judicial independence, the Court will once again have to distinguish between rights-determining functions that are truly judicial and those that are only quasi-judicial. In that kind of exercise, the fact that in *Bell Canada* and elsewhere the Court is now applying the "quasi-judicial" label indiscriminately to both would appear to present a considerable danger of confounding the analysis.

Confusing judicial rights-determining functions with quasi-judicial administrative rights-determining functions is even more serious, however, when it comes to the principle of judicial impartiality. Conceptually, one can have varying degrees of judicial *independence,* but with respect to a rights decider who is exercising a judicial function, there will be either reason for a reasonable apprehension of bias or not, and quasi-judicial rights deciders in the traditional sense can almost never be perceived to be impartial. Even if they have structural guarantees of independence, in exercising their rights-determining function they, like my energy board example and the Saltfleet Board of Health, will inevitably be understood to be appropriately defending their own interests.

Thus, the application of the "quasi-judicial" label indiscriminately both to bodies exercising true judicial rights-determining functions, such as the Canadian Human Rights Tribunal or residential landlord and tenant tribunals, and to bodies exercising the somewhat judicial but administrative rights-determining functions for which that label was originally coined, such as health boards, means either that impartiality will no longer be a requirement for the former or that it will become a new requirement for the latter. Since the rule of law will rule out the first possibility and common sense the second, it is apparent that the courts' application of the quasi-judicial label even to bodies exercising what are in fact judicial rights-determining functions is simply a mistake that will have to be fixed.

In summary, this doctrinal crinkle in the law of administrative justice must eventually be ironed out. The distinction between tribunal, judicial, and administrative rights-determining functions must be re-established. The former must be seen to be governed by a fixed set of rules of natural justice appropriate to the exercise of an authentic judicial function by an administrative tribunal, including the requirement of guaranteed independence and impartiality, and the latter by a variable set of rules of procedural fairness. The content of the latter rules would be tailored to fit the particular circumstances, but would, in any event, not include either independence or impartiality.

The Prescription for a Coherent Theory of Administrative Justice

Based on the foregoing, I believe that a coherent theory of administrative justice depends on acceptance of the following fundamental precepts:

1 The justice system comprises both the judicial – or court – justice system and the administrative justice system.
2 The administrative justice system comprises all non-court rights deciders authorized by statute to exercise *judicial* functions with respect to rights issues arising from the administration of government statutory rights enterprises.
3 Rights deciders must be seen to be exercising *judicial* functions whenever they are mandated to make final decisions and the issues they are deciding are justiciable issues, not administrative issues – that is, whenever the issues are to be determined by the decider judging what it is the *law* intends, thus invoking the treat-like-cases-alike principle and requiring an impartial decider.
4 The fact that a rights decider is mandated to decide an *inter partes* rights dispute, including a dispute between a private party and the government, will constitute *prima facie* evidence that the decider's function is a judicial function.
5 The administrative justice system does *not* encompass deciders exercising *administrative* rights-determining functions, even if those functions are of "quasi-judicial" nature in the original sense.
6 For the administrative justice system to be constitutionally legitimate, rights deciders exercising judicial functions must be seen to belong to the judicial branch of government and be constitutionally required to conform to at least the core structural and process norms that are indispensable to an authentic, rule-of-law-compliant, justice system.
7 The administrative aspect of the administrative justice system justifies significant adjustments of the structural and process norms that have traditionally pertained in the judicial justice system.

8 Such adjustments must not, however, impair the integrity of the core structural and process norms that the rule of law demands of an authentic justice system.

9 The core structural and process norms of an authentic administrative justice system are not variable but fixed. The content of those core norms essential to a rule-of-law-compliant administrative justice system remains to be worked out but must include, most significantly, objective, structural guarantees of independence and impartiality.

10 Although the essential core content of the rules of natural justice applicable to deciders exercising judicial functions is fixed (if not yet fully defined), deciders exercising *administrative* rights-determining functions, including quasi-judicial administrative rights-determining functions, are governed by rules of procedural fairness the content of which is variable.

11 The content of the rules of procedural fairness varies not only in accordance with the criteria specified in *Baker*[120] but also according to a rights-determining function's location on the spectrum of tribunal *functions.* This spectrum must now be seen to run from the administrative rights-determining functions that come closest to being purely executive in nature at one end, to the quasi-judicial administrative rights-determining functions that come *closest to being the judicial functions of a judicial tribunal* at the other end.[121]

The application of these basic precepts of a coherent administrative justice theory will require that courts reviewing decisions of non-court rights deciders in statutory rights enterprises do what the courts do in s. 96 cases: decide first whether the rights-determining function exercised by the decider is or is not a judicial function. If the function is held to be a judicial function, then the objections to the decision, to the decider, or to the process will be judged against the constitutional requirements of judicial independence and impartiality and the rules of natural justice pertinent to the exercise of a judicial function. If the function is found not to be a judicial function, the constitutional requirements will not apply and the objections will be judged against the variable rules of procedural fairness, with the content of those rules selected to fit the operational circumstances and role of the particular decider, as amended by any relevant legislative overrides.

Obviously, in distinguishing between judicial functions and other rights-determining functions, the difficulty will come at the interface between judicial rights-determining functions and quasi-judicial administrative rights-determining functions, where the distinction may be expected to fade to grey. But this is not a difficulty that can justify a strategy of adopting variable rules at that point. A decision will have to be made: is a particular rights decider exercising a judicial function or not? If the decider is exercising a judicial function, then that decider is part of the justice system/judicial branch and subject to the constitutional requirements of judicial independence and to the core rules of natural justice; if not, then not. There cannot be a sliding scale of constitutional justice-system/judicial branch *status* without subverting the integrity of the concept generally.

As we have seen, not all of these foundational precepts can be reconciled with the Supreme Court's current administrative justice jurisprudence. Therefore, if the authentic place of administrative justice in our justice system and our Constitution is to be finally recognized, the courts will have to reconsider.

With the context and terminology now clear, the concepts straight, and the prescription for a coherent theory of administrative justice identified, the development of concrete proposals for transformative reform of the administrative justice system begins to be possible. First, however, we need a better handle on the nature of administrative judicial tribunals and their critical role in our statutory rights enterprises.

3

Administrative Judicial Tribunals
The Inside Story

In this chapter, I turn to the administrative judicial tribunals themselves – to their generic characteristics, what they and their members actually do, the nature and importance of their systemic role in the statutory rights enterprises of which they are an integral part, and the institutional implications of the unique features of their operational environments. It is necessary to devote a considerable number of pages to this because only after this picture is clear will it be possible to fully understand the destructiveness of the executive branch's strategies and tactics for keeping their tribunals in thrall. Those strategies and tactics are not only incompatible with the tribunals' independence and impartiality and problematic for their competence but also destructive of their unique potential for contributing constructively to the work of the statutory enterprises of which they are the judicial arm.

The question of what proportion of the administrative tribunals in this country are judicial tribunals is inevitably a matter of conjecture. The *Trebilcock Report*,[1] for example, leaves the impression that they are a small group of exceptions, referring to them mainly in qualifying notes. The question will always be debatable at some level since, as I have said, at the margins, the categorization between administrative rights-determining functions and judicial functions will always be debatable. Nevertheless, a large proportion of administrative tribunals – indeed, by far a majority – are in fact judicial tribunals.[2]

A contemporary indicator is the current Ontario Ministry of Government Services classification of Ontario's "agencies." Of the approximately eighty-five "regulatory and adjudicative" agencies that the Ministry now classifies, nearly 75 percent are classified as "adjudicative," *not* as "regulatory."[3] For the purposes of its *Adjudicative Tribunals Accountability, Governance and Appointments Act, 2009*, the Ontario government has identified thirty-seven of its agencies as "adjudicative tribunals."[4]

"Major" Tribunals and "Boutique" Tribunals

In examining the nature, role, and significance of administrative judicial tribunals and what they do, it is necessary to distinguish between tribunals with large caseloads and tribunals with small caseloads. I will refer to the latter as "boutique" tribunals and to the former as "major" tribunals. Of the thirty-seven tribunals found in the Ontario government's current list of adjudicative tribunals, eleven may, I think, be fairly characterized as boutique and sixteen as major. I believe the major tribunals to be as follows:[5]

- Assessment Review Board
- Child and Family Services Review Board
- Consent and Capacity Board
- Criminal Injuries Compensation Board
- Dispute Resolution Services (within the Financial Services Commission)
- Grievance Settlement Board
- Health Professions Appeal and Review Board
- Human Rights Tribunal of Ontario
- Landlord and Tenant Board
- Physicians Payment Review Board
- Ontario Labour Relations Board
- Ontario Parole and Earned Release Board
- Ontario Review Board
- Public Service Grievance Board
- Social Benefits Tribunal
- Workplace Safety and Insurance Appeals Tribunal

In this chapter, I will make the case that the context in which administrative judicial tribunals do their work distinguishes them in seminal ways from courts; in this, I will refer principally to the operational context of the major tribunals. The operational context of the boutique tribunals is quite different, and its systemic implications will be examined later.[6]

What Judicial Tribunal Members Do – Exactly

To see plainly the special role and inherent importance of administrative judicial tribunals as surrogate courts in an authentic administrative justice system, one must begin by understanding what it is exactly that members of judicial tribunals, both major and boutique, do.[7] Their adjudicative function is, of course, substantially the same as the adjudicative function of trial-level civil court judges, but in an administrative judicial tribunal's special operational context, the performance of these functions has important institutional implications for both the tribunal (the corporate entity) and the statutory rights enterprise of which the tribunal is the judicial arm – implications that are not found in the work of trial court judges.

In the next few paragraphs, I shall explain what to experienced lawyers and judges will seem simple and obvious, perhaps even trite. But experienced lawyers and judges are prone to compare a judicial tribunal adjudicator's function and responsibilities – and his or her capacity for institutional influence or mischief – with those of a trial court judge, and in many important ways they are not comparable.

All adjudicators – judicial tribunal adjudicators and judges – may be said to do really only two things: make findings of fact and formulate legal opinions.[8]

"Findings" are the decisions on the factual issues. Findings emerge from an adjudicator's judgment about the relevance, credibility, and relative weight of the evidence that has been admitted, heard, and seen; findings are properly the business only of the individual adjudicators who have heard and seen that evidence.

When I say that the only other thing adjudicators do is formulate legal opinions, I am referring to the opinions they formulate in the course of making decisions other than *findings.* An adjudicator's legal opinion becomes a "decision" once the adjudicator decides in a final way that it is the opinion he or she finds most persuasive. At its root, every decision that is not a finding is the adjudicator's considered final opinion about what the law is or what the law requires.

I emphasize the opinion behind the decision to better evoke the intellectual, analytical, and personal content of an adjudicator's decision-making process, content that in the context of a tribunal, and particularly from an institutional perspective, is especially significant.

There are many categories of legal opinions to be formulated in judging a justiciable dispute about rights. The most prominent of these is, of course, the interpretation opinion – the opinion that adjudicators formulate about

how the substantive law applicable to the case (in the case of judicial tribunal adjudicators mainly the statutory provisions) is most convincingly
interpreted.

Perhaps of uncommon interest from a tribunal's perspective is the "issue
agenda" opinion – the opinion about which issues have to be addressed in
order to dispose properly of the case at hand. In tribunal proceedings, issue
agendas are not typically structured, as they are in lawsuits, through formal
pleadings. This is not an often-noted distinction but it is significant. In judicial tribunal cases, an adjudicator must always formulate an opinion about
which issues must be dealt with given the circumstances of the case – what
are the factual issues and what are the legal issues that this case necessarily
and fairly presents? It is true that frequently, perhaps most often, the issue
agenda is implicitly understood and nothing needs to be said about it. The
question is always implicit, however, and in a judicial tribunal context, much
more than in a trial court context, the nature of the proceedings is fundamentally determined by the adjudicator's final opinion, articulated or not, as
to what legal and factual issues have to be decided if the case is to be dealt
with on a fair and appropriate basis.

Then there are the opinions about burdens of proof and standards of
proof. Who has the burden? Does it shift? If so, when? To what standard
must the case, or a particular allegation in the case, be proved?

There are also opinions concerning the admissibility of evidence. To what
extent should admissibility be determined by the usual rules of evidence applicable in court proceedings? And, if not by those rules, then by what rules?
What is the effect of the chosen rules on the admissibility of a particular
piece of tendered evidence? What qualifies as relevant? What does not? (The
answers to these questions depend, of course, on the answers to the issue-
agenda question.)

The opinions formulated in the course of an adjudicative hearing as to
what the principles of natural justice require in response to the various
procedural issues arising in that hearing are of particular importance, and
here too there is often a significant difference between judicial tribunals
and courts. Almost always, the processes and procedures in the proceedings
of a judicial tribunal are not governed by enacted rules of procedure (beyond what may be specified in generic codes of procedure such as Ontario's
Statutory Powers Procedures Act) or by decades of precedent and tradition.
Tribunal hearings can offer opportunities for flexibility and innovation that
are not typically available to judges.[9]

Finally, there are the opinions concerning remedies: what can and should be done in crafting an appropriate and effective remedy, given the result and the circumstances of the case?

This, then, is what the members of an administrative judicial tribunal or the incumbents of administrative judicial offices do: they make findings and, with respect to these various categories of legal issues, they formulate the opinions that become their decisions.

The Unique Operational Environment of Major Judicial Tribunals

Exclusive Mandate, Narrow Field, High Volume

The contextual differences between the operational environment of major administrative judicial tribunals and that of civil courts present tribunals and their members with risks and responsibilities, as well as opportunities, that courts and judges do not share.

A major judicial tribunal's environment has three unique structural characteristics. First, the tribunal has been accorded an exclusive mandate to resolve in a final way all the legal and factual disputes arising in the administration of a particular statutory rights enterprise. This exclusive mandate gives the tribunal a central role in the operation of that enterprise and associates it in the public mind with the enterprise – a role and an association that courts do not have. Second, although often deep, the field of rights for which a judicial tribunal is typically responsible is always narrow: human rights, workers' compensation, labour relations, property assessment, mental competency, landlord and tenant disputes, and so on. Finally, although the field of rights is narrow, the number of disputes arising from it is, for reasons that are structurally innate, typically large, often very large. Ontario's Landlord and Tenant Board, for instance, adjudicates 85,000 cases a year.

These structural features of a major judicial tribunal's operational environment have a unique impact on the nature of the tribunal's institutional role and responsibilities and, most importantly, on the corporate responsibilities of its adjudicator members.

An Innately Hazardous Operational Environment

A major judicial tribunal's operational environment is also more hazardous from a political perspective than is generally true for a court. The statutory rights enterprises for which judicial tribunals are, and are seen to be, the judicial arm are typically the means of government intervention in key, often contentious aspects of a society's life. These interventions will reflect a political policy about which many people will have their own deeply held views, which then influence the way a tribunal's implementation of that policy is regarded. In addition, the individual decisions made in the course of such implementation are inherently controversial. Workers' compensation appeals tribunals, for instance, are engaged in restoring the livelihood of some badly injured people while at the same time denying it to other, equally badly injured people who happen not to have been injured at work; moreover, they restore workers' livelihoods at the expense of employers, who are not always enthusiastic at the prospect.

Other examples abound. One need only consider the activities of the Immigration and Refugee Board of Canada (IRB), welfare tribunals, human rights tribunals, labour relations boards, criminal code review panels, landlord and tenant tribunals, and so on, to be convinced that a pervasive aspect of the operational environments of most major judicial tribunals is a special vulnerability to political controversy. My earlier account of the recent travails of the BC Human Rights Tribunal member stemming from her McDonald's handwashing decision is a case in point (see "Idiosyncratic Removal at the BC Human Rights Tribunal, 2010" in Chapter 1, pages 80-86).

It is important to note that this vulnerability is significantly increased by the fact that all the controversial decisions in these narrow fields of rights will come exclusively from a single high-profile source – the tribunal; moreover, these decisions will come often. On a controversial issue, the courts might release one decision every year or two. On the other hand, because of the volume of its caseload in its narrow field, a major judicial tribunal might release several decisions on the same controversial issue in the course of a year – perhaps even hundreds. Thus, major judicial tribunals are not only especially susceptible to political controversy but also inherently more likely to trigger such controversy.

A Unique Legal Environment

Administrative judicial tribunals also operate in a legal environment that differs significantly from that in which the civil courts operate. In the first place, the doctrine of *stare decisis* does not typically apply. So, unlike judges, judicial tribunal adjudicators are not required, as far as the law is concerned, to follow previous decisions of their tribunal even if the previous decisions cannot be distinguished. This was recognized in the Supreme Court of Canada's 1993 decision in *Domtar Inc. v. Quebec (Commission d'appel en matière de lésions professionnelles),*[10] which held that the fact that two contemporaneous decisions from the same tribunal were in direct conflict with one another did not in itself provide grounds for a court to quash either decision – did not make either of them "unreasonable."[11]

Second, the rules of evidence applicable in court proceedings do not typically bind judicial tribunals. Third, the *functus officio* doctrine does not always apply to judicial tribunals. Most tribunals have been given – in my opinion rightly and wisely – the statutory power to reconsider and change their "final" adjudicative decisions.[12] And it is important to note here that it is typically the *tribunal* that has the power to reconsider, not the member who made the decision in the first instance.

Fourth, judicial tribunal decisions are not subject to appeal in the same way that the decisions of trial court judges are. Of course, the decisions of many tribunals are, in fact, subject to explicit statutory rights of appeal. But when one considers the reason for not assigning the tribunal's judicial function to the courts in the first place, those appeal rights have always been paradoxical. Professor Harry Arthurs's famous observation about the lack of justification for judicial review applies with special weight to *appeals*. "There is no reason to believe," he said in his 1983 Canadian Bar Review article "Protection Against Judicial Review," "that a judge who reads a particular regulatory statute once in his life, perhaps in worst-case circumstances, can read it with greater fidelity to legislative purpose than [a tribunal adjudicator] who is sworn to uphold that purpose, who strives to do so daily, and is well-aware of the effect upon that purpose of the various alternative interpretations."[13]

The paradoxical nature of appeal rights in administrative justice proceedings is being increasingly recognized. In British Columbia's modern administrative justice legislation, such rights have been removed entirely,[14] and the Supreme Court's decisions in *Dr. Q v. College of Physicians and Surgeons of British Columbia*[15] and *Law Society of New Brunswick v. Ryan*[16] have inaugurated a jurisprudence that will effectively convert tribunal appeals to the equivalent of judicial review applications – "appeals" to which the principles of deference will apply in the ordinary course.

The "It Matters" Factor

The final aspect of an administrative judicial tribunal's operational environment that bears particularly on the quality of its responsibilities and those of its members is the brute fact that, as I emphasized in the Introduction, *what tribunals do matters.* The courts themselves have acknowledged this fact. In *Baker v. Canada (Minister of Citizenship and Immigration),*[17] Justice L'Heureux-Dubé cited with approval the following 1994 statement of the English Court of Queen's Bench in *R. v. Higher Education Funding Council, ex parte Institute of Dental Surgery:* "In the modern state the decisions of administrative bodies can have a more immediate and profound impact on people's lives than decisions of courts, and public law has since *Ridge v. Baldwin,* [1963] 2 All E.R. 66, [1964] A.C. 40 been alive to that fact."[18]

Of course, the fact that the decisions of adjudicators *matter* is not unique to judicial tribunals. Obviously, it is equally true of the adjudicative decisions of courts and judges. Nevertheless, I make particular mention of it again in this context because, although it is a truth universally acknowledged for courts, when it comes to tribunals it is a truth that appears to be universally overlooked or ignored.

The Institutional Impact of What Members Do

The institutional impact of the opinions that judicial tribunal members formulate in the course of making their decisions in individual cases is an aspect of the administrative justice system that deserves more attention than it usually gets. And the opinions that come to mind first in this regard are, of course, the interpretation opinions.

The substantive statutory law that judicial tribunals are typically responsible for applying is, like all law, a set of rules that at some level are rules of general application intended to govern particular circumstances. Thus, for example, in a workers' compensation statute there is typically the general rule that workers are entitled to be compensated for injuries "arising out of and in the course of employment." A typical example of circumstances to which this general rule would apply would be a worker claiming compensation for lost earnings due to a broken leg suffered when the worker fell off a loading dock at his or her place of employment.

Now, as with all laws of general application, the general rule that injuries that arise out of and in the course of employment are to be compensated will have what Hart has famously described as a "core of certainty" surrounded by a "penumbra of doubt."[19] For cases that fall within the core of certainty, it is possible to say with certainty that the general rule applies, but for cases that fall within the penumbra of doubt there will, as Hart says, be reasons for both asserting and denying that the general rule applies. Thus, the broken leg case that I have just described clearly falls within the core of certainty of a workers' compensation system's general rule of compensability. If I were to add, however, the fact that the worker fell off the loading dock while being chased by a fellow employee in a bit of horseplay, suddenly we have reasons for both asserting and denying that the general rule applies. Further, if it appears that the accident occurred during an unpaid lunch break, we have yet another reason for questioning whether or not the general rule that injuries arising out of and in the course of *employment* are to be compensated applies.

The significant interpretative opinions formulated by administrative judicial tribunals will, of course, inevitably be about cases that fall within some general rule's penumbra of doubt. While such tribunals do not have discretionary powers to directly impact the nature or operation of their statutory rights enterprises in the sense of having a management or regulator's role, through the accumulation of the large volume of a major judicial tribunal's opinions about the applicability of an enterprise's general rule to cases within the penumbrae of doubt, the daily work of the tribunal does put the operational flesh on the legislative bones of the enterprise's policy, effectively determining the direction and nature of that policy's "maturation" over time.

In the field of workers' compensation, for instance, workers' compensation appeals tribunal decisions in individual cases will eventually determine the answer to generic questions such as whether injuries occurring during the course of unpaid lunch breaks are compensable, under what circumstances injuries caused by "accidents" arising out of horseplay will be seen as "arising out of and in the course of employment," whether or under what circumstances injuries caused by a fight between employees can be seen to have arisen out of and in the course of employment, and so on. At a more general level, those decisions will also determine whether, for an injury to be seen to "*arise out of* employment," the employment must be found to have been the *sole* cause of the injury, or whether it is sufficient that the employment was the dominant cause or enough that it made *a material contribution* to the injury – and so on and so forth.

And so it is with every judicial tribunal: the accumulation of its interpretation opinions will ultimately determine the outer margins and much of the practical content of the policy that the statutory rights enterprise was set up to implement.

This inevitable impact of a major judicial tribunal's daily exercise of its exclusive adjudicative jurisdiction over a large number of cases in a narrow field gives the tribunal a *de facto* policy role that the portfolio ministry, responsible to the legislature for that policy, cannot responsibly ignore. But disregarding the principles of justice is not an acceptable way of policing that role. There are other principled means by which portfolio ministries may assert a reasonable influence over the direction of the tribunal-driven maturation of their policy, and those means will be part of my proposal for reconciling and harmonizing the administrative side of the administrative justice system with its justice side.

What is true for interpretation opinions also holds for the accumulating opinions formulated by a judicial tribunal's members in making the various other kinds of legal decisions required in determining and disposing of the rights disputes within the tribunal's jurisdiction. All such decisions have comparable systemic implications.

Thus, the issue-agenda opinions will determine the nature – the character – and the extent of aspects of the tribunal's role that may not have been made clear in its constitutive statute and for which precedent and tradition may provide no ready answer. For example, where the judicial tribunal is a final "appeal" tribunal, is it the *correctness* of the first decider's decision or the *reasonableness* of that decision that is to be decided? The statute may not say. May – must – the issue agenda for the final decider include issues that were not addressed by the first decider? If there is an obvious issue that the parties have not raised , might that issue – in some circumstances, must that issue – nevertheless be included in the tribunal's issue agenda? Are there some issues that the tribunal must deal with, regardless of the parties' wishes?[20]

The tribunal members' accumulating opinions on burden-of-proof, standard-of-proof, and admissibility issues will also be very important. They will markedly influence the nature, fairness, and efficiency of the tribunal's proceedings and its reputation for fairness. They will ultimately determine the practical accessibility of the tribunal's proceedings. To what degree are the proceedings to be court-like and technical, as opposed to relaxed and informal? Will a party be able to function without a lawyer? The accumulating final opinions in individual cases will provide the answers.

Obviously, too, the accumulating opinions concerning the application of the principles of natural justice to in-hearing procedural and process issues will in due course determine, among other things, the extent to which unsophisticated parties come away from the proceedings confident of having been heard and whether an appropriate balance is typically struck between fairness and efficiency, between fairness and effectiveness.

Finally, the accumulating opinions of judicial tribunal members about remedies will determine the practical effectiveness of the underlying policy in the long run.

In summary, judicial tribunal adjudicators are members of an organization that is responsible for determining in a final way all legal and factual disputes arising in a particular statutory rights enterprise's administration of a narrow field of rights in which the volume of cases is large, the issues inherently contentious, and the reputation of the tribunal implicitly vulnerable. This is the environment in which tribunal adjudicators are asked to formulate legal opinions with respect to the various categories of issues I have mentioned: an environment that frees them from the discipline of the *stare decisis* and, often, the *functus officio* doctrines, and usually also from the rules of evidence, and where judicial review of their decisions is limited to proceedings in which the decisions are shielded by the deference principles from rigorous assessment.

The monopoly over the resolution of all legal or factual issues arising in the statutory rights enterprise's administration has been granted, it must be noted, to the judicial tribunal, the corporate entity. The tribunal is responsible for all the cases, individual members for only a proportion. It follows, therefore, that the special responsibilities classically arising from the grant of a monopoly are, first and foremost, the institutional responsibilities of the tribunal.

What are those special responsibilities? They must include ensuring: (1) that the tribunal's adjudication is not only performed at an optimal level of competence, and in accordance with the principles of fairness and impartiality, but is also perceived to be so performed; (2) that the tribunal's decisions are, if not always consistent, at least congruent; (3) that the tribunal and its procedures are accessible; (4) that the tribunal works as efficiently as possible but in ways that do not disproportionately impact fairness and access; and (5) that in its exclusive role as the judicial arm of its statutory rights enterprise – as the final arbiter of all the rights disputes arising in that enterprise – the tribunal is effective and influential.

The tribunal's systemic effectiveness will depend largely on the reputation the tribunal earns for expertise, competence, fairness, objectivity, efficiency, and effectiveness, not only within its user communities and among advocates representing members of those communities but, equally importantly, within the statutory enterprise itself – with the minister and deputy minister, with the professional managers of the enterprise, and within the ranks of the enterprise's first deciders.

In the long run, the effectiveness of a major administrative judicial tribunal depends in large measure on the institutional reputation that it is able to build and maintain among all of its stakeholders and client constituencies. To take an obvious example: a workers' compensation appeals tribunal that earns a general reputation among workers of having a culture of denial, or among employers as being biased against employer interests, or within its host ministry as being profligate with its resources cannot be effective in meeting its systemic responsibilities or even in standing up for its independence. Thus, there is much more at stake in the daily decisions of individual tribunal adjudicators than the interests of the parties to the disputes, important as those are.

What, then, are the systemic implications for a major administrative judicial tribunal's institutional responsibilities of its having to deal with a large volume of cases arising from a narrow field of politically sensitive rights?

One important negative implication is that there are numerous opportunities, arising very rapidly, for the tribunal to get itself into trouble, for conflicts and lack of congruency to arise among individual decisions on issues of special sensitivity. In such an environment, inconsistent or incongruent decisions will occur much more frequently than in the courts, and their flaws will therefore be more obvious. And when inconsistent or incongruent decisions do arise, it is not only a question of unfairness to an individual party but also of the impact not only on the reputation of the individual adjudicators but also on the *tribunal's* reputation for competent adjudication.

Experience tells us that if a judicial tribunal releases a poor decision on a sensitive issue, or one that cannot be logically reconciled with one released the week before, the most significant reaction from the various audiences for the tribunal's decisions is not that the tribunal member who wrote the decision has issued a poor decision but that the *tribunal* has issued a poor decision – not that the individual adjudicator has shown himself or herself to be incompetent or biased, although that may also be noted, but that the tribunal has produced incompetent or biased work. The tribunal's overall institutional effectiveness will have been negatively impacted by an individual adjudicator's decision.

The narrow field for which the tribunal is responsible also means that a greater proportion of the people judging the tribunal's performance will be specialists and experts themselves. This fact, combined with the large volume of cases and the relatively small size of the professional audience, means that community-wide negative perceptions pertaining to the tribunal's performance will be especially quick to develop.

The decisions to which I have been attributing the potential for trouble will, of course, be largely those based on interpretation opinions, but the high volume of cases arising from a narrow field also imbues the formulation of opinions in the other categories of issues with the potential for harm. The latter formulations are not likely to trigger political controversies on substantive matters, but to the extent that a large volume of individual decisions in similar cases on such matters as issue agendas, burden of proof, standard of proof, admissibility of evidence, fair-hearing questions, and remedies are consistent or congruent with one another, the content around which that consistency or congruency has gelled will effectively define the tribunal's adjudicative nature, and its efficiency, effectiveness, and accessibility. On the other hand, decisions that are inconsistent or incongruent on these issues will quickly lead to confusion over the tribunal's nature, create uncertainty as to its process, undermine confidence in its management, and impair its reputation and general effectiveness.

Contemplation of how Ontario's Medical Review Committee may have lost its users' respect for the fairness of its hearings, as noted in the Cory Report[21] that I referred to in Chapter 1, provides one useful context in which to think about the significance of the foregoing realities.

An administrative judicial tribunal's unique operational environment presents much more than special dangers, however. It also presents important, special opportunities – opportunities that, significantly, courts do not have. Because the tribunal's field of responsibility is narrow, it is within the grasp of the tribunal and its members to master it – to become, both in academic terms and in terms of a practical understanding of its realities, true experts in the subject matter. Moreover, because of the high caseload, this expertise is informed and enriched by a depth and breadth and currency of observation of the application of the statutory provisions in real-life situations that courts and judges can never match.

In his criticism of the courts' role in judicial review,[22] Professor Harry Arthurs referred to the unique "universe of discourse" that tribunal adjudicators inhabit, and to which, as a practical matter, courts and judges have no access. It is a universe that emerges naturally from the adjudicative responsibilities shared among a major judicial tribunal's relatively small corps of members, and from the depth and richness of their cumulative specialized experience in the resolution of a large caseload of disputes arising from their narrow field of specialization. Professor David Mullan, in explaining the justification for the courts' deference to tribunal decisions, has noted that this attitude "recognizes the reality that, in many instances, those working day to day in the implementation of frequently complex administrative schemes have or will develop a considerable degree of expertise or field sensitivity to the imperatives and nuances of the legislative regime."[23]

In addition to the richness and depth of experience that major judicial tribunals can bring to bear on their decisions, they also have a unique capacity for constructively adjusting their decisions on difficult issues in response to their developing experience. Viewed from the perspective provided by one set of facts, an interpretation opinion or an opinion on any of the other categories of standard issues might present itself as eminently persuasive, but shortcomings or deficiencies often appear when that opinion is viewed from the different perspective provided by another set of facts. Since previous tribunal decisions are not binding, and conflicting decisions are acceptable in law, the tribunal itself is readily able to correct its earlier opinions. Accordingly, in response to its growing experience in applying the statute to a range of real-life situations, the quality and sensitivity of its interpretation can mature in a sensible fashion.

Thus, the genius of the common law approach to the development of law finds a uniquely fertile field in a major administrative judicial tribunal, where, because of the narrow focus and large volume of cases, its advantages can be harvested on much shorter time lines than in the courts. It is akin to carrying out evolution-of-species experiments with fruit flies: a tribunal can work its way through generations of evolutionary developments in its opinion jurisprudence over a short time span because the cases come through its doors in large numbers and the life span of an established opinion on any particular issue can be as short or as long as may be warranted by the developing knowledge and tribunal-wide consensus.

Evidently, the special dangers inherent in a major judicial tribunal's assignment as the single judicial arm of a particular statutory rights enterprise and the unique opportunities and advantages presented by those same circumstances, have important implications for the corporate responsibilities of tribunal members. Most importantly, it will be impossible for the tribunal – the corporate entity – to either manage the dangers reasonably or realize the advantages effectively unless its individual adjudicators understand that their judicial function is the tribunal's function – inherently a corporate activity – in which they all have a stake and in which they are all engaged as members of a *team* of adjudicators.

If the tribunal is to be fully realized from an institutional perspective, its corps of adjudicators must be infused with a spirit of collegiality and cooperation; they must be adjudicators who thrive in a team environment and who are comfortable with capable leadership and effective institutional coordination. They must see themselves, and be seen by others, not as individual embodiments of the tribunal, as judges are of courts, but as the tribunal's agents doing the tribunal's business.

Fortunately, the courts have understood and responded to these special needs of judicial tribunals. In *IWA v. Consolidated-Bathurst Packaging Ltd.* and *Tremblay v. Quebec (Commission des affaires sociales)*,[24] the Supreme Court inaugurated a jurisprudence that authorizes and facilitates a co-ordinated team approach to tribunal adjudication. In this jurisprudence, the Court has highlighted the "necessity" of consistency and coherence in a tribunal's decisions – a consistency and coherence that is to be fostered by the tribunal[25] – while acknowledging the need for the common law evolution of those decisions through recognition of the legitimacy of conflicting decisions in the early going on any issue.[26] The Court has also acknowledged the propriety of individual adjudicators' taking these consistency and coherence requirements into account in their decision making, even though they are not bound by the principle of *stare decisis*.[27] The Court has recognized, as well, the appropriateness of members' being open to being influenced in the formulation of their opinions by the opinions of their colleagues in internal, structured institutional processes designed for the explicit purpose of informing and influencing their decision making.[28]

Especially pertinent to the concept that a judicial tribunal's judicial function is a team-based corporate function is the Supreme Court's observation in *Consolidated-Bathurst* that a situation in which the outcome of an appeal or application will depend only on which members of a tribunal happened to be assigned to the case "will be difficult to reconcile with the notion of equality before the law." The phrase "notion of equality before the law" is obviously another way of describing the treat-like-cases-alike principle. The *Consolidated Bathurst* Court considered this "notion" to be one of the "main corollaries of the rule of law, and perhaps also the most intelligible."[29]

With the systemic implications of the unique features of the operational context of a major administrative judicial tribunal thus laid bare, and with such a tribunal's adjudicative function recognized as necessarily an institutional function to be exercised by the tribunal's adjudicative members working as a team, the corporate responsibilities of these members, the institutional impact of their adjudicative activities, and the institutional responsibilities of the tribunal regarding the administration and management of the team all become clear.

One of the foremost implications of the tribunal's dependence on a vibrant team culture for the efficacy of its decision-making is its special vulnerability to members whose selection has been perniciously driven by political or patronage factors. A judicial tribunal's dependence on a viable and effective team culture prevents its adjudicative processes from coping with members who in their decision making are intent on pursuing partisan political or ideological goals. The special problem presented by partisan tribunal members was driven home to me personally by my experience in chairing tripartite adjudicative panels at the Ontario Workers' Compensation Appeals Tribunal. If I had wanted to manipulate the law to achieve the result that was most attractive from my own personal ideological or partisan perspective, then to maintain a viable and civilized dynamic in the panel discussions I would have had to actively mislead either my panel colleague the employer member or my panel colleague the worker member. Judicial tribunal adjudicators can work effectively as a team only if there is shared respect for the intellectual autonomy of one's colleagues, coupled with a shared confidence in the genuineness of each team member's contribution to the tribunal's legal conversations and in the non-partisan integrity of each team member's adjudicative goals. The disarray in the IRB's operations in 1993 when the pro-refugee "engagés" appointed by the Liberals found themselves working with the holdover, allegedly anti-refugee Conservative patronage appointees is a potent case in point.[30]

Boutique Tribunals: An Exception

"Boutique tribunals" is the label I adopted when the need to distinguish the major judicial tribunals from the others became clear.

Boutique tribunals are structurally much different from major tribunals, and in my view there is not much to commend them. The problem is their diminutive institutional footprint. Their caseloads are such that only a handful of part-time chairs and members can be justified; training budgets will be approved only grudgingly if at all; members will not have sufficient exposure to cases for a specialized expertise in the adjudicative role to develop or for a vibrant, collegial, institutional support environment to exist; Professor Arthurs's universe of discourse[31] will be nowhere to be found; and, typically sitting little and lonely in the very midst of their portfolio ministry's operational environment, boutique tribunals will find no justice-oriented collegial or institutional administrative or adjudicative support.

Dependency on the portfolio ministry will always be egregious, and the tribunal members will feel a vulnerability that is not conducive to robust decision making. Also, no "institutional" expertise is possible beyond the expertise of the individual members, and, due to the limited caseload, there is not much capacity for growth in expertise through the work. The portfolio ministries must therefore recruit only members who will bring their own home-grown expertise to the job – members who are then apt to be vulnerable to the *engagé* criticism that the *Globe and Mail* brought against the refugee experts appointed to the IRB in 1993.[32]

The adjudicative functions assigned to boutique tribunals need to be structured differently, and I will deal with that topic when I come to specifying my blueprint for reform.

4

Prelude to Reform

In previous chapters, I have examined the executive branch's strategies and tactics for ensuring that the exercise of judicial rights-determining functions within its domain remains within its control, identified the precepts underlying a coherent theory of administrative justice, and analyzed the unique operational environment in which administrative judicial tribunals and their members do their work. It is now possible to contemplate how the executive branch's administrative justice system might be fixed, but before we can usefully talk about specific reform proposals we need to deal with three important threshold issues: the issue of ideological judging, the constitutional issue, and the competence issue.

Ruling Out Ideological Judging

Anyone proposing a transformative reform of Canada's administrative justice system must begin by asking and answering this question: Is it right and necessary, or is it misguided and/or naïve, to expect that judicial tribunal adjudicators will not manipulate their decision making in pursuit of their own partisan or ideological goals? There can be no credible administrative justice system design that does not begin with a clear position on this issue.

A principal theme in this book is my argument that a principled administrative justice system requires merit-based, apolitical competitive appointment processes and merit-based, fair reappointment decisions based on objective performance evaluations, with the number of reappointments dependent solely on performance. The validity and weight of this argument depends initially on the validity of its premise: that adjudicators selected on merit in a competitive, apolitical selection process and whose independence is structurally guaranteed can be counted on not to manipulate the law or distort findings of fact in the service of their own partisan or ideological agendas. This premise is not universally accepted, however, particularly not with respect to the decision making of members of administrative tribunals.

The opposing view is that most adjudicators, if not all, consciously or subconsciously pursue their own personal agendas. In its extreme version, this theory goes to the extent of claiming that adjudicators, including judges, only pretend to be objectively applying the law, deliberately feigning impartiality even as they go about manipulating the law to suit themselves. If this view of the ideology of judging were accepted as valid, it would be impossible to justify an administrative justice system based on an objective, apolitical process of appointing and reappointing members of judicial tribunals.

Perhaps the best-known proponent of this "bad faith argument" is Harvard University's Duncan Kennedy, one of the principal members of the Critical Legal Studies movement. In his article "Toward a Critical Phenomenology of Judging,"[1] Kennedy takes the position that judges should "first decide how [they] want [their case] to come out" and then strive to find a convincing legal argument that will bring it out that way.[2] Kennedy finds that it facilitates appreciation of a theoretical analysis if one imagines a real situation against which the analysis can be played out, and the "real" situation he imagines in this article is a transit strike during which bus drivers are laying themselves down in front of their employer's bus garage as an obstructive tactic and the bus company has applied to the court for an injunction. Kennedy imagines himself as the "activist" judge whose own sense of justice leads him to want to decide against the employer and for the union. In the following passage, he describes what he sees to be the proper ideology of judging:

> Is not what I am doing illegitimate, from the standpoint of legality, right from the start? One could argue that since I think the law favors the company I have no business trying to develop the best possible case for the union. But this misunderstands the rules of the game of legality. All members of the [legal] community know that one's initial impression, that a

particular rule governs, and that when applied to the facts in Y yields X result, is often wrong. That's what makes law such a trip. What at first looked open and shut is ajar, and what looked vague and altogether indeterminate abruptly reveals itself to be quite firmly settled under the circumstances. So it is an important part of the judge's and the lawyer's role that they are to test whatever conclusions they have reached about the "correct legal outcome" by trying to develop the best possible argument on the other side. In my role as an activist judge I am just doing what I'm supposed to do when I test my first impression against the best pro-union argument I can develop. What would betray legality would be to adopt the wrong attitude at the end of the reasoning process, when I have reached a conclusion about "what the law requires" and find it still in conflict with how-I-want-it-to-come-out. But, for the moment, I am free to play around.[3]

My answer to Kennedy's very first question is a resounding yes. Of course, what his judge is doing is illegitimate. It is illegitimate because that judge is from the outset intent on going where his personal political or ideological agenda – his "sense of justice" – makes him want to go, and he proposes to go there unless it proves impossible to construct a presentable argument that will take him there. These are the goals of a biased judge. Kennedy is not wrong, however, in saying that it is necessary that a judge fully understand a party's best case before making his or her own decision.

In the years when I would speak or write about the judging process, as sometimes happened when I was chair of WCAT, I often talked about how a judge's proper initial approach to a decision on a contentious legal issue was comparable to Bertrand Russell's approach of first adopting an attitude of "hypothetical sympathy." In the introduction to his *History of Western Philosophy*, Russell describes the problem he had in deciding which philosophers were worthy of inclusion in his history. On those questions, his mind, like the minds of most adjudicators on first approaching a case, was far from open. He was a renowned philosopher in his own right, with decided views. Furthermore, his preconceived notions about a number of the philosophers he felt obliged to consider were less than flattering. As a scientist, however, he understood the importance of bringing an open mind to such an assessment. What was required, he said, was an attitude of "hypothetical sympathy":

> In studying a philosopher the right attitude is neither reverence nor contempt, but first a kind of hypothetical sympathy, until it is possible to know

what it feels like to believe in his theories, and only then a revival of the critical attitude. [This attitude of hypothetical sympathy] should resemble, as far as possible, the state of mind of a person abandoning opinions which he has hitherto held.[4]

I believe that such a tactic is necessary not only for the judging of philosophers but also for the exercise of judicial functions generally. Accordingly, it seems to me that it is clearly necessary for a judge to explore what Kennedy refers to as "legal fields" or "fields of answers" from which the possible answers must emerge – that is, the relevant statutory text, legislative history, precedent, jurisprudence, doctrinal literature, scholarly literature, and so on – with a view to developing a full understanding of each party's best case before reviving his or her critical attitude. Kennedy, however, does not admit to the necessity for any balance in the exercise. He does not pretend that he would put the same effort into understanding the best case that can be made on the employer's side of the obstruction issue. In his reasoning process, he is never influenced by even a hypothetical sympathy for the employer's case.

Obviously, one cannot search the law's "fields of answers" without having some goal in mind. If one is to look, one needs to know what one is looking for and be able to identify it when it turns up. The goal of Kennedy's imaginary judge is to find, if possible, an answer that puts striking workers in a better position vis-à-vis their right to interfere with an employer's means of production than the obvious answer would allow. As an adjudicator, I, on the other hand, would search the fields of answers for the same answer in the phase of my reasoning where I have adopted a hypothetical sympathy for the union's position, but I would also explore the fields with a different goal when I was in the exploratory mode of hypothetical sympathy for the employer's position.

Finally, I have to answer a few more questions. What am I doing at the point where, along with Russell, I revive the critical attitude? And how would I describe the answer I am ultimately looking for, the "opinion" that I must finally defend, the opinion that will become my decision?

In thinking about these questions, I was surprised to find much that was pertinent, in a backhanded way, in some of the Marxists' view of the rule of law, particularly as conveniently summarized by Hugh Collins in his book *Marxism and the Law*.[5] For instance, there can be no doubt that a judge engaged in legal reasoning must be, as the Marxists say, effectively involved in a "conversation" with the "dominant ideology"[6] and that the legal framework

of rules and doctrines provides a comprehensive interpretation and evaluation of social relationships and events that is in tune with the main themes
in the dominant ideology.[7] How could it be otherwise?

I also do not see how one could rationally quarrel with the Marxists and
other skeptics who say that "*autonomous* reasoning" is not a component of
modern legal systems. Indeed, for a democrat living in a democracy, the
claim that legal thought is *not* a "discrete, *non-instrumental,* and rational
investigation of justice" is obviously valid, and the portrayal of legal thought
as a "dialogue with the background dominant ideology *on the basis of the
formal constraints of coherence and consistency*" has in fact everything to
commend it. One must also agree that "the source of law and legal developments lies in the [dominant background] ideology," and that while judges
may claim to treat like cases alike, "*we can be sure the definitions of similar-
ity and differences are determined by criteria supplied by the dominant
ideology.*"[8] All of this, it seems to me, is bound to be true, provided – and this
is a big proviso – that the ideology we are talking about is the "background
dominant" ideology to which Collins's book refers.

The background dominant ideology of any democratic society must of
course allow for contests for control of that society's government – contests
among the "political ideologies" of the so-called right, left, or centre. The
political ideologies are indigenous to the dominant background ideology,
to which they all defer and whose core structures and rules they accept and
respect. And it is to this background ideology that the Marxists and I are
referring here, not the indigenous political ideologies.

Canada's dominant background ideology is characterized by a commitment to a system of democratic governance organized as a federation of
provinces and territories with universal suffrage; a system now recognized
to be implicitly based on the division of power between the legislative, executive, and judicial branches of government; a system bound by a written
constitution that defines the distribution of powers within the federation
and ensures that the fundamental rights and freedoms and the equality of
access to justice traditionally cherished in this society are protected from
being impaired or overridden by a government of the day; a system that,
subject to constitutional constraints, recognizes the paramount lawmaking
power of the legislative branch, assigns the determination of justiciable
rights disputes to adjudicators it expects to be independent and impartial,
and accepts as legitimate the common law system of lawmaking based on
that system's norms of legal reasoning and on the evolution of judicial precedent promoted by the doctrine of *stare decisis;* a system that embraces a

Westminster form of government inherited from the United Kingdom modified by the constraining role of a written constitution.

This is the "dominant background ideology" to which I refer, and where I depart from the Marxists' view is, of course, in their identification of the "dominant ideology" as a problem and the legal system's role in supporting and promulgating that ideology's "hegemony" as an obstacle. For me, and for any designer of an operational Canadian administrative justice system, Canada's dominant background ideology must be a given – must be the ideological context within which the administrative justice system must fit and operate, and whose principles and goals the system must be designed to respect and serve.

There is also no doubt in my view that, as the Marxists say, it will be the dominant background ideology to which any adjudicator will be consciously or subconsciously attuned to the criteria of alike and different, of coherence and incoherence. I can see no authentic alternative to this approach. Canadian courts and judges and administrative judicial tribunals and their adjudicator members are in the business of identifying and evolving the law within the discipline imposed by the common law's established norms of legal reasoning in a manner that is congruent with Canada's dominant background ideology; they are not political agents.

At the final stages of my reasoning process as an adjudicator, I, like Kennedy, am engaging in a notional conversation with the background authorities who have been in what Kennedy refers to as the "fields of answers" before me. This "conversation" engages the norms of legal reasoning fundamental to the dominant ideology, and my goal is to understand from the law that has gone before what is, in the application of those norms, most relevant to my issue.

As Kennedy says, legal reasoning may be usefully viewed as "a kind of work with a purpose," but his purpose is "to make the case come out the way [his] sense of justice tells [him] it ought to."[9] My purpose as an adjudicator, as a common law judge, would be to make the case come out the way that, of all the ways it could arguably come out, is *the one* way, in my professional judgment, that is the *most* consistent and coherent with what has gone before. In a typical administrative judicial tribunal setting, this will mean adopting the one answer that I believe is the *most* consistent and coherent with the intent of the legislature as discerned through application of the norms of legal reasoning, particularly the common law rules of statutory interpretation, to the evidence of such intent as principally found within the text of the applicable legislation. Whether or not engaging in this pursuit will produce a result I would have preferred myself, a result with which I would personally have been politically or morally more comfortable, is not a permissible consideration.

When Kennedy says that "the purpose here being to *make* the case come out the way my sense of justice tells me it ought to, in spite of what seems at first like resistance or opposition from 'the law,'" he is taking the very heart out of the rule of law and proving to the satisfaction of politicians and bureaucrats alike that adjudicative positions must indeed be filled by the government of the day's friends and allies.

I do not claim qualifications as a legal philosopher that would equip me to do credible battle in the theory of law with the likes of a Duncan Kennedy. I should like, therefore, to throw in my lot with Professor Raimo Siltala of the University of Helsinki. In his 2003 article "Whose Justice, Which Ideology?"[10] Siltala reviews Kennedy's book *A Critique of Adjudication*,[11] and delivers a stinging rejection of the Critical Legal Studies theory of adjudication that it presents. He characterizes it, among other things, as a "nightmare vision of the law," an "enforcement of politics in the thin disguise of law": "If such a fraudulent, Janus-faced model of legal adjudication were in fact adopted by the judiciary, the result would be a justice system that was an empty facade of false legality, failing rationality, and a faltering quest for legitimacy."

Any claim to *legitimacy* for political patronage appointments of members of administrative judicial tribunals obviously depends on the acceptance at some level of a Kennedyesque theory about the feigned impartiality of judges. Appointments based on the acceptance of that theory implicitly legitimize the concept that adjudication is in fact no more than, in Siltala's words, "the enforcement of politics in the thin disguise of law." And, of course, any appointment policy based on acceptance of that theory effectively turns the theory into a self-fulfilling prophecy.

This book is not concerned with assessing the respective merits of all the varying characterizations one finds in the literature about what judges are doing when they adjudicate. When one is challenging the legitimacy of an executive branch justice system, however, one must be clear where one stands on this one issue. I stand with those who believe that a concept of adjudication that positions judges and other adjudicators as manipulators of the law in the service of their personal or their patron's ideological or partisan agendas is one that is deeply incompatible with any principled theory of justice, and who believe that adjudicators must be committed as a matter of personal and professional integrity to going "where the evidence and the law fairly takes them."[12]

I also stand with Lawrence Solum, who argues in his article "Judicial Selection: Ideology versus Character"[13] that in a "normative" judicial appointment process, the key criterion for choosing a judge should be character. In his definition of the valid judicial character, he includes most importantly the "virtue of justice," which he equates roughly with a commitment to "impartial" or non-ideological judging.[14] His concluding paragraph provides a convincing response to the ideologists:

> Let me end by observing an ironic feature of the argument that I have made. It is the fact of ideological struggle that makes non-ideological judging necessary to realize the rule of law. It is the strife between opposing political ideologies that necessitates a neutral forum in which *the rules that contain the struggle* can be enforced. It is precisely because political ideology is so important that judges should be selected for their possession of the virtue of justice – the disposition to decide on the basis of the rules laid down rather than on the basis of their political preferences.[15]

My stand on this issue is, of course, predicated on the conviction that non-ideological judging does exist; that it can be generally ensured through embedding the concept in our society's political and legal culture and through apolitical, merit-based appointment processes and structural guarantees of independence and impartiality.

Nevertheless, before the vexed subject of ideological judging can be safely put behind us, a final "yes, but" question needs to be addressed: Yes, but what if one is a judicial tribunal adjudicator faced with enforcing a statute that one personally finds truly morally repugnant? What then?

Any argument against ideological judging must be premised on the assumption that the background dominant ideology to which judges and adjudicators are called to give their allegiance is not morally abhorrent. If it were morally abhorrent – for instance, as South Africa's was during the apartheid era – and our legal system had been recruited to support that ideology – if it had become what Professor David Dyzenhaus of the University of Toronto calls a "wicked legal system"[16] – the role of individual adjudicators would then be morally compromised. Right-thinking adjudicators would be faced with a choice between professional felicity to the law (assuming that the wicked system was being supported, as it was in South

Africa, by laws enacted in proper form by a complicit parliament) and their "personal moral impulse" to do what they can to confound that law.[17]

This is not our case, however. It was Aldous Huxley, I believe, who said that there are times and places where the only place for an honourable person is in jail, and there will be times and places, such as South Africa during the apartheid regime, where the only place for an honourable adjudicator will be, if not in jail, then off the bench, or, if on the bench, then in the role of an undercover operative striving to do as much as possible to restrain the morally compromised dominant ideology. Still, as long as we are not living in one of those places at one of those times, our democratic system of government requires that we be able to rely on our judges and judicial tribunal adjudicators as safe and tender guardians of the lawmaker's intent as determined through the application of the common law rules of statutory interpretation, regardless of the adjudicator's personal views on the substantive merit of such intent in a particular case.

Professor Dyzenhaus has written extensively about the role of judges, basing his analysis particularly on the conduct of the judiciary in South Africa during the apartheid era. In his book on South Africa's Truth and Reconciliation Commission's "Legal Hearing" (the hearing into the role of lawyers and judges during apartheid),[18] he begins with a review of a famous speech delivered in 1989, when apartheid was in full bloom, by Arthur Chaskalson, then the director of the South African Legal Resources Centre and an ardent opponent of apartheid. At the time of the Commission hearings, Chaskalson was the president of South Africa's new Constitutional Court. In that 1989 speech, he asserted that South African judges were duty bound to interpret statute law, insofar as was possible, in the light of the common law's "equitable principles."

Dyzenhaus characterizes Chaskalson's "suggestion that [common law] judges are under a duty to resort to common law presumptions in cases of alleged ambiguity in statutory language" as "controversial." It is controversial, he says, because "judges have to be predisposed towards using such presumptions before the presumptions will have any effect" – they have to "adopt a view of the rule of law which requires judges whenever possible to interpret statute law so as to make it consistent with fundamental principles of the common law because of the moral importance of these principles" – and many judges, Dyzenhaus believes, are "hostile" to that view of their role. He contrasts that view with the view that judges should be "plain fact judges," committed to looking only to "those parts of the public record that make it clear what the legislators as a matter of fact intended" and to give effect to that intention "without permitting their substantive convictions about justice to interfere."

My view of a judge's role, the view on which my recommendations concerning apolitical appointments and reappointments for administrative justice adjudicators is based, and the view that there is reason to think most judges in Canada probably accept,[19] is different.

In the first place, I believe that, in a common law system, it is plainly invalid to regard "legislative intent" as a *fact* to be ascertained on the basis of the best available evidence. Legislative intent is, rather, a legal construct to be determined by the assiduous application of the common law rules of statutory interpretation. If the interpretation of a statute in accordance with those rules led to a conclusion that was contrary to the known actual intention of the government when it proposed the legislation – contrary, perhaps, to the intention stated by the responsible minister when he or she, speaking in the legislature in which his or her government held a majority, proposed the bill for first reading – the rule-driven interpretation must nevertheless prevail. If this were not so, the legislative process of debate by the members of the legislature and enactment through successive votes would be a pointless exercise. Moreover, citizens, relying on the wording of the statute, perhaps years later and knowing nothing of the government's actual intention at the time of enactment or of the nature of the legislative debate, would not have the wherewithal to "know" the law, as our system requires them to do, and would be deprived of their right to organize their affairs in reliance upon the text of the statute as read and understood by them and their advisers.

Second, a judge's role in interpreting legislation in a manner congruent with the fundamental principles of the common law cannot, in my respectful view, be seen to depend on a particular judge being "predisposed" to do so. It is a role that is implicitly embedded in the rules of statutory interpretation that every judge is duty bound to respect. Perhaps the most pertinent example is the rule that legislatures must not be taken to have intended to override an established rule-of-law principle or an established right unless the statutory language makes such an intention unequivocally clear. Consider, for example, the following passages from the Supreme Court's 2003 decision in *Canadian Union of Public Employees (C.U.P.E.) v. Ontario (Minister of Labour)*, the retired judges' case, in which in a back-handed but very clear way the Court establishes that common law, rule of law principles cannot be abrogated by legislation except with language of unequivocal clarity:

... Affirming the rule of interpretation that "courts generally infer that Parliament or the legislature intended the tribunal's process to comport with principles of natural justice" (para. 21), the Court [in *Ocean Port*[20]] nevertheless concluded that "[i]t is not open to a court to apply a common law rule in the face of *clear* statutory direction" (para. 22) [emphasis added by the Court]. Further, "[w]here the intention of the legislature, as here, is *unequivocal*, there is no room to import common law doctrines of independence" (para. 27) [emphasis added by the Court].[21]

The reason for placing this interpretive burden of unequivocal clarity on those who would argue that a legislature intended that the requirements of procedural fairness or other established rule-of-law rights be disregarded is to ensure that established norms such as these are not swept away inferentially or consequentially as a result of the legislature's not paying enough attention. The point is made expressly in the following statement by the House of Lords in its 2000 decision in *R. v. Secretary of State for the Home Department, ex p. Simms*:

[T]he principle of legality means that Parliament must squarely confront what it is doing and accept the political cost. Fundamental rights cannot be overridden by general or ambiguous words. This is because there is too great a risk that the full implications of their unqualified meaning may have passed unnoticed in the democratic process. In the absence of express language or necessary implication to the contrary, the courts therefore presume that even the most general words were intended to be subject to the basic rights of the individual ...[22]

In summary, there is nothing in Canada's dominant background ideology that can possibly justify adjudicators assuming an activist judge's role; nothing to justify the manipulation of the law to support finding a legislative intent that fits more comfortably with their own moral compasses or political or personal agendas than the intent that a bona fide application of the rules of statutory interpretation would discern.

Of course, none of this argument in support of non-ideological judging applies to regulators – to members of regulatory agencies. Regulatory agencies are doing the executive branch's business and the executive branch is presumably entitled to appoint regulators who share its policy views in the regulatory agency's area of responsibility. Nevertheless, although regulators are not judges, once they have accepted appointment to a regulatory agency that the public has been assured is independent, they have at least an ethical duty to decide issues in a way that best comports with their own professional judgment. They too are not free to sell out to the government of the day's known preferences on particular issues.

Settling the Constitutional Issue

The Issue

The Supreme Court's eventual confirmation that the Constitution's so-called unwritten principle of judicial independence (first recognized by the Court in 1997 in the case referred to in this book as *PEI Reference*[23] and hereafter referred to as the "PEI principle of judicial independence" or "PEI principle") applies to administrative judicial tribunals is the prerequisite – the *sine qua non* – for the transcendent, transformative reform our executive branch administrative justice system demands. In an ideal world – one in which governments would readily acknowledge and respect their responsibility for conforming their executive branch justice system to the rule-of-law principles of justice – the constitutional issue would not be so pressing. As Professor Phillip Bryden has noted, however:

> The logic that drives our interest in the recognition of a constitutionally protected right to independent administrative tribunals is *the sense that the political system is either incapable of, or has lost interest in, providing the administrative justice machinery that Canadians deserve* ... If we had sufficient confidence in our legislative processes to put in place appropriate administrative justice machinery, we would not need to go beyond the traditional boundaries of the common law and impose systems of tribunal independence on legislatures contrary to the expressed (and, one might hope, well-considered) desires of those institutions.[24]

The reason for not having confidence that our legislatures will deliver the appropriate administrative justice structures is the executive branch's various and deeply rooted interests in maintaining the *status quo* of dependency and bias, and the acknowledged fact that, over the decades, the executive branch's defence of those interests has proven too strong for a vast array of concerted reform initiatives,[25] virtually all of which the executive branch has effectively ignored, defeated, finessed, or outlasted.

The latter experience should provide more than enough evidence that without a confirmed constitutional override, there is no realistic prospect for meaningful change. And if one needed more current evidence, one need look no further than the insouciant disrespect for the rule of law demonstrated by the Saskatchewan government in its structuring and administration of that province's administrative judicial tribunals, as chronicled in the 2010 decision of the Saskatchewan Court of Appeal in *Saskatchewan Federation of Labour v. Saskatchewan*,[26] the case that arose from the arbitrary mid-term discharge without cause of the Saskatchewan Labour Relations Board's chair and vice-chairs.

As a practical matter, therefore, Supreme Court confirmation that the PEI principle applies to administrative judicial tribunals and their members must be the first step in any meaningful reform. It is not a sufficient step, but it is the necessary first step. Fortunately, on both policy and doctrinal grounds, there is every reason for confidence that in due course this confirmation will come.[27] In my view, the case for constitutional protection of the independence and impartiality of administrative judicial tribunals and their members is effectively conclusive.

The New Context

The first thing to note is that Canada's modern-day administrative law provides an entirely new context for this constitutional debate. The context is new in two respects: first, the rule-of-law implications of a refusal of constitutional protection have changed dramatically; and, second, the conventional law conversation appears to be anticipating a judicial branch constitutional status for administrative judicial tribunals. Of course, there is never any mention of judicial branch status as such, but I would argue that the official acknowledgments of the tribunals' "justice system status" amounts to the same thing.

At the forefront of the modern debate in Canada concerning the constitutional status of administrative judicial tribunals must be the watershed nature of the change regarding the common law of judicial independence for administrative judicial tribunals ushered in by *Valente*,[28] the particulars of which I have previously discussed.[29]

As we have seen, prior to *Valente*, the courts presumed – that is, simply trusted – that anyone appointed to an adjudicative office was, as a practical matter, independent; that governments would respect their independence; and that appointed adjudicators could be counted on to act as though they were independent even when they were not. Post *Valente,* however, the *issue* of independence is no longer finessed by that presumption. The consequence, largely unnoticed thus far, is that the government/tribunal relationships of structural dependency that characterizes the administrative justice system as we know it are by and large now incompatible with the new *common law* of judicial independence.

Because of *Valente* and the judicial independence jurisprudence that followed *Valente,* the courts are now faced, for the first time in our history, with the question of whether they are prepared to be complicit in entrusting *judicial* functions to executive branch institutions and/or individuals who are not, in law, it is now clear, impartial. Post *Valente,* the courts must recognize that, if the PEI principle of judicial independence is held not to apply to protect the independence and impartiality of administrative judicial tribunals, then in Canada's administrative justice system, a system in which, everyone now agrees, *the bulk of the rights disputes of our citizens are decided,* the rule of law will have been found to be optional and therefore ineffectual – open to legislative override in any way at any time in the ordinary course.

The new context in which the issue of the applicability of a constitutional requirement of independence and impartiality to administrative judicial tribunals and their members is now to be decided also includes the fact that in the administrative law conversation in modern-day Canada, it has become conventional to attribute justice system status to administrative tribunals. The most direct, authoritative confirmation of this new norm can be found in the 2003 Supreme Court of Canada decision in *Paul v. British Columbia (Forest Appeals Commission),*[30] to which I have referred previously. There, in the course of reaffirming the inherent jurisdiction of administrative tribunals to decide *Charter* issues, and speaking for a unanimous Court, Justice Michel Bastarache confirmed that "the system of justice" encompasses "the ordinary courts, federal courts, statutory provincial courts *and administrative tribunals.*"[31]

Paul, together with its companion decision, *Nova Scotia (Workers' Compensation Board) v. Martin*[32] (issued at the same time), are the culminating decisions in the extended consideration by Canadian courts of whether administrative tribunals are implicitly authorized to decide *Charter* challenges to their constituent statutes. It is therefore fitting, and not unexpected, to find the first explicit judicial acknowledgment of the justice system status of tribunals appearing in this, the denouement in that line of cases. For it was the advent of the *Canadian Charter of Rights and Freedoms* in 1982, and the ensuing controversy over the tribunals' jurisdiction to apply it, that arguably pulled the issue of the justice system status of Canadian tribunals out of the shadows and onto the main stage.

After *Paul,* in 2005, in a majority judgment in *Christie v. British Columbia,*[33] the BC Court of Appeal, citing *Paul* and noting that administrative tribunals have become "important arbiters of legal rights and obligations in our society *in substitution for courts of law,*" held that, for purposes of "access to justice," tribunals are to be included "in the category of *the judiciary.*"[34] The Court of Appeal's decision was subsequently overturned by the Supreme Court of Canada on other grounds,[35] but it is not without interest in the context of this book that the Supreme Court did not find it necessary to challenge the categorization of administrative tribunals as part of the judiciary. More recently, the Supreme Court effectively confirmed in *Conway* that administrative tribunals qualify generically as "courts of competent jurisdiction" for the purpose of ordering remedies for *Charter* breaches under s. 24(1) of the *Charter.*[36]

Along with this developing jurisprudential recognition of the justice system status of tribunals have come the *ex cathedra* pronouncements to the same effect by senior members of the judiciary that I have described previously:[37] the statement by then Chief Justice of Canada Antonio Lamer to the Council of Canadian Administrative Tribunals (CCAT) conference in 1991,[38] the statement by Ontario Chief Justice Roy McMurtry to the Conference of Ontario Boards and Agencies (COPA) conference in 1997,[39] and the statement of the then soon-to-be Chief Justice of Canada Beverley McLachlin to the BC Council of Administrative Tribunals (BCCAT) conference in 1998.[40]

Of course, as I have noted before, the recognition in *Paul* of the justice system status of apparently all administrative tribunals, and of their status as courts of competent jurisdiction in *Conway,* perpetuated the Supreme Court's traditional resistance to acknowledging a distinction between tribunals exercising judicial functions and tribunals exercising administrative functions – between judicial tribunals and regulatory agencies. It is a resistance that will have to be abandoned when the time comes to address the constitutional requirement of tribunal independence and impartiality, since this requirement cannot apply to the latter even though it most certainly must apply to the former.

The Explicit Constitutional Requirements
There are important categories of administrative judicial tribunals where the applicability of a constitutional requirement of judicial independence

is already clear: where there are existing, *written,* constitutional or quasi-constitutional requirements of judicial independence that apply. The reference here is to ss. 11(d) and 7 of the *Canadian Charter of Rights and Freedoms;* the provincial constitutional requirement in s. 23 of the Quebec *Charter of Human Rights and Freedoms;* the quasi-constitutional requirement of ss. 2(e) and (f) of the *Canadian Bill of Rights;* and, possibly, the "due process" requirement under s. 1(a) of the *Alberta Bill of Rights.*

Thus, any tribunal exercising the function of trying persons charged with an "offence" is required by s. 11(d) of the *Charter* to be independent and impartial;[41] any tribunal whose decisions are dispositive of rights respecting "life, liberty or the security of the person" is required by s. 7 of the *Charter* (as interpreted by the Supreme Court) to be independent and impartial;[42] any Quebec tribunal that is deciding rights must be independent and impartial; and any federal tribunal that is "determining" a person's "rights and obligations" is required by the *Canadian Bill of Rights* to be independent and impartial, unless its constitutive statute provides otherwise;[43] and it remains to be seen whether the *Alberta Bill of Rights* requirement of due process includes adjudication by an independent and impartial tribunal.

The Implied Constitutional Requirement: The PEI Principle

A large proportion of our judicial tribunals do not fall within any of these written constitutional or quasi-constitutional provisions, however, and neither do provincial courts exercising civil law jurisdiction, such as the provincial family law courts, the small claims courts, or justices of the peace. Thus, we come to the so-called unwritten PEI principle of judicial independence[44] and to the current big question in Canadian administrative law: is *PEI Reference's* implicit constitutional requirement of judicial independence and impartiality that has been found to protect the independence of provincial tribunals exercising civil law judicial functions applicable to judicial tribunals ?

The Supreme Court's concern with the "gap" in the written constitutional protection of judicial independence that led it to fill that gap by recognizing an implicit constitutional requirement of judicial independence is seen in the following paragraphs from the judgment of Chief Justice Lamer, speaking for eight of the nine justices, in *PEI Reference:*

> However, upon closer examination, there are serious limitations to the view
> that the express provisions of the Constitution comprise an exhaustive and
> definitive code for the protection of judicial independence. The first and

most serious problem is that the range of courts whose independence is protected by the written provisions of the Constitution contains large gaps. Sections 96-100, for example, only protect the independence of judges of the superior, district, and county courts, and even then, not in a uniform or consistent manner. Thus, while ss. 96 and 100 protect the core jurisdiction and the financial security, respectively, of all three types of courts (superior, district, and county), s. 99, on its terms, only protects the security of tenure of superior court judges. Moreover, ss. 96-100 do not apply to provincially appointed inferior courts, otherwise known as provincial courts.[45]

To some extent, the gaps in the scope of protection provided by ss. 96-100 are offset by the application of s. 11(d), which applies to a range of tribunals and courts, including provincial courts. However, by its express terms, s. 11(d) is limited in scope as well – it only extends the envelope of constitutional protection to bodies which exercise jurisdiction over offences. As a result, when those courts exercise civil jurisdiction, their independence would not seem to be guaranteed. The independence of provincial courts adjudicating in family law matters, for example, would not be constitutionally protected. The independence of superior courts, by contrast, when hearing exactly the same cases, would be constitutionally guaranteed.[46]

The Court's solution is conveniently summarized in the following passage from the case report's head note.

Sections 96 to 100 of the Constitution Act, 1867, which only protect the independence of judges of the superior, district and county courts, and s. 11(d) of the Charter, which protects the independence of a wide range of courts and tribunals, including provincial courts, but only when they exercise jurisdiction in relation to offences, are not an exhaustive and definitive written code for the protection of judicial independence in Canada. Judicial independence is an unwritten norm, recognized and affirmed by the preamble to the Constitution Act, 1867 – in particular its reference to "a Constitution similar in Principle to that of the United Kingdom" – which is the true source of our commitment to this foundational principle. The preamble identifies the organizing principles of the Constitution Act, 1867 and invites the courts to turn those principles into the premises of a constitutional argument that culminates in the filling of gaps in the express terms of the constitutional text. The same approach applies to the protection of

judicial independence. Judicial independence has now grown into a principle that extends *to all courts*, not just the superior courts of this country.
(Emphasis added)

That the PEI principle enunciated by Chief Justice Lamer in *PEI Reference*
is now firmly established as a settled component of the constitutional law
of judicial independence can no longer be disputed.[47] This may be seen particularly in the Supreme Court's 2004 decision in *Re Application under
s. 83.28 of the Criminal Code*,[48] in which the Court had occasion to consider
the status of judicial independence in Canada generally. The pertinent passage reads as follows:

> This principle [of judicial independence] exists in Canadian law in a num-
> ber of forms. In the Constitution, it is explicitly referenced in ss. 96 to 100
> of the *Constitution Act, 1867* and in s. 11(*d*) of the *Charter.* The application
> of these provisions, however, is limited. The former applies to judges of
> superior courts, and the latter to courts and tribunals charged with trying
> the guilt of persons charged with criminal offences: *Reference re Remuner-
> ation of Judges of the Provincial Court of Prince Edward Island ...* at para. 84;
> *Ell ...* at para. 18. Judicial independence has also been implicitly recognized
> as a residual right protected under s. 7, as it, along with the remaining pro-
> tections in ss. 8 to 14, are specific examples of broader principles of funda-
> mental justice: *Re B.C. Motor Vehicle Act*, [1985] 2 S.C.R. 486, at p. 503.
> Moreover, the commitment to the "foundational principle" of judicial in-
> dependence has also been referenced by way of the Preamble to the *Con-
> stitution Act, 1867: Reference re Remuneration of Judges of the Provincial
> Court of Prince Edward Island*, at para. 109; see also *Ell*, at para. 19. *Judicial
> independence further represents the cornerstone of the common law duty of
> procedural fairness, which attaches to all judicial, quasi-judicial and ad-
> ministrative proceedings, and is an unwritten principle of the Constitution.*[49]

The only question remaining is whether and in what circumstances the
Supreme Court will apply the PEI principle to judicial tribunals.

The "All Courts" Question
The central focus of the continuing debate on the applicability of the PEI
principle to tribunals is the statement in *PEI Reference* that the principle applies to "all courts." This is, therefore, the question: does "all courts" in the
sense used by the Supreme Court include judicial tribunals?

In addressing that question, it is important at the outset to remember that the Court, in *PEI Reference*, knew that this would be a question and deliberately chose not to answer it. The question was explicitly raised in Justice Gérard La Forest's dissent:

> If one is to give constitutional protection to courts generally, one must be able to determine with some precision what the term "court" encompasses ... [W]hat are we to make of a general protection for courts such as that proposed by the Chief Justice? The word "court" is a broad term and can encompass a wide variety of tribunals. In the province of Quebec, for example, the term is legislatively used in respect of any number of administrative tribunals. Are we to include only those inferior courts applying ordinary jurisdiction in civil matters, or should we include all sorts of administrative tribunals, some of which are of far greater importance than ordinary civil courts? And if we do, is a distinction to be drawn between different tribunals and on the basis of what principles is this to be done?[50]

The majority could have responded to Justice La Forest's question with the conclusion that, it is frequently argued, the Court subsequently proffered in *Ocean Port*[51] (see below) – namely, that although the principle applies to provincial civil law courts, it does not apply to administrative tribunals of any kind. That they chose not to do so is significant. It at least demonstrates that the majority were not uncomfortable with leaving the question open or, in any event, unanswered.

Also, by 1997, when *PEI Reference* was decided, the Supreme Court had already established that it was comfortable with recognizing the "court" status of administrative tribunals even for constitutional purposes. In 1979, in *Attorney General of Quebec v. Blaikie*, it had held that Quebec's "tribunals" are "courts" for purposes of the language protections in s. 133 of the *Constitution Act, 1867*.[52] And in 1995, in *Weber v. Ontario Hydro*,[53] it confirmed that tribunals were "courts of competent jurisdiction" under s. 24(1) of the *Charter*, if they have jurisdiction over "the person, the subject matter and the remedy sought," which administrative judicial tribunals almost invariably do.

Ocean Port, Bell, and Ell

The Supreme Court first addressed the applicability of the PEI principle to administrative tribunals in its 2001 decision in *Ocean Port*.[54] In a unanimous judgment written by Chief Justice McLachlin, the Court overturned a

BC Court of Appeal decision that had quashed a decision of the BC Liquor Appeal Board on the grounds that the status of the Board's part-time members did not satisfy the procedural-fairness principle of judicial independence. Part-time members were appointed effectively at pleasure, and were therefore not independent. The Supreme Court, noting that the Liquor Appeal Board's constituent statute explicitly authorized at-pleasure appointments, concluded that in light of this provision the Court of Appeal's decision had effectively raised the common law requirement of judicial independence for the members of the Liquor Appeal Board to constitutional status, an elevation for which, in the Supreme Court's view, there was no authority.

The Court of Appeal had relied for its authority on the Supreme Court's decision in *2747-3174 Québec Inc. v. Quebec (Régie des permis d'alcool)*[55] that at-pleasure appointments are incompatible with the principle of judicial independence. As the Supreme Court pointed out in its *Ocean Port* decision, however, the Court in *Régie* was applying the Quebec *Charter's* written constitutional requirement of independence, whereas in British Columbia there was no constitutional requirement of independence. Thus, the statutory at-pleasure provision must be seen to be determinative.

Of course, *PEI Reference* was a possible authority for raising the common law requirement of judicial independence for the members of the Liquor Appeal Board to constitutional status. But *PEI Reference* had not figured at all in the Court of Appeal's decision. When the government appealed the Court of Appeal's decision to the Supreme Court, however, the respondent[56] invoked *PEI Reference* and argued that the PEI principle applied to the Liquor Appeal Board, rendering the legislation that authorized at-pleasure appointments of Board members constitutionally invalid. In rejecting that argument, the Supreme Court used comprehensive language that at first glance appears to flatly reject the applicability of the PEI principle to administrative tribunals of any kind, including administrative judicial tribunals.[57] Paragraph 24 of *Ocean Port* states:

> Administrative tribunals, by contrast [to judges], lack this constitutional distinction from the executive. They are, in fact, created precisely for the purpose of implementing government policy. Implementation of that policy may require them to make quasi-judicial decisions. They thus may be seen as spanning the constitutional divide between the executive and judicial branches of government. However, *given their primary policy-making function*, it is properly the role and responsibility of Parliament and

the legislatures to determine the composition and structure required by a tribunal to discharge the responsibilities bestowed upon it. While tribunals may sometimes attract *Charter* requirements of independence, as a general rule they do not. Thus, the degree of independence required of a particular tribunal is a matter of discerning the intention of Parliament or the legislature and ... this choice must be respected.[58]

However, while government lawyers continue to argue that *Ocean Port* is the authoritative answer to any claim that the PEI principle applies to judicial tribunals, it is clearly no longer a convincing argument; the Supreme Court's subsequent decisions in *Bell Canada* and in *Ell* tell a different story.

Moreover, as Mary McKenzie and I argue in our article on *Ocean Port* and the Saskatchewan Labour Relations Board,[59] notwithstanding the broad language in paragraph 24 of the *Ocean Port* judgment, the actual *ratio decidendi* in *Ocean Port* is only that the PEI principle does not apply to regulatory agencies. The Court understood that the tribunal whose independence was at issue in *Ocean Port* – the BC Liquor Appeal Board – was in fact a regulatory agency, not a judicial tribunal, and paragraph 33 of Chief Justice McLachlin's judgment makes this clear: "The *B.C. Liquor Appeal Board*" is "*first and foremost a licensing body*" and the licence suspension – the subject of the judicial review application – is "an incident of the Board's licensing function."[60] The paragraph concludes that "the exercise of power here at issue falls squarely within the executive power of the provincial government."

It is, of course, possible to argue that the BC Liquor Appeal Board, engaged as it was in hearing an appeal from the suspension of a hotel's liquor licence, was in fact a judicial tribunal exercising a judicial function, not a regulatory agency. Such an argument would strengthen the authority of *Ocean Port* when that decision is marshalled against the application of the PEI principle to judicial tribunals. And it does seem likely that the Board's functions, if looked at closely, would be seen to at least fall into the grey area referred to earlier, between functions that are clearly administrative or quasi-judicial administrative, and functions that are clearly judicial.

The Court does not address this question in *Ocean Port*, however. It finds, as indicated in paragraph 33, that the Board was exercising a licensing function, and so from a doctrinal perspective it does not matter how, on the facts, the Board's function should have been properly characterized. *Ocean Port* was decided on the basis of the Court's view that the Board was a licensing body; as a doctrinal authority, therefore, *Ocean Port* must remain a decision about a body exercising a licensing function.

In fact, the argument concerning the limited nature of the intended *ratio decidendi* of *Ocean Port* was accorded considerable weight by the Supreme Court itself when two years later, in its decision in *C.U.P.E.*,[61] it character-ized the *Ocean Port* decision as one involving the "adjudication of licensing violations in the context of government liquor policy," citing paragraph 33 of the *Ocean Port* judgment.[62] The *Ocean Port ratio decidendi* does not, therefore, address the applicability of the PEI principle to judicial tribunals, even though the paragraph 24 language seems broad enough to do so. If the words in paragraph 24 were in fact intended to encompass judicial tribu-nals, they must be discounted as classic *obiter dicta.* Thus, with respect to judicial tribunals, *Ocean Port* is not the doctrinal authority government lawyers have claimed it to be.

To argue that the Chief Justice intended in *Ocean Port* to lump regulatory agencies with administrative judicial tribunals is to assume also that she was intentionally rejecting the pre-*Ocean Port* Canadian *ex cathedra* recogni-tion of the important distinction between regulatory agencies and admin-istrative judicial tribunals. The argument also ignores the Supreme Court's previous linking of "courts" with "tribunals" in matters of a constitutional nature, as in *Blaikie* and *Weber.*[63]

But the most important reason for rejecting *Ocean Port* as an authority denying the application of the PEI principle to administrative judicial tribu-nals is the Supreme Court's own decision two years later in *Bell Canada.*[64]

In *McKenzie v. Minister of Public Safety and Solicitor General et al.,* the BC Supreme Court decision that I discussed at length in the Introduction and that held that the PEI principle did apply to British Columbia's Resi-dential Tenancy Arbitrators,[65] Justice McEwan found that the discrepancy between the categories of tribunals dealt with in *Ocean Port* and those dealt with in *Bell Canada* was sufficient in and of itself to distinguish *Ocean Port.* In his view, *Ocean Port's* rejection of the applicability of the PEI principle to tribunals could not possibly have been intended to apply to the "other tribu-nals" described in *Bell Canada* but not referenced in *Ocean Port.*[66] This was Justice McEwan's main ground for distinguishing *Ocean Port,* and the *Bell Canada* language he relied on reads as follows:

> [21] ... As this Court noted in Ocean Port ... administrative tribunals perform a variety of functions, and "may be seen as spanning the constitutional divide between the executive and judicial branches of government" (para. 24). *Some* administrative tribunals are closer to the executive end of the spec-trum: *their* primary purpose is to develop, or supervise the implementation

of, particular government policies. Such tribunals may require little by way of procedural protections. *Other tribunals, however,* are closer to the judicial end of the spectrum: *their* primary purpose is to adjudicate disputes through some form of hearing. Tribunals at this end of the spectrum may possess court-like powers and procedures. These powers may bring with them stringent requirements of procedural fairness, including a higher requirement of independence ..."

[23] ... The main function of the Canadian Human Rights Tribunal is adjudicative ... [It] *is not involved in crafting policy* ...[67]

It seems to me that Justice McEwan's judgment in this respect cannot be gainsaid. One cannot possibly read paragraph 21 of the *Bell Canada* decision without accepting that the Supreme Court was recognizing two categories of tribunals: "some closer to the executive end of the spectrum" whose "primary purpose" is to "develop, or supervise the implementation of, particular government policies" – the tribunals dealt with in *Ocean Port* – *and* "other tribunals," whose "primary purpose is to adjudicate disputes." *Bell Canada* must be seen as acknowledging that the *Ocean Port* decision, explicitly dealing only with the former category, had nothing directly to say about the latter.

It seems to me that this discrepancy between the two descriptions in *Ocean Port* and in *Bell Canada* is the strongest doctrinal ground for dispensing with *Ocean Port* as an authority of any kind respecting the applicability of the PEI principle to *Bell Canada*'s "other tribunals," but it is not the only one. In *Bell Canada*, the Court was presented with the perfect opportunity to confirm that it did intend that the PEI principle would not apply to judicial tribunals. Finding, however, that on the facts in *Bell Canada* it was not necessary to address that issue, the Court elected not to do so, thus leaving the definite impression that it did in fact still see that question to be open.[68]

And then in *Ell,*[69] issued on the same day as *Bell Canada*, the Court defined the generic scope of the PEI principle's range in general terms. In this decision, the Court extended the application of the PEI principle beyond the category of "all courts" to Alberta's "non-sitting justices of the peace," and in the course of doing so, laid down a general formula for identifying the office-holders to which the principle was to apply. "The scope of the unwritten principle of independence must be interpreted," it said, "in accordance with its underlying purposes," and its application to any particular office-holders "depends on whether they exercise judicial functions *that relate to the bases upon which the principle is founded.*"[70] Those bases were threefold: "impartiality in adjudication, preservation of our constitutional order, and public confidence in the administration of justice."[71]

If one takes the second of these three summary labels, "preservation of our constitutional order," out of context, it may appear that the office-holders the *Ell* Court saw as attracting the protection of the PEI principle must be only those that are engaged "in the preservation of our constitutional order," a somewhat lofty assignment for most office-holders or judicial tribunals – certainly too lofty for non-sitting justices of the peace. However, when one examines the context, and particularly paragraph 22 of the *Ell* judgment, it is apparent that the Court is applying this label to the need our "constitutional order" has for bodies exercising judicial functions to be separate from the legislative and executive branches of government. It is not that the judicial offices in question must be engaged in the preservation of our constitutional order, but that, if our constitutional order is to be preserved, the independence of those offices from the legislative and executive branches of government must be protected by the application of the PEI principle.

In my opinion, it is simply self-evident that judicial tribunals do exercise judicial functions that "relate to the bases" upon which *Ell* holds the principle to be founded. (Furthermore, the Court's explicit use in *Ell* of the phrase "courts or tribunals" in this context is only consistent with the Court's expectation that tribunals will be included among the office-holder candidates to which the principle may apply.[72]) More generally, as McKenzie and I argued, there are no discernible constitutionally relevant distinctions between administrative judicial tribunals such as the Canadian Human Rights Tribunal or the workers' compensation appeals tribunals, and provincial family law courts, non-sitting justices of the peace, small claims court judges appointed to short, renewable terms, and municipal judges, to all of whom the PEI principle has been held to apply.

It is also important from a policy perspective to note that a constitutional requirement of judicial independence for administrative judicial tribunals is no more onerous than the common law requirements; in fact, they are exactly the same. The only difference is that the former cannot be overridden by legislation.

In everything that follows, I am assuming that in due course it will become settled law that the PEI principle of judicial independence applies as a matter of course to the judicial functions exercised by judicial tribunals and their members, and also to adjunct judicial functions exercised by regulatory agencies. Without the activation of these constitutional norms, any reform effort will be futile.

The Competence Issue

The actual competence of adjudicators – of judges or of judicial tribunal members – is not a justice-system issue that comes up very often – never in the jurisprudence and rarely in the literature. One exception is the following observation by Professor Philip Bryden in his case comment on the BC Court of Appeal decision in *Ocean Port:*

> If our goal is to ensure that Canadians receive a high quality of administrative justice, enhancing the [independence] of tribunal members will not significantly advance that goal (if it will advance it at all) unless we are confident that these individuals have the skills and temperament to use their independence wisely and to render sound and just decisions.[73]

Another exception is the following observation by Professor David Mullan in his study of administrative tribunals for the Royal Commission on the Economic Union and Development Prospects for Canada:

> However, the current [tribunal member appointment] system does not ensure competence; nor does it ensure, where there is no protection from arbitrary removal, that there can exist the confidence to exercise one's competence without fear for one's position. Also, the processes by which appointments are made do not ensure that a sufficient number of those qualified to be members are given serious, or any, consideration for the positions in question.[74]

One could argue that adjudicator competence is as much a rule-of-law requirement as adjudicator impartiality, but it is not an argument for which there is likely to be an attentive audience, and not one for which I have space in this book. It is self-evident, however, that the quality of justice available in the administrative justice system depends in fact, if not in law, on optimizing the average competence of the adjudicator members and chairs of the system's judicial tribunals.

Courts and judges, as well as administrative judicial tribunals and their adjudicator members, are integral components of any theory or conception of formal justice.[75] At the legitimizing centre of every liberal theory of justice is a "judge" – an adjudicative body structured to be, and to be seen to be, a credible means of resolving the uncertainties attendant on cases that fall within every general rule's inevitable penumbra of doubt. Since every liberal theory of justice embraces the principle that the lawmaking authority must ultimately reside exclusively in the theory's accepted lawgiver, it is not surprising that concerns about the mechanisms, means, or protocols through which the lawgiver delegates to unelected judges the authority to interpret its laws have spawned a whole literature on the subject of what judges must do and how they must be seen to do it. This literature travels under the label "the ideology of judging" (a label that is distinct, it must be carefully noted, from "ideological judging"). I touched on this literature earlier when ruling out ideological judging.

Leaving aside the question of the substantive merit of the various theories about the ideology of judging, the point that is relevant to the argument that optimizing adjudicator competence must be a central goal of any reform proposal is that a recurring theme in all those theories is the importance of the quality of the justification that judges provide for their resolution of issues falling within a penumbra of doubt. In their reasons in support of their decisions, judges must justify their choice of authorities – authorities that are to be found among a range of possibly relevant and legitimate candidates in the multiple, complex, and often subtle "fields of answers" – and must credibly demonstrate the rational and congruent connection between the chosen authorities and their decisions. Regardless of where such justification is seen to come from or whatever it may be thought to consist of, it is on the quality of that justification that the credibility and legitimacy of the decision depends. This reality has emerged recently as a major theme in the Canadian administrative justice system, where the quality of the justification found in tribunal reasons has become more and more a key element in determining the quality of the deference that courts will accord to tribunal decisions.[76]

It follows, therefore, that the job the theorists inevitably assign to the judge – the job that is in many respects at the centre of their theories – is not a job for less than optimal talents. The validity of these theories must surely depend on the assumption that judges are by and large competent. One cannot expect to always have Dworkin's "Hercules," but neither can one validly posit a corps of adjudicators whose competence is by definition – a definition inherent, say, in a society's dysfunctional processes for appointing and re-appointing adjudicators – on average *less than optimal*.

One cannot contemplate the onerous, complex, sophisticated, and cardinal role that all conceptions of formal justice assign to judges without understanding that a system of judicial appointments that fails to optimize their competence – that carelessly or willfully allows the average competence among judges to be less than optimal – is a system that undermines and subverts citizens' rights in a way that no rational theory of justice can possibly justify. Accordingly, one of the principal goals of my reform proposals will be to install the structures necessary to ensure that the competence of judicial tribunal adjudicators and chairs is, on average, always optimal.

5 The Reform Proposal

The issue of how to reconcile the effective administration of policies entrusted to administrative tribunals with the conflicting principles of ministerial responsibility and judicial independence has been said to have "defied resolution."[1] In my opinion, however, this is not a fair statement. In reality, in Canada, resolution of this issue has rarely been attempted; indeed, there has been barely any recognition that such an issue exists.

The fact is that the conflicting principles and needs of ministerial responsibility on the one hand and those of judicial tribunal independence on the other can be easily reconciled. The appropriate means are readily available. They were marshalled for that purpose – if to some degree providentially – in the Ontario Workers' Compensation Appeals Tribunal (WCAT) structures described in the Introduction. All that is necessary is for the executive branch to decide to accord independence to judicial tribunals. In this chapter, I will show that it is both necessary justice policy and in the executive branch's own interest to do so, and, of course, constitutionally necessary as well.

The essence of a principled administrative justice system is that it is composed of judicial tribunals that are manifestly impartial – that is, manifestly independent and disinterested – and whose chairs and members are optimally competent. I propose, therefore, that we eliminate inappropriate executive branch influences, and install structures and laws that will guarantee independence and impartiality – both the fact and the appearance –

and ensure optimal competence. My proposal would, however, reconcile the judicial tribunals' requirement for independence and autonomy with the executive branch's need to influence the judicial-tribunal–driven maturation of the policy for which it is responsible.

It is a bold proposal that calls for the enactment in each province and territory and in the federal jurisdiction of an Administrative Justice Bill of Rights and for the presence in each jurisdiction of six new structures: (1) an independent Governing Council for Administrative Justice; (2) a Ministry of Administrative Justice; (3) an independent Tribunal Audit Board; (4) an Omnibus Judicial Tribunal; (5) a School of Applied Studies in Administrative Justice; and (6) for each judicial tribunal, and for each specialized division of the Omnibus Judicial Tribunal, a Community Advisory Panel. The proposal also restructures or relocates some traditional relationships and functions, makes some policies illegal, and introduces a number of new policies embedded in the Administrative Justice Bill of Rights.

The prospect of six new structures would lead any reasonable person to ask about the cost, but the cost impact should not be excessive. The members of the Community Advisory Panels will be volunteers pursuing their own interests. The new Ministry of Administrative Justice and the Omnibus Judicial Tribunal will assume responsibility for functions currently performed in various other places, and existing budgets would be transferred to them; moreover they should be able to exercise those functions more efficiently. The proposal's additional administrative costs will be mainly attributable to the Governing Council.

Once it becomes known that patronage opportunities have been stripped away, it may also be possible for smaller jurisdictions to contract for some of these functions from the appropriate institutions in neighbouring jurisdictions, or to collaborate with neighbouring jurisdictions in organizing collaborative, cross-jurisdiction institutions. An interesting precedent with regard to the latter is the federal government's long-standing practice of delegating the administration and adjudication of workers' compensation claims within its jurisdiction to the workers' compensation boards and appeals tribunals of the provinces and territories where such claims arise. There is no federal workers' compensation board.

Regulatory Agencies

It must be emphasized that this proposal for reform is not concerned with changes to regulatory agencies insofar as their exercise of administrative or even quasi-judicial administrative functions is concerned. It does, however, include transferring to judicial tribunals any *judicial* functions now exercised by regulatory agencies. In the case of such transfers, I propose, however, that the regulatory agency or responsible minister be given the authority to review the decisions made by the judicial tribunal with respect to the law, and in appropriate cases to install course corrections for future cases. Also, as first suggested in Chapter 2, a regulatory agency's need for control of its adjudicative decisions can perhaps be reconciled with the justice system's need for independent adjudication by separating the fact-finding portion of the decision-making process from the policy-driven portion and assigning only the former to a judicial tribunal.[2]

No doubt most readers will continue to have concerns about the practicality of distinguishing between judicial functions and rights-determining functions of a purely administrative or quasi-judicial administrative nature, and I concede that at the margins it will not be easy. Nevertheless, the distinction is indispensable. If our judicial system is to conform to the rule of law, judicial functions, wherever they may be found, must be accorded constitutional protection for their independence and impartiality. On the other hand, if our regulatory regimes are to function as they should, administrative rights-determining functions, regardless of where they are found and whether or not they are quasi-judicial, must not be restrained by the dictates of the constitutional protection accorded to judicial functions. Therefore, however difficult it is to make the distinction – in the marginal cases, that is – it must nevertheless be made.

No doubt, in the marginal cases, deciding in a judicial review proceeding whether or not a rights-determining function is a judicial function will prove to be more art than science. It will be rather like deciding the judicial review issues on the basis of whether an administrative tribunal's proceedings are "fair" or its decisions or reasons are "reasonable." To a large extent, in such cases the approach with respect to the "judicial or not" issue will have to be the same as the courts' approach to the "fair or reasonable, or not" issues. We will simply have to rely on the courts to recognize the circumstances when fairness requires an impartial adjudicator when they see them. Let us not lose sight of the fact, however, that in the vast majority of cases the nature of the function will be clear beyond dispute.

It is commonly argued that a regulatory agency should be staffed by persons who share the government's world view with respect to the subject matters within its jurisdiction. To those who see it that way, political/patronage appointments to such agencies, and the government's use of its reappointment power to filter out members whose decision-making proves to be incompatible with the government's own policy perspectives, appear defensible. Whatever may be said for such a view, however, its validity must be judged against principles other than justice principles. And since that view does not impact on any justice system issue, I have no reason to deal with it in this book and I have not done so.

An Administrative Justice Bill of Rights

The proposed Administrative Justice Bill of Rights will have quasi-constitutional status by means of provisions that override conflicting provisions in other statutes, including human rights codes, unless the other statutes contain an explicit "notwithstanding" clause that includes a proviso that the conflicting provision will expire five years after its proclamation.

Anticipating the Supreme Court's ultimate confirmation of the constitutional requirement of independence and impartiality for administrative bodies exercising judicial functions, the Bill of Rights' core provision will be that no one may lawfully exercise a judicial function unless their independence and impartiality is objectively guaranteed in accordance with the *Valente* principles of judicial independence.

This provision will require a careful definition of "judicial function" as it applies in an administrative justice system context. The definition will have to mark the distinctions between judicial functions exercised by courts and judicial functions exercised by administrative judicial tribunals and their adjudicators, or entrusted to government offices; between judicial functions and administrative functions (including quasi-judicial administrative functions); and between administrative judicial tribunals and regulatory agencies. The following attempt at draft language for the Bill of Rights provides the gist of what the proposal contemplates.

1 A statutory, rights-determining function assigned to a body that is not a judge or a court is an administrative judicial function for purposes of this Act if:
   a the function is not a legislative function;
   b the exercise of the function results in a final determination of the rights of a party or parties; and
   c the principle of equality in the law is seen to require that the function be exercised by a manifestly independent and impartial body focused on determining what the law intends or requires and not on what the body exercising the function considers advisable in its own interest.

2 The body to which an administrative judicial function is assigned, whether it be an organization, an office, or an individual, shall be referred to herein as a "judicial tribunal."

3 A "final" determination of the rights of a party or parties is one for which there is no legal recourse other than an application or appeal to a court.

The Governing Council for Administrative Justice

To have an independent administrative justice system, one must have at its centre – as its hub, as it were – an independent governing body. I propose that it be called the "Governing Council for Administrative Justice." The establishment of the Governing Council is the core component of my proposal for many reasons, but what makes such a council in fact indispensable is the inescapable need for expert and independent supervision – supervision of the appointment processes, of the evaluation of the performance of judicial tribunals and their members and chairs, of the discharge of members or chairs for cause, and of the non-renewal of members or chairs for failure to meet standards.

The Council is not a new or radical idea, far from it. The need for an independent "council" or "centre" with oversight responsibilities for the administrative justice system has been a recurring theme in Canadian reports and is an established component of the administrative justice systems in Quebec, the United Kingdom, and Australia.

The Canadian Experience with Administrative Justice Councils

Margot Priest, in her 1992 "tribunal from hell" paper,[3] identifies, within the multitude of Canadian reports and studies she had reviewed, a "general agreement" on the need for some sort of organizing body or council to carry out various functions.[4] These functions, she reported, are commonly "training, advising on appointments and developing conflict guidelines or model procedural codes for tribunals." She cites the following comment from H.W.R. Wade as having been noted by several of the studies: "A body is needed which can deal with complaints as they are, instead of leaving them to build up into a volume of public discontent which every twenty-five years or so, discharges itself in a special but temporary inquest by a committee which merely reports once and then dissolves."[5]

In a 1988 discussion paper on administrative justice, the Ontario Law Commission proposed for discussion the idea of establishing a "permanent supervisory body."[6] In 1989, Robert Macaulay, in his report to the Ontario

Management Board of Cabinet, to which I have referred previously, proposed the establishment of a "co-ordinating body" to be called the "Council
for Administrative Agencies"[7] (although he lumped regulatory agencies and
administrative judicial tribunals together in the administrative agencies category). Macaulay's Council was to have a full-time chair, with membership
that included chairs from existing agencies, members of the public, the
bench, the Law Society, academia, the civil service, and representatives of
the Attorney General and Management Board. The Council would report
to the Management Board "in relation to its operational functions" and to
the Attorney General in relation to matters of "procedure, law and equity."
It would have its own physical location, with facilities for "education and
research activities."

Macaulay's Council was to have its hands full, with responsibilities for
developing consistent agency rules; administering a centralized training
function both for new appointees and incumbent members; assisting the
legislature with the review of agency performance; developing performance standards; coordinating public education about the administrative
justice system; rationalizing resources; serving as a research centre on new
techniques in the adjudicative process; developing an inventory of qualified
candidates for agency positions; reviewing draft legislation that would have
a bearing on the system; developing standards for providing intervenor
funding; and advising the government on such matters as salary, tenure, and
appointment and reappointment processes.

Professor Ed Ratushny's report to the Canadian Bar Association on federal tribunals came a year later and recommended for the federal sphere
of administrative justice both a "Commissioner for Federal Tribunals and
Agencies" and a "Council of Tribunal and Agency Heads".[8] The Commissioner
was to have the rank of Deputy Minister, reside in the Ministry of Justice,
and be the person to whom the tribunals would look for administrative support and budget, thus eliminating the hosting role of portfolio ministries.
The Commissioner would also be responsible for the initial screening of candidates for appointment as tribunal members and for conducting periodic
assessments of the performance of individual tribunals and agencies, reporting on these to the Minister of Justice and to the Council of Tribunal
and Agency Heads.[9]

The Council was to consist of the heads of all administrative adjudicative
tribunals (judicial tribunals in my terminology), the heads of all the regulatory agencies, and an equal number of laypersons appointed by the Minister
of Justice after consultation with the opposition parties. Its responsibilities

were to include the review of any chair's decision not to recommend the renewal of an appointment; establishment of a code of conduct; mediation of issues between chairs and members at the instance of either; ordering the discipline, removal, or reinstatement of any member; inquiry into any complaints from the Minister of Justice or any member of the public; and recommendations arising from the Commissioner's performance assessments.[10] Ratushny also recommended the establishment of a "National Centre for Research and Education in relation to Administrative Tribunals and Agencies."[11]

In 1996, Margot Priest's interest in the administrative justice system resurfaced in Ontario. In a research study commissioned by the Ontario Law Reform Commission,[12] she reviewed the reports that had proposed the creation of some form of central body and concurred with the proposals. She recommended an "Administrative Justice System Council" with the mandate to investigate complaints, deal with the discipline of tribunal members and chairs, mediate conflicts between tribunals and government, develop and administer adjudicator performance appraisals, be a research centre, and develop policy.

In 1997, the *Wood Report*[13] recommended that all Ontario regulatory and adjudicative agency chairs should report to one Minister of the Crown and be responsible to that Minister for their agency's performance and the management of its funds, but that the management of the agencies' financial and administrative operations should be placed in the hands of an administrative "Chief" reporting to a committee of all agency chairs.

In 1998, again in Ontario, the *Guzzo Report*[14] called for central coordination of various aspects of the regulatory and adjudicative agencies' work, but did not specify the structure through which such coordination might be accomplished.

These recommendations from the many previous studies all ended up on the shelf, and to this day there is nothing resembling an administrative justice centre or council in any Canadian jurisdiction outside Quebec. Although British Columbia did have its Administrative Justice Office, that office was part of the Ministry of Attorney General and had no independence from government. Disbanded in 2008, its mandate stated that it was "to be an innovative centre of research, to analyze, report on and, where appropriate, lead administrative justice reform initiatives to support the very best administrative justice system for British Columbians and ensure that that system presents an effective dispute resolution alternative."[15]

The province of Quebec, on the other hand, has a bona fide independent council called Conseil de la justice administrative.[16] The council consists of the following members:

1) The president of the Administrative Tribunal of Québec;
2) A member of the Administrative Tribunal of Québec other than the vice-president, chosen after consultation with all the members of the Tribunal;
3) The president of the Commission des lésions professionnelles;
4) A member of the Commission des lésions professionnelles other than the vice-president, chosen after consultation with all the commissioners of that Commission;
5) The president of the Commission des relations du travail;
6) A member of the Commission des relations du travail other than the vice-president, chosen after consultation with all the commissioners of that Commission;
7) The chairman of the Régie du logement;
8) A member of the Régie du logement other than the vice-chairman, chosen after consultation with all the commissioners of the Régie;
9) Nine other persons who are not members of any of those bodies, two of whom only shall be advocates or notaries chosen after consultation with their professional order.[17]

The paragraph 2, 4, 6, 8, and 9 members are appointed by the government. All members are appointed to three-year terms, renewable only once.[18]

The functions of the Quebec council in respect of the Administrative Tribunal of Québec and its members are:

- To establish a code of ethics applicable to the members of the Tribunal;
- To receive and examine any complaint lodged against a member ...;
- To inquire, at the request of the Minister or of the president of the Tribunal, into whether a member is suffering from a permanent disability; and
- To inquire, at the request of the Minister, into any lapse raised as grounds for removal of the president or a vice-president of the Tribunal from his administrative office ...[19]

The Council may also report to the Minister on any matter the Minister may submit to the Council.[20]

History of Councils in Other Jurisdictions

For a relatively recent, detailed account of administrative justice systems and structures in the United Kingdom, Australia, and New Zealand (and also in Quebec and British Columbia), see the New Zealand Law Reform Commission's 2008 report.[21]

Since 1975, Australia has had an Administrative Review Council consisting of the Ombudsman, the president of the Australian Law Reform Commission, the president of the Council (appointed by the Governor General), and three to ten other members who meet the specified qualifications, also appointed by the Governor General. In general, its function is to keep the Commonwealth administrative law system under review, monitor developments in administrative law, and recommend to the responsible Minister improvements to the system.[22]

In the United Kingdom, there had been since 1958 a Council on Tribunals, which had principally an advisory role. In the radical restructuring of the architecture of the country's administrative justice system in 2007, the Council was replaced with the Administrative Justice and Tribunals Council (AJTC).[23] The AJTC's description of its strategic objectives reads as follows:

To focus first and foremost on the needs of users.

To keep under review and influence the development of administrative justice and tribunals through:

- giving authoritative and principled advice and guidance to government, the Tribunals Service and others within the administrative justice system on changes to legislation, practices and procedures to improve the working of administrative justice, tribunals and inquiries, including a framework of generally applicable principles;
- exploring and promoting the scope for new approaches to dispute resolution;
- seeking to build up influence over forthcoming legislation, in particular in advance of publication;
- recognising and responding to the diverse needs and circumstances of users, by applying effective monitoring arrangements and being alert to emerging issues;
- raising awareness of the different approaches within the UK legal systems.

To keep under review the work of the Tribunals Service, the tribunals within it and other tribunals:

- offering advice and assistance on wider policy issues that complement the Tribunals Service's own work programme or otherwise affect tribunals;
- commenting from time to time on Tribunals Service priorities, standards and performance measures;
- monitoring progress and performance of tribunals against common standards and performance measures.

To respond authoritatively to emerging issues and proposals that affect or involve administrative justice, tribunals and inquiries more generally:

- identifying and responding to perceived needs and current/prospective concerns in relation to all aspects of administrative justice;
- identifying priorities for, and encouraging the conduct of, relevant research;
- monitoring the relationships between first instance decision makers, ombudsmen, tribunals and the courts to ensure they are clear, complementary and flexible;
- promoting the accessibility of administrative justice and tribunals to users through open, fair and impartial procedures and high quality, user friendly information and advice;
- employing a range of communication methods to give an account of its work and disseminate its views.[24]

In 2010, with the advent of the new Conservative government in the United Kingdom and its commitment to radical budget restraint, the AJTC was identified as one of the non-government statutory bodies to be abolished. It was expected that the government would complete the formal steps necessary to abolish the Council in the spring of 2012; however, the government's plan has faced widespread opposition and, at the time of writing, the abolition of the Council had yet to be accomplished. The Hansard record of the long debate in the House of Lords over the plan to abolish the Council – a debate that ended in what I believe was an egregiously unfortunate result (the motion to delete the Council from the list of organizations to be abolished was defeated) – ironically makes a timely, closely reasoned, and highly persuasive case as to why it is absolutely necessary for any credible administrative justice system to have such a centre.[25]

The Governing Council for Administrative Justice: Structure, Financing, and Functions

Structure

In my proposal, the Governing Council for Administrative Justice is consti-tuted by the Administrative Justice Bill of Rights. It is governed by an independ-ent and representative Board of Governors consisting of fifteen Governors, including the Board's Chair. Each position has qualification criteria and se-lection protocol and prerogatives defined by the Bill of Rights. The following list of suggested positions will provide a flavour of what is contemplated:

- one position for the judiciary, to be filled by a judge or retired judge of the Provincial, Territorial, or Superior Court, appointed by the government
- three "tribunal" positions, to be filled by persons who have senior admin-istrative justice adjudicative experience and who are elected by judicial tribunal adjudicators in an election administered by the Canadian Bar Association or its provincial or territorial sections
- two "public interest" positions, to be filled by persons who are not law-yers and who may be reasonably seen as representative of the public in-terest, appointed by the government
- two "labour" positions, to be filled by persons with senior labour move-ment experience, selected by a designated labour movement organization
- two "business" positions, to be filled by persons who are experienced busi-ness persons, selected by a designated business community organization
- two "legal clinic" positions, to be filled by persons with senior legal aid clinic experience or its equivalent, selected by a designated legal aid organization (for example, the Association of Community Legal Services Clinics in Ontario)
- one "lawyer" position, to be filled by a person who is a practising member of the bar, selected by the Canadian Bar Association or its provincial or territorial sections
- one "academic" position, to be filled by a person who is a tenure-stream member of a local law faculty with expertise in administrative law, se-lected by a majority of the other Governors
- a Chair of the Board of Governors nominated by the government but whose appointment has been approved by a unanimous vote of the Governors. Judges or retired judges may not be appointed as Chair.[26]

I propose that the appointments to the Governor positions be three-year, order-in-council appointments renewable three times, and that the

appointment as Chair be a five-year, order-in-council appointment, also renewable three times. Reappointments of Governors shall be made upon the
recommendation of the Board Chair, and reappointment of the Chair upon
the recommendation of a two-thirds majority of the Governors voting by
secret ballot *in camera* in the absence of the Chair.

Governors might be paid a reasonable *per diem* for attendance at meetings and would be reimbursed for reasonable travelling expenses.

Direction and oversight of the day-to-day business of the Governing
Council would be provided principally by an executive committee of Gov-
ernors appointed by the Board, working with a full-time staff led by a
President and Chief Executive Officer.

The proposal contemplates that the President and Chief Executive Officer
would be appointed by the Board of Governors, and would be removable by
the Board during his or her term only for cause.

Financing: Inalienable Core Funding

Besides structuring the Board of Governors, and specifying the Governing
Council's functions and responsibilities, the Bill of Rights will also establish
inalienable core funding for the Council. To be and be seen to be fully independent, the Governing Council must be freed from dependence on the
government for its budget. The Bill of Rights will therefore require the government to provide the Council with an annual allotment of funds in the
amount of some specified percentage of the total of the annual budgets for
all of that government's regulatory agencies and administrative judicial tribunals. This percentage, set initially in the Bill of Rights, will, also by provision in the Bill of Rights, be subject to review at periodic intervals by the
Tribunal Audit Board (see below). I also propose that the Bill of Rights give
the Council the powers of a natural person, including the right to hold sur-
pluses for spending in future years as needed. The Council's other sources of
revenue will include charges for services provided to individual tribunals.

Functions

In my 1999 article "The Administrative Justice System in the New
Millennium: A Vision in Search of a Centre,"[27] I had occasion to give considerable thought to the functions that one would need to assign to what I
called a "Centre for Administrative Justice." There is not much that I would
change. My proposal gives the Governing Council duties and powers in
three categories of functions: oversight, research, and education.

The oversight category includes supervision of the congruency of the design and operation of the administrative justice system and its various components with rule-of-law, justice-system principles and standards, including, but not limited to, the right of prior approval of:

1 the accountability relationships and operational context respecting any person or institution that the government proposes be empowered to exercise a judicial function as defined in the Administrative Justice Bill of Rights
2 the length of the term of appointment of a judicial tribunal adjudicator or chair
3 the qualifications to be required of candidates for appointment as an adjudicator, or as the chair, of any particular judicial tribunal
4 the processes and protocols governing the recruitment, selection, and appointment of new judicial tribunal adjudicators and chairs
5 the processes, protocols, and standards governing evaluations in the ordinary course of the individual performance of judicial tribunal adjudicators and judicial tribunal chairs, or of the institutional performance of judicial tribunals
6 the terms of reference, processes, protocols, and standards governing episodic reviews of a judicial tribunal adjudicator's or chair's performance or conduct, or of a judicial tribunal's institutional performance
7 the processes, protocols, and standards governing the reappointment or non-reappointment of incumbent judicial tribunal adjudicators and chairs
8 the processes, protocols, and standards governing the termination of an appointment of a judicial tribunal adjudicator or chair for lack of capacity, misconduct, or other common law justifications for discharge
9 the structural design and operational plans and the constitutive legislation for new or reconfigured judicial tribunals, and of the disposition or reassignment of adjudicators or chairs whose positions have been affected by any reconfiguration or discontinuation of a judicial tribunal.

The Governing Council will also have the exclusive right to:

1 design, establish, and supervise public complaints processes for judicial tribunals
2 designate the persons who are to conduct any episodic review of a judicial tribunal adjudicator's or chair's performance or conduct, or of a

judicial tribunal's performance, and to initiate such reviews on its own motion at any time

3 specify tribunal reporting requirements respecting institutional performance of judicial functions

4 review and approve a judicial tribunal's education and training programs

5 issue public reports on any administrative justice issue, at any time.

The Council will also be authorized to mediate disputes between judicial tribunals and the Ministry of Administrative Justice (see below) over job classification issues and other administrative accountability issues, and between judicial tribunal adjudicators and their chairs.

The Council's research functions may include:

1 an online, always current administrative justice bibliography covering administrative justice literature, including conference papers and studies and reports from all relevant administrative justice jurisdictions

2 an administrative justice reporting service covering significant decisions of generic interest to the administrative justice system from Canadian tribunals and from Canadian, UK, and other courts or tribunals

3 a periodic news service designed to keep judicial tribunals and their adjudicators up-to-date on relevant developments in their own and other administrative justice jurisdictions

4 banks of best practices information

5 compilation of judicial tribunal rules and practice guidelines

6 the commissioning of administrative justice research projects.

I also propose that the Bill of Rights give the Council a general oversight jurisdiction concerning the education and training of adjudicators and chairs, including the authority to promote and accredit programs. It would be expected to work in this regard with those organizations already active in the field, such as the Society of Ontario Adjudicators and Regulators (SOAR), Osgoode Hall Law School, the BC Council of Administrative Tribunals (BCCAT), the Council of Canadian Administrative Tribunals (CCAT), Alberta's Foundation of Administrative Justice, and so on, and to play a direct role in educating the public about the administrative justice system, particularly in communities of potential users. The Council's jurisdiction would include the accreditation of the programs offered by the proposed new School of Applied Studies in Administrative Justice (see below) and other post-secondary, college, or university programs devoted to the training and accreditation of judicial tribunal adjudicators and chairs.

A Ministry of Administrative Justice

One of the core components of my proposal for reform is the elimination of the structural integration of administrative judicial tribunals and portfolio ministries. These close-knit relationships are the antithesis of both institutional and individual independence; replete with conflicts of interest, they cannot be reconciled with any perception of impartiality. As we have seen, one can no longer pretend, as governments now do, and as the legal system itself did at one time,[28] that the conflicts of interest and the lack of judicial independence inherent in the integration of a judicial tribunal's structures with its host ministry's structures are, from a justice perspective, benign – legally or otherwise.

The need for judicial tribunals to be administratively accountable to government will continue, however, and my proposal specifies a new point of contact. At first glance, the most obvious choice would have been the Ministries of Attorney General (among which I include the federal Department of Justice and Attorney General), but this is not my choice. My proposal calls for the transfer of the responsibility for hosting administrative judicial tribunals to a new Ministry of Administrative Justice in each province or territory as well as federally.

The creation of a specialized Ministry of Administrative Justice is a novel idea but an important one.[29] Nothing could better give the administrative justice system in all of the jurisdictions in Canada outside of Quebec the standing and priority the system obviously requires but has never had. The creation of such a ministry in each jurisdiction would mark, in a major and public way, a point of renewal and provide a fresh, high-profile focus for the administrative justice component of our justice system.

There is also a strong case to be made against using Ministries of Attorney General as the new point of contact. In the past, reformers concerned about the debilitating conflicts of interest inherent in having portfolio ministries host their own tribunals have always proposed transferring hosting responsibilities to the Attorney General, but this was a strategy born principally of the absence of anything else in the nature of a safe harbour. With a Ministry of Administrative Justice in view, the shortcomings of the Attorney General ministries for this role become evident.

In the first place, Attorneys General have no history of interest in the administrative justice system *per se*. Because of their heavy responsibilities for the courts and the criminal justice system and for handling constitutional issues, the administrative justice system has been for them a largely unregarded – indeed, unrecognized – topic. The absence of Attorney General intervention in administrative justice system issues, as opposed to their dealing with the problems of the particular tribunals that they themselves are hosting, has always been a feature of their work. That lacuna speaks volumes about the need for a new ministry with a single-minded administrative justice focus. Indeed, it has been Attorney General and Justice lawyers who, since the Supreme Court of Canada's decision in *PEI Reference*,[30] have always led the charge against the recognition of any constitutional protection for the independence of judicial tribunals. And, of course, the Ontario Criminal Injuries Compensation Board justice system train wreck occurred on the watch of a long list of Ontario Attorneys General.

The Ontario Provincial Auditor's report of his value-for-money audit of the Ministry of Community and Social Services' first-level adjudication of claims under the Ontario Disability Support Program (ODSP), to which I will be referring later,[31] evidences the type of "tin ear" that is often found within the executive branch bureaucracy when it comes to administrative judicial tribunals. And the Ministries of Attorney General are not immune.

Especially compelling evidence of the typical tuned-out position of Attorneys General vis-à-vis judicial tribunals is provided by the multitude of studies with which the country's Attorneys General have recently been involved concerning the problem of "access to civil justice" – studies in which the role of judicial tribunals has never figured. For example, in 2006 the Ontario Attorney General appointed Coulter Osborne, former Associate Chief Justice of Ontario, to lead the Civil Justice Reform Project. It tasked Osborne with developing options to "reform the civil justice system to make it more accessible and affordable for Ontarians," yet nowhere in his terms of reference or in his report will one find any reference to tribunals.

Thus, we have numerous studies devoted to considering every possible avenue for improving access to the civil justice system yet judicial tribunals are never in the picture. This is despite the fact that access to judicial tribunals is itself inherently a part of the access to civil justice problem and, historically, tribunals have always been seen as one of the solutions to such access problems; indeed, the latter perception largely accounts for their existence. Nevertheless, it is as though, in the first decade of the twenty-first century, for Canada's Attorneys General the administrative justice system had ceased to exist.

Finally, moving the hosting of judicial tribunals to the Ministries of Attorney General would not solve the conflict problem. An Attorney General's client is the government. When the government is a party to a dispute being heard by a judicial tribunal, it is the Ministry of Attorneys General's lawyers who appear on behalf of the government. Attorneys General and Justice Department lawyers also act for governments when they challenge tribunal decisions through judicial review applications or appeals.

I concede that the latter criticism applies equally to the long-standing responsibility of Attorneys General for the administration of the courts, and I would argue that the same criticism is valid there. This has been recognized in the United Kingdom by the recent transfer of responsibility for the courts from the Lord Chancellor to a Ministry of Justice, and it is a view shared by the Canadian Judicial Council.[32] But that is a concern for another day and someone else's book. My reform proposal envisages a new day for the administrative justice system, and there is no reason to mar that day by a reflexive adherence to traditions that are not defensible in principle. Accordingly, my proposal is that the hosting of all administrative judicial tribunals be assigned to a new Ministry of Administrative Justice in each relevant jurisdiction.

This hosting role as I envisage it will not be as invasive as has been the case with portfolio ministries. Judicial tribunal chairs will be their tribunal's chief executive officers in the fullest sense of the term, and judicial tribunal chief administrative officers and chief financial officers will report to the tribunal chair, not to the Ministry. Only the tribunal chair will report to the Ministry. Judicial tribunal staff will be employees of the tribunal, not members of the public service.

The new Ministry will not provide administrative support services, which will be provided either by autonomous in-house tribunal departments or, where the size of the tribunal makes this impracticable, by the new Omnibus Judicial Tribunal (see below). Nor will the new Ministry have the right of prior approval for the various judicial tribunal strategies and instruments of accountability, governance, and communications, such as those that Ontario's *Adjudicative Tribunals Accountability, Governance and Appointments Act* currently assigns to the host ministers. Under my proposal, it will be the Governing Council's responsibility to ensure that instruments of this type meet system standards.

The judicial tribunals' administrative budgets will be developed and defended by the tribunals and their chairs and will not be part of a Ministry of Administrative Justice's budget. The Ministry's jurisdiction, however, will include review and approval of the tribunal budgets and the shepherding of those budgets through the government's budget approval processes. It will also include the administration of tribunal funding, and oversight responsibilities concerning tribunal administrative accountability. The new Ministry will be able to intervene whenever a judicial tribunal appears to be in trouble from an administrative perspective.

The responsibilities of the Ministry of Administrative Justice would also include:

- being the host ministry for the Governing Council for Administrative Justice, the Omnibus Judicial Tribunal, and the Tribunal Audit Board
- administration of the order-in-council appointments and reappointments of judicial tribunal adjudicators and chairs
- administration of financial audits and other tribunal administrative accountability mechanisms
- collaboration with the Governing Council in the approval and design of all new administrative justice judicial functions and the initial drafting of all legislation related to administrative justice
- working with the Omnibus Judicial Tribunal and the Governing Council in identifying and disseminating best practices
- promoting standards of excellence within the administrative justice system generally
- advising the government on administrative justice issues
- administering the Administrative Justice Bill of Rights
- working with the Governing Council to identify and champion new administrative justice strategies and structures.

The Omnibus Judicial Tribunal

The Proposal

The Omnibus Judicial Tribunal is of the genre sometimes referred to as "super tribunals." Such tribunals have been a recurring subject of discussion within administrative justice communities since Australia created its Administrative Appeals Tribunal in 1975. My proposal contemplates the creation of the Omnibus Judicial Tribunal by the Administrative Justice Bill of Rights as the home of the judicial rights-determining functions now exercised by boutique tribunals and by major tribunals whose functions could be conveniently and effectively folded into one large tribunal organization. The new tribunal would also become the source of administrative and other support services now typically provided by the portfolio ministries.

In the past, I have had two occasions to write about the value of such a tribunal. The more recent article explored my reasons at some length,[33] and I draw on it extensively in the discussion that follows.

"Omnibus Judicial Tribunal" is a useful generic description but as the title of an actual operating tribunal it falls flat. In Ontario, I would call such a tribunal "the Provincial Tribunal," and that is what I called it in my previous articles. To emphasize its generic nature, however, I will in the following paragraphs use the "Omnibus Judicial Tribunal" label, or "Omnibus Tribunal" for short.

The principal feature of the Omnibus Tribunal from which most of the advantages would flow is its scale. In Ontario it might eventually assume the functions of twenty to thirty existing tribunals. Australia's omnibus tribunal deals with issues arising in more than 350 different statutes. Naturally, the first thing that comes to mind is the cost savings that might result. If one takes twenty or thirty management structures and collapses them into one, one might well anticipate cost savings. Several factors, however, suggest that such savings might prove elusive. These include the greater sophistication and complexity of the Omnibus Tribunal's management structure, the need to structure the Tribunal with specialized divisions and subdivisions so that the specialization and expertise that are the hallmark advantages of an administrative justice system will not be lost, and the modernization of adjudicator compensation levels that would be required in a tribunal of this stature.

Much more to the point are the other important advantages that such a tribunal's pre-eminent stature and high public profile would be sure to deliver. Its stature would, for instance, require, and attract, leaders with impeccable qualifications and reputations, and the Tribunal would have to be provided with the wherewithal to ensure that compensation packages reflect fairly those qualifications and status. The Omnibus Tribunal's size, status, and profile would also necessitate a sophisticated and effective management structure.

The necessarily high public profile of the Omnibus Tribunal would also provide the administrative justice system for the first time with a focused public persona that would bring the system to the surface of public consciousness. Administrative justice in the hands of the Omnibus Judicial Tribunal would become more the general public's business than at present, when each of a large number of small tribunals impacts only on a small segment of the public. Such a profile would create pressures to achieve performance excellence that would be difficult to resist; the quality of administrative justice would have the potential for becoming an actual political issue.

The scale of the Tribunal and its responsibilities for adjudication of justiciable rights disputes arising in a number of different statutory enterprises would tend to dilute its public association with any particular enterprise and thus ameliorate the stress experienced by single tribunals arising from their public association with one statutory rights enterprise. As we have seen, one of the problems with single-focus tribunals is their inherent vulnerability to political undermining by disgruntled parties and their allies. They are also hard-pressed to achieve and maintain the public reputation that results in controversial decisions being accepted, even by those who think them wrong, as at least a good faith and probably competent fulfillment of a tribunal's duty.

In addition, the scale of the Omnibus Judicial Tribunal would foster the development of sophisticated technology, and allow for the intelligent, centralized management of common resources and support services that are now spread in small isolated pieces in twenty or thirty different places. The scale of operations would also result in greater efficiencies and effectiveness in the utilization of adjudicative resources. Proportional process, the deployment of adjudicators at varying and appropriate skill levels, and the enhanced flexibility that comes with cross-appointments and internal seconding would all be possible.

The physical size of the Tribunal, the societal significance of its mandate, and the political clout that goes with all of that, as well as the price that would be paid by such a tribunal, its high-profile leaders, and the government of the day should its public reputation falter, would motivate the Tribunal to work with the Governing Council to resist the patronage culture of appointments and to embrace competitive and objective selection processes and appropriate qualification standards.

With all of these adjudicators operating in one cost centre, it will also no longer be possible to hide the actual cost of ill-considered policies. Take, for example, the policy of the federal government, and the policy recently adopted by the Ontario government, of arbitrarily limiting the service of an appointee in any one judicial tribunal position to a maximum of ten years. Experienced adjudicators are to be arbitrarily dismissed after ten years of service. No effort has been made to justify this policy, nor has there been any attempt to calculate the cost. The cost will be paid in the loss of tribunal efficiency, the distraction of management, the expense of running repetitive recruitment and training activities, the dilution of the quality of decision making through reduction in the average experience level of tribunal adjudicators, and, most importantly, the discouragement of potential career-minded adjudicator candidates. One does not have to think very hard about this to know that, over an entire system, the cost of such a policy, both in dollars and in the quality and fairness of decisions, will be significant.[34] In an Omnibus Tribunal context, such costs would immediately be seen to be intolerable.

The Omnibus Judicial Tribunal will be especially important as a home for the boutique tribunals and for the adjunct judicial functions now being exercised by regulatory agencies. The Fairness Committee's proposal to assign the adjudicative functions of the Ontario Securities Commission to a new and independent adjudicative tribunal might have been implemented had there been an existing omnibus tribunal with a known reputation to which those functions could have been conveniently transferred.[35]

Over time, as they proved their worth and competence, Omnibus Judicial Tribunals could be expected to become the workhorses of the administrative justice system: efficient, expert, competent, independent, robust, and accessible, and perhaps eventually accommodating a large proportion of the administrative justice judicial functions now housed in a variety of small, medium, and large but isolated tribunals – in fact, tribunals with the potential to grow into the type of far-reaching super tribunals now found in Quebec and Australia and recently created in the United Kingdom.

The Experience with Super Tribunals in Other Jurisdictions
Australia's Administrative Appeals Tribunal (AAT) commenced operations on 1 July 1976. The description of its functions, powers, and jurisdiction as it appears on the Tribunal's website reads:

The Tribunal is an independent body that reviews a wide range of administrative decisions made by Australian Government ministers, officials, authorities and other tribunals. The Tribunal can also review administrative decisions made by state government and non-government bodies in limited circumstances.

Merits review of an administrative decision involves its reconsideration. On the facts before it, the Tribunal decides whether the correct – or, in a discretionary area, the preferable – decision has been made in accordance with the applicable law. It will affirm, vary or set aside the decision under review.

The Tribunal is not always the first avenue of review of an administrative decision. In some cases, it cannot review a decision until an internal review has been conducted by the body that made the primary decision. In other cases, review by the Tribunal is only available after intermediate review by a specialist tribunal. For example, in the area of social security, an application may be made to the Tribunal only after review by the Social Security Appeals Tribunal.

Section 33 of the AAT Act requires that proceedings of the Tribunal be conducted with as little formality and technicality, and with as much expedition, as the requirements of the Act and a proper consideration of the matters before the Tribunal permit. The Tribunal is not bound by the rules of evidence and can inform itself in any manner it considers appropriate.

The Tribunal does not have a general power to review decisions made under Commonwealth legislation. The Tribunal can only review a decision if an Act, regulation or other legislative instrument provides specifically that the decision is subject to review by the Tribunal. Jurisdiction is generally conferred by the enactment under which the reviewable decision was made.

The AAT has jurisdiction to review decisions made under approximately 400 separate Acts and legislative instruments. Decisions in the areas of social security, taxation, veterans' affairs and workers' compensation constitute the bulk of the Tribunal's workload. The Tribunal also reviews decisions in areas such as bankruptcy, civil aviation, corporations law, customs, freedom of information, immigration and citizenship, industry assistance and security assessments undertaken by the Australian Security Intelligence Organisation.[36]

For Canadians, the most relevant other administrative justice jurisdiction is the United Kingdom, which has recently made earth-shaking reforms in the structures of its administrative justice system. In the first stage of these reforms, the United Kingdom enacted the *Constitutional Reform Act 2005* (CRA),[37] which, among other things (such as transferring the judicial functions of the House of Lords to a new Supreme Court), created an independent Judicial Appointments Commission for the appointment of judges and gave that Commission responsibility for selecting and appointing tribunal adjudicators (now called "administrative law judges" and appointed to *life-tenured positions*).

Next, in 2006, the conflicts of interest between portfolio ministries and their tribunals were ended. All tribunal administrative support was transferred from the portfolio ministries to an independent single agency, "Tribunals Service," located in the new Ministry of Justice.

Then the super tribunal concept was introduced. In 2007, the British Parliament enacted the *Tribunals, Courts and Enforcement Act 2007* (TCEA).[38] In a speech to the University of Toronto Symposium on the Future of Administrative Justice in January 2008, Lord Justice Carnwath, the United Kingdom's Lord Justice of Appeal and the newly appointed Senior President of Tribunals, described the effect of the TCEA as it relates to the super tribunal concept:

> The TCEA creates two new, generic tribunals, the *First-tier Tribunal* and the *Upper Tribunal,* into which existing tribunal jurisdictions can be transferred. The First-tier will hear first instance cases, and will deal with fact and law. The Upper Tribunal is intended to be primarily, but not exclusively, an appellate tribunal from the First-tier Tribunal. The Act also provides for the establishment of "chambers" within the two tribunals so that the many jurisdictions that will be transferred into the new tribunals can be divided into groups with related interests. Each chamber will be headed by a Chamber President and overall leadership will be provided by the Senior President of Tribunals.[39]

The UK government has now implemented virtually all of the radical recommendations of the *Leggatt Report,*[40] thus fully justicizing an executive branch justice system that five years ago appears to have suffered from many of the deficiencies of Canada's executive branch administrative justice system as described in these pages.

New Zealand's government proposed a similar justicizing of its administrative justice structure,[41] and, as appears from the review of the systems of "other jurisdictions" in the New Zealand Law Commission's 2008 report "Tribunals in New Zealand,"[42] the various Territories of Australia have now adopted structures akin to the Commonwealth's Administrative Appeals Tribunal.

The Canadian Experience with Omnibus Tribunals

The Australian experience with its super tribunal had no impact in Canada until 1994, when New Brunswick might be said to have partially embraced the concept of a super tribunal when it created its Labour and Employment Board. That Board's jurisdiction includes the adjudication of disputes under six major statutes: the *Industrial Relations Act,* the *Public Service Labour Relations Act,* the *Fisheries Bargaining Act,* the *Employment Standards Act,* the *Pension Benefits Act,* and the *Human Rights Act.*[43]

The Australian precedent was first specifically considered in Quebec, in the planning of the major restructuring of its administrative justice system preceding the introduction of the Tribunal administratif du Québec (TAQ, Quebec Administrative Tribunal) in 1996. TAQ is a super administrative appeals tribunal that is at least a close relative to the Australian model. As Professor France Houle tells us, the Ouellette report[44] considered but rejected the Australian model and proposed instead the creation of four super tribunals, each specializing in a particular area of the law. Subsequently, the Garant report[45] proposed one tribunal with four divisions, and this is what was accepted. TAQ's four divisions are the Social Affairs Division, the Immovable Properties Division, the Territory and Environment Division, and the Economic Affairs Division.[46]

In Ontario, the Australian precedent itself attracted little attention but in 1998-99, with little fanfare, the government created in three different areas of adjudication what might well be called omnibus or super tribunals: the Licence Appeal Tribunal,[47] the Agriculture, Food and Rural Affairs Appeal Tribunal,[48] and the Health Services Appeal and Review Board.[49]

The scope of the jurisdiction of these amalgamated tribunals is exemplified by the Licence Appeal Tribunal's website description of its mandate:

> The mandate of LAT is to provide fair, impartial and efficient decisions concerning compensation claims and licensing activities regulated by several ministries of the provincial government including Ministry of Government Services, Ministry of Children and Youth Services, Ministry of Training, Colleges and Universities, Ministry of Transportation, and Ministry of Municipal Affairs and Housing and Ministry of Community Safety and Correctional Services.
>
> LAT gets its enabling powers from 21 statutes that include a right of appeal to this Tribunal.[50]

In February 2001, the Ontario Labour Ministry presented for public consultation a formal proposal for the creation of an Ontario omnibus tribunal: the "Unified Workplace Tribunal." The proposal contemplated the merger of the Human Rights Commission, the Labour Relations Board, and the

Workplace Safety and Insurance Appeals Tribunal, among others. After about five months of public controversy, the government concluded that there was no "consensus of support" within the stakeholder communities and the proposal was formally withdrawn.[51]

The current Ontario government has evinced a continuing interest in the concept of "clustering" – bringing together a number of related tribunals in a cooperative working environment. A limited version of this concept was first applied in the late 1990s to the Ontario Labour Relations Board and the Workplace Safety and Insurance Appeals Tribunal. For a number of years, the two tribunals have been located on adjacent floors in the same building and have been sharing reception services, library resources, and hearing rooms.

More recently, in September 2006, the government announced the Agency Cluster Project and appointed Kevin Whitaker (then chair of the Ontario Labour Relations Board and now a Justice of the Ontario Superior Court) as the "Agency Cluster Facilitator" to work with five tribunals in the municipal, environment, and land planning sector with a view to finding ways to improve services through "cross-agency cooperation and coordination of operations, administration and dispute resolution services while respecting the unique roles and mandates of each." The tribunals in question were the Assessment Review Board, the Conservation Review Board, the Board of Negotiation, the Environmental Review Tribunal, and the Ontario Municipal Board.

Following the Facilitator's final report,[52] this clustering became operational on a cooperative basis in 2009. The concept of clustering received formal approval and statutory authorization in Ontario's 2009 *Adjudicative Tribunals Accountability, Governance and Appointments Act*.[53] In 2010, the Ontario government announced its intention to form a second cluster, this time bringing together the Human Rights Tribunal, the Landlord and Tenant Board, the Social Benefits Tribunal, and two boutique tribunals, and this has now been accomplished. In these clustering arrangements, each clustered tribunal retains its own structure and responsibilities as defined by its existing constitutive legislation, which continues in force, but with another layer of senior, coordinating management added. It is still too early to tell whether this will prove to be a successful concept.[54]

An issue with omnibus tribunals and clustered tribunals that has not received much attention is the problems obviously inherent in combining in one super or clustered tribunal the jurisdictions of both judicial tribunals and regulatory agencies. Ontario's three amalgamated tribunals referred to above are examples of organizations that would seem to have been assigned both judicial and regulatory functions. When the time comes to determine what their "principal" function is for purpose of assessing the level of independence they require – as the Supreme Court had to do in *Bell Canada* with respect to the Canadian Human Rights Tribunal[55] – the complications involved in combining tribunals that belong in different categories will have to be faced.

The Proposed Structure

In the 1997 article in which I first talked about a Provincial Tribunal in Ontario,[56] I proposed a specific structure and described it in considerable detail. Looking back on it now, I remain convinced that it was a good proposal, perhaps a bit too creative at the margins but respectable overall. It was written without the idea of the Governing Council in mind, and so with regard to the handling of disputes between tribunal members and tribunal chairs there is some overlap between the responsibilities I envisioned then for the Provincial Tribunal's Board of Governors and those that I would now assign to the Governing Council. Subject to this change, I remain satisfied with that earlier proposal as far as it went. There is no reason to repeat it here in all its detail; however, to complete the picture of the restructuring of the administrative justice system that my reform proposal contemplates, I would highlight the following:

- The Omnibus Tribunal is conceived as an expert, stand-alone, multi-layered judicial tribunal so structured as to be readily expandable to effectively accommodate the transfer to it of any number of specialized judicial functions of whatever size.
- Created by the Administrative Justice Bill of Rights, it would be structured, effectively, as a Crown corporation, with the contractual, financial management, and investment powers of a natural person.
- Its Board of Directors would have positions with specified selection criteria and appointment protocols much like the Board of Governors proposed above for the Governing Council (although with fewer members). In the provinces, the corporation might be called "The Provincial Tribunal."
- The Bill of Rights would give the government the statutory power to effect the transfer of judicial functions from existing tribunals to the Omnibus Tribunal by regulations at any time that it proves convenient or expedient to do so.

- The Bill of Rights would authorize the Tribunal to make or review any judicial decisions affecting legal rights or obligations in Ontario, or elsewhere, provided only that the jurisdiction to make or review such decisions is not exclusive to the courts and that it has been assigned to the Tribunal by law *or by the agreement of the parties to a dispute.*
- The dispute resolution functions of the Tribunal would be devoted principally to the adjudicative work of administrative judicial tribunals whose jurisdiction has been assigned to it. However – and this is a particularly novel aspect of the proposal – the Tribunal's expert adjudicative services would also be available to other sectors, such as universities, municipalities, or the private sector, on a fee-for-service basis.
- The Tribunal would, as well, have the authority to conduct public inquiries requested by the government, also on a fee-for-service basis.
- To accommodate the need to maintain the benefits of the flexibility and specialized expertise inherent in the administrative justice system, the Bill of Rights would provide for the Tribunal to be structured in divisions and subdivisions of specialization headed by Tribunal adjudicators appointed as Division Chairs who would have responsibilities within their divisions akin to a judicial tribunal chair's responsibilities for a tribunal's adjudication.
- It would be necessary for the Omnibus Tribunal to retain the current system's capacity to fashion unique responses to unique challenges, but in the Omnibus Tribunal those unique aspects could be rationally developed against the backdrop of a common and familiar context.
- To help maintain the confidence of user communities, each division would work with a separate Community Advisory Panel (see below).
- The inaugural transfer of judicial tribunals or other adjudicative functions to the Omnibus Judicial Tribunal might prudently be confined to the functions of three or four tribunals that would provide the Tribunal with a core business that it could readily assimilate and around which it could develop its organization, resources, and skills.
- The Omnibus Tribunal would be authorized by the Bill of Rights to establish from time to time multi-member Review Panels consisting of senior Tribunal adjudicators designated by the Tribunal Chair.[57] The enabling legislation would provide that decisions of Review Panels would be binding in future cases with respect to the same issues, but only in future cases.
- Review Panels would not hear appeals by parties of decisions in individual cases; instead, they would review and determine generic issues referred by the Chief Adjudicator or a Division Chair in much the way

that courts sometimes hear "stated cases." These would be issues of general systemic interest to the Tribunal or to one or more categories of parties to the Tribunal's proceedings. A Review Panel's determination would not affect the rights of parties in previously decided cases, including the case from which the referral may have originated.

• The review and determination of a generic issue by a Review Panel would be separate from the Tribunal's usual processes for exercising its reconsideration powers regarding the outcome in a particular case. The latter powers would be exercised at the Division level.
• The act would authorize the Tribunal to establish a two-tier system of adjudication for any particular categories of cases. In such a system, the second tier would perform an appeals function accessible by the parties, but perhaps only with leave of the Tribunal.
• Tribunal decisions would be final. There would be no *appeal* to the courts on either fact or law. The Act, however, would contemplate judicial review by the courts in the ordinary course.

Omnibus Tribunal Funding

With respect to the adjudication functions transferred to the Omnibus Tribunal, the Bill of Rights would provide for funding of the Tribunal on the basis of a multi-year contract with fixed prices for the estimated caseload, automatically adjustable annually in response to cost-of-living increases; the Tribunal would have the right to reopen the contract's pricing provision in response to unexpected increases in caseload. The first contract would cover a five-year period.

To minimize the Tribunal's financial dependency on the government's goodwill, the financial supervision mandate of the new Tribunal Audit Board (see below) would apply to the Tribunal. The Tribunal Audit Board would be responsible, as well, for evaluating the Tribunal's compliance with its agreed-upon performance parameters.

As mentioned above, the funding would also be supplemented by the profits from the Omnibus Tribunal's "business" of offering its expert – and independent – adjudication services and *ad hoc* inquiry services to the government and to other sectors, including the private sector, on a fee-for-service basis.

The Omnibus Judicial Tribunal's Role as Provider of Support Services to Other Tribunals

There is one aspect of the Omnibus Judicial Tribunal's jurisdiction that was not suggested in my earlier article but is now part of my reform proposal. This concerns giving the Omnibus Judicial Tribunal a tribunal services function: exclusive jurisdiction over the delivery of tribunal services, including legal services, to autonomous administrative judicial tribunals that are not large enough to support viable in-house services. This will be an important improvement. The Omnibus Judicial Tribunals will be engaged in the ordinary course in creating and delivering such services for their own needs and so could easily provide those same services to the tribunals that need them. This would also solve the problem of inappropriate dependencies arising from the provision of administrative support and legal services by government ministries.

The Tribunal Audit Board

My proposal calls for a guarantee of competitive compensation levels and reasonable separation packages for adjudicators and chairs, and I will talk about all of that shortly. However, while competitive and guaranteed compensation levels and separation packages for individual adjudicators are a good and necessary thing, financially speaking they are not enough. What is also needed is a means of assuring the financial well-being of the tribunals themselves.

Throughout Canadian history, funding has always been an issue for judicial tribunals. What happens when a portfolio ministry starves a tribunal of the funding it requires to fulfill its mandate in a reasonable manner was made painfully clear in the Ontario Ombudsman's report of his investigation of that province's Criminal Injuries Compensation Board.[58] The dismal story of Canadian human rights commissions perennially deprived of the funding they needed to deal reasonably with their mandates is written for all to see in the persistent backlogs and shameful processing times that have been a consistent feature of their record. In fact, unacceptable processing times and debilitating, reputation-destroying backlogs have been frequent experiences for all but the most favoured of tribunals.

An explanation for executive branch underfunding of judicial tribunals is found in Chapter 1. For judicial tribunals, dealing with their governments on funding issues presents serious independence issues – the same issues, in fact, as those identified by the courts in the *PEI Reference* jurisprudence regarding how disputes about salary levels between judges and the government might be resolved without impairing or being seen to impair judicial independence.[59] It is a problem that clearly needs a structural solution, and I propose we take a leaf from the Supreme Court's idea of placing "remuneration commissions" between judges and the government and place similar commissions between *tribunals* and the government.

My reform proposal, therefore, includes the creation by the Bill of Rights of a "Tribunal Audit Board" whose goals would be: to minimize a judicial tribunal's financial dependency on the government's goodwill; to minimize the impact on the perception of tribunal independence of a public tribunal/ government battle over budget issues; and to enhance the public credibility of tribunals regarding the competence of their management of their budget. Consisting of independent members with tribunal, user, and public and private financial and auditing backgrounds, the Audit Board would be mandated to monitor the financial performance and cost structures of administrative judicial tribunals and to issue public reports.

The Bill of Rights would also provide that, upon request of either the government or a tribunal, the Audit Board would publish a reasoned and expert opinion concerning the soundness of any budget proposals that may have become an issue between a tribunal and the government. Both the periodic reporting and the public budget proposal opinions would contribute to an environment conducive to the resolution of funding issues without undermining either the perception or the substance of the tribunals' judicial independence.

Presumably, the Audit Board Chair and members would be part-time, and they would be assisted by a professional and administrative support staff.

A School of Applied Studies in Administrative Justice

As we shall see, the reform proposal envisions an administrative justice system employing a cadre of professional career administrative justice adjudicators. For this reason, an effective strategy of professional accreditation and continuing education is essential. I therefore propose the creation of a School of Applied Studies in Administrative Justice that would be responsible for professional continuing legal education programs for judicial tribunal members and chairs. Once the concept of judicial tribunal adjudication as a viable career becomes widely accepted, it might then be feasible for the School, perhaps in association with one of the law schools, to offer degrees in applied studies in administrative justice, or advocacy training for advocates appearing before judicial tribunals. The Governing Council would accredit the School's programs.

Obviously, it would not be necessary to have a School of Applied Studies in Administrative Justice in every jurisdiction. As long as a School was accredited by a jurisdiction's Governing Council, it would not matter very much where it was physically located, especially in this modern era of sophisticated distance education technology.

Community Advisory Panels

The proposal also includes an Administrative Justice Bill of Rights requirement for a Community Advisory Panel to be associated with each of the judicial tribunals, including each division of the Omnibus Judicial Tribunal. The Bill of Rights would not specify the structure or the number of positions for any particular panel, but would make the Chair of each tribunal responsible for establishing a panel for his or her tribunal that the Governing Council approves as satisfying the Bill of Rights' requirements.

Community Advisory Panels would promote the confidence and buy-in of the user communities, and minimize strains between them and judicial tribunals arising from misunderstandings. They would be solely advisory panels, and tribunal management would be under no obligation to implement their recommendations. However, the Bill of Rights would require tribunals to provide panels with all the information about the tribunal's administration and performance that it was lawful to transmit; to commit their chairs and senior management to participating in good faith in regular meetings with their Panels (organized by the tribunal); and to consult with their Panels regarding any proposed major administrative, process, or policy change. Also, if a Panel were to make a formal recommendation for a change in practice or policy and the tribunal was unable or unwilling to implement it, the Bill of Rights would require the tribunal chair to provide the Panel with written reasons.

The Bill of Rights would authorize Community Advisory Panels to apply to the Governing Council for the enforcement of their "rights." The Panels might also double as the Tribunals' "selection committees" in the appointment process (see below).

Terms of Appointment

One of the reform proposal's central themes – and one of the critical points of departure from the policies of the current administrative justice system – is the embrace of professionalism. Tribunal adjudicators in the new system will be, and will be seen to be, professionals committed to long-term adjudicative careers. However, the proposal retains the policy of appointing tribunal members and chairs to renewable fixed terms of relatively short duration, typically three or five years, but – and this is of critical importance – with no limit on the number of reappointments.

The proposed retention of the short-term appointment policy reflects my view that the Quebec and UK governments made a mistake when they converted their judicial tribunal members to administrative "judges" and appointed them to life-tenured positions. The appointment of tribunal members to life-tenured positions does not, in my view, accord with an administrative justice system's unique needs.[60]

In the administrative justice system, individual tribunal members must continue to be accountable to the tribunal year in and year out for the performance of their corporate responsibilities, including their participation as effective team players in the tribunal's exercise of its institutional judicial responsibilities. Life-tenured members may not be personally well disposed towards the institutional, team-focused nature of their role, nor can one be assured that they will voluntarily adapt themselves to the institutional restrictions and discipline that their role entails. And, of course, tribunal chairs must themselves account to the government – in my proposal, to the Ministry of Administrative Justice – for the continued excellence of their tribunal's performance. Thus, for both tribunal adjudicators and tribunal chairs, I am proposing that fixed-term renewable appointments continue to be the norm.

This has many systemic implications. For one, it makes periodic reappointment decisions and their administrative accoutrements a permanent feature of the system. Second, it requires the system to be dedicated to the routine harvesting of the important advantages that fixed-term renewable appointments present for optimizing competence and ensuring continuing compliance with standards of excellence. These advantages must be harvested for they are what will justify the system of short-term renewable appointments that would otherwise not be warranted in a justice system. There must therefore be an ongoing institutional capacity – and stomach – for routinely refusing to reappoint adjudicators who fail to meet the tribunal's standards or who prove unwilling to comply in good faith with its corporate adjudicative strategies. I am not talking here of dismissal for shortcomings so serious as to amount to "cause" in the ordinary common law meaning of that concept. I am talking about the system being able to rid itself periodically of adjudicators who, although not guilty of anything amounting to cause, are consistently failing to meet the tribunal's standards and reasonable performance expectations.

For the competence of the administrative justice system to be optimized, however, the system must be able to compete in the professional marketplace for the best candidates, and short-term appointments are a natural obstacle. Accordingly, the policy of short-term appointments subject to non-renewal for failure to perform must be matched by a reappointment regime that is, and is seen to be, impervious to abuse. The regime must be so structured as to give candidates absolute confidence that if appointed they can count on routine reappointments until they retire, as long as they continue to meet the tribunal's reasonable performance requirements.

And it is here that we must face the fact that routine evaluations of the performance of individual judicial tribunal adjudicators are indisputably necessary. They are necessary because the principle of judicial independence and rules of fairness require that reappointment decisions be data-based, objective, and fair.

Security of Tenure

Eliminating Discretion in Reappointments

Of all the ways in which the executive branch impairs the individual independence of administrative justice adjudicators and discourages interest from the most competent potential candidates, the arbitrary reappointment regime is particularly egregious.[61] No system of adjudication that deliberately leaves its adjudicators exposed to secret and arbitrary retaliation from the government and its influential friends can call itself a justice system.

This shameful blot on Canada's justice system and its international reputation simply cannot stand. By itself it disqualifies our executive branch administrative justice system from any claim to be a justice system, and its removal is an essential feature of any reform proposal. Thus, my proposal calls for an open, objective, and merit-based reappointment process in which members will be denied reappointment only because of a demonstrated persistent failure to meet their tribunal's performance standards, and in which members faced with such a prospect will have a fair opportunity to challenge their evaluations in an independent and objective process.

Dealing with Mid-Term Dismissals

There can also be no perception of independence or impartiality if it is known that judicial tribunal adjudicators or chairs may be dismissed at any time, without cause. Thus, the Administrative Justice Bill of Rights will rule out at-pleasure appointments, eliminate any possible perception that adjudicators are no more than employees of government subject to dismissal at any time merely upon payment in lieu of notice, and provide that adjudicators or chairs may not be terminated during their term except for cause.

Discharge-for-Cause Procedures

Both a rational justice policy and the existing common law principles of judicial independence require that there be legislated procedural protection for members or chairs of judicial tribunals facing discharge for alleged cause – protection that entitles them to a full, fair hearing before an independent adjudicator, possibly a judge.[62]

One solution would be to expand the jurisdiction of the Canadian Judicial Council to encompass such cases, but there is some merit in having flexibility in the process, depending on the circumstances of each case. I therefore propose that the Administrative Justice Bill of Rights specify a general entitlement to an independent review and a fair hearing, with the particulars of the process and the identity of the reviewer to be decided by the Governing Council on a case-by-case basis. It would not be appropriate for the Governing Council to undertake a review and hearing itself because, in light of its other responsibilities, it could not be seen to be entirely disinterested.

Optimizing Competence

The Agenda

The competence-optimizing strategy as I conceive it has two distinct components. The first is to define "adjudicative competence" – to specify what the system must look for in its candidates and expect in its chairs and members in the way of skills, knowledge, aptitude, temperament, training, and experience. The second is to identify and install the structural arrangements necessary to ensure that the average adjudicative competence of a particular tribunal's roster of members, as measured against the foregoing standard qualifications, is always as good as it can reasonably be. The measure of a tribunal's compliance with a justice-system imperative of optimized adjudicative competence will be the presence of the latter structures in appropriate degree, rather than the level of competence of any particular tribunal member. A justice system that, either willfully or through indifference, fails to provide such structures is, in my opinion, no more acceptable in justice terms than one that fails to guarantee impartiality.

Space does not permit me to address in minute detail the requirements implicit in the justice imperative of optimal adjudicative competence. The agenda would not be difficult to imagine, however, and would include the following requirements that would be specified in the Administrative Justice Bill of Rights:

- as a prerequisite for the filling of any vacancy, the specification of a set of qualifications relevant to that vacancy, including, as a standard item, an aptitude for judging, all as approved by both the tribunal chair and the Governing Council
- open, qualifications-driven, widely advertised *competitions* for appointments, headed by the chair of the recruiting tribunal, or, in the case of the selection of a tribunal chair, headed by a person selected by the Governing Council
- no limits on the number of reappointments, provided adjudicators continue to meet their tribunal's performance standards at a certain level of excellence as certified by the Governing Council
- appropriate, objective, and fair performance evaluation strategies for both individual judicial tribunal members and the tribunal itself
- independent, transparent, merit-based, and fair reappointment processes
- fair and objective processes for dealing with complaints about the conduct or capacity of judicial tribunal chairs and members, similar to the Canadian Judicial Council process for judges
- mechanisms for ensuring competitive but proportionate compensation levels for judicial tribunal members and chairs (see "Ensuring Competitive Compensation" below)
- reasonable separation packages for outgoing chairs and members (see "Separation Packages" below)
- realistic training programs for new appointees, and regular continuing education programs for experienced members, all under the principal direction and control of the members' tribunals but subject to the approval of the Governing Council
- a requirement that administrative judicial tribunals give written reasons for their decisions, subject to possible exemptions approved by the Governing Council, and that they provide public access to reasons that is amenable to standard research techniques
- a limitation on the use of part-time members in judicial tribunals to situations where the arrangements for their deployment are compatible with maintaining their own and their tribunal's competence and independence, all as approved by the Governing Council.[63]

Thus, it is not difficult to identify what systemic structural changes it would take to optimize the adjudicative competence of judicial tribunals and their members.

The Influence of Reasons

In the current administrative justice system, one of the most promising influences for good from the point of view of bolstering commitments to optimizing competence is the courts' increasing reliance on tribunal reasons in judicial review proceedings. The courts have now established that good-quality written reasons form an essential basis for a court's assessment of the reasonableness of a tribunal's decision, and therefore an element of the common law of procedural fairness. On the latter point, as mentioned in Chapter 1, the Supreme Court's seminal decision on the law of judicial review in *Dunsmuir v. New Brunswick*[64] is especially significant.

Ruling Out Patronage Appointments

The executive branch's strategy for ensuring that its administrative judicial tribunals will be reliably responsive to the government's needs and interests through the appointment of friends, and supporters to adjudicator and chair positions is incompatible with impartial adjudication as well as with any commitment to optimizing the system's competence. For both reasons, these practices, including the seconding of public servants to either chair or adjudicator positions,[65] will be ruled out by the Administrative Justice Bill of Rights provisions governing appointments.

Mandating an Appropriate and Competitive Selection Process

To serve the goal of optimizing the competence of both judicial tribunals and their adjudicator corps and of eliminating patronage influences, I propose that the Administrative Justice Bill of Rights require an objective and competitive process for recruiting and selecting the "best" tribunal members and chairs that can be found. Since the quality of a selection process can be judged only from its details, I will now spell out the selection/appointment processes to be specified in the Bill of Rights.

The intention to fill a vacancy, and the qualifications required of candidates, should be widely advertised well in advance of the selection process, in accordance with criteria approved by the Governing Council.

No person should be appointed as a tribunal adjudicator unless first recommended for appointment after a fair and competitive selection process conducted by a representative, non-partisan selection committee composed of members with relevant interests in the outcome and headed by the chair of the tribunal to which the appointment will be made, all as approved and authorized by the Governing Council. It may be convenient for a tribunal chair to nominate the Community Advisory Panel as the tribunal's selection committee, perhaps augmented by representation from the tribunal itself.

The tribunal chair should have the casting vote in the selection committee, and no person should be recommended for appointment unless a majority of the selection committee has recommended that appointment and it has been approved by the tribunal chair. Thus the chair would have a veto, but so would a majority of the non-partisan selection committee.

The Bill of Rights would require the government to advise the Governor-in-Council or the Lieutenant Governor-in-Council to appoint the candidate selected through the competitive selection process and recommended by the tribunal chair unless there are reasons satisfactory to the Prime Minister or Premier for declining that recommendation; such reasons must then be shared with the chairs of the Governing Council and the tribunal, but would remain confidential. In summary, the government would have a reasoned veto on selections, but nothing more.[66]

I also propose that the Bill of Rights specify that the selection and appointment of the chair of an administrative judicial tribunal be governed by the same rules applicable to the selection and appointment of a tribunal adjudicator, except that the structure and make-up of the selection committee shall be as determined by the Governing Council and shall include at least two members nominated by the Ministry of Administrative Justice, one of whom shall be the chair of the committee. The candidates for tribunal chair positions shall be required to have the same adjudicative qualifications required for the tribunal's adjudicators, coupled with such additional administrative and management skills as the Ministry of Administrative Justice may specify.

Relevant Qualifications

The Bill of Rights will require that qualifications for appointment to an adjudicator position be explicitly determined, prior to the competition, by the head of the organization in which the vacancy is located, in consultation with that organization's selection committee and approved by the Governing Council. Unless the Governing Council specifically approves some modification for a particular vacancy, the Bill of Rights will require the standard qualifications to include at least the following:

- at least six years of in-depth experience that may be reasonably considered significantly relevant to the adjudicative function in question
- substantial experience in interpreting and applying legislation

- a good understanding of the justice system and of administrative law and the principles governing a fair hearing
- sound judgment and demonstrated superior analytical, conceptual, problem-solving, and decision-making skills
- a temperament that is respectful of diversity and attuned to listening actively and being open to fair and impartial consideration of evidence or submissions that are novel or at odds with the candidate's previously held views
- an ability to formulate reasoned decisions and to communicate the reasons effectively, orally and/or in writing, in a timely manner
- a clear commitment to pursuing professional development as necessary to enhance and/or maintain adjudicative skills and expertise and to become and/or remain current in the fields of knowledge relevant to the work of the organization to which the candidate seeks appointment
- the self-confidence, self-control, and sensitivity to the diverse interests of parties, and their sometimes disparate capacities, necessary to maintain effective and fair control of hearings in confrontational and stressful situations
- computer literacy.

Ensuring Competitive Compensation

Compensation levels are an important issue when one is seeking to optimize the competence of tribunals by competing in the employment market for the most qualified candidates and retaining them once they have been appointed. Moreover, as we have seen, financial security is both a common law and constitutional requirement of judicial independence. We must therefore have need for structural guarantees of financial security and appropriate compensation levels.[67] The absence of financial security for administrative judicial tribunal members cannot be reconciled with the independence of tribunal members under either the common law or constitutional principles of independence, and also cannot support a commitment to optimal competence. It is obvious that the current deficiencies in this respect will have to be addressed.

I therefore propose that the *Valente* guarantee of financial security be enforced by specific compensation provisions in the Administrative Justice Bill of Rights.[68] These provisions will require the compensation and benefit levels for administrative judicial tribunal adjudicators and chairs to be equal to the public service levels for positions with comparable responsibilities. I also propose that the comparability of positions be determined ultimately by the public service's regular job classification regime in consultation with the Tribunal Audit Board. This is a statutory guarantee that will obviate the need for independent remuneration commissions for individual tribunal adjudicators or chairs.

Separation Packages

Guaranteeing compensation levels is not enough. An administrative justice system that is dependent on the recruitment and retention of professional, career adjudicators but also committed to optimizing competence through the periodic removal of adjudicators who are no longer meeting the system's standards of excellence must also have a structured system of advance notice of non-renewal combined with generous separation packages. The design of such packages will have to take into account a number of end-of-employment factors that are unique to adjudicators.

First, because of issues of perceived bias, as long as adjudicators continue to adjudicate they cannot be involved in a job-hunting exercise among the communities to whom their tribunal provides adjudicative services.[69] Second, when an adjudicator's term expires, he or she will typically have a standing workload of unwritten decisions that both the tribunal and the parties will need to have completed. No one can do that for them. And, third, there will always have to be a rule preventing adjudicators who leave their positions from accepting employment in advocacy roles in their tribunal's field of interest for some fixed period following the release of their last decision. These restrictions now typically apply for six months.

Although these unique factors will necessitate separation packages that are more costly than typical separation packages, including some level of compensation even for those leaving voluntarily, they ought not to present much of a cost burden from an overall perspective.

Since adjudication is an interesting and challenging job with many attractive features from the adjudicator's perspective, with the introduction of competitive selection processes, the promise of an uninterrupted career as a professional adjudicator contingent only on continued performance, and guaranteed, competitive compensation and benefits, individuals appointed to adjudicator positions can be counted on to maintain their performance at the required level and continue as adjudicators. Moreover, most of those who see themselves falling short of the required standards will not wait to be told that their appointment will not be renewed. They will quietly move into other areas of employment.

Of all the full-time and part-time appointments to the vice-chair position during my twelve years as chair of the Ontario Workers' Compensation Appeals Tribunal (where we enjoyed an ideal merit-based selection process with no limit on the number of reappointments), I can think of only four or five who failed to meet the tribunal's standards. I also cannot remember more than one or two of the successful vice-chairs leaving the tribunal for other career opportunities, other than to accept an appointment to the bench or promotion to a senior public service position.

Evaluating Adjudicator Performance
Perhaps the most important strategy for optimizing tribunal competence is a policy of short-term appointments supported by a reappointment process that routinely refuses reappointment to adjudicators and chairs when they cease to meet performance standards. As we have seen, however, it is vital that such refusals be decided, and be seen to be decided, pursuant to a demonstratively fair and objective process, a process that must depend on objective performance evaluations.

Evaluating the performance of adjudicators is inherently controversial, of course, for there is the the obvious question: how is it possible to preserve the independence of an adjudicator if that adjudicator's decision making is subject to a superior's evaluation? Nevertheless, once one accepts that reappointment decisions must be made pursuant to a merit-based, objective, and fair process – which is at the very heart of a properly designed administrative justice system – performance evaluations become indispensable. Doing without them is not an option. To be sure, I am not proposing that the "correctness" of an adjudicator's decisions be reviewed (other than in accordance with procedures provided by law for that purpose, namely, applications for reconsideration or for judicial review), but in fairness to the adjudicator and in the interests of the tribunal, reappointment decisions must be made on the basis of objective evidence of performance measured against defined standards. Obviously, this does not pertain to judicial tribunal adjudicators appointed to life-tenured terms in other systems, but for adjudicators appointed to renewable terms the principles of justice make performance assessments inescapable.

There is a convenient precedent for the appropriateness of such an evaluation. In *Rai v. Ontario (Provincial Court)*, a 2005 case of the Ontario Divisional Court, a senior judge of the Ontario Provincial Court who was charged by statute with responsibility for deciding whether a deputy judge of the Small Claims Court should have his three-year term renewed was obviously working with some objective information. The judgment indicates that the senior judge provided the deputy judge, whose renewal she refused, with "reasons" – reasons that, on judicial review, the Ontario Divisional Court found acceptable.[70]

Also leading the way on this issue are the performance evaluation procedures at Quebec's Administrative Tribunal (TAQ). This evaluation procedure was described by Professor France Houle of the University of Montreal in her 2009 paper on the province's new administrative justice structure:[71]

> Designing a performance evaluation program that can manage adjudicator performance without compromising independence is not easy. The TAQ established a pilot project performance review procedure and since February 2006, this project is on-going. TAQ members agreed to participate to [*sic*] this project and they formed a Committee which is in charge of the procedure. This Committee works with the ENAP (School for Public Administration in Québec).
>
> The ENAP manages the project within the tribunal. The other important point is that this process is completely confidential – ENAP doesn't know the names of the members who are evaluated. Numbers have been assigned to each file and it is only the Chair of the Tribunal who has the key to this codification (only the Chair can match the # with the name of the Board member).
>
> For each member, ENAP [sends] a questionnaire to parties, lawyers *and colleagues*. The evaluation is done in the form of a survey, based on numbers which are statistically valid. The questionnaires are filled in and sent back to ENAP which analyses the results.

There is also a long-established and, by all accounts, successful system of formal, routine evaluations of tribunal adjudicators at the BC Workers' Compensation Appeals Tribunal and also at the IRB.

It is important to note, however, that with respect to judicial tribunal adjudicators, it is not only the quality of the adjudicator's decision-making and his or her conduct of hearings that count. As we have seen, there is much more to the job of a tribunal adjudicator than hearing and deciding cases. Judicial tribunal adjudicators must participate in good faith in the tribunal's decision-institutionalizing processes; conform themselves to the tribunal's institutional hearing culture; abide by its hearing strategies, tactics, and practice; make decisions that are readable, analytically sound, and congruent with the decisions of their colleagues even though not bound by the doctrine of *stare decisis;* be reliable in meeting tribunal production standards with respect to both the number and timeliness of decisions; follow the tribunal's institutional styles and format of decision writing; keep current with the tribunal's developing jurisprudence and with other developments in the law relating to their field; and continue to be a contributing, collegial team player.

A tribunal member who consistently fails to accept the latter responsibilities is not someone whose appointment a tribunal can afford to have renewed, however good his or her actual decision making may be. And if the quality of the performance of these responsibilities is to influence the reappointment decision, then once again it cannot be just a matter of a tribunal chair's impressions based on anecdotal evidence gathered behind closed doors or in casual hallway conversations; objective evidence of the member's shortcomings must be collected. Naturally, the chair's supervisory and training responsibilities will require that as a first priority such evidence be shared with the members affected, to give them the opportunity to adjust their performance in response to the evidence, or to challenge its validity.

Obviously, in any process for evaluating the performance of tribunal members, the tribunal chair – the tribunal's CEO – must be deeply involved. However, chairs must accept the need for a responsible and viable system that includes a fair and objective grievance procedure when members find themselves in serious disagreement with their chair regarding their performance. Also, the principles of independence and impartiality, and the need to give competent adjudicators ironclad assurances about their job security, absolutely precludes any government involvement in the evaluation process or in an aggrieved member's course of action in the event of a dispute with the chair over an evaluation.

In principle, these evaluation functions can be exercised only by independent and expert assessors known to have no axe to grind and no agenda but the pursuit of excellence in the administrative justice system.

Finally, the evaluation methods for tribunal *chairs* will be established by the Ministry of Administrative Justice with the approval of the Governing Council.

The Reappointment Process

My proposal includes a Bill of Rights requirement that the government advise the Governor-in-Council or Lieutenant Governor-in-Council to reappoint any administrative justice adjudicator whose reappointment has been earned by continued performance unless the Premier has specific reasons for declining to so.

If the chair does not propose to recommend reappointment for reasons that do not amount to cause, or if the Premier intends to refuse to advise the Lieutenant Governor-in-Council to reappoint pursuant to the recommendation, six months' advance notice of such intentions and of the reasons therefor should be given to the judicial tribunal adjudicator in question, who may then elect to have the issue of his or her reappointment reviewed by the Governing Council. The Council will thereupon initiate a procedure for hearing the issue in which the aggrieved adjudicator, the tribunal chair, and a representative of the Ministry of Administrative Justice will have the right to participate as parties. The identity of the person or persons who will hear the issue will be decided by the Council. If the aggrieved adjudicator so elects, his or her referral of the issue to the Council will be held in confidence and the hearing held *in camera.*

After the hearing and the reviewer's decision, the Council will either recommend that the adjudicator be reappointed in the ordinary course – or with conditions – or not. In the former case, the government may or may not accept the recommendation; if they do not, written reasons will be shared with the Council's Chair and, at the request of the adjudicator but not otherwise, the Council's recommendation and its reasons will be made public.

Failure of a tribunal chair or the government to give an administrative justice adjudicator notice of an intention not to reappoint at least six months prior to the expiration of his or her current term will result in an automatic one-year extension of that term. An adjudicator whose appointment is not renewed for failure to meet performance standards will be entitled to a generous separation package equivalent to one year's salary and the continuation of benefits for twelve months.

The possible non-renewal of a tribunal chair's appointment would require a different procedure. Based on data from evaluation of the chair, either the Minister of Administrative Justice or the Governing Council's Chair would initiate a discussion of the advisability of reappointing the chair. If these discussions confirm that there is an issue, the chair will be advised and can choose between accepting a separation package or challenging the evaluation. In the latter case, the process will be a customized process agreed upon by the Ministry, the Council, and the chair. If the chair so elects, the fact that there is an issue, the procedure for resolving the issue, and the ultimate decision will all be held in confidence.

To bolster a judicial tribunal chair's personal sense of independence, the Bill of Rights will provide that a chair whose appointment is not renewed for his/her or the tribunal's failure to meet performance standards will be entitled to a separation package equivalent to eighteen months' salary and continuation of benefits for the same period, subject, however, to salary from new employment being set off.

Reviewing the Institutional Performance of Tribunals and Chairs
In addition to proposing appropriate means for evaluating the performance of individual adjudicators, and chairs, I propose both episodic and periodic reviews of the institutional performance of the judicial tribunals themselves. Tribunal institutional goals include: reasonable accessibility; a competent, consistent, and congruent body of decisions; appropriate and proportionate process; efficiency and fairness of administration; effectiveness as a statutory rights enterprise's judicial arm; timeliness of decision making, and so on. Naturally, the extent to which tribunals are effective in meeting those goals can vary over time and from tribunal to tribunal. Inevitably, there will also be occasions when the tribunal or its chairs have become the subject of a public controversy that can be resolved only by an objective performance review or inquiry.

It has always been the practice to assign such episodic tribunal reviews or inquiries to outsiders. In this book so far, you will have seen references to Professor Paul Weiler's review of the Ontario workers' compensation system; former Justice Peter Cory's review of the Medical Review Committee; the Ontario Ombudsman's review of the Criminal Injuries Compensation Board; the Fairness Committee's review of the Ontario Securities Commission's adjudicative process; and the Green Paper review of the performance of WCAT when I was chair (to which I referred in the Introduction) conducted by the private consulting firm Coopers and Lybrand. Institutional reviews are typically initiated in response to a perceived problem, and, as we have seen, are conducted by someone chosen by the government.

Ad hoc reviews or inquiries by outsiders present a number of systemic, justice-system issues. When the government chooses the moment, selects the reviewer, and defines the reviewer's terms of reference, there cannot always be complete confidence in the objectivity of the review and there will often be grounds for suspicion about its real purpose. The reviewer's independence from government is also not always clear. These issues obviously do not arise in the case of an Ombudsman-initiated review, nor do they arise where the chosen reviewer is sufficiently august, as was the case with former Justice Cory's review of the Medical Review Committee.

A second problem is that *ad hoc* reviewers typically do not come to the review with any particular expertise in, informed understanding of, or perhaps any empathy with the work of judicial tribunals in an administrative justice system setting. This is potentially equally true of an ombudsman, a retired judge, or a consulting firm.

Consider, for example, the following indication of such lack of knowledge or empathy in the office of Ontario's Auditor General. An Ontario *ad hoc* Administrative Justice Working Group had occasion some time ago to express concerns about the Auditor General's apparent lack of administrative justice system expertise and understanding as demonstrated in his reports on his "value-for-money" audit of the adjudicative activities of the first-level deciders in the administration of the Ministry of Community and Social Services' Ontario Disability Support Program (ODSP).[72] In the Working Group's opinion, the Auditor General demonstrated little understanding of the adjudicative culture. He appeared to ignore the norms of structural independence that properly govern the relationships at play in the ODSP adjudicative regime. He misconstrued the standards of proof applicable in adjudicative processes. And he showed no appreciation of the necessary differences in process between the first and final levels of adjudication, or of the nature of the responsibilities of the final-level tribunal (the Social Benefit Tribunal).[73]

From a justice policy perspective, it is inappropriate in principle, and often not helpful in practice, for the government or the ombudsman to initiate, on their own, either an episodic or periodic review of the performance of a judicial tribunal or its chair. I therefore propose that the Administrative Justice Bill of Rights explicitly prohibit reviews of the performance of administrative judicial tribunals or their chairs or members except as initiated or approved, as well as directed and supervised, by the Governing Council.

For any independent organization, there must, however, be a means of providing objective reassurances to the public and the government that all is well behind the independent structures. I therefore propose routine reviews of the performance of judicial tribunals and their chairs, and of the tribunal's continuing relevance, at regular intervals, perhaps every six or seven years – reviews that would be conducted under the independent supervision and direction of the Governing Council and the Tribunal Audit Board.

The Portfolio Ministries' Role: From Covert to Overt

It is too much to expect, but there is every reason for the executive branch to view my proposed reforms in a positive light. These are reforms that will ensure that the decisions of the judicial arm of their statutory rights enterprises are competent and well informed, with a high potential for contributing constructively to the successful administration of their statutory rights enterprises. The reformed structures will also make it perfectly clear that the portfolio ministry is not responsible for the tribunal's decisions in individual cases. On the other hand, the new structures provide the ministries with effective tools for influencing those decisions in a general way, and for administering principled course corrections when they see tribunal decisions taking a policy turn they believe not to have been contemplated by the legislature.

Cutting the ties between portfolio ministries and their administrative judicial tribunals, taken together with other aspects of my proposal, will put all judicial tribunals safely beyond the reach of the portfolio ministries' traditional means of influence and control, but a portfolio ministry's ability to influence the policy-maturation process must continue. The justice side of the administrative justice system must be harmonized with the administrative side.

As we have seen, a judicial tribunal's role as the exclusive judicial arm of a statutory rights enterprise means that what it decides, day in and day out, eventually determines in many important respects the policy's ultimate shape and direction. Having deprived the portfolio ministries of their traditional means of controlling that shape and direction, my proposal must provide an appropriate and effective substitute – official channels through which they may exert the needed influence in a manner that is overt and that is compatible with the rule of law.

In considering this question, I have found of particular interest my experience in dealing with the relationship between WCAT and the workers' compensation system's "portfolio ministry" – that is, the Workers' Compensation Board (WCB) (as the Ontario Workplace Safety and Insurance Board was then called). (In workers' compensation statutory rights enterprises, the policy and administrative role that is usually played by a portfolio ministry is played by the Board.)

As a statutory rights enterprise's judicial arm, judicial tribunals have, as we have seen, institutional responsibilities that go beyond dispensing justice in individual cases. Their hearing and decision-making processes and their decisions in large numbers of individual cases are not only the means of maturing the policy but they are, or should be, one of the principal means through which the enterprise itself develops its understanding of the intricacies of the law and policy that it is administering. There is nothing like the scrutiny that a competent and objective adjudicative hearing brings to bear on the question of how an enterprise's law and policy and administration is working – on the ground, in individual cases – to enlighten the enterprise's administrators as to the strengths and weaknesses, as well as the lawfulness, of its rules and of its day-to-day administration. In an ideal world, the tribunal's decisions would be welcomed by the administrator as providing a unique daily window into how the enterprise is working and what adjustments may be needed. In reality, however, the typical relationship between the administrator and the tribunal is adversarial, often exacerbated by the administrator's ingrained lack of respect for the tribunal – a lack of respect stemming perhaps most importantly in our current system from the long-standing government tradition of appointing tribunal members apparently without sufficient regard for their qualifications.

Obviously, when the enterprise's administrator and his or her staff instinctively see tribunal decisions as public criticisms of themselves and their policies by people who are undeserving, unqualified, and probably only marginally competent, the potential for the tribunal to be a constructive influence on the enterprise is lost. Instead, one can count on the administrators' taking all available steps to minimize or reverse the effects of those decisions, to the extent they cannot be ignored.

In his 1980 report on Ontario's workers' compensation system in which he recommended the creation of WCAT, Professor Weiler had this problem much in mind, and he made two radical suggestions. First, to minimize the effect of simple misunderstandings on the relationship, Weiler proposed that the WCAT chair be an *ex officio* non-voting member of the WCB board of directors. Second, and most surprisingly, he proposed that the final say on the interpretation of "the policy and general law" of the *Workers' Compensation Act*,[74] be given to the WCB board of directors. Both proposals were accepted. The WCAT chair was made a non-voting member of the WCB, and s. 86n (subsequently s. 93) of the revised *Act* contained the following provisions:

> (1) Where a decision of the Appeals Tribunal turns upon an interpretation of the policy and general law of this Act, the board of directors

... may in its discretion review and determine the issue of interpretation ... and may direct the Appeals Tribunal to reconsider the matter
in light of the determination of the board of directors.

(2) Where the board of directors ... in the exercise of its discretion under
subsection (1) considers that a review is warranted, it shall either
hold a hearing and afford the parties likely to be affected by its determination an opportunity to make oral and written submissions or it
may dispense with a hearing if it permits the parties ... to make written submissions, as the board may direct.

(3) The board of directors ... shall give its determination and direction,
if any, under this section in writing together with its reasons
therefor.

(4) Pending its determination, the board of directors ... with respect to
the decision that is the subject-matter of the review, may stay the
enforcement or execution of the order made under the decision or
may vacate the order if it has been implemented.

According the Board the power to review WCAT's decisions was bitterly
resented by the injured/worker/labour community as being incompatible
with the concept of an independent tribunal. As the chair of the tribunal,
however, I thought it an especially insightful provision. For one thing, the
tribunal was as much in the business of influencing the WCB's administration as it was of ensuring that justice be done in individual cases, and this
provision had the merit of making the tribunal's decisions inescapably part
of the board of directors' business.

It was also, I thought, naïve to believe that a decision of a single tribunal
panel could be effective in causing a billion-dollar corporation to change its
direction in any major way unless that change was actually embraced by the
corporation's administrators. Giving the WCB board of directors the final
say on interpretation issues integrated the tribunal into the WCB's decision-
making process and presupposed that the WCB would consider itself bound
by the tribunal's interpretations unless the board of directors opted to exercise its review power.

The specified review process, with its requirement for participation by
the parties in an oral or written hearing coupled with the WCB's obligation
to give reasons if it directed the tribunal to reconsider, also ensured that if
the WCB disagreed with the tribunal, it would have to do so after a full
consideration of the tribunal's reasons and with a public explanation in a

decision that could itself be challenged through judicial review proceedings. It was a process that promised to give the important issues a full airing at the highest levels of the enterprise.

Finally, one knew that, from a logistical perspective, it was not a procedure that a board of directors would invoke except in the most serious of cases.

As it turned out, the power was exercised on, as I recall, only two occasions. In both, the WCB board elected to give effect to WCAT's decision as far as the individual worker was concerned, and to challenge only the generic interpretation. Ultimately, however, the board of directors deadlocked over the exercise of the power. The worker/union members of the eventually bilateral board would not vote in favour of exercising the power in any case, and the employer members would not approve policy changes that would bring the WCB's policies in line with WCAT's decisions without first exercising the power. The effect of this deadlock was to effectively create a bifurcated workers' compensation system in Ontario, where some benefits that were absolutely ruled out at the WCB were potentially available on appeal. Compensation for disabilities caused by chronic stress in the workplace was perhaps the most prominent example.

Thus, in practice, that aspect of the Weiler design did not turn out to work particularly well.[75] Nevertheless, the experience of seeing up close how the design worked, did not work, and might have worked has convinced me that a viable administrative justice system must have structures that will effectively harmonize the work of administrative judicial tribunals with the work of the portfolio ministries.

The Portfolio Ministries' Channels of Overt Influence

What is needed, in my view, are appropriate, overt channels through which portfolio ministries may appropriately challenge or influence a tribunal's decisions on issues that impact directly on such ministries' policies. In this context, my use of the term "portfolio ministries" encompasses the regulatory agencies whose judicial functions have, under these proposed reforms, been transferred to a judicial tribunal, thus replicating the situation I have described in workers' compensation systems, where the workers' compensation boards are the equivalent of portfolio ministries. Since it is, in broad terms, the body that is responsible for the policy of the statutory rights enterprise that I propose be given access to the overt channels of influence, in what follows I will use the term "policy body" to encompass either the portfolio ministries or the relevant regulatory agencies.

The proposed channels of influence are:

- Regular meetings, perhaps every quarter, between the judicial tribunal's leadership and the policy body's leadership, thus giving the latter the same access and role as the Community Advisory Panels vis-à-vis the tribunal. Of course, discussion of current or pending cases would be off limits in these meetings, but with the tribunal safely at actual arm's length from the policy body, such meetings would no longer be problematic from a rule-of-law perspective.
- The traditional "enactment" channels that can be included in any tribunal's constitutive statute, and often are – that is, the power of the policy body to make regulations that may influence the direction the policy is taking, and/or to issue to the tribunal timely, ministerial "directions" on generic issues of interpretation. These powers are obviously appropriate from a justice perspective and would continue. (Each of these can be challenged on judicial review if they are not seen to be authorized by the statute.) These channels would also include the always present option of amending the legislation in response to a tribunal decision, but timely legislative reform is not always practicable.
- Participation of the policy body in the tribunal's proceedings as a party in an effort to openly influence the decision through in-hearing case advocacy. I would provide every policy body with the opportunity to participate as a party at that policy body's election with the authority for this direct participation in the tribunal's adjudicative process being confirmed by statute. (Where the tribunal is both in fact and in appearance independent from the policy body, as would be the case if my reform proposals were adopted, this channel of influence becomes unobjectionable in principle and valuable in practice.)
- Authority to request the tribunal chair to refer a generic interpretation issue to a tribunal review panel if such a review is authorized under the tribunal's constitutive statute. The chair would be free to accept or refuse the request. (This would apply particularly to the Omnibus Judicial Tribunal Chair, who would have the statutory authority to refer a generic interpretation issue to a senior tribunal "review panel," a procedure akin to a "stated case" procedure. This authority would be a useful addition to the institutionalizing tools of any judicial tribunal – a way of conducting a leading case strategy without imposing an undue burden on an actual set of parties.)

- Authority for the policy body to participate as a party in any such review ordered by the tribunal's chair.
- Authority for the portfolio minister to order a "Ministerial Review" of any particular tribunal interpretation of the law.

I appreciate the radical and largely unprecedented nature of the last proposal,[76] but if such a Ministerial Review were governed by the following conditions, it would, in my opinion, be compliant with the rule of law.

- The Ministerial Review would be available only for issues of law or procedure or the appropriateness of the remedy ordered by the tribunal; the tribunal's findings of fact would stand.
- The review procedure would allow for participation as "parties" by the parties to the original proceedings, the tribunal, the Governing Council, and other interested parties, including a regulatory agency affected by the decision.
- The review's conclusion regarding the interpretation issue would have the same authoritative status in future tribunal cases as a decision of a superior court. It would not affect the outcome in the case or cases that had provoked the Ministerial Review or in any past cases.
- The Ministerial Review decision and the written reasons in support of the decision would be required to be made public; if they differed materially from the tribunal's reasons (but not otherwise), the decision would be subject to judicial review as though it were a decision of a tribunal. The Administrative Justice Bill of Rights would specify, however, that the standard of the judicial review relative to the differences between the Ministerial Review decision and the tribunal decision would be correctness; that is, the review decision's reasons for disagreeing with the tribunal's decision would be reviewed against a standard of "correctness."
- A judicial review of the Ministerial Review decision would be available on the initiative of a party to the original tribunal decision, of the tribunal itself, or of the Governing Council for Administrative Justice.

I also propose that the Bill of Rights authorize the policy body to initiate *judicial* reviews of any judicial tribunal decision and to participate as a party in those proceedings or in any judicial review proceedings initiated by others. The Bill of Rights would also confirm the standing of the tribunal as a full party in any judicial review of a tribunal decision.

The costs that the parties to the original tribunal decision reasonably incur in participating in a Ministerial Review, in a judicial review of the Ministerial Review decision, or in a judicial review of the tribunal's decision on the initiative of a policy body, would be payable by the government as advance costs.

One can readily anticipate, of course, that some or all of these channels of government or regulatory agency intervention will be considered unnecessary and/or inappropriate with respect to many judicial tribunal functions. Where there is agreement on that point, it can be reflected in the tribunal's constitutive statute.

6

Implementing the Reform Proposal
A Strategy for Change

If you have read my reform proposal all the way through, I have no doubt that your reaction will have been, "Well, that's not going to happen."

But hold on a minute. In the past two decades, reforms quite as revolutionary as my proposals have in fact been implemented in Canada – twice. They were implemented, as we have seen, in Quebec, in 1996, but also, in 1998, in Canada's military justice system.

Following the Supreme Court's finding in 1992 in *R. v. Généreux*[1] that the Canadian military's court-martial tribunal structures were not independent and impartial as required by s. 11(d) of the *Canadian Charter of Rights and Freedoms*, the military justice system underwent a complete overhaul and transformative restructuring to bring it into compliance with the *Valente* principles of judicial independence.[2] The principal vehicle of that reform was a 1998 amendment of the *National Defence Act*. Parliament's intent to effect a transformative reform may be seen from the following excerpt from the summary at beginning of the amending act:

This enactment reforms and modernizes the National Defence Act and, in particular, the Code of Service Discipline. Key components of the enactment include: clarification of the roles and responsibilities of the principal actors in the military justice system, including the Minister of National Defence and the Judge Advocate General, and the establishment of *clear standards of institutional separation* between the investigative, prosecutorial, defence and judicial functions ...[3]

And, almost equally surprising, the same revolution has recently occurred in the United Kingdom, with essentially the same result as in Quebec and in Canada's military justice system. In each case, the existing system of dependent and biased rights-determining tribunals lost its constitutional validity. This was done voluntarily in Quebec, with the enactment of the Quebec *Charter of Human Rights and Freedoms* and its specific requirement that all tribunals be independent and impartial, whereas the revolution in the Canadian military justice system was compelled by the Supreme Court's finding that its structures were unconstitutional. In the United Kingdom, the constitutional requirement for independent and impartial tribunals appears to have emerged as a direct result of that country's new relationship with the European Union.

Article 6 of the *European Convention on Human Rights*[4] provides explicitly that "[i]n the determination of his civil rights and obligations or of any criminal charge against him, everyone is entitled to a fair and public hearing within a reasonable time *by an independent and impartial tribunal* established by law." When it became clear that the United Kingdom's judicial tribunal structures would now be tested against this requirement of independence and impartiality, something had to be done. In due course, the British Parliament enacted its own *Human Rights Act 1998*, effectively integrating the *European Convention* with British law,[5] whereupon the tribunals found their constitutive statutes and the validity of their decisions open to challenge on the grounds that the tribunals' structures or process did not satisfy the requirements of Article 6. It was therefore not surprising that in May 2000, the same year the *Human Rights Act* came into force, the Lord Chancellor appointed Sir Andrew Leggatt to "undertake a review of tribunals" and gave him ten months to report.

Leggatt's report and its radical recommendations were published in August 2001, and by 2007 the recommendations had been largely implemented.[6] That the recommendations were revolutionary was not unexpected, for Leggatt had been given a licence to think big. The terms of reference set by the Lord Chancellor obviously anticipated the need for major structural changes. I find it of special interest, moreover, that the Lord Chancellor's terms of reference struck most of the notes that have been struck throughout this book. They read as follows:

To review the delivery of justice through tribunals other than ordinary courts of law, constituted under an Act of Parliament by a Minister of the Crown or for purposes of a Minister's functions; *in resolving disputes, whether between citizens and the state, or between other parties,* so as to *ensure* that:

- There are fair, timely, proportionate and effective arrangements for handling those disputes, within an effective framework for decision-making which encourages the systematic development of the area of law concerned, and *which forms a coherent structure, together with the superior courts, for the delivery of administrative justice;*
- The administrative and practical arrangements for supporting those decision-making procedures *meet the requirements of the European Convention on Human Rights for independence and impartiality;*
- There are adequate arrangements for improving people's knowledge and understanding of their rights and responsibilities in relation to such disputes, and that tribunals and other bodies function in a way which makes those rights and responsibilities a reality;
- The arrangements for the funding and management of tribunals and other bodies by Government departments are efficient, effective and economical; and *pay due regard both to judicial independence,* and to ministerial responsibility for the administration of public funds;
- *Performance standards for tribunals are coherent, consistent, and public; and effective measures for monitoring and enforcing those standards are established; and*
- *Tribunals overall constitute a coherent structure for the delivery of administrative justice.*

The review may examine, insofar as it considers it necessary, administrative and regulatory bodies which also make judicial decisions as part of their functions.[7]

Thus, it all comes down to the constitutional issue. Once the Supreme Court confirms the application of *PEI Reference*'s constitutional principle of judicial independence and impartiality[8] to judicial tribunals, all the elements of Canada's existing system of executive branch "justice" that are incompatible with the rule of law will become constitutionally insupportable. Canadian governments will then be faced with the same imperative for fundamental reform as that faced by Quebec, by Canada's military justice system, and by the United Kingdom.

7

Meanwhile, a Toolkit for Litigators

Meanwhile, as we await the definitive constitutional decision, in the contemplation of day-to-day challenges to tribunal decisions there is much for activist litigators to think about. Much of it I have already touched on, but it may be useful to pull the main concepts together once more. It is easily argued, for instance, that most of Canada's judicial tribunals outside Quebec do not conform to the modern, *common law* principles of judicial independence and impartiality, which leaves their decisions vulnerable to judicial review. Because of the nature of the executive branch's administrative justice strategies and tactics, most administrative judicial tribunals fail to meet one or more of the common law conditions for judicial independence. Moreover, many of those strategies and tactics will be found not to have been authorized by unequivocally clear statutory provisions.

First, in breach of the *Valente* principles of independence,[1] the tenure of judicial tribunal adjudicators is not secure. Consider the following:

- Judicial tribunal adjudicators are appointed to terms of short duration and the reappointment regimes are universally in breach of at least the spirit of the *Valente* principles as well as in flagrant breach of the objective, merit-based, and fair renewal process requirement arguably established in *The Attorney General of Québec v. Barreau du Montréal.*[2] The Ontario Court of Appeal's 2012 decision in *Ontario Deputy Judges'*

Association v. Ontario (Attorney General)[3] may also be of some help here. In that decision, the Court of Appeal held that if the renewal of the Ontario Small Claims Court Deputy Judges' three-year terms had been in the discretion of the "Executive Branch" rather than a Senior Judge, that would have been a renewal arrangement that would not have satisfied *Valente*'s security-of-tenure condition of judicial independence.[4] Of course, Small Claims Court Deputy Judges are not technically members of a judicial tribunal, but given the nature of their assignments and their three-year terms of appointment, it is difficult to see any relevant point of distinction.

- It may be possible to show that particular reappointment decisions do not adhere to the proper purpose requirements for the exercise of statutory discretions as established in *Roncarelli v. Duplessis* and revisited in *Canadian Union of Public Employees (C.U.P.E.) v. Ontario (Minister of Labour)*.[5]

- The practice of idiosyncratic removals has created an environment throughout the administrative justice system in which judicial tribunal adjudicators have ample reason to fear reprisals for decisions that are unpopular with the government or its influential friends. It can therefore be argued that any objective and fully informed observer would have a reasonable apprehension of bias in the decision making of any judicial tribunal in such a system.

- All judicial tribunal members are subject to discharge for cause without the statutory guarantee of an independent, objective, and full hearing that the *Valente* principles require.[6]

- The members and/or chairs of some judicial tribunals still hold their positions at pleasure.

- Part-time judicial tribunal members have no security of tenure of any kind. Their continued assignment to cases is effectively dependent on the tribunal chairs' continuing to find their decisions satisfactory on a case-by-case basis.

Second, judicial tribunal members typically have no objectively guaranteed financial security:

- The nature and amount of compensation are typically left entirely to the discretion of the executive branch, and the history of executive branch abuse of such discretion is well known.

- The *level* of compensation may be inconsistent with judicial independence. This was addressed by the Ontario Court of Appeal in *Deputy Judges Assn. v. Ontario (Attorney General).*[7]
- In Ontario, government policy stipulates that persons appointed as judicial tribunal adjudicators should not expect "competitive" compensation – indeed, need not be paid anything except reimbursement for reasonable expenses.[8]
- Again, part-time members of judicial tribunals are a special case. In fact, they have zero financial security. As a practical matter, whether or not they receive any further remuneration is entirely at the discretion of the tribunal chair.

Finally, the adjudicative processes of some judicial tribunals are so controlled by the executive branch that the administrative control condition of judicial independence cannot be met. It is not unheard of, for example, for a tribunal's registrar function to be exercised by host ministry officials, including the assignment of adjudicators to particular cases, or for the ministry to dictate whether or not the tribunal will provide written reasons, or to stipulate the amount of time to be budgeted for each case. The administrative arrangement whereby the funds available for the administration of the Ontario Criminal Injuries Compensation Board were reduced by the amount of each of its substantive monetary awards is an egregious example.[9] The Employment Insurance Commission's administrative control over the Boards of Referees as described by Professor Gaile McGregor is another.[10] And the portfolio ministries' pervasive control of all aspects of a tribunal's administration as specified in Ontario's *Adjudicative Tribunals Accountability, Governance and Appointments Act* will impact in a variety of ways on the institutional independence of judicial tribunals.

It is also useful to note that it is possible to challenge a failure to comply with the principles of procedural fairness by attacking the system itself, rather than by making sport of individual adjudicators.[11]

Pending resolution of the constitutional issues, litigators seeking to rely on the common law's procedural fairness requirements of judicial independence will likely find themselves butting up against a government's allegation that the interpretation of some statute authorizes the offending policy or practice and thus trumps the common law requirement. It is important, therefore, to keep in mind the significant interpretation burden that any government faces in attempting to make that case. The standard rules of statutory interpretation include the principle that legislatures should be presumed not to have intended to legislate in a way that does not accord with established legal norms.[12] This principle would seem to be particularly rigorous for interpretations of statutes that a government argues overrides rule-of-law principles of natural justice and procedural fairness, perhaps especially interpretations that are alleged to override the foundational principle of judicial independence.

A particularly helpful articulation of the law on this point may be found in passages from the Supreme Court's decision in *CUPE* that I referred to on this same point in Chapter 4.[13] Helpful, as well, is the affirmation of that principle and the explanation of the importance of this rule by the House of Lords in its decisions in *R. v. Secretary of State for the Home Department, ex p. Simms*, and in *Morgan Grenfell & Co. v. Income Tax Special Commissioner*, dated 2000 and 2002, respectively, also referred to previously.[14]

Finally, it seems to me that judicial tribunals' non-compliance with the rule of law, as demonstrated in this book, presents an important standard-of-review issue that, as far as I know, has yet to be raised in any court.

As confirmed in *Dunsmuir v. New Brunswick*, the Supreme Court's deference to the decision of tribunals is now thought by the Court to be based on Dyzenhaus's "deference as respect."

> We agree with David Dyzenhaus where he states that the concept of "deference as respect" requires of the courts "not submission but a respectful attention to the reasons offered or which could be offered in support of a decision": "The Politics of Deference: Judicial Review and Democracy", in M. Taggart, ed., *The Province of Administrative Law* (1997), 279, at p. 286 (quoted with approval in *Baker*, at para. 65, *per* L'Heureux-Dubé J.; *Ryan*, at para. 49).[15]

My question is this: how can the courts "respect" tribunals that are exercising judicial functions when the tribunals' structured bias is, in law, clear for all to see? How can a court apply a reasonableness standard of review to the exercise of a judicial function, or deem a tribunal decision emerging from that exercise to be "reasonable," when the decision in question has been made in the exercise of a judicial function by a body that is in law transparently neither independent nor impartial?

Even if Canadian legislatures were seen to be constitutionally empowered to create such bodies and authorize them to exercise judicial functions, can it be right – is it constitutionally sound – for our courts to allow themselves to be complicit in the bypassing of rule-of-law requirements in the exercise of judicial functions? Are they constitutionally entitled to defer to the decisions of adjudicative bodies where core rule-of-law structural requirements are known to be absent?

One cannot read the Saskatchewan Court of Appeal's decision in the 2010 *Saskatchewan Federation of Labour v. Saskatchewan* case[16] without knowing that the Saskatchewan Labour Relations Board is at least in law a biased tribunal. If I were practising law in Saskatchewan, I would be arguing that the reasonableness standard of review cannot reasonably or constitutionally be seen to apply to the decisions of a biased tribunal, and can therefore no longer be justified in judicial reviews of the Saskatchewan Labour Relations Board's decisions. I would be asking the courts not only to apply the standard of correctness to any review of those decisions but also to place the burden on respondents to show that both the Board's interpretation and application of the law, *and its findings of fact,* are *correct.*[17]

I would be making the same arguments in British Columbia with respect to the judicial review of any of that province's judicial tribunals. Since the BC Court of Appeal decision in *McKenzie v. British Columbia (Minister of Public Safety and Solicitor General),*[18] the BC government has been claiming a statutory right to dismiss any tribunal member in mid-term without cause and without reasons. I would particularly make these arguments with regard to the judicial review of decisions of the staff of the BC housing ministry, who since 2006 have been exercising the judicial functions of a court in dealing with landlord and residential tenant disputes, with no pretense of any separation from government.[19]

And to those who would argue that British Columbia's statutory standards of review precluded a correctness standard, I would reply that those legislated standards are themselves constitutionally invalid because they seek to interfere with the courts' own adjudicative process, contrary to the *Valente* principles.[20] In Ontario, I would make the same argument based on the degree of dependency of Ontario judicial tribunals on the government evidenced in the *Adjudicative Tribunals Accountability, Governance and Appointments Act, 2009.*

Well, that is likely more than enough.

Eventually, the Supreme Court will confirm that Canada's Constitution does not permit judicial functions to be exercised by tribunals dependent on and controlled by the executive branch. When that day comes, the proposals for reform contained in Chapter 5, which at first blush no doubt appeared naïve and impossibly radical, might then be viewed in a different light.

Notes

INTRODUCTION

1 Admittedly, only a photocopy, but still ... As you might imagine, this is not the first time I have told this story. Judith McCormack, a former Ontario Labour Relations Board chair, references it in her 1998 article "The Price of Administrative Justice," 6 C.L.E.L.J. 1 at 1, and I published it myself in my article "The Corporate Responsibilities of Tribunal Members – CCAT 2008" (2009) 22 Can. J. Admin. L. & Prac. 1 at 12.

2 Administrative Justice Working Group (AJWG), *Submission to the Ontario Law Reform Commission on Research Priorities* (March 2007) [unpublished].

3 Convenience dictates that one speaks as though in Canada we had only one administrative justice system, but, of course, each province and territory – and municipality – has its own, and there is also a federal system. With the exception of Quebec, however, these systems are virtually identical in their conception and administration, and for convenience I will continue to talk about *a* system with the expectation that readers will extrapolate the analysis to the particular system with which they are most familiar. In doing so, I adopt the practice uniformly found in Canadian administrative justice literature.

4 In the federal jurisdiction, the components of the executive branch are referred to as "departments," whereas in the provinces they are called "ministries." For convenience, I will use the term "ministry" in all cases.

5 See "Quasi-judicialism – The Cuckoo Chick in the Administrative Justice Nest" in Chapter 2, "Administrative *Justice*," at 170-84.

6 *British Columbia v. Imperial Tobacco Canada Ltd.*, [2005] 2 S.C.R. 473 [*Imperial Tobacco*].

7 *Ibid.*, para. 58 [citations omitted].

8 *Ibid.*, para. 59 [emphasis added; citations omitted].

9 Since 1997, I have written and published or presented at administrative law conferences over two dozen articles on administrative justice issues.

10 I left the program in January 2009 with a doctorate degree. My dissertation title was
   "Executive Branch Justice: Canada's 'Official Courts.'"

11 *Workers' Compensation Act*, R.S.O. 1980, c. 539, as revised, particularly by S.O. 1984,
   c. 58.

12 Appointed to the position initially by the Progressive Conservative government of
   Frank Miller, I was reappointed twice by the Liberal government of David Peterson
   and once by the New Democratic Party government of Bob Rae. Under the last appointment, I served for the first twenty-one months of Premier Mike Harris's term
   as Premier.

13 See reference in Workers' Compensation Appeals Tribunal, *Annual Report 1991*
   (Toronto: Workers' Compensation Appeals Tribunal, 1991) at 3.

14 Emphasis in original. Les Liversidge is an employers' counsel whose firm specializes
   in workers' compensation matters and whose experience as an employers' workers'
   compensation advocate predates 1985. His *e-Letter* is sent regularly to his employer
   clients.

15 I must note that these administrative responsibilities were always shared with my
   "Alternate Chair" – of whom I had several over the years, commencing with Jim
   Thomas – and, of course, with other colleagues in senior administrative or counsel
   positions.

16 Over the course of the twelve years, in addition to my administrative and management duties, I chaired WCAT adjudicative panels and wrote the panels' reasoned
   decisions in approximately 150 cases.

17 By 1997, WCAT's budget (by the end of that year WCAT had been renamed WSIAT
   – the Workplace Safety and Insurance Appeals Tribunal) had topped $13 million
   and the tribunal dealt with about 5,100 appeals per year. See "Statement of Operations, Year Ended December 31, 1997," Workplace Safety and Insurance Appeals
   Tribunal, *Annual Report 1997* (Toronto: Workplace Safety and Insurance Appeals
   Tribunal, 1998) at 56.

18 "Host ministry" is common administrative law parlance for the ministry or department responsible to the legislature for ensuring that a tribunal is operating effectively and efficiently in accordance with its mandate.

19 "Vice-Chair" is a confusing designation. In some tribunals, such as the Ontario
   Labour Relations Board and WCAT, it identifies a purely adjudicative position – the
   "neutral" chair of the tribunal's tripartite hearing panels. Typically, in those tribunals
   there will be a large number of "Vice-Chairs." In other tribunals, a vice-chair is at
   least in part an administrative position similar to a vice-president, and there is usually only one or two.

20 See, *e.g.*, Robert Macaulay, *Directions: Report on a Review of Ontario's Regulatory
   Agencies* (Ontario Management Board of Cabinet, 1989) [*Macaulay Report*] at 2-20.

21 Paul Weiler, *Reshaping Workers' Compensation for Ontario* (Report submitted to
   Robert G. Elgie, MD, Minister of Labour, November 1980) (Toronto: Ministry of
   Labour, 1980) [*Weiler Report*] at 112.

22 For a review of the UK and European Court authorities on the principle that, where
   the initial decision maker is not independent or impartial or its process does not

otherwise comply with the principles of natural justice, no objection will be taken provided parties ultimately have access to a review tribunal with a "full" review jurisdiction (including, where a decision turns on factual issues, the jurisdiction to review the findings of fact). See *Begum (FC) v. London Borough of Tower Hamlets*, [2003] U.K.H.L. 5 [*Begum*].

23 *De novo* hearings are those in which the case is tried again from the beginning, including the rehearing of evidence and the consideration of new evidence. In "appeal" hearings, only potential errors in law are typically considered.

24 In 1979, out of 460,000 initial claims adjudicator decisions, Professor Weiler reported that the Claims Review Branch reviewed 20,000 decisions and corrected 8,000, the Appeal Adjudicators disposed of 3,600 appeals, and in approximately 1,200 of those cases the outcome of the appeal was wholly or partially positive for the appellant. The Appeals Commissioners, in their turn, heard in that same year some 1,500 appeals, and in 40 percent of them the decision of the Appeal Adjudicator was revised or reversed. *Weiler Report, supra* note 21 at 95.

25 The *Workers' Compensation Act* designated tribunal staff as "Crown employees."

26 Staff salaries and benefits were by statute equal to public service salaries and benefits. The salary and benefit levels for the Chair, Vice-Chairs, and members were set by the Management Board of Cabinet in consultation with the Ministry of Labour.

27 In Ontario, in 1989, 70 percent of tribunals did not have their own budgets but were financed through their line ministries' budgets. See *Macaulay Report, supra* note 20 at 2-12.

28 For an account of this activity, see Ontario, Workers' Compensation Appeals Tribunal, *Annual Report 1995 and 1996* (Toronto: Workers' Compensation Appeals Tribunal, 1996) at 12.

29 Ian Strachan, whose selection as the new Chair was the good news during my last trying days at the tribunal. He had been a colleague and WCAT Vice-Chair since 1986.

30 The speech was subsequently published. See S. Ronald Ellis, "An Administrative Justice System in Jeopardy: Ontario's Appointments Policies" (1998) 6 C.L.E.L.J. 53.

31 The Conference of Ontario Boards and Agencies (COBA) organized under the leadership of Dr. Ratna B. Ray, at the time the chair of the Rent Review Hearings Board.

32 This was an adaptation of an earlier selection process involving a "Minister's Advisory Committee," which I will be describing at greater length later.

33 R.S.B.C. 1996, c. 384 (as amended). Section 14.9(3) was added to the *Public Sector Employers Act* effective 28 May 2003, by s. 54 of the *Administrative Tribunals Appointment and Administration Act*, S.B.C. 2003, c. 47 [*ATAAA*].

34 These letters were attached to the petition materials filed in May 2005. They were not letters negotiated as part of any settlement arrangement but were provided in response to McKenzie's request for references in the ordinary course.

35 *McKenzie v. Minister of Public Safety and Solicitor General et al.* 2006 B.C.S.C. 1372 (CanLII), 272 D.L.R. (4th) 455 (B.C.S.C.), [2006] 12 W.W.R. 404, 52 C.C.E.L. (3d) 191, 145 C.R.R. (2d) 192, 61 B.C.L.R. (4th) 57 [*McKenzie*].

36 *McKenzie v. British Columbia (Minister of Public Safety and Solicitor General)* 2007 B.C.C.A. 507 (CanLII) [*McKenzie appeal*] at paras. 25-47. The mootness was said to have arisen because of legislation, enacted after the lower court judgment but before

the hearing of the appeal, which transferred the jurisdiction to adjudicate residential tenancy disputes – including, it may be noted, the jurisdiction to issue eviction orders – from the Residential Tenancy Arbitrators to members of the BC housing ministry's staff.

37   *Ibid.* at paras. 6-7 and 31-37.

38   McKenzie and the government had negotiated a settlement of her reinstatement rights and her potential civil suit, but this agreement was made on the condition that the settlement would not bar her from continuing as a party in the appeal and in any subsequent proceedings before the Supreme Court of Canada. At the same time, a companion agreement included a unique provision for the government to pay McKenzie a predetermined amount as "advance costs" of the appeal.

39   *Ocean Port Hotel Ltd. v. British Columbia (General Manager, Liquor Control and Licensing Branch)*, [2001] 2 S.C.R. 781 [*Ocean Port*].

40   *Bell Canada v. Canadian Telephone Employees Association*, [2003] 1 S.C.R. 884 [*Bell Canada*].

41   *Ell v. Alberta*, [2003] 1 S.C.R. 857 [*Ell*].

42   *Reference re Remuneration of Judges of the Provincial Court of Prince Edward Island; Reference re Independence and Impartiality of Judges of the Provincial Court of Prince Edward Island; R. v. Campbell; R. v. Ekmecic; R. v. Wickman; Manitoba Provincial Judges Assn. v. Manitoba (Minister of Justice)*, [1997] 3 S.C.R. 3 [*PEI Reference*].

43   Ron Ellis, "Fair Hearings in an Ocean Port World – a Textured Concept" (2003) 18 J.L. & Soc. Pol'y 45.

44   Now Mr. Justice Pearlman of the BC Supreme Court.

45   Among other things, the order-in-council cancelling the appointment must be published in the *Official Gazette*. Newspaper or social network coverage will be inevitable.

46   My speaking notes for that debate may be found among the 2009 conference papers in the CCAT website (http://www.ccat-ctac.org/en/conferences/papers.php).

47   As we shall see below, a year and a half later, the reappointment of that respected but outspoken chair was refused by the BC government.

48   Except for Quebec.

49   As reported on the front page of the Toronto *Saturday Star* of 14 June 2003.

50   As I recall, $105,000.

51   See, *e.g., R. v. Valente*, [1985] 2 S.C.R. 673 [*Valente*] at para. 31, and especially *2747-3174 Québec Inc. v. Quebec (Régie des permis d'alcool)*, [1996] 3 S.C.R. 919 [*Régie*] at para. 67.

52   Established by the Supreme Court in *Borowski v. Canada (Attorney General)*, [1989] 1 S.C.R. 342 [*Borowski*].

53   *Ibid.*, at paras. 29-42.

54   *McKenzie appeal, supra* note 36 at paras. 45 and 46.

55   The reform was introduced by Bill 130, *An Act Respecting Administrative Justice*, enacted in December 1996 (S.Q. 1996, c. 54). The new legislation created TAQ – the *Tribunal administratif du Québec* – and its supervising council, the *Conseil de la justice administratif*, and assigned to the new tribunal the adjudicative responsibilities of a high proportion of Quebec tribunals. For a convenient, authoritative description of TAQ, see the Quebec Court of Appeal's judgment in *The Attorney General of*

Québec v. Barreau du Montréal, [2001] J.Q. No. 3882 (C.A.), leave to appeal refused (2002), 2002 CarswellQue 2078 (S.C.C.), reconsideration refused (2002), 2002 CarswellQue 2683 [*Barreau*], cited to J.Q. (C.A). See also France Houle, "A Brief Historical Account of the Reforms to the Administrative Justice System in the Province Of Quebec" (2009) 22 Can. J. Admin. L. & Prac. 47; and Gaston Pelletier, "Status of the Members of Bodies Established by the Québec Legislature to Exercise Adjudicative Functions within the Administrative Branch" (2010) 23 Can. J. Admin. L. & Prac. 41.

56　*Charter of Human Rights and Freedoms*, R.S.Q. c. C-12, s. 23.

57　Convenience dictates that I continue to refer to the administrative justice structures in the rest of Canada, and to the problems with those structures, under the generic "Canadian" label, but in what follows, references to "Canada" or to "Canadian" agencies or tribunals are intended to respectfully exempt Quebec and Quebec agencies and tribunals.

58　Ombudsman Ontario (André Marin, Ombudsman of Ontario), *Investigation into the Treatment of Victims by the Criminal Injuries Compensation Board: "Adding Insult to Injury"* (Toronto: Ombudsman Ontario, February 2007).

59　Andrew J. Roman, "Structure and Accountability of Administrative Agencies" in *Law Society of Upper Canada Special Lectures, 1992, Administrative Law, Principles, Practices and Pluralism* (Toronto: Carswell, 1992) at 63.

60　H. W. Arthurs, *Without the Law: Administrative Justice and Legal Pluralism in Nineteenth Century England* (Toronto and Buffalo: University of Toronto Press, 1985) [Arthurs, *Without the Law*].

61　H. Arthurs, "Jonah and the Whale: The Appearance, Disappearance and Reappearance of Administrative Law" (1980) 30 U.T.L. J. 225 [Arthurs, "Jonah and the Whale"].

62　The Right Honourable Lord Hewart of Bury, Lord Chief Justice of England, *The New Despotism* (New York: Cosmopolitan Book Corporation, 1929) at 8.

63　Albert Venn Dicey, *Lectures Introductory to the Study of Law of the Constitution*, 1st ed. (London: Macmillan, 1885).

64　See, *e.g.*, John Willis, "The McRuer Report: Lawyers' Values and Civil Servants' Values" (1968) 18 U.T.L.J. 351.

65　Arthurs, "Jonah and the Whale," *supra* note 61 at 229.

66　J.A. Corry, "Administrative Law and the Interpretation of Statutes" (1935-36) 1 U.T.L.J. 286. Corry's labels for tribunals and their members were "state agencies" and "officials."

67　*Ibid.* at 288.

68　See, *e.g.*, Harry Arthurs, "Protection against Judicial Review" (1983) 43 Can. Bar Rev. 277, and Willis, *supra* note 64 at 360.

69　With apologies to Professor Arthurs; see Arthurs, *Without the Law, supra* note 60.

CHAPTER 1: DEFEATING THE RULE OF LAW IN THE ADMINISTRATIVE JUSTICE SYSTEM

1　Gunnar Helgi Kristinsson, "Parties, States and Patronage" (1996) 19 Western European Politics 433-57 (footnote references omitted). For a concise account of the roots of Canada's virulent culture of patronage in the appointment of public officials, see Jack Stilborn, *Political Patronage: A Newly Troubled Tradition*, Research backgrounder (Ottawa: Research Branch of the Library of Parliament, 1989).

2 "[P]olitical patronage has been ... rampant for years in the naming of members to administrative tribunals": D.J. Mullan, "Administrative Tribunals: Their Evolution in Canada from 1945 to 1984" in I. Bernie and A. Lajoie, eds., *Regulations, Crown Corporations and Administrative Tribunals* (Toronto: University of Toronto Press, 1985) at 184.
3 Randy Colwell and Paul G. Thomas, "Parliament and the Patronage Issue" (1987) 22 Journal of Canadian Studies 163.
4 Chris Skelcher, *The Appointed State: Quasi-Governmental Organizations and Democracy* (Buckingham, PA: Open University Press, 1998) at 82.
5 *Ibid.* at 95, 97.
6 *Ibid.* at 97. Even the language of government reflects this, with appointments being often formally described as being "in the gift of the Minister."
7 S.N. Eisenstadt and L. Roniger, *Patrons, Clients and Friends: Interpersonal Relations and the Structure of Trust in Society* (Cambridge: Cambridge University Press, 1984) at 33-34.
8 Skelcher, *supra* note 4 at 98-99.
9 *Ibid.* at 82-83. (For the term "responsive competence," Skelcher credits B.G. Peters, *The Politics of Bureaucracy: A Comparative Perspective,* 4th ed. (New York: Longman, 1995).
10 *Ibid.* at 83 [emphasis added].
11 Ontario, Legislative Assembly, *Official Report of Debates [Hansard]* (11 October 1995) at 216.
12 See column by James Rusk, *Globe and Mail* (12 October 1995).
13 Whether parole boards are to be properly considered judicial tribunals is, perhaps, debatable. It is one of those tribunals at the margins of the "judicial tribunal" category. In my view, they are indeed judicial tribunals – part of the justice system. The basis for arguing this issue will be seen in my definition of a "judicial function" later in the book.
14 Reported in the *Globe and Mail* on 9 May 1990 [emphasis added].
15 See Introduction at 24.
16 *Toronto Star* (6 January 1994).
17 *Globe and Mail* (7 October 1994).
18 See Ed Ratushny, *Report on the Independence of Federal Administrative Tribunals and Agencies* (Presented to President John R. Jennings at the annual general meeting commemorating the seventy-fifth anniversary of the Canadian Bar Association, London England, 1990) (Ottawa: Canadian Bar Association, 1990) [*Ratushny Report*].
19 *Ibid.* at 10.
20 *Ibid.;* "Reconfiguration of Tribunals and Tenure" at 11-16.
21 Robert E. Hawkins and David M. Shoemaker, "Reputational Review II: Administrative Agencies, Print Media and Content Analysis" (1998-99) 12 Can. J. Admin. L. & Prac. 1.
22 *Ibid.* at 38.
23 *Ibid.* at 41.
24 Agency Reform Commission on Ontario's Regulatory and Adjudicative Agencies (Gary Guzzo, Chair), *Everyday Justice* (Toronto: Queen's Printer for Ontario, 1998) [*Guzzo Report*].

25 *Ibid.* at vii.

26 *Ibid.* at 4.

27 *Ibid.* at 15 [emphasis added].

28 *Ibid.* at 16 [emphasis added].

29 McConnell was commenting on the Nova Scotia Law Reform Commission's comprehensive survey of Nova Scotia's agencies, boards, and commissions as reported in its "1997 Final Report, Reform of the Administrative Justice System in Nova Scotia" [emphasis added].

30 Cited in Manitoba Law Reform Commission, *Improving Administrative Justice in Manitoba: Starting with the Appointments Process* (Report no. 21) (Winnipeg: Manitoba Law Reform Commission, November 2009) [*Manitoba Appointments Report*] at 22.

31 *Keddy v. New Brunswick (Workplace Health, Safety and Compensation Commission)* (2002), 212 D.L.R. (4th) 84 (N.B.C.A.), judgment of Robertson J.A. at para. 27.

32 New Brunswick Commission on Legislative Democracy, *Final Report and Recommendations* (Fredericton: Government of New Brunswick, December 2004) [*New Brunswick Commission Report*] at 84.

33 *Infra* at 79 – *Matkowski v. Saskatchewan.*

34 *Globe and Mail* (8 March 2008).

35 *Saskatchewan Federation of Labour v. Saskatchewan,* 2010 SKCA 27 [*SFL v. Sask CA 2010*] at paras. 12, 56, 57, 67, 68, 71, 72, and 73. The legislation in question became *The Trade Union Act,* R.S.S. 1978, c. T-17 ("Bill 6"), *The Construction Industry Labour Relations Act, 1992,* S.S. 1992, c. C-29.11 ("Bill 80"), and the new *Public Service Essential Services Act,* S.S. 2008, c. P-42.2 ("Bill 5").

36 *Ibid.* at para.12, quoting Premier Brad Wall.

37 *Globe and Mail, supra* note 34.

38 Section 20(1) of *The Interpretation Act, 1995,* S.S. 1995, c. I-11.2, states:

> Subject to subsection (2), notwithstanding any other enactment or any agreement, if a person is a member of a board, commission or other appointed body of the Government of Saskatchewan or any of its agencies or Crown corporations on the day on which the Executive Council is first installed following a general election as defined in The Election Act, the term of office for which that person was appointed is deemed to end on the earlier of: (a) the last day of the term for which the person was appointed; or (b) a day designated by the Lieutenant Governor in Council or the person who made the appointment.

39 *SFL v. Sask CA 2010, supra* note 35 at para. 55.

40 *Ibid.,* citing Legislative Assembly of Saskatchewan, *Debates and Proceedings* [*Hansard*] (5 July 1982) at 491.

41 The Second Reading occurred on 5 July 1982, ten weeks after Grant Devine's Progressive Conservative Party had swept the NDP out of power.

42 *SFL v. Sask CA 2010, supra* note 35 at para. 58.

43 See Ron Ellis, "Saskatchewan Takes the Justice out of Justice," *Lawyers Weekly* (6 April 2010).

44 *The Saskatchewan Federation of Labour, and the Saskatchewan Government and General Employees' Union, and The Saskatchewan Joint Board Retail, Wholesale*

and Department Store Union v. Saskatchewan (Attorney General, Department of Advanced Education, Employment and Labour), and The Saskatchewan Labour Relations Board, 2010 SKQB 390 (CanLII) [*SFL v. Saskatchewan*] at para. 75.

45 In the interests of full disclosure, I am one of the co-counsel for the appellants in that appeal.

46 *Manitoba Appointments Report, supra* note 30.

47 *Ibid.* at 2, fn 8.

48 *New Brunswick Commission Report, supra* note 32 at 84.

49 *Ibid.* at 87.

50 New Brunswick, Government of, *An Accountable and Responsible Government, a New Generation of Canadian Leadership ... The Government's Response to the Final Report of the Commission on Legislative Democracy ... Renewing Democracy in New Brunswick* (Fredericton: Government of New Brunswick, 2007).

51 *Adjudicative Tribunals Accountability, Governance and Appointments Act, 2009,* S.O. 2009, c. 33, sch. 5 [*Adjudicative Tribunals Governance Act*].

52 Ontario Bar Association, "Adjudicative Tribunals Accountability, Governance and Appointments Act, 2009 – Cause for Concern – The Tribunal Independence Issue" (2011) 24 Can. J. Admin. L. & Prac. 225 [OBA, *Cause for Concern*].

53 S.B.C. 2003, c. 47.

54 See Introduction at 24.

55 Canada, House of Commons, 35th Parliament – 2nd Session, Standing Committee on Citizenship and Immigration. *Information Session Regarding the Ministerial Advisory Committee on the Selection of Members of the Immigration and Refugee Board,* Parliament of Canada Record of Evidence 18 June 1996, at records .1540, .1545, .1550, .1555, .1600, .1605, .1610, .1615, .1620, and .1625 [Standing Committee Record].

56 27 October 2011.

57 Standing Committee Record, *supra* note 55 at .1540.

58 My interview with Peter Showler, 27 October 2011.

59 Standing Committee Record, *supra* note 55 at .1540.

60 See Introduction at 24.

61 Standing Committee Record, *supra* note 55 at .1540.

62 *Ibid.*

63 *Ibid.,* in response to a question from Meredith.

64 *Ibid.* at .1545, .1555, and .1600, through questioning from MPs Meredith (twice), Minna, and Nunez.

65 I had resigned several months earlier.

66 Citizenship and Immigration Canada, News Release (9 July 2007).

67 S.A. 2009, c. A-31.5 [emphasis added].

68 *Ibid.* at s. 15.

69 Peter Aucoin and Elisabeth Goodyear-Grant, "Designing a Merit Based Process for Appointing Boards of ABCs: Lessons from the Nova Scotia Reform Experience" (2002) 45 Canadian Public Administration 301 at 311.

70 *Ibid.* at 314.

71 "Terms of Reference for Advisory Committees on Adjudicative Boards and Selection Criteria to Be Used by Advisory Committees on Adjudicative Boards," online:

Government of Nova Scotia <http://www.gov.ns.ca/exec_council/abc/pubs/Terms -of-Reference.pdf>.

72 *Supra* note 51.

73 By the new IRB chair, Brian Goodman. Fleury had resigned.

74 *Canadian Press* (8 April 2008).

75 *Pelletier v. Canada (Attorney General)*, 2008 FCA 1 (CanLII) at para. 33.

76 *R. v. Valente*, [1985] 2 S.C.R. 673 [*Valente*] (previously cited).

77 *British North America Act, 1867* (U.K.), 30-31 Vict., c. 3, ss. 96, 99, and 100.

78 It is a tradition that did seem to exist for actual judges but in fact never existed for adjudicative members of judicial tribunals.

79 *Reference re Justices of the Peace Act; Re Currie and Niagara Escarpment Commission*, [1984] O.J. No. 3393 (Ont. C.A.) [*Currie*].

80 *Ibid.* at paras. 28-32 [emphasis added].

81 The tribunal was trying a soldier charged with an offence under the *Narcotics Control Act.*

82 *R. v. MacKay*, [1980] 2 S.C.R. 370 [*MacKay*]. It is remarkable but, as far as I have been able to discern, true that there is no Canadian case in which the independence of a judge or adjudicator was ever actually at issue until *MacKay.*

83 *Canadian Bill of Rights (An Act for the Recognition and Protection of Human Rights and Fundamental Freedoms)*, S.C. 1960, c. 44 at s. 2(f).

84 *MacKay, supra* note 82 at 379.

85 *Ibid.* at 395.

86 *Ibid.* at 404 [emphasis added].

87 *R. v. Valente (No. 2)* (1983), 2 C.C.C. (3d) 417 (Ont. C.A.) [*Valente No. 2*].

88 In retrospect, it is perverse that the Court of Appeal decision that led to the iconic Supreme Court decision that is now always referred to as "*Valente*" is named "*Valente (No. 2).*" Still, there it is.

89 *Valente, supra* note 76 at paras. 27 (security of tenure), 40 (financial security), and 47 (administrative control).

90 *Ibid.* at para. 22. See also *Charkaoui v. Canada (Citizenship and Immigration)*, [2007] S.C.J. No. 9 [*Charkaoui*] at para. 32.

91 Section 11 states: "Any person charged with an offence has the right ... (d) to be presumed innocent until proven guilty according to law in a fair and public hearing *by an independent and impartial tribunal*" [emphasis added].

92 *IWA v. Consolidated-Bathurst Packaging Ltd.*, [1990] 1 S.C.R. 282 [*Consolidated-Bathurst*] at 332, per Gonthier J.

93 *Canadian Pacific Ltd. v. Matsqui Indian Band*, [1995] 1 S.C.R. 3 [*Matsqui*] at para. 79, per Lamer C.J.C.

94 *R. v. Généreux*, [1992] 1 S.C.R. 259 [*Généreux*].

95 *Ibid.* at 292-93.

96 *Valente, supra* note 76 at para. 31.

97 The 1992 trial court judgment seems not to have been reported but is described in the ensuing Court of Appeal judgment: *Preston v. British Columbia* (1994), 116 D.L.R. (4th) 258 (B.C.C.A.) [*Preston*].

98 *Interpretation Act*, R.S.B.C. 1979, c. 206, s. 22(a) and (b).

99 *Preston, supra* note 97 at para. 14.

100 *Hewat v. Ontario* (1996), 32 O.R. (3d) 622 (Ont. Div. Ct.).

101 *Hewat v. Ontario* (1998), 37 O.R. (3d) 161 (Ont. C.A.) *[Hewat]*.

102 *Ibid.* at para. 22.

103 *Interpretation Act,* R.S.A. 2000, c.I-8, s. 20(4) [emphasis added]. This wording was first introduced to the Alberta *Interpretation Act* in 1999, a year after the Ontario Court of Appeal decision in *Hewat, supra* note 101. See S.A. 1999, c. 32, s. 10(2)(b).

104 *Administrative Tribunals Appointment and Administration Act,* S.B.C. 2003, c. 47.

105 R.S.B.C. 1996, c. 384, amended by s. 54 of the *Administrative Tribunals Appointment and Administration Act, ibid.*

106 *McKenzie v. Minister of Public Safety and Solicitor General et al.,* 2006 B.C.S.C. 1372 (CanLII), 272 D.L.R. (4th) 455 (B.C.S.C.), [2006] 12 W.W.R. 404, 52 C.C.E.L. (3d) 191, 145 C.R.R. (2d) 192, 61 B.C.L.R. (4th) 57 *[McKenzie]* (previously cited).

107 See page 47.

108 *Ibid.*

109 An example of this came to the public's attention in January 2008 when the federal government "terminated" the designation of Linda Keen as president and CEO of the Canadian Nuclear Safety Commission. The *Nuclear Safety and Control Act,* S.C. 1997, c. 9, provided for the appointment of the Commission's members to fixed terms on good behaviour, but for only the "designation" of a member as president.

110 *Dunsmuir v. New Brunswick,* [2008] 1 S.C.R. 190 *[Dunsmuir]*.

111 For a full counter-argument, see Ron Ellis, "*Dunsmuir* and the Independence of Adjudicative Tribunals" (2010) 23 Can. J. Admin. Law & Prac. 203.

112 Alan D. Levy, "A Review of Environmental Assessment in Ontario" (2001) 11 J. Envtl. L. & Prac. 173.

113 *Ibid.* at 258.

114 *Ibid.* at 259.

115 Robert Macaulay, *Directions: Report on a Review of Ontario's Regulatory Agencies* (Ontario Management Board of Cabinet, 1989) *[Macaulay Report]* (previously cited) at 2-21.

116 Ontario, Legislative Assembly, *Official Report of Debates [Hansard]* (31 March 1998) at A-798ff.

117 *Ahumada v. Canada (Minister of Citizenship & Immigration)* (2001), 199 D.L.R. (4th) 103 (Fed. C.A.).

118 As quoted in Ron Ellis, "Appointments Policies in the Administrative Justice System: Lessons from Ontario: Four Speeches" (1998) 11 Can. J. Admin. L. & Prac. 205 [Ellis, "Lessons from Ontario"] at 250-52.

119 *Ibid.*

120 Rosalie Silberman Abella, "Canadian Administrative Tribunals: Towards Judicialization or Dejudicialization" (1988) 2 Can. J. Admin. L. & Prac. 1 at 10.

121 Fortunately, the termination of her arbitration appointment in British Columbia did not end McKenzie's adjudicative career. She was able to secure an adjudicative appointment with a major tribunal in another jurisdiction, and at the time of writing has been a respected member of that tribunal for several years.

122 *Administrative Tribunals Appointment and Administration Act, supra* note 105 at ss. 3(1) and 3(2).

123 In his statement of claim, the ousted vice-chair describes a meeting with the Deputy Minister of Labour and the Board chair at the time he was in the process of deciding in the first instance whether to give up his practice as a lawyer, mediator, and arbitrator and accept a full-time appointment to the Board. At that meeting, he was anxious to establish that he would be free to be independent in his decision making without jeopardizing subsequent reappointments, and he alleges that he was assured that if he made decisions in accordance with the law and the facts, he could count on reappointments for as long as the [NDP] government was in power. See the passages from the statement of claim cited in *Matkowski v. Saskatchewan*, [2007] S.J. No. 81 (Q.B.) [*Matkowski*].

124 But permitted reappointments to further terms.

125 *Matkowski, supra* note 123. The basis for the allegations of labour-movement influence in the decision not to reappoint may be seen in the affidavit filed in the case. There is also a Hansard record, both amusing and telling, of the Saskatchewan Minister of Labour's wry attempt to skate around questions in the Saskatchewan legislature concerning the unions' influence on the decision not to reappoint. See *Saskatchewan Hansard* (3 May 2006) at 1499-1501, and (8 May 2006) at 1553-55.

126 *Supra* note 16 and accompanying text.

127 *In the matter of the Mental Health act, RSO 1990, Chapter M-7 and in the matter of JS, a patient in the Penetanguishene Mental Health Center, Penetanguishene, Ontario* – a decision by [the] ... Acting Chairman of the Panel of the Review Board having jurisdiction for Penetanguishene Mental Health Center, dated at North York, 25 March 1994.

128 *Brar v. College of Veterinarians of British Columbia*, 2011 BCSC 486 (CanLII) [*Brar*].

129 *Datt v. McDonald's Restaurants (No. 3)*, 2007 BCHRT 324 [*Datt*].

130 Ezra Levant, "Enough's Enough: Exclusive Excerpt: How McDonald's Hand-Washing Policy Was Overruled" (2 April 2009), online: Macleans.ca <http://www2.macleans.ca/2009/04/02/enough%E2%80%99s-enough/>.

131 *Emergency Health Services Commission v. Cassidy*, 2011 BCSC 1003 (CanLII) at para. 38.

132 "If You Love Human Rights Clap Your Hands" *Lawyers Weekly* (5 July 2002).

133 *Brar and Others v. BCVMA and Osborne (No. 17)*, 2010 BCHRT 260 at para. 9.

134 *Brar, supra* note 128 at paras. 21-90.

135 *Ibid.* at para. 83

136 *Ibid.* at para. 84.

137 The BCVMA was, as we have seen, the principal respondent in the discrimination claim.

138 At para. 64.

139 *Brar, supra* note 128 at paras. 81, 83, 87, and 89-90.

140 Ron Lebi and Elizabeth Mitchell, "The Decline in Trade Union Certification in Ontario: The Case for Restoring Remedial Certification" (2003) 10 C.L.E.L.J 472 at 475 and 484.

141 *Ibid.* at 475 (footnote references omitted).

142 *Ibid.* at 484.

143 After leaving WCAT in June 1997, I returned to private practice. In my capacity as a solo practitioner, I had occasion over the following three years to advise or consult

with individuals who had suffered idiosyncratic removals from Ontario judicial tribunal adjudicative positions on five different occasions.

144 Ontario, Management Board of Cabinet, "Appointment Agreement for Regulatory & Adjudicative Agencies" in "Tools, Templates and Guides" (November 2000) [unpublished] [emphasis added]. This was one of the "tools" contained in the binder presented to the November 2000 Conference of Ontario Boards and Agencies meeting by the Attorney General and the chair of the Management Board of Cabinet. See page 122.

145 And no wonder. In *Caperton v. A.T. Massey Coal Co., Inc,* 129 S. Ct. 2252, 2009 U.S. LEXIS 4157 (2009), by a 5-4 margin the US Supreme Court vacated a verdict of the West Virginia Supreme Court of Appeals that had overturned a $50 million jury verdict against the nation's fourth-largest coal mining company in the circumstances where the deciding vote in the West Virginia Supreme Court of Appeals' 3-2 decision was by a judge who had recently won an election contest over an incumbent judge with the assistance of $3 million worth of campaign funds from the CEO of the coal company. John Grisham's novel *The Appeal* (New York: Doubleday, 2008) tells essentially the same story in a fictional form, but without the happy, if near-run, outcome in *Caperton.*

146 "Watch Dogs Describe Coming 'Under Attack' by Conservative Government" *Globe and Mail* (26 January 2010).

147 See the report by *Toronto Star* immigration reporter Nicholas Keung concerning an application to the Federal Court by two Roma families for judicial review of the IRB's rejection of their refugee appeal. The application alleges bias and relies on the Minister's comments and the statistical evidence concerning the impact of those comments on the rejection rate of Roma appeals: *Toronto Star* (30 November 2010) A12.

148 See Introduction at 6.

149 *2747-3174 Québec Inc. v. Quebec (Régie des permis d'alcool),* [1996] 3 S.C.R. 919 [*Régie*].

150 See Introduction, note 51.

151 *The Attorney General of Québec v. Barreau du Montréal,* [2001] J.Q. No. 3882 (C.A.), leave to appeal refused (2002), 2002 CarswellQue 2078 (S.C.C.), reconsideration refused (2002), 2002 CarswellQue 2683, cited to J.Q. (C.A) [*Barreau*] (previously cited).

152 *Régie, supra* note 149.

153 *Barreau, supra* note 151 at para. 174.

154 Section 49 of the *Act Respecting Administrative Justice,* S.Q. 1996, c. 54, provided for the renewal of a term of office to be "examined" according to a procedure to be established by regulation. Subsequently, the regulation required the forming of a committee that would "determine" whether the member still fulfilled the necessary criteria for appointment and recommend to the Minister of Justice whether or not the appointment should be renewed. See *Regulation Respecting the Procedure for the Recruitment and Selection of Persons Apt for Appointments as Members of the Administrative Tribunal of Québec and for the Renewal of their Term of Office,* Order-in-Council 317-98, 18 March 1998 (1998) 130 G.O.Q. II 1800, Division IX, Renewal of Terms of Office, s. 25-29. The third member of the committee was a "representative of the legal community."

155 *Barreau, supra* note 151 at paras. 172-90.

156 The TAQ members' association and a number of individual members had inter-
vened in the decision to challenge the fixed-term appointments as being incompatible with the requirement of independence.

157 *Barreau, supra* note 151 at paras. 170-90. But compare the judgment of the Military
Court in *R. v. Corporal R.P. Joseph*, 2005 CM 41, where it was held that the appointment of military judges to fixed renewable terms was not compatible with the requirement of independence and impartiality. In the latter case, no consideration was
given to the possibility of a fair, merit-based, and objective renewal process. See,
more recently, the decision of the Quebec Superior Court in *Association des juges
administratifs de la Commission des lesions professionnelles, et al. v. Procureur general du Québec*, 2011 QCCS 1614 (CanLII) (1 April 2011), which holds that fixed
terms of adjudicative tribunal members are incompatible with the principles of judicial independence, distinguishing *Barreau* on this point. Whether the Quebec Court
of Appeal's affirmation in *Barreau* that fixed terms are compatible with the requirements of independence provided there is a merit-based, open, fair, and independent
reappointment process will be reasserted in this appeal remains to be seen.

158 *An Act Respecting Administrative Justice*, R.S.Q., c. J-3, as amended to 13 May 2003,
contains the applicable post-*Barreau* provision. See s. 49 dealing with appointment
renewals.

159 As recommended, for instance, in the *Ratushny Report, supra* note 18, recommendation 38 at 62.

160 R. Dussault and L. Borgeat, *Administrative Law*, 2d ed., vol. 1 (Toronto: Carswell,
1985). It may be noted, however, that subsequent to the 2003 post-*Barreau* amendments to the renewal committee provisions, the National Assembly finally opted for
life-tenured appointments for TAQ members. See *An Act to Amend the Act Respecting Administrative Justice*, S.Q. 2005, c. 17, s. 2. The amended *Act* now provides
for TAQ members "to hold office during good behaviour."

161 In *Reference re Remuneration of Judges of the Provincial Court of Prince Edward
Island; Reference re Independence and Impartiality of Judges of the Provincial Court
of Prince Edward Island; R. v. Campbell; R. v. Ekmecic; R. v. Wickman; Manitoba
Provincial Judges Assn. v. Manitoba (Minister of Justice)*, [1997] 3 S.C.R. 3 [*PEI
Reference*] (previously cited).

162 This principle is conveniently summarized by the Alberta Court of Queen's Bench
in *Canada Safeway Limited v. Alberta Human Rights and Citizenship Commission*,
2000 ABQB 897 (CanLII) at para. 66:

> In *Régie*, and the Supreme Court's earlier decisions in *Ruffo v. Conseil de la
> Magistrature* 1995 CanLII 49 (S.C.C.), (1995), 130 D.L.R. (4th) 1 (S.C.C.) at
> para. 38 ("*Ruffo*") and *Canadian Pacific Ltd. v. Matsqui Indian Band*, 1995
> CanLII 145 (S.C.C.), [1995] 1 S.C.R. 3 at para. 62 ("*Matsqui*"), the Supreme
> Court held that the administrative law principles of natural justice and the duty
> to be fair incorporate the same principles of adjudicative independence and im-
> partiality as s.23 of the Quebec *Charter* and ss.7 and 11(d) of the Canadian
> *Charter of Rights and Freedoms*. Therefore, the Supreme Court of Canada deci-
> sions dealing with these principles, whether under the Quebec *Charter*, admin-
> istrative law, or ss.7 and 11(d) of the *Charter*, are applicable.

163 René Dussault, a principal author of, for instance, the administrative law treatise: Dussault and Borgeat, *supra* note 160.

164 *Alberta Bill of Rights*, R.S.A. 2000, c. A-14. The Alberta courts do not appear to have had occasion to examine whether the due process of law required under s. 1(a) before an individual may be deprived of the right to liberty, security of the person, and enjoyment of property includes independent and impartial tribunals.

165 See page 42.

166 Cédric P. Lamarche, "Saskatchewan Announces the Likely Dissolution of Its Human Rights Tribunal" (17 March 2010), online: Whitten and Lublin <http://blog.toronto -employmentlawyer.com/>.

167 See page 46.

168 *Weatherill v. Canada (Attorney General)*, [1999] F.C.J. No. 787 [*Weatherill*].

169 Canada, House of Commons, *Debates*, 36th Parliament, 1st Session, Edited Hansard No. 42 (Tuesday, 2 December 1997) at 1435. According to press reports, the "hear, hear" in Hansard in fact referenced a "standing ovation from members on both sides of the house": *Globe and Mail* (22 January 1998).

170 Federal Court Justice Louis Marcel Joyal.

171 *Globe and Mail* (22 January 1998).

172 *Weatherill v. Canada (Attorney General)* (1998), 6 Admin. L.R. (3d) 137 (F.C.) at para. 30.

173 *Weatherill, supra* note 168 at paras. 56-97.

174 *Judges Act*, R.S.C 1985, c. J-1, as amended.

175 He had been appointed chair of the Canada Labour Relations Board on 9 March 1989 by order of the Governor-in-Council, to hold office during good behaviour for a term of ten years commencing 1 May 1989. The appointment was authorized by s. 10 of the *Canada Labour Code*, R.S.C., 1985, c. L-2.

176 *Wedge v. Canada (Attorney General)* (1995), 133 F.T.R. 277 [*Wedge*].

177 *Weatherill, supra* note 168 at para. 87.

178 *Ibid.* at para. 88.

179 At CCAT's annual conference in 2000 the late Keith Oleksiuk, at the time recently the chair of the BC Labour Relations Board, spoke on the problem of reconciling the accountability of tribunals and their members with the need for independence. He described the "high level of antagonism" between the parties in the BC labour relations environment and the "highly charged atmosphere" in which individual members of the BC Labour Relations Board were being asked to decide controversial union/management issues. He reported that during his four years as chair, the average tribunal vice-chair stayed for a "little over one [three-year] term"; that, as of that time, no BC Labour Relations Board chair had ever completed a five-year term; and that the government had notorious difficulty finding people willing to accept an appointment as Labour Relations Board chair.

180 *Ahumada, supra* note 117 and accompanying text at 76.

181 As we have seen, Macaulay's 1989 study reported that, in Ontario, 70 percent of tribunals did not have their own budgets but were financed through the portfolio ministry's budget. See *Macaulay Report, supra* note 115. There is nothing to suggest that those arrangements have changed in the intervening twenty years.

182 *Macaulay Report, supra* note 115.

183 *Ibid.* at 10-11 (in the Overview of the report) [emphasis added].

184 Paul Aterman, "What's Not New in Administrative Justice: Macaulay and Ouellette – Remember Them?" (2005) 18 Can. J. Admin. L. & Prac. 251 at 288, quoting Ron Ellis speaking notes for an address to the 1989 Conference of Ontario Boards and Agencies.

185 *Adjudicative Tribunals Governance Act, supra* note 51.

186 *Ibid.* at s. 1 [emphasis added].

187 OBA, *Cause for Concern, supra* note 52. I was a member of the OBA Administrative Law Section task force that worked on that commentary.

188 *Ibid.* at 228 – "Provisions that give us Concern," para. 9.

189 In 2006, the BC government did exactly that: it tore down the façade of independence for the adjudicators of residential landlord and tenant disputes and transferred the adjudication of those disputes to the portfolio ministry's staff. See *Tenancy Statutes Amendment Act, 2006*, S.B.C. 2006, c. 35.

190 The federal government is reported to have had 640 positions that could be filled by Governor-in-Council appointments in 2002. Of these, 270 were IRB adjudicative positions. See author's interview with Peter Showler, 27 October 2011.

191 Lorne Sossin, *The Independent Board and the Legislative Process* (Edmonton: Alberta Federation of Labour, 2006). For the litigation of the issue in the Alberta Court of Queen's Bench, see *Communications, Energy and Paperworkers Union of Canada, Local 707 v. Alberta (Labour Relations Board)*, [2004] Alta. L.R.B.R. 1.

192 *Ibid.* at 16.

193 The story is told and, apocryphal or not, generally believed (I have personally heard the story from two Alberta chairs who purported to have been there) that a few years ago, when the chairs of Alberta tribunals proposed to organize a circle of chairs somewhat similar to SOAR in Ontario, BCCAT in British Columbia, or CCAT federally, the Alberta government advised the chairs that if they were to go ahead with the proposal, they would all be fired.

194 S.A. 2009, c. A-31.5.

195 *Ibid.* at ss. 7(1) and (2) [emphases added].

196 *Ibid.* at s. 1(1)(d).

197 Gaile McGregor, "Anti-Claimant Bias in the Employment Insurance Appeals System: Causes, Consequences, and Public Law Remedies" (2002) 15 Can. J. Admin. L. & Prac. 229.

198 *Ibid.* at 232.

199 *Ibid.* at 258-59.

200 *Ibid.* at 259-64.

201 *Ibid.* at 264.

202 *Ibid.* at 267-68.

203 *Ibid.* at 258-69 and 275-82.

204 The reference to *Lippé* is *R. v. Lippé*, [1991] 2 S.C.R. 114 [*Lippé*] at para. 60.

205 *McGregor, supra* note 197 at 280-83.

206 *Ibid.* at 239.

207 *Ibid.* at 241.

208 *Tenant Protection Act, 1997,* S.O. 1997, c. 24 [since repealed].

209 Advocacy Centre of Tenants Ontario (ACTO) and the Legal Clinics Housing Issues Committee (LCHIC). *Submission to the Ombudsman Ontario – Concerning the Failure of the Tenant Protection Act and the Rules and Procedures of the Ontario Rental Housing Tribunal to Meet Ombudsman Fairness Standards* (20 June 2002) [*Fairness Complaint*]. The *Fairness Complaint* was released to the media on the same day. See also the analysis of the Tribunal's record on evictions reported by Jennifer Ramsay in her article "Provincial Agency Creating Homelessness" *Toronto Star* (30 June 2000).

210 *Ibid.* at 9.

211 *Tenant Protection Act, supra* note 208 at ss. 175(2) and 177(2)(a).

212 *Ibid.* at ss. 177(1) and 192(1).

213 *Ibid.* at ss. 192(2) and 192(4). See *Dovale v. Metropolitan Toronto Housing Authority,* 2001 CanLII 28024 (S.C.D.C.) at paras. 36 and 37.

214 In the tight market for affordable rental housing that prevailed during this period in most of Ontario, vacant apartments could be readily filled with new tenants.

215 In the study reported by Ramsay, *supra* note 209, of the evicted tenants interviewed, 29 percent claimed not to have received a copy of the notice of the application to evict.

216 *Statutory Powers Procedure Act,* R.S.O. 1990, c. S.22 at s. 6(1).

217 *Supra* note 211.

218 This persisted for four years, despite complaints from the legal clinics. In a large box at the top printed in bold, the form announced itself as a Notice of Hearing, specifying the place, date, and time of the hearing, and then below, less prominently, it noted that the hearing would take place only if the tenant filed a written dispute within five days. See *Fairness Complaint, supra* note 208, "Notice of Hearing Not Clear and Understandable" at 20.

219 ORHT Guidelines provided that a respondent was expected to "seek help [within the two or three business days available to them] if they cannot read or understand" the Notice of Hearing. See *ibid.,* "Setting Aside a Default Eviction Order" at 10.

220 Only one of the Tribunal's pamphlets was written primarily for tenants ("Termination of a Tenancy by a Tenant"). There were none to assist tenants in responding to a landlord's application even though tenants were respondents in 91 percent of the Tribunal's cases, but several pamphlets were written primarily for landlord applicants (*e.g.,* "Terminating a Tenancy," "Reasons for Terminating a Tenancy by a Landlord," "Terminating a Tenancy in a Care Home," and "If a Tenant Doesn't Pay Rent"). There is no pamphlet titled "If Your Landlord Applies for an Eviction Order" or "If Your Landlord Locks You Out of Your Rental Unit." See *ibid.,* "No Public Information Materials to Assist Tenants" at 28-31.

221 Under s. 84 of the *Tenant Protection Act,* the Tribunal had the discretion to refuse to evict "unless satisfied, having regard to all the circumstances, that it would be unfair to refuse," and also the discretion to order the postponement of the enforcement of an eviction order on terms. And, while the absence of published decisions prevented a precise determination of the frequency of the Tribunal's exercise of these discretions, the impression left with clinic advocates was that the Tribunal believed that landlords were entitled to eviction orders almost regardless of the seriousness of the tenant's breach of the *Act.* This did not accord with the weight of jurisprudence

where, when it was the Superior Court issuing the eviction orders, the Court was willing to balance the seriousness of the breach against the severity of the eviction remedy. Housing rights organizations had also noted the failure of ORHT adjudicators to exercise their discretion to not evict in a manner that would recognize the personal circumstances of a tenant facing a shortage of affordable housing if evicted. The Centre for Equality Rights in Accommodation, reporting to the City of Toronto as part of the city's eviction prevention project, contrasted the ORHT's seemingly routine issuance of eviction orders for arrears of rent with the much slower, more measured approach of lending institutions when a mortgage or other financing payment is missed. The Centre submitted that, just as foreclosure and repossession are remedies of last resort for financial institutions, the ORHT should exercise its discretion to relieve against eviction in appropriate arrears cases so that eviction is also a remedy of last resort. The authors of the *Fairness Complaint* were of the view that many evictions could have been avoided if the Tribunal had been willing to exercise its discretion in appropriate cases. Given that "84% of all eviction applications ... are for arrears, and that 50% of arrears eviction orders are for amounts of $800 or less," the authors felt that there was "every reason to think that many [eviction] applications could be resolved through an ordered repayment schedule." See *ibid.*, "Failure to Appropriately Exercise Discretion" at 34-36.

222 *Ibid.*, "Tribunal Decisions Not Available" at 31-34.

223 *Ibid.*, "Mediation Process Not Designed to Facilitate Fair Settlements" at 12 and 24-28.

224 The average hearing time was ten to fifteen minutes per case; in Toronto, with the introduction of "express" hearing blocks for eviction applications by landlords, the Tribunal was able to reduce that average to eight minutes. See *ibid.*, "Efficiency Valued over Accessibility and Fairness" at 16-18.

225 That speed and efficiency had pride of place in the Tribunal's priorities may be seen in the following paragraph from the Tribunal's 1999-2000 annual report as quoted in the *Fairness Complaint:*

> The Tribunal has been successful in resolving applications quickly. On average the Tribunal maintains only one month's receipts as open files. We were even more efficient this past fiscal year. We focused on the files that had no disputes and issued default orders as quickly as possible. Our statistics indicate that over all, we were able to issue default orders within one to two days after the dispute deadline [of five calendar days]. In addition, we issued most orders within 21 days of the application being filed, and even more complex orders were issued within 23 to 25 days.

The pressure the Tribunal was under to speed up the eviction process may be seen from the KPMG Consulting report following KPMG'S December 1999 internal review, in which the Tribunal is urged to target a consistent 70 percent rate of default orders. Following the KPMG recommendations, the ORHT apparently took steps to increase the speed of its default eviction process by having staff telephone landlords to obtain any missing documentation necessary to support a signed eviction order. The government also amended the legislation, as recommended by KPMG, to allow Tribunal staff, not adjudicators, to sign default orders. See *ibid.*

226 See, *e.g.*, Paul Stuart Rapsey, "See No Evil, Hear No Evil, Remedy No Evil: How the Ontario Rental Housing Tribunal Is Failing to Protect the Most Fundamental Rights of Residential Tenants" (2000) 15 J. L. & Soc. Pol'y 163. See also *Jung v. Toronto Community Housing Corp.*, [2007] O.J. No. 4363 (Ont. Div. Ct.) at paras. 25-27. The latter decision dealt with the review of an eviction application heard by the ORHT concerning a long-time occupant of public housing, which resulted in an eviction order that was challenged on judicial review. The Divisional Court was of the view that the transcript of the hearing disclosed that virtually all the rules of natural justice had been violated. The Court concluded: "The Tribunal appeared biased. The person most at risk was denied a hearing. It was, as [tenant's counsel] said, a 'trial by ambush.' The decisions must be set aside."

227 Fairness Committee (The Honourable Justice Coulter A. Osbourne, QC, Chair; Professor David J. Mullan and Bryan Finlay, QC, Members), "Report of the Fairness Committee to David A. Brown, Q.C., Chair of the Ontario Securities Commission" (5 March 2004) [unpublished].

228 *Ibid.*, "Conclusion" at 32 [emphasis added].

229 Readers may be wondering how the Ontario Securities Commission's enforcement of its rules can be appropriately classified as the exercise of a judicial function. It is an arguable point with the function sitting at the intersection of the categories of administrative quasi-judicial functions and judicial functions. However, its characterization as a judicial function derives, in my opinion, from the fact that enforcement procedures in the securities field are often strongly akin to criminal proceedings. Liberty of the person is not involved, but issues implicitly engaging allegations of moral turpitude, very substantial "fines," and very serious consequences for the reputation and careers of individuals are typically potentially at risk in these proceedings. My view in that respect is bolstered by the OSC's own Fairness Committee's recommendation for an independent adjudicative process. I also note that the decision to "convict" or not in these cases is not likely to present the same degree of polycentric issues inherent in less criminal-style regulatory proceedings.

230 Paul Weiler, *Reshaping Workers' Compensation for Ontario* (Report submitted to Robert G. Elgie, MD, Minister of Labour, November 1980) (Toronto: Ministry of Labour, 1980) [*Weiler Report*] (previously cited).

231 But not without support for the recommendation from the Ontario legislature. Recommendation Five in the 2004 *Report on the Five-Year Review of the Securities Act* by the Ontario Legislative Assembly's Standing Committee on Finance and Economic Affairs reads: "The adjudicative function of the Ontario Securities Commission should be separated from its other functions, based on the recommendations of the Fairness Committee." And, in fairness, one of the factors that may have delayed action on this recommendation is the legislature's anticipation of the establishment of a National Securities Commission.

232 Ombudsman Ontario (André Marin, Ombudsman of Ontario). *Investigation into the Treatment of Victims by the Criminal Injuries Compensation Board: "Adding Insult to Injury."* (Toronto: Ombudsman Ontario, February 2007).

233 *Ibid.* [emphasis added].

234 The Ombudsman's reference here to the CICB's being a "quasi-judicial" tribunal is in line with the terminology now prevailing in the Supreme Court's jurisprudence,

but what he describes is clearly a "judicial" tribunal. I will address the Courts' "misuse" of the "quasi-judicial" terminology in Chapter 2.

235 As will be seen, this is, in miniature, precisely what has happened with respect to the administrative justice system writ large.

236 The intervention of the Ombudsman can change that, as occurred in the case of Ontario's Criminal Injuries Compensation Board (see *supra* note 232 and text at 111-13).

237 A. Freedman, *Patronage: An American Tradition* (Chicago: Nelson-Hall Publishers, 1994) at 12 [emphasis added].

238 Ontario, Legislative Assembly, Standing Committee on the Ontario Legislature (Michael J. Breaugh, Chair), *Report on Appointments in the Public Sector, 1986* (Toronto: Government of Ontario, 1986) [*Breaugh Report*] at 13-14. (This is the report that led to the establishment in Ontario of the current Standing Legislative Committee review of proposed tribunal appointments.)

239 It is noteworthy that the committee that developed this report was formed after the Liberal Party formed the government with the help of the NDP in 1985. The Committee thus had a majority of Liberal or NDP members.

240 *Breaugh Report, supra* note 238 at 13-14 [emphasis added].

241 For a debunking of the popular view that imposing a maximum on the number of reappointments of adjudicators is good policy from a "new blood" perspective, see S. Ronald Ellis, "Administrative Justice System Reform: The Term of Appointment Issue" (1996) 10 Can. J. Admin. L. & Prac. 1.

242 This statement appears in a document published by the Progressive Conservative government in its so-called implementation of the *Guzzo Report*. See Ontario, Management Board of Cabinet, "Learning Strategy" in "Tools, Templates and Guides" (November 2000) [unpublished] at 1 [emphasis added]. This was one of the "tools" contained in the binder presented to the November 2000 Conference of Ontario Boards and Agencies meeting by the Attorney General and the chair of the Management Board of Cabinet. See *infra* note 270 and text at 122. Note that the reference in the passage to "appointees" encompassed appointees to both adjudicative and regulatory positions.

243 Management Board Secretariat, Corporate Policy Branch, Program Management and Estimates Division, "Corporate Management Directive" (November 1994).

244 Online: Public Appointments Secretariat <http://www.pas.gov.on.ca/scripts/en/Home.asp>. Click the "Compensation" Quick Link.

245 See "Ontario Government Appointees Directive, Management Board of Cabinet" (1 May 2011) [unpublished] at 4.

246 In Ontario, this glaring deficiency appeared to have been finally addressed in June 2006 when a new directive was issued tying tribunal member and chair remuneration directly to specified levels of the public service compensation structure. See "Addendum to the Government Appointees Directive" issued in 2006 under the *Management Board of Cabinet Act*, R.S.O. 1990, c. M.1. Now see "Ontario Government Appointees Directive, Management Board of Cabinet" (1 May 2011) [unpublished] at 6-7.

247 Andrew J. Roman, "Structure and Accountability of Administrative Agencies" in *Law Society of Upper Canada Special Lectures, 1992, Administrative Law, Principles, Practices and Pluralism* (Toronto: Carswell, 1992) 63 at 64 (previously cited).

248 Of course, the quality of appointments to Ontario tribunals has never been uniform. The actual selection process and the level of concern for appropriate levels of qualifications and standards of competence varies from ministry to ministry, from minister to minister, and from government to government. See in the Introduction my description of the Ministry of Labour's traditional approach to appointments. And appointments to "elite" tribunals like the Securities Commission and the Labour Relations Board and a handful of others have traditionally been perceived by their client communities as sound, and often very good indeed. Nevertheless, Margot Priest's "Tribunal from Hell" paper – "Structure and Accountability of Administrative Agencies" in *Law Society of Upper Canada Special Lectures, 1992, Administrative Law, Principles, Practices and Pluralism* (Toronto: Carswell, 1992) – reflected the unprincipled appointment processes pertaining to the great majority of Ontario administrative tribunals at the time the Guzzo Commission commenced its study (at that time the total was approximately seventy).

249 An ad hoc group of approximately fifteen tribunal chairs who had been meeting together on a regular basis since 1987 for the purpose of sharing and discussing their common problems.

250 Priest, *supra* note 248 at 14.

251 In Ontario, where the two-terms-and-out rule was applied (but not consistently), a simple mathematical analysis will show that the average experience of a tribunal's incumbent members at any point in time could never exceed approximately three years. This is the average that mathematically pertains under the rule if one assumes that every member is reappointed once, and all members serve out their final, second term. Of course, in real life both assumptions hold only in a proportion of cases. The *Macaulay Report, supra* note 115, indicates that in 1989, in Ontario, the average number of years of service for the members of the tribunals surveyed was "4-4.5." This included members of those tribunals such as WCAT, the Labour Relations Board, the Ontario Municipal Board, and others to which the two-terms-and-out policy had never been applied. Macaulay also reports (at 2-13) that the tribunal chairs he surveyed were of the opinion that it took a new appointee 1.5 years to get to the point of full performance. As mentioned earlier, under the current government in Ontario, the maximum years of service in one tribunal position is ten.

252 The Harper government's refusal of reappointments to established and performing members of the IRB in 2006 as mentioned earlier is one particularly telling piece of evidence of government unconcern with continuity in the work of judicial tribunals. The Saskatchewan Party's dismissal of experienced tribunal members is another.

253 Recent statutory provisions specifying merit-based appointments are regarded as breakthroughs but also viewed with suspicion.

254 The *Macaulay Report*'s survey of Ontario "regulatory" agencies (which included judicial tribunals) indicated that 66 percent of members were part-time (*supra* note 115 at 2-13). In a survey of BC tribunals, Bryden and Hatch report that 48 percent of the forty-six tribunals that they surveyed (those with at least some adjudicative function) were composed exclusively of part-time members, and a further 30 percent were composed of a full-time chair and part-time members. Only 22 percent of the tribunals surveyed had more than one full-time member. See Philip Bryden and

Ron Hatch, "British Columbia Council of Administrative Tribunals Research and Policy Committee – Report on Independence, Accountability and Appointment Processes in British Columbia" (1998-99) 12 Can. J. Admin. L. & Prac. 235 at 248.

255 On a personal note, in 1996, I was earning $105,000 as chair of WCAT, while some senior staff were earning in the $120,000 range.

256 Their pensions are still not portable and neither are their disability or life insurance policies.

257 An incumbent adjudicator who actively seeks employment within a community of potential employers who do business with the adjudicator's tribunal will be seen to have created a reasonable apprehension of bias. See *Golden Valley Golf Course Ltd. v. British Columbia*, 2001 BCCA 392 (CanLII).

258 This remains invariably true.

259 Prior consultation with chairs is now a more common practice, but far from universal.

260 The existence of published qualifications has become more common.

261 See, *e.g.*, the following statutory provision not infrequently found in the constitutive statutes of Ontario administrative justice tribunals: "Members of the [tribunal] holding a hearing shall not ... communicate directly or indirectly in relation to the subject-matter of the hearing with any person or with any party or representative of the party except upon notice to and with opportunity for all parties to participate, but the [tribunal] may seek legal advice from an adviser independent from the parties and in such case the nature of the advice should be made known to the parties in order that they may make submissions as to the law." For a particular example, see s. 23(2) of the *Health Insurance Act*, R.S.O. 1990, c. H.6, as amended, incorporated by reference in s. 9.11(13) of the *Charitable Institutions Act*, R.S.O. 1990, c. C.9 (as amended). Whether this statutory language would be interpreted as prohibiting discussions with tribunal colleagues or in-house counsel who did not participate in the hearing is perhaps not clear.

262 Still true, of course.

263 Tribunal chairs and members are deemed to be in the same position in this respect as judges. However, partisan advocates and parties – and the media – do not feel the same traditional constraints in their criticism of tribunals and their chairs and members as they do in their criticism of judges. They perceive the former to be beneficiaries of a patronage appointment system and therefore not deserving of their respect. See, for example, Ezra Levant's unwarranted criticism of the BC Human Rights Tribunal decision in *Datt v. McDonald's Restaurants* and of its author, *supra* note 129 and text at 81-83.

264 For a startling example of this problem, see the Ontario Ombudsman's report on the budget woes of the Criminal Injuries Compensation Board (Ombudsman Ontario, *supra* note 232 and text at 111-13).

265 As we have seen, this remains a pervasive systemic problem.

266 See Roman, *supra* note 247 at 77; Sheridan Scott, "The Continuing Debate Over the Independence of Regulatory Tribunals" in *Law Society of Upper Canada Special Lectures, 1992, Administrative Law, Principles, Practices and Pluralism* (Toronto: Carswell, 1992) at 79; and George M. Thomson, "Agencies, Boards and Commissions:

Accountability and Independence" in *Law Society of Upper Canada Special Lectures, 1992, Administrative Law, Principles, Practices and Pluralism* (Toronto: Carswell, 1992) at 93.

267 Scott, *ibid.* at 80.

268 Thomson, *supra* note 266 at 93.

269 This was a reference to Priest's listing of the truly shocking number of official studies and reports about tribunals over the years without much if anything to show for them. Roman had also expressed surprise and shock at the number of the relevant studies and reports that Priest had cited. See Priest, *supra* note 248 at 14-41.

270 Ontario, Management Board of Cabinet, "Tools, Templates and Guides" (November 2000) [unpublished].

271 As noted in the joint statement dated 16 November 2000, signed by Chris Hodgson, Chair, Management Board of Cabinet, and James Flaherty, Attorney General and Minister Responsible for Native Affairs, on the occasion of their release of the binder of implementation instruments.

272 Society of Ontario Adjudicators and Regulators, "Towards Maintaining and Improving the Quality of Adjudication: SOAR Recommendations for Performance Management in Ontario's Administrative Justice System" (1995) 9 Can. J. Admin. L. & Prac. 179.

273 Ontario, Ministry of Government Services, *Governance Tools for Agencies, 2007,* online: Ministry of Government Services <http://www.gov.on.ca/MGS/en/AbtMin/157218.html>.

274 *Guzzo Report, supra* note 24 at 2.

275 *Supra* note 242 and text at 123.

276 See, for example, the case of the full-time tribunal vice-chair adjudicator reappointed against his tribunal chair's recommendation, notwithstanding the vice-chair's having demonstrated an inability to be an adjudicator. This was a subject of a question by a Liberal MPP in the Ontario legislature during Question Period on Tuesday, 10 December 2002 (Hansard at 721, paras. 662-65). This is also known to have been a not uncommon experience at the Immigration and Refugee Board. It will be remembered that in his interview with the *Toronto Star* referred to in the Introduction (see Introduction, note 49 and accompanying text at 24), retired IRB chair Peter Showler had said: "[S]erving members who get mediocre or even bad [performance] ratings can find themselves appointed to a second term because of political connections, while members who have excelled are sometimes denied a second term."

277 R.S.O. 1990, c. H.6, as amended, at s. 5.

278 Peter deC. Cory, *Study, Conclusions and Recommendations Pertaining to Medical Audit Practice in Ontario* (Submitted to the Honourable George Smitherman, Minister of Health and Long-Term Care, Government of Ontario, 21 April 2005) at 12.

279 *Ibid.*

280 *Ibid.* at 165.

281 *Ibid.*

282 See *Health Insurance Act*, R.S.O. 1990, c. H.6, as amended by S.O. 2007, c. 10, Sched. G, s. 2(1), at s. 5.1.

283 Ron Ellis, "Saskatchewan Takes the Justice out of Justice," *Lawyers Weekly* (6 April 2010).

284 Priest, *supra* note 248.

285 Thomson, *supra* note 266 at 93.

286 This Commission made recommendations only with respect to reform of the Railway Committee. However, since the Railway Committee was the first and only tribunal in Canada at the time, this report qualifies as a review of the genre, as it then was.

287 The section titled "Law, Society and the Economy."

288 Québec, Ministère de la justice, Groupe de travail sur les tribunaux administratifs (1987), Yves Ouellette [unpublished].

289 Québec, Ministère de la justice, Groupe de travail sur certaines questions relatives à la réforme de la justice administrative, *Une justice administrative pour le citoyen* (Québec: Publications officielles, 1994).

290 I am indebted to Margot Priest for her scholarly work in digging out much of the information concerning the pre-1992 federal studies and reports, and reporting that information extensively in her famous "tribunal from hell" article, *supra* note 247. See also the following reports from other jurisdictions: the *U.K. Donoughmore Report* in 1932; United Kingdom, *Report of the Committee on Administrative Tribunals and Enquiries by Chairman, The Rt Hon Sir Oliver Franks, GCMG KCB CBE)*, Cmnd 218 (July 1957) [*Franks Report*]; and Sir Andrew Leggatt, *Tribunals for Users One System, One Service (Report of the Review of Tribunals)* (March 2001), online: UK National Archives <http://webarchive.nationalarchives.gov.uk/+/http://www.tribunals-review.org.uk/leggatthtm/leg-00.htm> [*Leggatt Report*]; the Australian *Kerr Committee Report* in 1968 that lead to the substantial administrative justice reforms in that country in the mid-1970s; and recent New Zealand Reports. In 2004, the New Zealand Law Commission produced a report called *Delivering Justice for All* (NZLC R85), in which it recommended the rationalization of tribunals into a unified framework; this was followed in January 2008 with "Issues Paper 6, Tribunals in New Zealand," which was issued contemporaneously with the New Zealand Ministry of Justice report *Tribunals in New Zealand: The Government's Preferred Approach to Reform* (Wellington: Government of New Zealand, 2008).

291 Roman, *supra* note 247 at 63.

292 *Ibid.* at 77.

293 The BC Administrative Justice Project and its white paper did produce some improvements: a "merit-based," but not competitive, appointment process, with chair involvement in the appointment of new members, but, significantly, not in their reappointment. (See the *Administrative Tribunals Act*, S.B.C. 2004, c. 45, and compare s. 3[1] with s. 3[2]). The improvements did not last, however. See, for example, Frank Falzon, "The Integrated Administrative Tribunal" (2006) 19 Can. J. Admin. L. & Prac. 239 at 243-46. By contrast, the recent UK reports have led to substantive reform.

294 Priest, *supra* note 248 at 42.

295 *Ibid.* at 46.

296 Gerald Heckman and Lorne Sossin, "How Do Canadian Administrative Law Protections Measure Up to International Human Rights Standards? The Case of Independence" (2005) 50 McGill L.J. 193 at 200 [citations omitted].

CHAPTER 2: ADMINISTRATIVE *JUSTICE*

1 That is, organizes and cares for.

2 Frank Falzon, "The Integrated Administrative Tribunal" (2006) 19 Can. J. Admin. L. & Prac. 239 at 248.

3 This change first appeared in the Ontario Management Board Secretariat's "Agency Establishment and Accountability Directive," issued in February 2000.

4 S.O. 2009, c. 33, sch. 5.

5 Ontario, Royal Commission Inquiry into Civil Rights (James Chalmers McRuer, Chair), *Report No. 1, Vol. 1* (Frank Fogg, Queen's Printer, 1968) [*McRuer Report*] (previously cited) at 120-23.

6 See, for example; *Attorney General of Quebec v. Udeco Inc. et al.,* [1984] 2 S.C.R. 502 at 512; *Boulis v. Minister of Manpower and Immigration,* [1974] S.C.R. 875 at 885; *R. v. MacKay,* [1980] 2 S.C.R. 370 (previously cited) at 407.

7 Ed Ratushny, *Report on the Independence of Federal Administrative Tribunals and Agencies* (Presented to President John R. Jennings at the annual general meeting commemorating the seventy-fifth anniversary of the Canadian Bar Association, London England, 1990) (Ottawa: Canadian Bar Association, 1990) [*Ratushny Report*] at 31.

8 Antonio Lamer, "Administrative Tribunals – Future Prospects and Possibilities" (1991) 5 Can. J. Admin. L. & Prac. 107.

9 Beverley McLachlin, "The Roles of Administrative Tribunals and Courts in Maintaining the Rule of Law" (1998) 12 Can. J. Admin. L. & Prac. 171 at 176.

10 *Bell Canada v. Canadian Telephone Employees Association,* [2003] 1 S.C.R. 884 [*Bell Canada*] (previously cited) at para. 22.

11 *Ibid.* at para. 23.

12 Michael J. Trebilcock, Leonard Waverman, and J. Robert S. Prichard, "Markets for Regulation: Implications for Performance Standards and Institutional Design" in *Government Regulation: Issues and Alternatives 1978* (Canada: Ontario Economic Council, 1978) [*Trebilcock Report*].

13 *Ibid.* at 36.

14 *Ibid.* at 37.

15 *Ibid.* at 38-39.

16 *Ibid.* at 38 [emphasis added].

17 See the Introduction at 12 for my description of the Ontario Workers' Compensation Board's four levels of adjudication and, for the UK authority, see the Introduction, note 22.

18 A *de novo* hearing is a hearing in which all the factual issues in a case as well as the issues of law are retried as though for the first time.

19 In Quebec, the point of departure in this respect may have been the publication of Québec, Groupe de travail sur les tribunaux administratifs (René Dussault, Chair), *Les tribunaux administratifs au Québec: rapport du Groupe de travail sur les tribunaux administratifs* (Québec: Ministère de la Justice, 1971) [*Dussault Report*].

20 Ann Marshall Young, "Evaluation of Administrative Law Judges: Premises, Means, and Ends" (1997) 17 Journal of the National Association of Administrative Law Judges 1 at 1.

21 United Kingdom, *Report of the Committee on Administrative Tribunals and Enquiries by Chairman, The Rt Hon Sir Oliver Franks, GCMG KCB CBE)*, Cmnd 218 (July 1957) (previously cited) at para. 40.

22 As reported by The Honourable Sir Gerard Brennan, AC, KBE, first president of Australia's Administrative Appeals Tribunal, in a speech given in Canberra in August 2006 on the occasion of the Tribunal's thirtieth anniversary.

23 W.A. Robson, "Essays" in R.E. Wraith and P.G. Hutchesson, eds., *Administrative Tribunals* (London: George Allen and Unwin, 1973) at 197, and referred to in Frans Slatter, *Parliament and Administrative Agencies in Law Reform: A Study Paper Prepared for the Law Reform Commission of Canada* (Ottawa: Minister of Supply and Services, 1982).

24 William Wade and Christopher Forsythe, *Administrative Law*, 8th ed. (Oxford: Oxford University Press, 2000) at 885, 887.

25 *Ibid.* at 888-89.

26 Sir Andrew Leggatt, *Tribunals for Users One System, One Service (Report of the Review of Tribunals)* (March 2001), online: UK National Archives <http://webarchive.nationalarchives.gov.uk/+/http://www.tribunals-review.org.uk/leggatthtm/leg-00.htm> [*Leggatt Report*] (previously cited) at c. 2, para. 2.18.

27 Robson, *supra* note 23. Of course, British Columbia did have its Administrative Justice Project, which in 2003 led to a set of legislative reforms. Even after that project's long and thorough study of the subject, however, the BC legislature was ultimately not prepared to "rise to the height of a general proposition" concerning "the principles which should inform a system of administrative justice." Consider, for instance, the failure to subject the tribunal member reappointment process to the merit principle, or to resolve the egregious conflicts of interest inherent in portfolio ministry hosting of administrative justice tribunals. See, in the latter respect: S. Ronald Ellis, "Administrative Justice Reform – Disturbing Omissions in the British Columbia White Paper," Parts I, II, and III, *Lawyers Weekly* (17, 24, and 31 January 2003).

28 Falzon, *supra* note 2 at 247 ("A single Great Heresy stands as an obstacle ... that administrative tribunals are properly understood as servants of the executive branch").

29 Barry Bresner, Timothy Leigh-Bell, Michael J. Trebilcock, and Leonard Waverman, "Ontario's Agencies, Boards, Commissions, Advisory Bodies and Other Public Institutions: An Inventory (1977)," in *Government Regulation: Issues and Alternatives 1978* (Canada: Ontario Economic Council, 1978) 207 at 207, fn1 [emphasis added].

30 Lamer, *supra* note 8 [emphasis added].

31 As quoted in Ron Ellis, "Appointments Policies in the Administrative Justice System: Lessons from Ontario: Four Speeches" (1998) 11 Can. J. Admin. L. & Prac. 205 [Ellis, "Lessons from Ontario"] at 250-52.

32 I was present at the conference, and this was my personal impression of the audience's reaction.

33 See McLachlin, *supra* note 9 at 176.

34 "While there are distinctions between administrative tribunals and courts, both are part of the system of justice. Viewed properly, then, the system of justice encompasses the ordinary courts, federal courts, statutory provincial courts and administrative

tribunals": *Paul v. British Columbia (Forest Appeals Commission)*, [2003] 2 S.C.R. 585 [*Paul*] at para. 22.

35 Arguably, from the formation of the first "tribunal" (the federal Board of Railway Commissioners) in 1903 to Chief Justice Dickson's seminal judgment in *C.U.P.E. v. New Brunswick Liquor*, [1979] 2 S.C.R. 227.

36 See, for example, John Willis, "The McRuer Report: Lawyers' Values and Civil Servants' Values" (1968) 18 U.T.L.J. 351, and H.W. Arthurs, "Protection against Judicial Review" (1983) 43 Can. Bar Rev. 277.

37 J.A. Corry, "Administrative Law and the Interpretation of Statutes" (1935-36) 1 U.T.L.J. 286 (previously cited).

38 For an especially telling example of the lack of empathy among Canadian administrative law scholars for the rule-of-law, justice role of administrative tribunals, see the late Professor John Willis's published defence of his personal covert collaboration with prosecuting counsel when Willis was a part-time member of the Ontario Securities Commission and in the midst of chairing disciplinary hearings at which those same counsel were prosecuting on behalf of the Commission: John Willis, "Canadian Administrative Law in Retrospect" (1974) 24 U.T.L.J. 225 at 241-42.

39 *Constitution Act (An Act for the Union of Canada, Nova Scotia, and New Brunswick, and the Government thereof; and for Purposes connected therewith) 1867*, 30 and 31 Vict., c. 3 (originally known as the *British North America Act*).

40 See *Reference re Act to Amend Chapter 401 of the Revised Statutes, 1989, the Residential Tenancies Act, S.N.S. 1992, c. 31* (sub nom. *Reference re Amendments to the Residential Tenancies Act*), [1996] 1 S.C.R. 186; *MacMillan Bloedel Ltd. v. Simpson*, [1995] 4 S.C.R. 725; and *Sobeys Stores Ltd. v. Yeomans*, [1989] 1 S.C.R. 238.

41 *The Attorney General of Québec v. Barreau du Montréal*, [2001] J.Q. No. 3882 (C.A.), leave to appeal refused (2002), 2002 CarswellQue 2078 (S.C.C.), reconsideration refused (2002), 2002 CarswellQue 2683 [*Barreau*] (previously cited).

42 *Ibid.* at para. 53.

43 See Chapter 1, "The Sea Change in the Law of Judicial Independence: *Valente*, 1985," at 66-71.

44 Ontario's recent embrace of a "clustering" policy for some groups of tribunals might be seen as a commitment to the idea of organizing some tribunals in a collection of subject-oriented mini-systems.

45 Joel Feinberg, *Social Philosophy* (Englewood Cliffs, NJ: Prentice Hall, 1973) at 99.

46 H.L.A. Hart, *Concept of Law* (London: Oxford University Press, 1961) at 155-56.

47 *Ibid.* at 160.

48 *Ibid.* at 161 [emphasis added].

49 *Reference re Remuneration of Judges of the Provincial Court of Prince Edward Island; Reference re Independence and Impartiality of Judges of the Provincial Court of Prince Edward Island; R. v. Campbell; R. v. Ekmecic; R. v. Wickman; Manitoba Provincial Judges Assn. v. Manitoba (Minister of Justice)*, [1997] 3 S.C.R. 3 [*PEI Reference*] (previously cited) at paras. 9-10.

50 *Canadian Union of Public Employees (C.U.P.E.) v. Ontario (Minister of Labour)*, [2003] 1 S.C.R. 539 [*CUPE*] at 189.

51 See Chapter 1, note 76 and text at 66.

52 *R. v. Valente*, [1985] 2 S.C.R. 673 [*Valente*] (previously cited) at paras. 27 (security of tenure), 40 (financial security), and 47 (administrative control). These "essential conditions" are sometimes referred to as the three "core characteristics" or "mechanisms" of judicial independence.

53 *Ibid.* at para. 22. See also *Charkaoui v. Canada (Citizenship and Immigration)*, [2007] S.C.J. No. 9 [*Charkaoui*] at para. 32.

54 *MacKeigan v. Hickman*, [1989] 2 S.C.R. 796 at para. 56.

55 See Chapter 1, note 150 and accompanying text.

56 See, *e.g.*, *PEI Reference, supra* note 49 at paras. 118-25; see also, among others, *Beauregard v. Canada*, [1986] 2 S.C.R. 56 at paras. 21-24; *Ell v. Alberta*, [2003] 1 S.C.R. 857 [*Ell*] (previously cited) at para. 28, and *R. v. Lippé*, [1991] 2 S.C.R. 114 [*Lippé*] (previously cited).

57 *Valente, supra* note 52 at para. 20.

58 *Lippé, supra* note 56 at para. 51. This appears in the dissenting judgment of Chief Justice Lamer speaking for himself and Justices John Sopinka and Peter Cory, but on this point the rest of the Court agreed – see the judgment of Justice Charles Gonthier speaking for the majority at paras. 87-96.

59 *Ibid.* at para. 60.

60 This statement will have given the informed reader pause since conventional wisdom has it that regulatory agencies typically exercise both administrative and judicial functions, but I argue (at length later) that most functions of regulatory agencies that have been conventionally characterized as "judicial" are in fact administrative – quasi-judicial, perhaps, but still administrative.

61 See for example, the *Ontario Energy Board Act, 1998*, S.O. 1998, c. 15, sch. B [*Energy Board Act*] at s. 44(1)(b)(i).

62 *Reference re Ontario Residential Tenancies Act*, [1981] 1 S.C.R. 714 [*Ontario RTA Reference*].

63 *Labour Relations Board of Saskatchewan v. John East Iron Works, Limited*, [1949] A.C. 134 (P.C.).

64 *Ibid.* at 149.

65 *Ontario RTA Reference, supra* note 62 at 735.

66 Arguably, the Workers' Compensation Board, which rejected the workers' claim, is also a party.

67 It is unlikely, of course, to be an *identical* decision, since in the real world each worker's rights will typically be decided by different judges. Thus, the actual results can be expected only to fall with the range of variance attributable to the innate differences in the idiosyncrasies of each judge.

68 Hart, *supra* note 46 [emphasis added].

69 *Baker v. Canada (Minister of Citizenship and Immigration)*, [1999] 2 S.C.R. 817 [*Baker*].

70 *R. v. Higher Education Funding Council, ex parte Institute of Dental Surgery*, [1994] 1 All E.R. 651 (QB) at 667 [emphasis added].

71 *Ontario RTA Reference, supra* note 62 at 744.

72 The jurisprudence also establishes that the fact that a tribunal exercises an "inquisitorial" adjudicative function does not detract from the judicial nature of that

function. See *Charkaoui, supra* note 53 at paras. 50-51 ("there are two types of judicial systems ...").

73 See Chapter 4 at 207.

74 *Langenburg (Town) v. Gamey,* 2010 SKCA 11 (CanLII).

75 *Burzminski v. Burzminski,* 2010 SKCA 16 (CanLII).

76 *R. v. Toy,* 2010 SKCA 6 (CanLII).

77 *Whatcott v. Saskatchewan (Human Rights Tribunal),* 2010 SKCA 26 (CanLII).

78 In Report No. 5 (1982) of Ontario's Standing Procedural Affairs Committee.

79 Lon Fuller, "The Forms and Limits of Adjudication" (1978) 92 Harv. L. Rev. 350 at 394.

80 *Pushpanathan v. Canada (Minister of Citizenship and Immigration),* [1998] 1 S.C.R. 982 at para. 31. While the Supreme Court credits P. Cane with the concept, there would appear to be no doubt that it originated with Fuller.

81 *McRuer Report, supra* note 5 at 232.

82 See *Energy Act,* R.S.O. 1990, c. E.16, ss. 23(1), (2), and (4) and s. 25(1).

83 Fuller, *supra* note 79 at 400.

84 *Newfoundland Telephone Co. v. Newfoundland (Board of Commissioners of Public Utilities),* [1992] 1 S.C.R. 623 [*Newfoundland Telephone*].

85 The Court did take notice of the fact that standards of bias will vary depending on the nature of the tribunal, but it held in the end that, at the point where the Board embarked on its "hearing," its members' conduct was to be measured against the standard of a reasonable apprehension of bias – a court and judicial tribunal standard.

86 *Committee for Justice and Liberty et al. v. National Energy Board et al.,* [1978] 1 S.C.R. 369 [*National Energy Board*].

87 *Ibid.* at 391. *Szilard v. Szasz,* [1955] S.C.R. 3, involved a bias question respecting an arbitrator in a commercial arbitration exercising what was patently a judicial function [emphasis added].

88 *National Energy Board, supra* note 86 at 401 [emphasis added].

89 *Ocean Port Hotel Ltd. v. British Columbia (General Manager, Liquor Control and Licensing Branch),* [2001] 2 S.C.R. 781 (previously cited) at para. 24.

90 *Bell Canada, supra* note 10 at para. 21.

91 Even though, in my view remarkably, with respect to Saskatchewan's Labour Relations Board, the Saskatchewan Court of Queen's Bench would beg to differ. See *The Saskatchewan Federation of Labour, and the Saskatchewan Government and General Employees' Union, and The Saskatchewan Joint Board Retail, Wholesale and Department Store Union v. Saskatchewan (Attorney General, Department of Advanced Education, Employment and Labour), and The Saskatchewan Labour Relations Board,* 2010 SKQB 390 (CanLII) [*SFL v. Saskatchewan*].

92 Fairness Committee (The Honourable Justice Coulter A. Osbourne, QC, Chair; Professor David J. Mullan and Bryan Finlay, QC, Members), "Report of the Fairness Committee to David A. Brown, Q.C., Chair of the Ontario Securities Commission" (5 March 2004) [unpublished] (previously cited). See Chapter 1 at 110-11.

93 Paul Weiler, *Reshaping Workers' Compensation for Ontario* (Report submitted to Robert G. Elgie, MD, Minister of Labour, November 1980) (Toronto: Ministry of Labour, 1980) [*Weiler Report*] (previously cited).

94 *Nicholson v. Haldimand Norfolk (Regional) Police Commissioners*, [1979] 1 S.C.R. 311 [*Nicholson*].

95 *Re Knapman and the Board of Health for the Township of Saltfleet*, [1954] O.R. 360 (S.C.O., Gale J.); [1955] O.W.N. 615 (C.A.) aff'g the judgment of Justice Gale; aff'd by the S.C.C. in *Saltfleet (Township) Board of Health v. Knapman*, [1956] S.C.R. 877, aff'g judgments of Court of Appeal and Gale J. [*Saltfleet*].

96 *Ontario RTA Reference, supra* note 62.

97 *Saltfleet, supra* note 95 at 369-70 [emphasis added].

98 *McRuer Report, supra* note 5 at 29 [emphasis added].

99 *Howarth v. Canada (National Parole Board)*, [1976] 1 S.C.R. 453 [*Howarth*].

100 *Federal Court Act*, R.S.C. 1970 (2nd Supp.), c. 10.

101 *Howarth, supra* note 99 at 471 [emphasis added].

102 As quoted by the Court in *ibid*. [emphasis added].

103 *Ibid.* [emphasis added].

104 *Ibid.* at 459 [emphasis added].

105 *Minister of National Revenue v. Coopers and Lybrand*, [1979] 1 S.C.R. 495.

106 *Ibid.* at 500.

107 *Ibid.* at 505 [emphasis added].

108 *Nicholson, supra* note 94 at 325 [emphasis added]. See also *Knight v. Indian Head School Division No. 19*, [1990] 1 S.C.R. 653 at 669 [*Knight*].

109 *Knight, ibid.*

110 See in particular *Syndicat des employés de production du Québec et de l'Acadie v. Canada (Human Rights Commission)*, [1989] 2 S.C.R. 879.

111 *Bell Canada, supra* note 10.

112 *Ibid.* at paras. 21 and 22.

113 *Ontario RTA Reference, supra* note 62 and accompanying text.

114 Bill 160 – *The Saskatchewan Human Rights Code Amendment Act, 2010.*

115 *Nicholson, supra* note 94 at 324.

116 *Paul, supra* note 34 [emphasis added].

117 *R. v. Conway*, [2010] 1 S.C.R. 765 [*Conway*].

118 *Valente, supra* note 52 – the decision that established the modern definition of judicial independence as it applies to tribunals.

119 See, *e.g., Ell, supra* note 56 at para. 20: "The scope of the unwritten [constitutional] principle of [judicial] independence must be interpreted in accordance with its underlying purposes. In this appeal, its extension to the office held by the respondents *depends on whether they exercise judicial functions* that relate to the bases upon which the principle is founded ..." [emphasis added].

120 *Baker, supra* note 69.

121 It will be remembered that the Supreme Court's configuration of that "spectrum" in *Bell Canada, supra* note 10 at para. 21, specified "closest to *the courts*" [emphasis added], as marking the juridical end of the administrative spectrum.

CHAPTER 3: ADMINISTRATIVE JUDICIAL TRIBUNALS

1 Michael J. Trebilcock, Leonard Waverman, and J. Robert S. Prichard, "Markets for Regulation: Implications for Performance Standards and Institutional Design" in

Government Regulation: Issues and Alternatives 1978 (Canada: Ontario Economic Council, 1978) [*Trebilcock Report*] (previously cited).

2 "[T]he decisions of most tribunals are in truth judicial rather than administrative": William Wade and Christopher Forsythe, *Administrative Law,* 8th éd. (Oxford: Oxford University Press, 2000).

3 This information appeared in the Ministry of Government Services' "List of Classified Government Agencies," dated 1 May 2008.

4 General, O. Reg. 126/10, issued under the Ontario *Adjudicative Tribunals Accountability, Governance and Appointments Act, 2009,* S.O. 2009, c. 33, sch. 5.

5 I am not concerned at this stage with great precision in the allocation of tribunals between the major and boutique categories; it is enough to recognize that there are major tribunals (characterized by high caseloads) and it is useful to identify the Ontario judicial tribunals that appear likely to fall within that category.

6 See *infra* at 202-3.

7 In the following paragraphs, I rely heavily on my article, "The Corporate Responsibility of Tribunal Members – CCAT 2008" (2009) 21 Can. J. Admin. L. & Prac. 1, in which I cover the same ground.

8 S.R. Ellis, "Findings and Opinions: The Agencies' Only Stock in Trade" in Philip Anisman and Robert Franklin Reid, eds., *Administrative Law Issues and Practice* (Toronto: Carswell, 1995).

9 For an example of court deference to a tribunal's unusual but practicable choice of procedure, see Leonard Marvy and David A. Wright, "'Master of Its Own House': Procedural Fairness and Deference to Ontario Labour Relations Board Procedure: Case Comment on *International Brotherhood of Electrical Workers, Local 1739 v. International Brotherhood of Electrical Workers* [86 O.R. (3d) 508 (Div. Ct.)] and *Amalgamated Transit Union Local 113 v. Ontario Labour Relations Board* [88 O.R. (3d) 361 (Div. Ct.)]" (2008) 21 Can. J. Admin. L. & Prac. 361.

10 *Domtar Inc. v. Quebec (Commission d'appel en matière de lésions professionnelles),* [1993] 2 S.C.R. 756 at para. 94. And see particularly *Essex County Roman Catholic School Board v. O.E.C.T.A.* (2001) 56 O.R. (3d) 85 (C.A.) at 94.

11 Here you may be thinking, "How can one square this tolerance of conflicting tribunal decisions with the application of the 'like-cases' principle? On judicial review, should the courts not have the duty to fix this?" I answer as follows. First, an effective adherence to the like-cases principle does not guarantee the exact results even in cases that are identical on the facts. The principle calls for "like" results in "like" cases and these are assured when the law is applied, as Hart says, without "prejudice, interest, or caprice," and applied, I would add, by a competent adjudicator. The practical fact that the "like" cases will inevitably be adjudicated by different judges means that there will be differences in the interpretation of the law and in the findings of fact arising from the good-faith idiosyncrasies of the individual judges. The principle will be confirmed as having been applied authentically so long as both results fall within the range of results that are reasonable, relative to the law and the evidence. Moreover, when neither of the conflicting decisions can be said to be "unreasonable," it would not be appropriate for the courts to intervene. Faced with two conflicting but reasonable decisions, a court, to intervene, would have to decide that one of the reasonable decisions was not in its view "correct," thus abrogating the

standard of review appropriate for that tribunal and effectively usurping the tribunal's specialized and expert role in the interpretation of its statute. The reconciling of inconsistent tribunal decisions must be left to the tribunal itself, otherwise its essential mandate as the judicial arm of a statutory rights enterprise is emasculated. The tools this book proposes for accomplishing this include the usual tribunal strategies and structures for "institutionalizing" its decisions – educational and collegial consultation strategies and the like – plus the typical power to reconsider, as well as some additional provisions of a like nature in the reform proposals to follow.

12 See, *e.g.*, s. 21.2(1), *Statutory Powers Procedure Act*, R.S.O. 1990, c. S-22, as amended by S.O. 1997: "A tribunal may, if it considers it advisable and if its rules made under section 25.1 deal with the matter, review all or part of its own decision or order, and may confirm, vary, suspend or cancel the decision or order."

13 Harry Arthurs, "Protection against Judicial Review" (1983) 43 Can. Bar Rev. 277 at 286.

14 They have been replaced by a discretionary right of a tribunal to refer a question of law to the court in the form of a stated case. See *Administrative Tribunals Act*, S.B.C. 2004, c. 45 at s. 43(2).

15 *Dr. Q v. College of Physicians and Surgeons of British Columbia*, [2003] 1 S.C.R. 226.

16 *Law Society of New Brunswick v. Ryan*, [2003] 1 S.C.R. 247.

17 *Baker v. Canada (Minister of Citizenship and Immigration)*, [1999] 2 S.C.R. 817 [*Baker*] at para. 25.

18 *R. v. Higher Education Funding Council, ex parte Institute of Dental Surgery*, [1994] 1 All E.R. 651 (QB) at 667.

19 H.L.A. Hart, *Concept of Law* (London: Oxford University Press, 1961) (previously cited) at 123.

20 See, *e.g.*, the Ontario Residential Tenancy Commission's statutory duty to decide "on the real merits and justice of the case" and to "ascertain the real substance of all transactions and activities" as referred to by Dickson J. in *Reference re Ontario Residential Tenancies Act*, [1981] 1 S.C.R. 714 (previously cited). See Chapter 2 at 159.

21 Peter deC. Cory, *Study, Conclusions and Recommendations Pertaining to Medical Audit Practice in Ontario* (Submitted to the Honourable George Smitherman, Minister of Health and Long-Term Care, Government of Ontario, 21 April 2005) (previously cited). For earlier discussion, see Chapter 1 at 124-26.

22 Arthurs, *supra* note 13 and page 193.

23 D.J. Mullan, "Establishing the Standard of Review: The Struggle for Complexity?" (2004) 17 Can. J. Admin. L. & Prac. 59 at 93.

24 *IWA v. Consolidated-Bathurst Packaging Ltd.*, [1990] 1 S.C.R. 282 [*Consolidated-Bathurst*] (previously cited); *Tremblay v. Quebec (Commission des affaires sociales)*, [1992] 1 S.C.R. 952 [*Tremblay*].

25 *Consolidated-Bathurst, ibid.* at para. 74.

26 *Tremblay, supra* note 24 at para. 45. Ordinarily, precedent is developed by the actual decision makers over a series of decisions. A tribunal hearing a new question may thus render a number of contradictory judgments before an institutional consensus naturally emerges.

27 *Consolidated-Bathurst, supra* note 24 at para. 81.

28 *Ibid.* at para. 95.

29 Yves-Marie Morissette, "Le contrôle de la compétence d'attribution: thése, antithése et synthése" (1986) 16 R.D.U.S. 591, cited with approval in *Consolidated-Bathurst, supra* note 24 at para. 74.
30 Robert E. Hawkins and David M. Shoemaker, "Reputational Review II: Administrative Agencies, Print Media and Content Analysis" (1998-99) 12 Can. J. Admin. L. & Prac. 1 (previously cited). See Chapter 1 at 42-43.
31 Arthurs, *supra* note 13. Also *supra* note 22 and text at 199-200.
32 Hawkins and Shoemaker, *supra* note 30. See Chapter 1 at 42-43.

CHAPTER 4: PRELUDE TO REFORM

1 Duncan Kennedy, "Toward a Critical Phenomenology of Judging" in Allan C. Hutchinson and Patrick Monahan, eds., *The Rule of Law: Ideal or Ideology* (Toronto: Carswell, 1987) at 141-67 [Kennedy, "Phenomenology of Judging"].
2 *Ibid.* at 145.
3 *Ibid.* at 146.
4 Bertrand Russell, *History of Western Philosophy* (New York: Simon and Schuster, 1945) at 39.
5 Hugh Collins, *Marxism and Law* (Oxford: Oxford University Press, 1984).
6 *Ibid.* at 135-36.
7 *Ibid.* at 50.
8 *Ibid.* [emphases added].
9 Kennedy, "Phenomenology of Judging," *supra* note 1 at 149.
10 Raimo Siltala, "Whose Justice, Which Ideology?" (2003) 16 Ratio Juris 123 at 123-30.
11 Duncan Kennedy, *A Critique of Adjudication: Fin de Siecle* (Cambridge, MA: Harvard University Press, 1997).
12 See s. 51 of the Society of Ontario Adjudicators and Regulators, *Model Code of Professional and Ethical Responsibilities* (Toronto: Society of Ontario Adjudicators and Regulators, 1996): "An adjudicator shall apply the law to the evidence in good faith and to the best of his/her ability. The prospect of disapproval from any person, institution, or community must not deter an adjudicator from making the decision which he or she believes is correctly based on the law and the evidence. *Adjudicators must be prepared to go where the evidence and law fairly takes them*" [emphasis added].
13 Lawrence B. Solum, "Judicial Selection: Ideology versus Character" (2004) 26 Cardozo L. Rev. 659.
14 *Ibid.* at 677.
15 *Ibid.* at 689 [emphasis added].
16 David Dyzenhaus, *Hard Cases in Wicked Legal Systems: South Africa Law in the Perspective of Legal Philosophy* (Oxford: Clarendon Press, 1991) at 57.
17 See Robert Cover, *Justice Accused: Antislavery and the Judicial Process* (New Haven, CT: Yale University Press, 1975) at 226-29, as cited and quoted in David Dyzenhaus, *Judging the Judges, Judging Ourselves – Truth, Reconciliation and the Apartheid Legal Order* (Oxford: Hart Publishing, 1998; as reprinted in paperback with amendments in 2003) [Dyzenhaus, *Judging the Judges*] at 73.
18 Dyzenhaus, *ibid.* at 16.

19 Ian Greene, with Carl Baar, Peter McCormick, George Szablowski, and Martin Thomas, *Final Appeal: Decision-Making in Canadian Courts of Appeal* (Toronto: Lorimer, 1998).

20 *Ocean Port Hotel Ltd. v. British Columbia (General Manager, Liquor Control and Licensing Branch)*, [2001] 2 S.C.R. 781 [*Ocean Port*] (previously cited).

21 *Canadian Union of Public Employees (C.U.P.E.) v. Ontario (Minister of Labour)*, [2003] 1 S.C.R. 539 [*CUPE*] (previously cited) at para. 117.

22 *R. v. Secretary of State for the Home Department, ex p. Simms*, [2000] 2 A.C. 115 (H.L.) at 131. See also *Morgan Grenfell & Co. v. Income Tax Special Commissioner*, [2002] 2 All E.R. 1 (H.L.) at para. 8. (I am indebted to Frank Falzon for bringing these authorities to my attention and providing this felicitous phrasing of the argument.)

23 *Reference re Remuneration of Judges of the Provincial Court of Prince Edward Island; Reference re Independence and Impartiality of Judges of the Provincial Court of Prince Edward Island; R. v. Campbell; R. v. Ekmecic; R. v. Wickman; Manitoba Provincial Judges Assn. v. Manitoba (Minister of Justice)*, [1997] 3 S.C.R. 3 [*PEI Reference*] (previously cited). Characterizing a constitutional requirement as *unwritten* is perhaps not an ideal way of putting it. It is clear from *PEI Reference* that the Court found the constitutional requirement of judicial independence for provincial courts to be, as a matter of interpretation, implicitly part of the written constitution, and thus an *implicit* requirement or principle, not an *unwritten* requirement. "Unwritten" is, however, the Court's word.

24 Philip Bryden, "A Common Law Constitutional Principle of Tribunal Independence? A Comment on Ocean Port Hotel Ltd. v. British Columbia" (2002) 22 Admin. L.R. (3d) 43 at 58 [emphasis added].

25 See the description of the executive branch strategy of defeating or finessing reform recommendations: Chapter 1 at 127-32.

26 *Saskatchewan Federation of Labour v. Saskatchewan*, 2010 SKCA 27 (CanLII) [*SFL v. Sask CA 2010*] (previously cited).

27 For a full doctrinal and policy argument in support of the applicability of the unwritten constitutional principle of judicial independence to administrative justice tribunals, see S. Ronald Ellis and Mary E. McKenzie, "Ocean Port or the Rule of Law? The Saskatchewan Labour Relations Board" (2009) 22 Can. J. Admin. L. & Prac. 267.

28 *R. v. Valente*, [1985] 2 S.C.R. 673 (previously cited).

29 See Chapter 1, "The Sea Change in the Law of Judicial Independence: *Valente*, 1985," at 66-71.

30 *Paul v. British Columbia (Forest Appeals Commission)*, [2003] 2 S.C.R. 585 [*Paul*] (previously cited).

31 *Ibid.* at para. 22 [emphasis added].

32 *Nova Scotia (Workers' Compensation Board) v. Martin*, [2003] 2 S.C.R. 504.

33 [2005] B.C.C.A. 631.

34 *Ibid.*, majority judgment of Newbury, J.A., at para. 75 [emphasis added].

35 *Christie v. British Columbia*, [2007] 1 S.C.R. 873.

36 *R. v. Conway*, [2010] 1 S.C.R. 765 [*Conway*] (previously cited). See also the Court's recognition in *Tranchemontagne v. Ontario (Director, Disability Support Program)*, [2006] 1 S.C.R. 513, of the general jurisdiction of administrative tribunals to rule

statutory provisions invalid for non-compliance with provincial or federal human rights codes.

37   See Chapter 2 at 137-38.

38   Antonio Lamer, "Administrative Tribunals – Future Prospects and Possibilities" (1991) 5 Can. J. Admin. L. & Prac. 107 (previously cited).

39   As quoted in Ron Ellis, "Appointments Policies in the Administrative Justice System: Lessons from Ontario: Four Speeches" (1998) 11 Can. J. Admin. L. & Prac. 205.

40   Beverley McLachlin, "The Roles of Administrative Tribunals and Courts in Maintaining the Rule of Law" (1998) 12 Can. J. Admin. L. & Prac. 171 (previously cited).

41   This requirement is confined to tribunals exercising penal jurisdiction. See *R. v. Wigglesworth*, [1987] 2 S.C.R. 541.

42   The s. 7 *Charter* requirement that no one may be deprived of such rights except in accordance with the principles of "fundamental justice" has been taken to encompass the principles of procedural fairness, including a hearing by an independent and impartial tribunal. See, *e.g.*, *Re B.C. Motor Vehicles Act*, [1985] 2 S.C.R. 486; *R. v. Lyons*, [1987] 2 S.C.R. 309 at 361; and *Chiarelli v. Canada (Minister of Employment and Immigration)*, [1992] 1 S.C.R. 711 at 743.

43   *Canadian Bill of Rights*, S.C. 1960, c. 44, s. 2.

44   As first recognized in *PEI Reference, supra* note 23.

45   *Ibid.* at para. 85.

46   *Ibid.* at para. 86.

47   See, *e.g.*, *Ell v. Alberta*, [2003] 1 S.C.R. 857 [*Ell*] (previously cited) at para.19; *Re Application under s. 83.28 of the Criminal Code*, [2004] 2 S.C.R. 248 [*S. 83.28 Application*] at para. 81; *British Columbia v. Imperial Tobacco Canada Ltd.*, [2005] 2 S.C.R. 473 [*Imperial Tobacco*] (previously cited) at paras. 44-51; and *Charkaoui v. Canada (Citizenship and Immigration)*, [2007] S.C.J. No. 9 [*Charkaoui*] at para. 32.

48   *S. 83.28 Application, ibid.*

49   *Ibid.* at para. 81 [emphasis added; citations for *PEI Reference* and *Ell* have been omitted]. It should be noted that the last sentence in this passage appears to provide another example of the Court's conflation of "quasi-judicial and administrative proceedings" with "judicial" proceedings.

50   *PEI Reference, supra* note 23 at para. 323 [emphasis added].

51   *Ocean Port, supra* note 20.

52   *Attorney General of Quebec v. Blaikie*, [1979] 2 S.C.R. 1016 at 1030 [*Blaikie*].

53   *Weber v. Ontario Hydro*, [1995] 2 S.C.R. 929 [*Weber*]. See also *R. v. 974649 Ontario Inc.*, [2005] 3 S.C.R. 575 at para. 15ff. Compare *Mooring v. Canada (National Parole Board)*, [1996] 1 S.C.R. 575.

54   *Ocean Port, supra* note 20.

55   *2747-3174 Québec Inc. v. Quebec (Régie des permis d'alcool)*, [1996] 3 S.C.R. 919 [*Régie*] (previously cited).

56   Ocean Port Hotel Ltd.

57   *Ocean Port, supra* note 20, particularly at paras. 23, 24, and 29-31.

58   *Ibid.* at para. 24 [emphasis added]. The last two lines read: "... a matter of discerning the intention of Parliament or the legislature and, absent constitutional constraints, this choice must be respected." Taken at face value, the phrase "absent constitutional constraints" might suggest that the Court intended to leave open the possibility of

the PEI principle's applying to some tribunals. It seems clear from the context, however, that the Court was referring in *Ocean Port* to confirmed constitutional constraints such as those explicit in s. 11(d) and implicit in s. 7 of the *Charter.*

59 Ellis and McKenzie, *supra* note 27.

60 *Ibid.* at para. 33 [emphasis added].

61 *CUPE, supra* note 21.

62 *Ibid.* at paras. 119 and 120.

63 *Blaikie, supra* note 52 and accompanying text.

64 *Bell Canada v. Canadian Telephone Employees Association,* [2003] 1 S.C.R. 884 [*Bell Canada*] (previously cited).

65 *McKenzie v. Minister of Public Safety and Solicitor General et al.* 2006 B.C.S.C. 1372 (CanLII), 272 D.L.R. (4th) 455 (B.C.S.C.), [2006] 12 W.W.R. 404, 52 C.C.E.L. (3d) 191, 145 C.R.R. (2d) 192, 61 B.C.L.R. (4th) 57 [*McKenzie*] (previously cited). Justice McEwan held that the principle applied and rendered unconstitutional and therefore invalid the statutory provision that the government had argued authorized it to terminate arbitrator appointments at any time without cause. As seen in the Introduction at 19-20 and 25-26, the BC Court of Appeal, preferring mootness to substance, forestalled review of that decision on its merits at any higher level of court. Justice McEwan's decision still stands, therefore, never challenged on its merits.

66 *Ibid.* at para. 134.

67 *Bell Canada, supra* note 64 at paras. 21 and 23 [emphases added].

68 *Ibid.* at paras. 29-30.

69 *Ell, supra* note 47.

70 *Ibid.* at para. 20 [emphasis added].

71 *Ibid.* at para. 24.

72 *Ibid.* at paras. 22 and 30-32.

73 Philip Bryden, "A Common Law Constitutional Principle of Tribunal Independence? A Comment on Ocean Port Hotel Ltd. v. British Columbia" (2002) 22 Admin. L.R. (3d) 43 at 57.

74 D.J. Mullan, "Administrative Tribunals: Their Evolution in Canada from 1945 to 1984" in I. Bernie and A. Lajoie, eds., *Regulations, Crown Corporations and Administrative Tribunals* (Toronto: University of Toronto Press, 1985) at 184.

75 See, *e.g.,* "Theory of Justice: Justice as Fairness" in John Rawls, *A Theory of Justice* (Cambridge, MA: Belknap Press, 1971) as adjusted by himself in John Rawls, "Justice as Fairness as a Political Conception of Justice" from 'Justice as Fairness: Political Not Metaphysical' (1985)" in Robert C. Solomon and Mark C. Murphy, eds., *What Is Justice? Classic and Contemporary Readings,* 2d ed. (New York: Oxford University Press, 2000) at 339-45.

76 See now, *e.g., Dunsmuir v. New Brunswick,* [2008] 1 S.C.R. 190 (previously cited) at para. 47.

CHAPTER 5: THE REFORM PROPOSAL

1 H. W. Arthurs, *Without the Law: Administrative Justice and Legal Pluralism in Nineteenth Century England* (Toronto and Buffalo: University of Toronto Press, 1985) (previously cited) at 128.

2 See the discussion in Chapter 2 at 165-67 in connection with my hypothetical energy board's determination of whether or not to revoke a gas-marketing licence, and at 173 in connection with the Saltfleet Board of Health having been possibly assigned a judicial function that would be appropriately exercised only by a judicial tribunal.

3 Margot D. Priest, "Structure and Accountability of Administrative Agencies" in *Law Society of Upper Canada Special Lectures, 1992, Administrative Law, Principles, Practices and Pluralism* (Toronto: Carswell, 1992) 11 (previously cited).

4 *Ibid.* at 43.

5 H.R. Wade, *Administrative Law,* 5th ed. (Oxford: Clarendon Press, 1982) at 795.

6 Hudson N. Janisch, "Administrative Tribunals and the Law" (1988-89) 2 Can. J. Admin. L. & Prac. 262 at 284-85.

7 Robert Macaulay, *Directions: Report on a Review of Ontario's Regulatory Agencies* (Ontario Management Board of Cabinet, 1989) [*Macaulay Report*] (previously cited) at 8-130 to 8-150. The description in the following paragraphs of the role for the Council proposed by *Macaulay* may be found at 8-150.

8 Ed Ratushny, *Report on the Independence of Federal Administrative Tribunals and Agencies* (Presented to President John R. Jennings at the annual general meeting commemorating the seventy-fifth anniversary of the Canadian Bar Association, London England, 1990) (Ottawa: Canadian Bar Association, 1990) [*Ratushny Report*] (previously cited), recommendation 8.

9 *Ibid.,* recommendations 69-70.

10 *Ibid.,* recommendations 9-13, 37, 60(d) and 61, 65-67, 68, 71, and 56.

11 *Ibid.,* recommendation 56.

12 Margot Priest, *Fundamental Reforms to the Ontario Administrative Justice System in Rethinking Civil Justice* (Research studies for the Civil Justice Review, Law Reform Commission of Ontario, 1996) (Toronto: Law Reform Commission of Ontario, 1996).

13 Ontario, Government Task Force on Agencies, Boards and Commissions (Bob Wood, Chair). *Report on Restructuring Regulatory and Adjudicative Agencies* (Toronto: Ministry of Government Services, February 1997) [*Wood Report*].

14 Agency Reform Commission on Ontario's Regulatory and Adjudicative Agencies (Gary Guzzo, Chair), *Everyday Justice* (Toronto: Queen's Printer for Ontario, 1998) [*Guzzo Report*].

15 Online: <http://www.gov.bc.ca/ajo/popt/about_the_ajo.htm>.

16 *Administrative justice, An Act respecting,* R.S.Q. c. J-3, s. 165.

17 *Ibid.,* s. 167.

18 *Ibid.,* s. 168.

19 *Ibid.,* s. 177.

20 *Ibid.*

21 See Chapter 1, note 289. For the United Kingdom, see especially Gavin Drewry, "The Judicialisation of 'Administrative' Tribunals in the UK: From Hewart to Leggatt," (2009) No. 28 E SI/2009 *Transylvanian Review of Administrative Sciences* 45 at 45-64.

22 Australia, *Administrative Appeals Tribunal Act 1975 (as amended),* Part V, Administrative Review Council, ss. 47-58.

23 *Tribunals, Courts and Enforcement Act 2007* (U.K.), 2007, c. 15, Part 1, Chapter 5, s. 44(1), Schedule 7, Part 2.

24 *Ibid.*, Schedule 7, Part 2, for the statutory definition of the AJTC's function. The AJTC's strategic objectives as set out above are online: <http://www.ajtc.gov.uk/about/strategic-objectives.htm>.

25 Volume 722, Part No. 74, Lords Hansard text, for 29 November 2010, Committee (2nd day) re *Public Bodies Bill,* Amendment 17: "Schedule 1, page 16, line 4, leave out 'Administrative Justice and Tribunals Council,'" moved by Lord Borrie, columns 1321-38 (a one-and-a-half hour debate).

26 No disrespect for judges or retired judges is intended. It is a question of not confusing the optics or blurring the culture between the courts and the judicial tribunals.

27 Ron Ellis, "The Administrative Justice System in the New Millennium: A Vision in Search of a Centre" (1999-2000) 13 Can. J. Admin. L. & Prac. 171. [Ellis, "Administrative Justice System"].

28 See Chapter 1, "The Sea Change in the Law of Judicial Independence: *Valente*, 1985," at 66-71.

29 I should make clear that it is not my idea. The suggestion surfaced at a meeting of Ontario's Administrative Justice Working Group with executive branch officials in 2008 where I was present. I cannot now recall where the credit should lie.

30 *Reference re Remuneration of Judges of the Provincial Court of Prince Edward Island; Reference re Independence and Impartiality of Judges of the Provincial Court of Prince Edward Island; R. v. Campbell; R. v. Ekmecic; R. v. Wickman; Manitoba Provincial Judges Assn. v. Manitoba (Minister of Justice),* [1997] 3 S.C.R. 3 *[PEI Reference]* (previously cited).

31 *Infra* at 275.

32 Canadian Judicial Council, *Alternative Models of Court Administration* (September 2006) [unpublished], online: Canadian Judicial Council <http://www.cjc-ccm.gc.ca>.

33 Ron Ellis, "Super Provincial Tribunals: A Radical Remedy for Canada's Rights Tribunals" (2001) 15 Can. J. Admin. L. & Prac. 15 [Ellis, "Super Provincial Tribunals"].

34 For an attempt at closely considering the implications of such a policy, see S. Ronald Ellis, "Administrative Justice System Reform: The Term of Appointment Issue" (1996) 10 Can. J. Admin. L. & Prac. 1 [Ellis, "Term of Appointment Issue"].

35 Fairness Committee (The Honourable Justice Coulter A. Osbourne, QC, Chair; Professor David J. Mullan and Bryan Finlay, QC, Members), "Report of the Fairness Committee to David A. Brown, Q.C., Chair of the Ontario Securities Commission" (5 March 2004) [unpublished] (previously cited). See Chapter 1 at 110-11.

36 Online: <http://www.aat.gov.au/AboutTheAAT/IntroductionToTheAAT.htm>. It must be noted, however, that in Australia it has long been held to be actually unconstitutional for a judicial function to be assigned to any institution other than a court, so the jurisdiction of the AAT is confined to a merit review of administrative decisions. See the paper ("World Report #1") presented by the Honourable Justice Garry Downes, AM, President of the Australian Administrative Appeals Tribunal, Judge of the Federal Court of Australia, to the Canadian Council of Administrative Tribunals Fourth International Conference, Vancouver, 2007 [unpublished].

37 *Constitutional Reform Act 2005* (U.K.), 2005, c. 4.

38 *Tribunals, Courts and Enforcement Act 2007* (U.K.), 2007, c. 15.

39 Carnwath, Lord Justice, Lord Justice of Appeal, Senior President of Tribunals, Address (University of Toronto Symposium on the Future of Administrative Justice, Toronto, January 2008) [unpublished] at para. 9.

40 Sir Andrew Leggatt, *Tribunals for Users One System, One Service (Report of the Review of Tribunals)* (March 2001), online: UK National Archives <http://webarchive. nationalarchives.gov.uk/+/http://www.tribunals-review.org.uk/leggatthtm/leg-00. htm> [*Leggatt Report*] (previously cited).

41 New Zealand, Ministry of Justice, *Tribunals in New Zealand: The Government's Preferred Approach to Reform* (Wellington: Government of New Zealand, 2008). However, it appears from the public record that the push for reform of the administrative justice system in New Zealand may have faltered following a change of government in November 2008.

42 *Ibid.*

43 *Labour and Employment Board Act,* S.N.B. 1994, c. L-0.01.

44 Québec, Ministère de la justice, Groupe de travail sur les tribunaux administratifs (1987), Yves Ouellette [unpublished].

45 Québec, Ministère de la justice, Groupe de travail sur certaines questions relatives à la réforme de la justice administrative, *Une justice administrative pour le citoyen* (Québec: Publications officielles, 1994).

46 France Houle, "A Brief Historical Account of the Reforms to the Administrative Justice System in the Province Of Quebec" (2009) 22 Can. J. Admin. L. & Prac. 47 (previously cited) at 62-65.

47 *Licence Appeal Tribunal Act, 1999,* S.O. 1999, c. 12, Sched. G.

48 *Ministry of Agriculture, Food and Rural Affairs Act,* R.S.O. 1990, c. M.16, as amended by S.O. 1999, c. 12, Sched. A, s. 20(2).

49 *Ministry of Health Appeal and Review Board Act,* 1998, S.O. 1998, c.18.

50 Online: <http://www.lat.gov.on.ca/english/index.htm>.

51 For an account of the reasons for the failure of this proposal, and why its failure casts no shadow over the super tribunal idea itself, see Ellis, "Super Provincial Tribunals," *supra* note 33 at 16-18.

52 Kevin Whitaker, *Final Report of the Agency Cluster Facilitator for the Municipal, Environment and Land Planning Tribunals* (22 August 2007) [unpublished].

53 *Adjudicative Tribunals Accountability, Governance and Appointments Act, 2009,* S.O. 2009, c. 33, ss. 15-20.

54 For a recent assessment, see Michael Gottheil and Doug Ewart, "The Potential of Ontario's Clustering Model to Advance Administrative Justice" (2011) 24 Can. J. Admin. L. & Prac. 161.

55 *Bell Canada v. Canadian Telephone Employees Association,* [2003] 1 S.C.R. 884 (previously cited).

56 Ellis, "Super Provincial Tribunals," *supra* note 33.

57 This is an innovation that would be a helpful addition to the institutionalizing strategies for any rights tribunal, super tribunal or otherwise.

58 See Chapter 1 at 111-13.

59 *PEI Reference, supra* note 30.

60 For a full elucidation of that view, see Ron Ellis, "Misconceiving Tribunal Members: A Memorandum to Québec" (2005) 18 Can. J. Admin. Law & Prac. 189.

61 See the discussion about idiosyncratic removals in Chapter 1.

62 See *R. v. Valente*, [1985] 2 S.C.R. 673 [*Valente*] (previously cited) at paras. 30-31; *Therrien (Re)*, [2001] 2 S.C.R. 3 at para. 39. But see contra *Weatherill v. Canada (Attorney General)*, [1999] F.C.J. No. 787 [*Weatherill*] (previously cited) at para. 88, and *Wedge v. Canada (Attorney General)* (1995), 133 F.T.R. 277 [*Wedge*] (previously cited) (see Chapter 1 at 94-98).

63 Regular part-time members with assured assignments to a significant number of specified hearing days per month would be an example of such an arrangement.

64 *Dunsmuir v. New Brunswick*, [2008] 1 S.C.R. 190 [*Dunsmuir*] (previously cited) at paras. 47, 48, and 151.

65 I am referring to the secondment of members of the public service to the administrative justice system on the basis of a leave of absence. Obviously, once tribunal adjudication becomes a secure and valued career, experienced public servants may well be motivated to transfer from the public service and pursue an adjudicative career.

66 This is a proposal has been made previously. See Peter Aucoin and Elisabeth Goodyear-Grant, "Designing a Merit Based Process for Appointing Boards of ABCs: Lessons from the Nova Scotia Reform Experience" (2002) 45 Canadian Public Administration 301 at 311.

67 *PEI Reference, supra* note 30 at para. 135; and *Deputy Judges Assn. v. Ontario (Attorney General)* (2006), 80 O.R. (3d) 481(C.A.) at para. 22.

68 *Valente, supra* note 62.

69 See, for instance, the decision of the BC Court of Appeal in *Golden Valley Golf Course Ltd. v. British Columbia*, 2001 BCCA 392 (CanLII) (previously cited).

70 *Rai v. Ontario (Provincial Court)* (2005), 76 O.R. (3d) 641 (Div. Ct.). There are also elements of good-quality judicial tribunal decisions that can be assessed objectively. See WCAT's "Hallmarks of Decision Quality" in S. Ronald Ellis, "Misconceiving Tribunal Members: A Memorandum to Quebec" (2005) 18 Can. J. Admin. L. & Prac. 189 (previously cited) at 204-5.

71 Houle, *supra* note 46 at 70-71.

72 The Ontario Auditor General's value-for money-audit of the Ontario Disability Support Program was conducted initially in 2004, with a follow-up audit in 2006.

73 Administrative Justice Working Group, "The Provincial Auditor and the Administrative Justice System" (Submission to the Auditor General of Ontario, 9 March 2007, subsequently published) (2010) 23 Can. J. Admin. L. & Prac. 237. (I should note that I was one of the principal authors of this submission.)

74 *Workers' Compensation Act*, R.S.O. 1980, c. 539.

75 Having fallen into disuse, the review provision was removed from the *Act* in 1996.

76 It is not entirely unprecedented, however. It is reflective of the s. 86(n) powers of review of the WCB board of directors referred to above. It is also akin to – but, from a justice policy perspective, infinitely preferable to – the statutory right of appeal to cabinet that one finds in some tribunals' statutes.

CHAPTER 6: IMPLEMENTING THE REFORM PROPOSAL

1 [1992] 1 S.C.R. 259 (previously cited), overruling *R. v. MacKay*, [1980] 2 S.C.R. 370 (previously cited). See Chapter 1 at 70-71.

2 *R. v. Valente*, [1985] 2 S.C.R. 673 [*Valente*] (previously cited).

3 *Act to amend the National Defence Act and to Make Consequential Amendments to
   other Acts*, S.C. 1998, c. 35 [emphasis added]. For a full account of the jurisprudence
   from *Généreux* up to the amendment of the *National Defence Act* in 1998 and later,
   see *R. v. Corporal H.P. Nguyen*, 2005 CM 57. For the denouement of this reform
   process, see *Security of Tenure of Military Judges Act*, S.C. 2011, c. 22, s. 2, making
   appointments of members of court-martial tribunals life-tenured appointments.
4 *Convention for the Protection of Human Rights and Fundamental Freedoms*, 4
   November 1950, 213 U.N.T.S. 221 at 223, Eur. T.S. 5 [*European Convention on
   Human Rights*] [emphasis added].
5 *Human Rights Act 1998* (U.K.) ,1998, c. 2.
6 For a description, see Chapter 5 at 252-53.
7 Sir Andrew Leggatt, *Tribunals for Users One System, One Service (Report of the
   Review of Tribunals)* (March 2001), online: UK National Archives <http://
   webarchive.nationalarchives.gov.uk/+/http://www.tribunals-review.org.uk/
   leggatthtm/leg-00.htm> [*Leggatt Report*] (previously cited) [emphasis added].
8 *Reference re Remuneration of Judges of the Provincial Court of Prince Edward Island;
   Reference re Independence and Impartiality of Judges of the Provincial Court of Prince
   Edward Island; R. v. Campbell; R. v. Ekmecic; R. v. Wickman; Manitoba Provincial
   Judges Assn. v. Manitoba (Minister of Justice)*, [1997] 3 S.C.R. 3 [*PEI Reference*] (previously cited).

CHAPTER 7: MEANWHILE, A TOOLKIT FOR LITIGATORS

1 *R. v. Valente*, [1985] 2 S.C.R. 673 [*Valente*] (previously cited).
2 *The Attorney General of Québec v. Barreau du Montréal*, [2001] J.Q. No. 3882 (C.A.),
   leave to appeal refused (2002), 2002 CarswellQue 2078 (S.C.C.), reconsideration refused (2002), 2002 CarswellQue 2683, cited to J.Q. (C.A.) [*Barreau*] (previously
   cited). See Chapter 1 at 91-92.
3 2012 ONCA 437 (CanLII).
4 *Ibid.* at paras. 7-9.
5 *Roncarelli v. Duplessis*, [1959] S.C.R. 121; *Canadian Union of Public Employees
   (C.U.P.E.) v. Ontario (Minister of Labour)*, [2003] 1 S.C.R. 539 [*CUPE*] (previously
   cited).
6 See "Discharge without Recourse" in Chapter 1 at 94-99.
7 *Deputy Judges Assn. v. Ontario (Attorney General)* (2006), 80 O.R. (3d) 481(C.A.)
   (previously cited) at para. 22. See also *Reference re Remuneration of Judges, of the
   Provincial Court of Prince Edward Island; Reference re Independence and Impartiality
   of Judges of the Provincial Court of Prince Edward Island; R. v. Campbell; R. v.
   Ekmecic; R. v. Wickman; Manitoba Provincial Judges Assn. v. Manitoba (Minister of
   Justice)* [1997] 3 S.C.R. 3 [*PEI Reference*] (previously cited) at para. 135.
8 Online: Public Appointments Secretariat <http://www.pas.gov.on.ca/scripts/en/
   Home.asp>. Click the "Compensation" Quick Link.
9 See Chapter 1 at 111-13.
10 Gaile McGregor, "Anti-Claimant Bias in the Employment Insurance Appeals System:
   Causes, Consequences, and Public Law Remedies" (2002) 15 Can. J. Admin. L. &
   Prac. 229 (previously cited).

11 In *CUPE, supra* note 5, the unions were successful in challenging the generic appointments *process* rather than a particular application of that process. See also in this regard *R. v. Lippé*, [1991] 2 S.C.R. 114 (previously cited), and *Barreau, supra* note 2. *Barreau* also supplies a useful precedent for bar associations or other professional bodies that seek standing to challenge the independence and impartiality of administrative judicial tribunals. And now see also *Canada (Attorney General) v. Downtown Eastside Sex Workers United against Violence Society*, [2012] SCC 45 (CanLII).

12 See, *e.g., Joplin v. Chief Constable of the City of Vancouver* (1982), 144 D.L.R. (3d) 285 (B.C.S.C.), aff'd (1985), 20 D.L.R. 4th 314 (B.C.C.A.) (legislature presumed not to have intended rule-making power to be used to exclude a common law duty of fairness); *ATCO Gas & Pipelines Ltd. v. Alberta (Energy & Utilities Board)*, [2006] 1 S.C.R. 140 at para. 79 (the principle against confiscating property); and *Dikhranian v. Attorney General of Quebec*, [2005] 3 S.C.R. 530 at paras. 32-36 (the principle against interfering with vested rights).

13 *CUPE, supra* note 5. See Chapter 4 at 213-14.

14 *R. v. Secretary of State for the Home Department, ex p. Simms*, [2000] 2 A.C. 115 (H.L.) (previously cited); *Morgan Grenfell & Co. v. Income Tax Special Commissioner*, [2002] 2 All E.R. 1 (H.L.) (previously cited). See Chapter 4 at 214.

15 *Dunsmuir v. New Brunswick*, [2008] 1 S.C.R. 190 [*Dunsmuir*] (previously cited) at para. 48.

16 *Saskatchewan Federation of Labour v. Saskatchewan*, 2010 SKCA 27 (CanLII) (previously cited).

17 For an account of the English and European jurisprudence on the principle that if the lower-level decision maker is not independent or impartial, the principles of natural justice can be satisfied only if the review tribunal has a "full" review jurisdiction, including, where a decision turns on factual issues, the jurisdiction to review the findings of fact, see *Begum (FC) v. London Borough of Tower Hamlets*, [2003] U.K.H.L. 5 (previously cited).

18 *McKenzie v. British Columbia (Minister of Public Safety and Solicitor General)*, 2007 B.C.C.A. 507 (CanLII) (previously cited).

19 British Columbia's Bill 72, the *Tenancy Statutes Amendment Act, 2006* (previously cited).

20 See Chapter 1 at 70. I appreciate that the Supreme Court has now conceded the legislature's power to set standards of review, but, in my respectful view, that concession was hasty from a constitutional perspective and will have to be revisited in due course.

Select Bibliography

LEGISLATION

Act Respecting Administrative Justice, R.S.Q. c. J-3

Act to amend the National Defence Act and to Make Consequential Amendments to other Acts, S.C. 1998, c. 35

Adjudicative Tribunals Accountability, Governance and Appointments Act, 2009, S.O. 2009, c. 33, sch. 5

Administrative Tribunals Act, S.B.C. 2004, c. 45

Administrative Tribunals Appointment and Administration Act, S.B.C. 2003, c. 47

Alberta Bill of Rights, R.S.A. 2000, c. A-14

Alberta Public Agencies Governance Act, S.A. 2009, c. A-31.5

British North America Act, 1867 (U.K.), 30-31 Vict., c. 3

Canada Labour Code, R.S.C., 1985, c. L-2

Canadian Bill of Rights (An Act for the Recognition and Protection of Human Rights and Fundamental Freedoms), S.C. 1960, c.44

Charter of Human Rights and Freedoms, R.S.Q. c. C-12

Constitutional Reform Act 2005 (U.K.), 2005, c. 4

Federal Courts Act, R.S.C. 1985, c. F-7

Health Insurance Act, R.S.O. 1990, c. H.6

Human.Rights Act 1998 (U.K.) ,1998, c. 2

Human Rights Code, R.S.B.C. 1996, c. 210

Interpretation Act, R.S.A. 2000, c.I-8

Interpretation Act, R.S.B.C. 1979, c. 206

The Interpretation Act, 1995, S.S. 1995, c. I-11.2

Judges Act, R.S.C. 1985, c. J-1

Labour and Employment Board Act, S.N.B. 1994, c. L-0.01

Licence Appeal Tribunal Act, 1999, S.O. 1999, c. 12

Ministry of Agriculture, Food and Rural Affairs Act, R.S.O. 1990, c. M.16, as amended by S.O. 1999, c. 12

Ministry of Health Appeal and Review Board Act, 1998, S.O. 1998, c.18

Nuclear Safety and Control Act, S.C. 1997, c. 9

Ontario Energy Board Act, 1998, S.O. 1998, c. 15, sch. B

Public Sector Employers Act, R.S.B.C. 1996, c. 384

Public Service Essential Services Act, S.S. 2008, c. P-42.2

Residential Tenancies Act, 2006, S.O. 2006, c. 17

Security of Tenure of Military Judges Act, S.C. 2011, c. 22

Statutory Powers Procedure Act, R.S.O. 1990, c. S.22

Tenancy Statutes Amendment Act, 2006, S.B.C. 2006, c. 35

The Construction Industry Labour Relations Act, 1992, S.S. 1992, c. C-29.11

The Trade Union Act, R.S.S. 1978, c. T-17

Tribunals, Courts and Enforcement Act 2007 (U.K.), 2007, c. 15

Workers' Compensation Act, R.S.O. 1980, c. 539

JURISPRUDENCE

2747-3174 Québec Inc. v. Quebec (Régie des permis d'alcool), [1996] 3 S.C.R. 919.

Ahumada v. Canada (Minister of Citizenship & Immigration) (2001), 199 D.L.R. (4th) 103 (Fed. C.A.)

Association des juges administratifs de la Commission des lesions professionnelles, et al. v. Procureur general du Québec, 2011 QCCS 1614 (CanLII)

ATCO Gas & Pipelines Ltd. v. Alberta (Energy & Utilities Board), [2006] 1 S.C.R. 140

Attorney General of Quebec v. Blaikie, [1979] 2 S.C.R. 1016

Attorney General of Quebec v. Udeco Inc. et al., [1984] 2 S.C.R. 502

Baker v. Canada (Minister of Citizenship and Immigration), [1999] 2 S.C.R. 817

Beauregard v. Canada, [1986] 2 S.C.R. 56

Begum (FC) v. London Borough of Tower Hamlets, [2003] U.K.H.L. 5 *[Begum]*.

Bell Canada v. Canadian Telephone Employees Association, [2003] 1 S.C.R. 884.

Borowski v. Canada (Attorney General), [1989] 1 S.C.R. 342.

Boulis v. Minister of Manpower and Immigration, [1974] S.C.R. 875

Brar and others v. BCVMA and Osborne (No. 17), 2010 BCHRT 260

Brar v. College of Veterinarians of British Columbia, 2011 BCSC 486 (CanLII)

British Columbia v. Imperial Tobacco Canada Ltd., [2005] 2 S.C.R. 473

Canada (Attorney General) v. Downtown Eastside Sex Workers United against Violence Society, [2012] SCC 45 (CanLII)

Canada Safeway Limited v. Alberta Human Rights and Citizenship Commission, 2000 ABQB 897 (CanLII)

Canadian Pacific Ltd. v. Matsqui Indian Band, [1995] 1 S.C.R. 3

Canadian Union of Public Employees (C.U.P.E.) v. Ontario (Minister of Labour), [2003] 1 S.C.R. 539

Caperton v. A.T. Massey Coal Co., Inc, 129 S. Ct. 2252, 2009 U.S. LEXIS 4157 (2009)

Charkaoui v. Canada (Citizenship and Immigration), [2007] S.C.J. No. 9

Chiarelli v. Canada (Minister of Employment and Immigration), [1992] 1 S.C.R. 711

Christie v. British Columbia, [2005] B.C.C.A. 631

Christie v. British Columbia, [2007] 1 S.C.R. 873

Committee for Justice and Liberty et al. v. National Energy Board et al., [1978] 1 S.C.R. 369

Communications, Energy and Paperworkers Union of Canada, Local 707 v. Alberta (Labour Relations Board), [2004] Alta. L.R.B.R. 1

Datt v. McDonald's Restaurants (No. 3), 2007 BCHRT 324

Deputy Judges Assn. v. Ontario (Attorney General) (2005), 78 O.R. (3d) 504 (Sup. Ct.)

Deputy Judges Assn. v. Ontario (Attorney General) (2006), 80 O.R. (3d) 481 (C.A.)

Dikhranian v. Attorney General of Quebec, [2005] 3 S.C.R. 530

Domtar Inc. v. Quebec (Commission d'appel en matière de lésions professionnelles), [1993] 2 S.C.R. 756

Dr. Q v. College of Physicians and Surgeons of British Columbia, [2003] 1 S.C.R. 226

Dunsmuir v. New Brunswick, [2008] 1 S.C.R. 190

Ell v. Alberta, [2003] 1 S.C.R. 857

Essex County Roman Catholic School Board v. O.E.C.T.A. (2001), 56 O.R. (3d) 85 (C.A.).

Golden Valley Golf Course Ltd. v. British Columbia, 2001 BCCA 392 (CanLII)

Hewat v. Ontario (1998), 37 O.R. (3d) 161 (C.A.)

Howarth v. Canada (National Parole Board), [1976] 1 S.C.R. 453

In the matter of the Mental Health act, RSO 1990, Chapter M-7 and in the matter of JS, a patient in the Penetanguishene Mental Health Center, Penetanguishene, Ontario – a decision by [the] ... Acting Chairman of the Panel of the Review Board having jurisdiction for Penetanguishene Mental Health Center, dated at North York, 25 March 1994

IWA v. Consolidated-Bathurst Packaging Ltd., [1990] 1 S.C.R. 282

Joplin v. Chief Constable of the City of Vancouver (1982), 144 D.L.R. (3d) 285 (B.C.S.C.), aff'd (1985), 20 D.L.R. 4th 314 (B.C.C.A.)

Jung v. Toronto Community Housing Corp., [2007] O.J. No. 4363 (Ont. Div. Ct.)

Kane v. Board of Governors of the University of British Columbia, [1980] 1 S.C.R. 1105

Keddy v. New Brunswick (Workplace Health, Safety and Compensation Commission) (2002), 212 D.L.R. (4th) 84 (N.B.C.A.), judgment of Robertson J.A.

Knight v. Indian Head School Division No. 19, [1990] 1 S.C.R. 653

Labour Relations Board of Saskatchewan v. John East Iron Works, Limited, [1949] A.C. 134 (P.C.)

Law Society of New Brunswick v. Ryan, [2003] 1 S.C.R. 247

MacKeigan v. Hickman, [1989] 2 S.C.R. 796

MacMillan Bloedel Ltd. v. Simpson, [1995] 4 S.C.R. 725

Matkowski v. Saskatchewan, [2007] S.J. No. 81 (Q.B.)

McKenzie v. British Columbia (Minister of Public Safety and Solicitor General) 2007 B.C.C.A. 507 (CanLII), 287 D.L.R. (4th) 313 (B.C.C.A.); application for leave to appeal to the S.C.C. dismissed, [2007] C.S.C.R. no. 601

McKenzie v. Minister of Public Safety and Solicitor General et al. 2006 B.C.S.C. 1372 (CanLII), 272 D.L.R. (4th) 455 (B.C.S.C.), [2006] 12 W.W.R. 404, 52 C.C.E.L. (3d) 191, 145 C.R.R. (2d) 192, 61 B.C.L.R. (4th) 57

Minister of National Revenue v. Coopers and Lybrand, [1979] 1 S.C.R. 495

Mooring v. Canada (National Parole Board), [1996] 1 S.C.R. 575

Morgan Grenfell & Co. v. Income Tax Special Commissioner, [2002] 2 All E.R. 1 (H.L.)
Newfoundland Telephone Co. v. Newfoundland (Board of Commissioners of Public Utilities), [1992] 1 S.C.R. 623
Nicholson v. Haldimand Norfolk (Regional) Police Commissioners, [1979] 1 S.C.R. 311
Nova Scotia (Workers' Compensation Board) v. Martin, [2003] 2 S.C.R. 504
Ocean Port Hotel Ltd. v. British Columbia (General Manager, Liquor Control and Licensing Branch), [2001] 2 S.C.R. 781
Ontario Deputy Judges' Association v. Ontario (Attorney General), 2012 ONCA 437 (CanLII)
Paul v. British Columbia (Forest Appeals Commission), [2003] 2 S.C.R. 585
Preston v. British Columbia (1994), 116 D.L.R. (4th) 258 (B.C.C.A.)
Pushpanathan v. Canada (Minister of Citizenship and Immigration), [1998] 1 S.C.R. 982
R. v. 974649 Ontario Inc., [2005] 3 S.C.R. 575
R. v. Conway, [2010] 1 S.C.R. 765
R. v. Corporal H.P. Nguyen, 2005 CM 57
R. v. Généreaux, [1992] 1 S.C.R. 259
R. v. Higher Education Funding Council, ex parte Institute of Dental Surgery, [1994] 1 All E.R. 651 (QB)
R. v. Lippé, [1991] 2 S.C.R. 114
R. v. Lyons, [1987] 2 S.C.R. 309
R. v. MacKay, [1980] 2 S.C.R. 370
R. v. Secretary of State for the Home Department, ex p. Simms, [2000] 2 A.C. 115 (H.L.)
R. v. Valente (No. 2) (1983), 2 C.C.C. (3d) 417 (Ont. C.A.)
R. v. Valente, [1985] 2 S.C.R. 673
R. v. Wigglesworth, [1987] 2 S.C.R. 541
Rai v. Ontario (Provincial Court) (2005), 76 O.R. (3d) 641 (Div. Ct.)
Re Application under s. 83.28 of the Criminal Code, [2004] 2 S.C.R. 248
Re B.C. Motor Vehicles Act, [1985] 2 S.C.R. 486
Re Knapman and the Board of Health for the Township of Saltfleet, [1954] O.R. 360 (S.C.O., Gale J.); [1955] O.W.N. 615 (C.A.) aff'g the judgment of Justice Gale; aff'd by the S.C.C. in *Saltfleet (Township) Board of Health v. Knapman,* [1956] S.C.R. 877, aff'g judgments of Court of Appeal and Gale J.
Reference re Act to Amend Chapter 401 of the Revised Statutes, 1989, the Residential Tenancies Act, S.N.S. 1992, c. 31 (sub nom. *Reference re Amendments to the Residential Tenancies Act),* [1996] 1 S.C.R. 186
Reference re Justices of the Peace Act; Re Currie and Niagara Escarpment Commission, [1984] O.J. No. 3393 (Ont. C.A.).
Reference re Ontario Residential Tenancies Act, [1981] 1 S.C.R. 714
Reference re Remuneration of Judges of the Provincial Court of Prince Edward Island; Reference re Independence and Impartiality of Judges of the Provincial Court of Prince Edward Island; R. v. Campbell; R. v. Ekmecic; R. v. Wickman; Manitoba Provincial Judges Assn. v. Manitoba (Minister of Justice) [1997] 3 S.C.R. 3
Roncarelli v. Duplessis, [1959] S.C.R. 121

Saskatchewan Federation of Labour v. Saskatchewan, 2010 SKCA 27 (CanLII)
Sobeys Stores Ltd. v. Yeomans, [1989] 1 S.C.R. 238
Syndicat des employés de production du Québec et de l'Acadie v. Canada (Human Rights Commission), [1989] 2 S.C.R. 879
The Attorney General of Québec v. Barreau du Montréal, [2001] J.Q. No. 3882 (C.A.), leave to appeal refused (2002), 2002 CarswellQue 2078 (S.C.C.), reconsideration refused (2002), 2002 CarswellQue 2683
The Saskatchewan Federation of Labour, and the Saskatchewan Government and General Employees' Union, and The Saskatchewan Joint Board Retail, Wholesale and Department Store Union v. Saskatchewan (Attorney General, Department of Advanced Education, Employment and Labour), and The Saskatchewan Labour Relations Board, 2010 SKQB 390 (CanLII)
Therrien (Re), [2001] 2 S.C.R. 3
Tranchemontagne v. Ontario (Director Disability Support Program), [2006] 1 S.C.R. 513
Tremblay v. Quebec (Commission des affaires sociales), [1992] 1 S.C.R. 952
Weatherill v. Canada (Attorney General), [1999] F.C.J. No. 787
Weber v. Ontario Hydro, [1995] 2 S.C.R. 929
Wedge v. Canada (Attorney General) (1995), 133 F.T.R. 277

STUDIES AND REPORTS

Administrative Justice Working Group. *Submission to the Ontario Law Reform Commission on Research Priorities* (March 2007) [unpublished].
–. "The Provincial Auditor and the Administrative Justice System" (Submission to the Auditor General of Ontario, 9 March 2007, subsequently published) (2010) 23 Can. J. Admin. L. & Prac. 237.
Advocacy Centre of Tenants Ontario (ACTO) and the Legal Clinics Housing Issues Committee (LCHIC). *Submission to the Ombudsman Ontario – Concerning the Failure of the Tenant Protection Act and the Rules and Procedures of the Ontario Rental Housing Tribunal to Meet Ombudsman Fairness Standards* (20 June 2002).
Agency Reform Commission on Ontario's Regulatory and Adjudicative Agencies (Gary Guzzo, Chair). *Everyday Justice* (Toronto: Queen's Printer for Ontario, 1998).
Bresner, Barry, Timothy Leigh-Bell, Michael J. Trebilcock, and Leonard Waverman. "Ontario's Agencies, Boards, Commissions, Advisory Bodies and Other Public Institutions: An Inventory (1977)" in *Government Regulation: Issues and Alternatives 1978* (Toronto: Ontario Economic Council, 1978).
Canada, House of Commons, 35th Parliament – 2nd Session, Standing Committee on Citizenship and Immigration. *Information Session Regarding the Ministerial Advisory Committee on the Selection of Members of the Immigration and Refugee Board*, Parliament of Canada Record of Evidence 18 June 1996.
Canadian Judicial Council. *Alternative Models of Court Administration* (Ottawa: Canadian Judicial Council, September 2006).
Cory, Peter deC. *Study, Conclusions and Recommendations Pertaining to Medical Audit Practice in Ontario* (Submitted to the Honourable George Smitherman,

Minister of Health and Long-Term Care, Government of Ontario, 21 April 2005).

Fairness Committee (The Honourable Justice Coulter A. Osbourne, QC, Chair; Professor David J. Mullan and Bryan Finlay, QC, Members). "Report of the Fairness Committee to David A. Brown, Q.C., Chair of the Ontario Securities Commission" (5 March 2004) [unpublished].

Leggatt, Sir Andrew. *Tribunals for Users One System, One Service (Report of the Review of Tribunals)* (March 2001), online: UK National Archives <http://webarchive.nationalarchives.gov.uk/+/http://www.tribunals-review.org.uk/leggatthtm/leg-00.htm>.

Macaulay, Robert. *Directions: Report on a Review of Ontario's Regulatory Agencies* (Toronto: Ontario Management Board of Cabinet, 1989).

Manitoba Law Reform Commission. *Improving Administrative Justice in Manitoba: Starting with the Appointments Process* (Report no. 21) (Winnipeg: Manitoba Law Reform Commission, November 2009).

New Brunswick Commission on Legislative Democracy. *Final Report and Recommendations* (Fredericton: Government of New Brunswick, December 2004).

New Brunswick, Government of. *An Accountable and Responsible Government, a New Generation of Canadian Leadership ... The Government's Response to the Final Report of the Commission on Legislative Democracy ... Renewing Democracy in New Brunswick* (Fredericton: Government of New Brunswick, 2007).

New Zealand, Ministry of Justice. *Tribunals in New Zealand: The Government's Preferred Approach to Reform* (Wellington: Government of New Zealand, 2008).

Ombudsman Ontario (André Marin, Ombudsman of Ontario). *Investigation into the Treatment of Victims by the Criminal Injuries Compensation Board: "Adding Insult to Injury."* (Toronto: Ombudsman Ontario, February 2007).

Ontario Bar Association. "Adjudicative Tribunals Accountability, Governance and Appointments Act, 2009 – Cause for Concern – The Tribunal Independence Issue" (2011) 24 Can. J. Admin. L. & Prac. 225.

Ontario, Government Task Force on Agencies, Boards and Commissions (Bob Wood, Chair). *Report on Restructuring Regulatory and Adjudicative Agencies* (Toronto: Ministry of Government Services, February 1997).

Ontario, Legislative Assembly, Standing Committee on the Ontario Legislature (Michael J. Breaugh, Chair). *Report on Appointments in the Public Sector, 1986* (Toronto: Government of Ontario, 1986).

Ontario, Management Board of Cabinet. "Tools, Templates and Guides" (November 2000) [unpublished].

Ontario, Ministry of Government Services. *Governance Tools for Agencies, 2007,* online: Ministry of Government Services <http://www.gov.on.ca/MGS/en/AbtMin/157218.html>.

Ontario, Royal Commission Inquiry into Civil Rights (James Chalmers McRuer, Chair). *Report No. 1, Vol. 1* (Toronto: Frank Fogg, Queen's Printer, 1968).

Ontario, Workers' Compensation Appeals Tribunal. *Annual Report 1995 and 1996.* (Toronto: Ontario Workers' Compensation Appeals Tribunal, 1996).

Osborne, Coulter A. *Civil Justice Reform Project: Summary of Findings and Recommendations* (November 2007), online: Ontario Ministry of the Attorney General <http://www.attorneygeneral.jus.gov.on.ca/english/about/pubs/cjrp/>.

Priest, Margot. *Fundamental Reforms to the Ontario Administrative Justice System in Rethinking Civil Justice* (Research studies for the Civil Justice Review, Law Reform Commission of Ontario, 1996 (Toronto: Law Reform Commission of Ontario, 1996).

Québec, Groupe de travail sur les tribunaux administratifs (René Dussault, Chair). *Les tribunaux administratifs au Québec: rapport du Groupe de travail sur les tribunaux administratifs* (Québec: Ministère de la Justice, 1971).

Ratushny, Ed. *Report on the Independence of Federal Administrative Tribunals and Agencies* (Presented to President John R. Jennings at the annual general meeting commemorating the seventy-fifth anniversary of the Canadian Bar Association, London, England, 1990). (Ottawa: Canadian Bar Association, 1990).

Society of Ontario Adjudicators and Regulators. *Model Code of Professional and Ethical Responsibilities* (Toronto: Society of Ontario Adjudicators and Regulators, 1996).

–. "Towards Maintaining and Improving the Quality of Adjudication: SOAR Recommendations for Performance Management in Ontario's Administrative Justice System" (1995) 9 Can. J. Admin. L. & Prac. 179.

Sossin, Lorne. *The Independent Board and the Legislative Process* (Edmonton: Alberta Federation of Labour, 2006).

Trebilcock, Michael J., Leonard Waverman, and J. Robert S. Prichard. "Markets for Regulation: Implications for Performance Standards and Institutional Design" in *Government Regulation: Issues and Alternatives 1978* (Toronto: Ontario Economic Council, 1978).

United Kingdom, *Report of the Committee on Administrative Tribunals and Enquiries by Chairman, The Rt Hon Sir Oliver Franks, GCMG KCB CBE)*, Cmnd 218 (July 1957).

Weiler, Paul. *Reshaping Workers' Compensation for Ontario* (Report submitted to Robert G. Elgie, MD, Minister of Labour, November 1980). (Toronto: Ministry of Labour, 1980).

Whitaker, Kevin. *Final Report of Agency Cluster Facilitator for the Municipal, Environment and Land Planning Tribunals* (22 August 2007) (Toronto: Ministry of Labour, 2007).

Ontario Legislative Assembly, Standing Procedural Affairs Committee Reports
Between 1978 and 1996, the Standing Procedural Affairs Committee and its successor committees (the Standing Committee on Procedural Affairs and Agencies, Boards and Commissions; and the Standing Committee on Government Agencies) were mandated to select each year a number of government agencies for review by the Committee. The results of these reviews were reported in a series of annual reports titled *Report on Agencies, Boards and Commissions* and numbered consecutively from 1 to 23. The final three reports (21, 22, and 23) were all issued in 1996,

reflecting a hiatus in the reporting from 1993 to 1996. These reports are referred to below as the "Ontario Standing Committee Reports" and are individually identified by number and date:

Ontario Standing Committee Report No. 1 (1978)
Ontario Standing Committee Report No. 5 (1982)
Ontario Standing Committee Report No. 6 (1983)
Ontario Standing Committee Report No. 7 (1984)
Ontario Standing Committee Report No. 10 (1987)
Ontario Standing Committee Report No. 12 (1990)

BOOK AND ARTICLES

Abella, Rosalie Silberman. "Canadian Administrative Tribunals: Towards Judicialization or Dejudicialization" (1988) 2 Can. J. Admin. L. & Prac. 1.

Allison, John W.F. "Theoretical and Institutional Underpinnings" in Michael Taggart, ed., *The Province of Administrative Law* (Oxford: Hart Publishing, 1977).

Arthurs, H. "Jonah and the Whale: The Appearance, Disappearance and Reappearance of Administrative Law" (1980) 30 U.T.L. J. 225.

Arthurs, H.W. *Without the Law: Administrative Justice and Legal Pluralism in Nineteenth Century England* (Toronto and Buffalo: University of Toronto Press, 1985).

Arthurs, Harry. "Protection against Judicial Review" (1983) 43 Can. Bar Rev. 277.

Aucoin, Peter, and Elisabeth Goodyear-Grant. "Designing a Merit Based Process for Appointing Boards of ABCs: Lessons from the Nova Scotia Reform Experience" (2002) 45 Canadian Public Administration 301.

Bryden, Philip. "A Common Law Constitutional Principle of Tribunal Independence? A Comment on Ocean Port Hotel Ltd. v. British Columbia" (2002) 22 Admin. L.R. (3d) 43.

Bryden, Philip, and Ron Hatch. "British Columbia Council of Administrative Tribunals Research and Policy Committee – Report on Independence, Accountability and Appointment Processes in British Columbia" (1998-99) 12 Can. J. Admin. L. & Prac. 235.

Carnwath, Lord Justice, Lord Justice of Appeal, Senior President of Tribunals. Address (University of Toronto Symposium on the Future of Administrative Justice, Toronto, January 2008) [unpublished].

Carnwath, Lord Justice, Lord Justice of Appeal, Senior President of Tribunals. "Developments in the UK" (Paper presented to the CCAT conference Administrative Justice without Borders, Vancouver, May 2007) [unpublished].

Collins, Hugh. *Marxism and Law* (Oxford: Oxford University Press, 1984).

Colwell, Randy, and Paul G. Thomas. "Parliament and the Patronage Issue" (1987) 22 Journal of Canadian Studies 163.

Corry, J.A. "Administrative Law and the Interpretation of Statutes" (1935-36) 1 U.T.L.J. 286.

Cover, Robert. *Justice Accused: Antislavery and the Judicial Process* (New Haven, CT: Yale University Press, 1975).

Dicey, Albert Venn. *Lectures Introductory to the Study of Law of the Constitution,* 1st ed. (London: Macmillan, 1885).

Downes, The Hon. Justice Garry, AM, President of the Australian Administrative Appeals Tribunal, Judge of the Federal Court of Australia. "World Report #1" (Paper presented to the Canadian Council of Administrative Tribunals Fourth International Conference, Vancouver, 2007) [unpublished].

Drewry, Gavin. "The Judicialisation of 'Administrative' Tribunals in the UK: From Hewart to Leggatt," (2009) No. 28 E SI/2009 *Transylvanian Review of Administrative Sciences* 45.

Dussault, R., and L. Borgeat. *Administrative Law,* 2d ed., vol. 1 (Toronto: Carswell, 1985).

Dyzenhaus, David. *Hard Cases in Wicked Legal Systems: South Africa Law in the Perspective of Legal Philosophy* (Oxford: Clarendon Press, 1991).

–. *Judging the Judges, Judging Ourselves – Truth, Reconciliation and the Apartheid Legal Order* (Oxford: Hart Publishing, 1998; as reprinted in paperback with amendments in 2003).

Eisenstadt, S.N., and L. Roniger. *Patrons, Clients and Friends: Interpersonal Relations and the Structure of Trust in Society* (Cambridge: Cambridge University Press, 1984).

Ellis, Ron. "Appointments Policies in the Administrative Justice System: Lessons from Ontario: Four Speeches" (1998) 11 Can. J. Admin. L. & Prac. 205.

–. "*Dunsmuir* and the Independence of Adjudicative Tribunals" (2010) 23 Can. J. Admin. Law & Prac. 203.

–. "Fair Hearings in an Ocean Port World – a Textured Concept" (2003) 18 J. L. & Soc. Pol'y 45.

–. "Saskatchewan Takes the Justice Out of Justice" *Lawyers Weekly* (6 April 2010).

–. "Super Provincial Tribunals: A Radical Remedy for Canada's Rights Tribunals" (2001) 15 Can. J. Admin. L. & Prac. 15.

–. "The Administrative Justice System in the New Millennium: A Vision in Search of a Centre" (1999-2000) 13 Can. J. Admin. L. & Prac. 171.

Ellis, S. Ronald. "Administrative Justicie Reform – Disturbing Omissions in the British Columbia White Paper," Parts I, II, and III, *Lawyers Weekly* (17, 24, and 31 January 2003).

–. "Administrative Justice System Reform: The Term of Appointment Issue" (1996) 10 Can. J. Admin. L. & Prac. 1.

–. "An Administrative Justice System in Jeopardy: Ontario's Appointments Policies" (1998) 6 C.L.E.L.J. 53.

–. "Misconceiving Tribunal Members: A Memorandum to Québec" (2005) 18 Can. J. Admin. Law & Prac. 189.

–. "Restructuring the Administrative Justice System: The Provincial Tribunal" (1997) 10 Can. J. Admin. L. & Prac. 175.

–. "The Corporate Responsibilities of Tribunal Members – CCAT 2008" (2009) 22 Can. J. Admin. L. & Prac. 1.

Ellis, S. Ronald, and Mary E. McKenzie. "Ocean Port or the Rule of Law? The Saskatchewan Labour Relations Board" (2009) 22 Can. J. Admin. L. & Prac. 267.

Falzon, Frank A.V. "The Integrated Administrative Tribunal" (2006) 19 Can. J. Admin. L. & Prac. 239.

Feinberg, Joel. *Social Philosophy* (Englewood Cliffs, NJ: Prentice Hall, 1973).

Freedman, A. *Patronage: An American Tradition* (Chicago: Nelson-Hall Publishers, 1994).

Friedland, Robert. "If You Love Human Rights Clap Your Hands" *Lawyers Weekly* (5 July 2002).

Fuller, Lon. "The Forms and Limits of Adjudication" (1978) 92 Harv. L. Rev. 350.

Gottheil, Michael, and Doug Ewart. "The Potential of Ontario's Clustering Model to Advance Administrative Justice" (2011) 24 Can. J. Admin. L. & Prac. 161.

Hart, H.L.A. *Concept of Law* (London: Oxford University Press, 1961).

Hawkins, Robert E., and David M. Shoemaker. "Reputational Review II: Administrative Agencies, Print Media and Content Analysis" (1998-99) 12 Can. J. Admin. L. & Prac. 1.

Heckman, Gerald, and Lorne Sossin. "How Do Canadian Administrative Law Protections Measure Up to International Human Rights Standards? The Case of Independence" (2005) 50 McGill L.J. 193.

Hewart, The Right Honourable Lord of Bury, Lord Chief Justice of England. *The New Despotism* (New York: Cosmopolitan Book Corporation, 1929).

Houle, France. "A Brief Historical Account of the Reforms to the Administrative Justice System in the Province Of Quebec" (2009) 22 Can. J. Admin. L. & Prac. 47.

Janisch, Hudson N. "Administrative Tribunals and the Law" (1988-89) 2 Can. J. Admin. L. & Prac. 262.

Kennedy, Duncan. *A Critique of Adjudication: Fin de Siecle* (Cambridge, MA: Harvard University Press, 1997).

–. "Toward a Critical Phenomenology of Judging" in Allan C. Hutchinson and Patrick Monahan, eds., *The Rule of Law: Ideal or Ideology* (Toronto: Carswell, 1987).

Kristinsson, Gunnar Helgi. "Parties, States and Patronage" (1996) 19 Western European Politics 433.

Lamer, Antonio. "Administrative Tribunals – Future Prospects and Possibilities" (1991) 5 Can. J. Admin. L. & Prac. 107.

Lebi, Ron, and Elizabeth Mitchell. "The Decline in Trade Union Certification in Ontario: The Case for Restoring Remedial Certification" (2003) 10 C.L.E.L.J. 472.

Levy, Alan D. "A Review of Environment Assessment in Ontario" (2001) 11 J. Envtl. L. & Prac. 173.

McConnell, Moira. "Commentary on the Law Reform Commission's '1997 Final Report, Reform of the Administrative Justice System in Nova Scotia'" (Paper presented to CCAT Conference, Ottawa 1998) [unpublished].

McCormack, Judith. "The Price of Administrative Justice" (1998) 6 C.L.E.L.J. 1.

McGregor, Gaile. "Anti-Claimant Bias in the Employment Insurance Appeals System: Causes, Consequences, and Public Law Remedies" (2002) 15 Can. J. Admin. L. & Prac. 229.

McLachlin, Beverley. "The Roles of Administrative Tribunals and Courts in Maintaining the Rule of Law" (1998) 12 Can. J. Admin. L. & Prac. 171.

Morissette, Yves-Marie. "Le contrôle de la compétence d'attribution: thése, antithése et synthése" (1986) 16 R.D.U.S. 591.

Mullan, D.J. "Administrative Tribunals: Their Evolution in Canada from 1945 to 1984" in I. Bernie and A. Lajoie, eds., *Regulations, Crown Corporations and Administrative Tribunals* (Toronto: University of Toronto Press, 1985).

–. "Establishing the Standard of Review: The Struggle for Complexity?" (2004) 17 Can. J. Admin. L. & Prac. 59.

Pelletier, Gaston. "Status of the Members of Bodies Established by the Québec Legislature to Exercise Adjudicative Functions within the Administrative Branch" (2010) 23 Can. J. Admin. L. & Prac. 41.

Priest, Margot D. "Structure and Accountability of Administrative Agencies" in *Law Society of Upper Canada Special Lectures, 1992, Administrative Law, Principles, Practices and Pluralism* (Toronto: Carswell, 1992).

Ramsay, Jennifer. "Provincial Agency Creating Homelessness" *Toronto Star* (30 June 2000).

Rapsey, Paul Stuart. "See No Evil, Hear No Evil, Remedy No Evil: How the Ontario Rental Housing Tribunal Is Failing to Protect the Most Fundamental Rights of Residential Tenants" (2000) 15 J. L. & Soc. Pol'y 163.

Rawls, John. *A Theory of Justice* (Cambridge, MA: Belknap Press, 1971).

–. "Justice as Fairness as a Political Conception of Justice" from 'Justice as Fairness: Political Not Metaphysical' (1985)" in Robert C. Solomon and Mark C. Murphy, eds., *What Is Justice? Classic and Contemporary Readings*, 2d ed. (New York: Oxford University Press, 2000).

Robson, W.A. "Essays" in R.E. Wraith and P.G. Hutchesson, eds., *Administrative Tribunals* (London: George Allen and Unwin, 1973).

Roman, Andrew J. "Structure and Accountability of Administrative Agencies" in *Law Society of Upper Canada Special Lectures, 1992, Administrative Law, Principles, Practices and Pluralism* (Toronto: Carswell, 1992).

Russell, Bertrand. *History of Western Philosophy* (New York: Simon and Schuster, 1945).

Scott, Sheridan. "The Continuing Debate over the Independence of Regulatory Tribunals" in *Law Society of Upper Canada Special Lectures, 1992, Administrative Law, Principles, Practices and Pluralism* (Toronto: Carswell, 1992).

Skelcher, Chris. *The Appointed State: Quasi-Governmental Organizations and Democracy* (Buckingham, PA: Open University Press, 1998).

Siltala, Raimo. "Whose Justice, Which Ideology?" (2003) 16 Ratio Juris 123.

Slatter, Frans. *Parliament and Administrative Agencies in Law Reform: A Study Paper Prepared for the Law Reform Commission of Canada* (Ottawa: Minister of Supply and Services, 1982).

Solum, Lawrence B. "Judicial Selection: Ideology versus Character" (2004) 26 Cardozo L. Rev. 659.

Stilborn, Jack. *Political Patronage: A Newly Troubled Tradition*, Research backgrounder (Ottawa: Research Branch of the Library of Parliament, 1989).

Thomson, George M. "Agencies, Boards and Commissions: Accountability and Independence" in *Law Society of Upper Canada Special Lectures, Administrative Law, Principles, Practices and Pluralism* (Toronto: Carswell, 1992).

United States, Office of Personnel Management. *1989 Program Handbook for Administrative Law Judges* (Washington, DC: US Office of Personnel Management, 1989).

Wade, H.R. *Administrative Law,* 5th ed. (Oxford: Clarendon Press, 1982).

Wade, William, and Christopher Forsythe. *Administrative Law,* 8th ed. (Oxford: Oxford University Press, 2000).

Willis, John. "Canadian Administrative Law in Retrospect" (1974) 24 U.T.L.J. 225.

–. "The McRuer Report: Lawyers' Values and Civil Servants' Values" (1968) 18 U.T.L.J. 351.

Young, Ann Marshall. "Evaluation of Administrative Law Judges: Premises, Means, and Ends" (1997) 17 Journal of the National Association of Administrative Law Judges 1.

Index

ruled out except for cause, 263; Community Advisory Panels, 261; compensation, 268; discharge for cause, 264; executive branch channels for influencing tribunals on policy issues, 279-82; Governing Council for Administrative Justice, 241, 242; idiosyncratic removals, 272-74; judicial function defined, 234-35; Omnibus Judicial Tribunal, 248, 256; optimizing competence, 264-65; quasi-constitutional status for Bill of Rights, 234; patronage appointments, 266; performance evaluation of adjudicators, 275; performance evaluation of tribunals, 275; qualifications, 267-68; reappointments process, 272-74; separation packages, 274; Tribunal Audit Board, 260

Reform Proposal, budgets (tribunals'), 247. *See also* Reform Proposal, Tribunal Audit Board

Reform Proposal, boutique tribunals, 248, 251, 255

Reform Proposal, Community Advisory Panels, 232, 257, 261, 266

Reform Proposal, constitutional protection of the independence of judicial tribunals is a prerequisite, 277, 285

Reform Proposal, executive branch overt channels of influence, 232, 276-82; costs to parties of government interventions, 282; course corrections by legislation, regulations, directives, 233, 280; judicial review, 281-82; judicial tribunals' traditional relationships with administrators of their statutory rights enterprises, 276-77; lessons from author's experience with WCB's "final say" power to review WCAT decisions, 276-79; meet-

ings (regular) between policy bodies and judicial tribunals, 280; Ministerial Reviews, 281; party status for policy bodies in judicial tribunal hearings, 280; "policy bodies," 279; policy maturation, tribunals' role, 195-96, 276; policy bodies' referral of decisions to tribunals for reconsideration, 281; principled course corrections, 276

Reform Proposal, financial security, 268-70

Reform Proposal, general principles, 231

Reform Proposal, Governing Council for Administrative Justice, 232, 235-45, 265, 266, 267, 272, 273, 275, 281; Canadian experience with administrative justice councils, 235-39; financing, inalienable core funding, 242; functions, 242-45; history of councils in other jurisdictions, 239-40; structure, 241-42

Reform Proposal, independence and impartiality, 231, 233, 234, 263, 284-85

Reform Proposal, Ministry of Administrative Justice, 232, 244, 245-48, 262, 267, 272, 273; functions, 247-48; ministries of the attorney general, the case against, 245-47

Reform Proposal, Omnibus Judicial Tribunal, 232, 247, 248-59, 261, 280; advantages, 249-51; adjunct judicial functions, 251; boutique tribunals, 251; Canadian history with omnibus tribunals, 253-56; combining regulatory functions with judicial functions, a problem, 255; funding, 258; structure, 256-58; omnibus tribunal experience in other jurisdictions, 251-53; support services for other tribunals, 258-59

About the Author

Ron Ellis is a lawyer, academic, teacher, labour arbitrator, and former tribunal adjudicator and administrator. He has been teaching, speaking, studying, and writing about administrative justice system issues for most of his career and has published widely in this area. His administrative justice background includes a PhD in administrative justice from York University, Osgoode Hall Law School (Osgoode); twelve years as the inaugural Chair and CEO of Ontario's Workers' Compensation Appeals Tribunal (WCAT); seven years as an associate professor of law at Osgoode; eleven years as a management labour lawyer with Osler Hoskin & Harcourt; and several years as a part-time labour arbitrator. While at Osgoode he was, for a number of years, director of Osgoode's storefront poverty law clinic, Parkdale Community Legal Services. From 1981 to 1985 he was director of education for the Law Society of Upper Canada and the Federation of Law Societies. Ellis was the inaugural president of the Society of Ontario's Adjudicators and Regulators (SOAR), and a member of the original Board of Directors of the Council of Canadian Administrative Tribunals (CCAT), and is a recipient of both the SOAR and CCAT medals. He is currently an adjunct professor in Osgoode's professional LLM Program in Administrative Law.

Donn Short
"Don't Be So Gay!" Queers, Bullying, and Making Schools Safe (2013)

Melissa Munn and Chris Bruckert
On the Outside: From Lengthy Imprisonment to Lasting Freedom (2013)

Emmett Macfarlane
*Governing from the Bench: The Supreme Court of Canada and
the Judicial Role* (2013)

Ron Ellis
Unjust by Design: The Administrative Justice System in Canada (2013)

David R. Boyd
The Right to a Healthy Environment: Revitalizing Canada's Constitution
(2012)

David Milward
*Aboriginal Justice and the Charter: Realizing a Culturally Sensitive
Interpretation of Legal Rights* (2012)

Shelley A.M. Gavigan
Hunger, Horses, and Government Men: Criminal Law on the Aboriginal Plains, 1870-1905 (2012)

Steven Bittle
Still Dying for a Living: Corporate Criminal Liability after the Westray Mine Disaster (2012)

Jacqueline D. Krikorian
International Trade Law and Domestic Policy: Canada, the United States, and the WTO (2012)

Michael Boudreau
City of Order: Crime and Society in Halifax, 1918-35 (2012)

David R. Boyd
The Environmental Rights Revolution: A Global Study of Constitutions, Human Rights, and the Environment (2012)

Lesley Erickson
Westward Bound: Sex, Violence, the Law, and the Making of a Settler Society (2011)

Elaine Craig
Troubling Sex: Towards a Legal Theory of Sexual Integrity (2011)

Laura DeVries
Conflict in Caledonia: Aboriginal Land Rights and the Rule of Law (2011)

Jocelyn Downie and Jennifer J. Llewellyn (eds.)
Being Relational: Reflections on Relational Theory and Health Law (2011)

Grace Li Xiu Woo
Ghost Dancing with Colonialism: Decolonization and Indigenous Rights at the Supreme Court of Canada (2011)

Fiona Kelly
Transforming Law's Family: The Legal Recognition of Planned Lesbian Motherhood (2011)

Colleen Bell
The Freedom of Security: Governing Canada in the Age of Counter-Terrorism (2011)

Andrew S. Thompson
In Defence of Principles: NGOs and Human Rights in Canada (2010)

Aaron Doyle and Dawn Moore (eds.)
Critical Criminology in Canada: New Voices, New Directions (2010)

Joanna R. Quinn
The Politics of Acknowledgement: Truth Commissions in Uganda and Haiti (2010)

Patrick James
Constitutional Politics in Canada after the Charter: Liberalism, Communitarianism, and Systemism (2010)

Louis A. Knafla and Haijo Westra (eds.)
Aboriginal Title and Indigenous Peoples: Canada, Australia, and New Zealand (2010)

Janet Mosher and Joan Brockman (eds.)
Constructing Crime: Contemporary Processes of Criminalization (2010)

Stephen Clarkson and Stepan Wood
A Perilous Imbalance: The Globalization of Canadian Law and Governance (2009)

Amanda Glasbeek
Feminized Justice: The Toronto Women's Court, 1913-34 (2009)

Kimb Brooks (ed.)
Justice Bertha Wilson: One Woman's Difference (2009)

Wayne V. McIntosh and Cynthia L. Cates
Multi-Party Litigation: The Strategic Context (2009)

Renisa Mawani
Colonial Proximities: Crossracial Encounters and Juridical Truths in British Columbia, 1871-1921 (2009)

James B. Kelly and Christopher P. Manfredi (eds.)
Contested Constitutionalism: Reflections on the Canadian Charter of Rights and Freedoms (2009)

Catherine Bell and Robert K. Paterson (eds.)
Protection of First Nations Cultural Heritage: Laws, Policy, and Reform (2008)

Hamar Foster, Benjamin L. Berger, and A.R. Buck (eds.)
The Grand Experiment: Law and Legal Culture in British Settler Societies (2008)

Richard J. Moon (ed.)
Law and Religious Pluralism in Canada (2008)

Catherine Bell and Val Napoleon (eds.)
First Nations Cultural Heritage and Law: Case Studies, Voices, and Perspectives (2008)

Douglas C. Harris
Landing Native Fisheries: Indian Reserves and Fishing Rights in British Columbia, 1849-1925 (2008)

Peggy J. Blair
Lament for a First Nation: The Williams Treaties of Southern Ontario (2008)

Lori G. Beaman
Defining Harm: Religious Freedom and the Limits of the Law (2007)

Stephen Tierney (ed.)
Multiculturalism and the Canadian Constitution (2007)

Julie Macfarlane
The New Lawyer: How Settlement Is Transforming the Practice of Law (2007)

Kimberley White
Negotiating Responsibility: Law, Murder, and States of Mind (2007)

Dawn Moore
Criminal Artefacts: Governing Drugs and Users (2007)

Hamar Foster, Heather Raven, and Jeremy Webber (eds.)
Let Right Be Done: Aboriginal Title, the Calder *Case, and the Future of Indigenous Rights* (2007)

Dorothy E. Chunn, Susan B. Boyd, and Hester Lessard (eds.)
Reaction and Resistance: Feminism, Law, and Social Change (2007)

Margot Young, Susan B. Boyd, Gwen Brodsky, and Shelagh Day (eds.)
Poverty: Rights, Social Citizenship, and Legal Activism (2007)

Rosanna L. Langer
Defining Rights and Wrongs: Bureaucracy, Human Rights, and Public Accountability (2007)

C.L. Ostberg and Matthew E. Wetstein
Attitudinal Decision Making in the Supreme Court of Canada (2007)

Chris Clarkson
Domestic Reforms: Political Visions and Family Regulation in British Columbia, 1862-1940 (2007)

Jean McKenzie Leiper
Bar Codes: Women in the Legal Profession (2006)

Gerald Baier
Courts and Federalism: Judicial Doctrine in the United States, Australia, and Canada (2006)

Avigail Eisenberg (ed.)
Diversity and Equality: The Changing Framework of Freedom in Canada (2006)

Randy K. Lippert
Sanctuary, Sovereignty, Sacrifice: Canadian Sanctuary Incidents, Power, and Law (2005)

James B. Kelly
Governing with the Charter: Legislative and Judicial Activism and Framers' Intent (2005)

Dianne Pothier and Richard Devlin (eds.)
Critical Disability Theory: Essays in Philosophy, Politics, Policy, and Law (2005)

Susan G. Drummond
Mapping Marriage Law in Spanish Gitano Communities (2005)

Louis A. Knafla and Jonathan Swainger (eds.)
Laws and Societies in the Canadian Prairie West, 1670-1940 (2005)

Ikechi Mgbeoji
Global Biopiracy: Patents, Plants, and Indigenous Knowledge (2005)

Florian Sauvageau, David Schneiderman, and David Taras,
with Ruth Klinkhammer and Pierre Trudel
The Last Word: Media Coverage of the Supreme Court of Canada (2005)

Gerald Kernerman
Multicultural Nationalism: Civilizing Difference, Constituting Community (2005)

Pamela A. Jordan
Defending Rights in Russia: Lawyers, the State, and Legal Reform in the Post-Soviet Era (2005)

Anna Pratt
Securing Borders: Detention and Deportation in Canada (2005)

Kirsten Johnson Kramar
Unwilling Mothers, Unwanted Babies: Infanticide in Canada (2005)

W.A. Bogart
Good Government? Good Citizens? Courts, Politics, and Markets in a Changing Canada (2005)

Catherine Dauvergne
Humanitarianism, Identity, and Nation: Migration Laws in Canada and Australia (2005)

Michael Lee Ross
First Nations Sacred Sites in Canada's Courts (2005)

Andrew Woolford
Between Justice and Certainty: Treaty Making in British Columbia (2005)

John McLaren, Andrew Buck, and Nancy Wright (eds.)
Despotic Dominion: Property Rights in British Settler Societies (2004)

Georges Campeau
From UI to EI: Waging War on the Welfare State (2004)

Alvin J. Esau
The Courts and the Colonies: The Litigation of Hutterite Church Disputes (2004)

Christopher N. Kendall
Gay Male Pornography: An Issue of Sex Discrimination (2004)

Roy B. Flemming
Tournament of Appeals: Granting Judicial Review in Canada (2004)

Constance Backhouse and Nancy L. Backhouse
The Heiress vs the Establishment: Mrs. Campbell's Campaign for Legal Justice (2004)

Christopher P. Manfredi
Feminist Activism in the Supreme Court: Legal Mobilization and the Women's Legal Education and Action Fund (2004)

Annalise Acorn
Compulsory Compassion: A Critique of Restorative Justice (2004)

Jonathan Swainger and Constance Backhouse (eds.)
People and Place: Historical Influences on Legal Culture (2003)

Jim Phillips and Rosemary Gartner
Murdering Holiness: The Trials of Franz Creffield and George Mitchell (2003)

David R. Boyd
Unnatural Law: Rethinking Canadian Environmental Law and Policy (2003)

Ikechi Mgbeoji
Collective Insecurity: The Liberian Crisis, Unilateralism, and Global Order (2003)

Rebecca Johnson
Taxing Choices: The Intersection of Class, Gender, Parenthood, and the Law (2002)

John McLaren, Robert Menzies, and Dorothy E. Chunn (eds.)
Regulating Lives: Historical Essays on the State, Society, the Individual, and the Law (2002)

Joan Brockman
Gender in the Legal Profession: Fitting or Breaking the Mould (2001)

Printed and bound in Canada by Friesens

Set in Futura Condensed and Warnock by Artegraphica Design Co. Ltd.

Copy editing and proofreading: F & M Chow Consulting